Software Testing and Continuous Quality Improvement

Software Testing and Continuous Quality Improvement

William E. Lewis

Software Testing Associates, Inc.
Plano, Texas

AUERBACH

Boca Raton   London   New York   Washington, D.C.

Library of Congress Cataloging-in-Publication Data

Lewis, William E.
        p.   cm.
    Software testing and continuous quality improvement / William E. Lewis.
    Includes bibliographical references and index.
    ISBN 1-8493-9833-9 (alk. paper)
    1. Computer software—Testing—Standards. 2. Computer software—Quality
    control—Standards. I. Title.
QA76.76.T48L495 2000
005.1′4—dc21   99-086186
                                                                                    CIP

Visit the CRC Press Web site at www.crcpress.com

© 2000 by CRC Press LLC
Auerbach is an imprint of CRC Press LLC

No claim to original U.S. Government works
International Standard Book Number 0-8493-9833-9
Library of Congress Card Number 99-086186
Printed in the United States of America   5 6 7 8 9 0
Printed on acid-free paper

About the Author

William E. Lewis holds a B.A. in mathematics and an M.S. in operations research and has 34 years' experience in the computer industry. Currently, as a senior technology engineer for Technology Builders, Inc., Atlanta, Georgia, he trains and consults in the requirements-based testing area, focusing on leading-edge testing methods and tools.

He is a certified quality analyst (CQA) and certified software test engineer (CSTE) sponsored by the Quality Assurance Institute (QAI), Orlando, Florida. Over the years, he has presented several papers to conferences. In 1998 he presented a paper to QAI's Annual International Information Technology Quality Conference, entitled "Spiral Testing," an excerpt from Section III of this book. He also speaks at meetings of the American Society for Quality and the Association of Information Technology Practitioners.

Mr. Lewis was an assistant director with Ernst & Young, LLP, located in Las Colinas, Texas. He joined E & Y in 1994, authoring the company's software configuration management, software testing, and application evolutionary handbooks, and helping to develop the Navigator/Fusion Methodology application improvement routemaps. He was the quality assurance manager for several application development projects and has extensive experience in test planning, test design, execution, evaluation, reporting, and automated testing. He was also the director of the ISO initiative, which resulted in ISO9000 international certification for Ernst & Young.

Lewis also worked for the Saudi Arabian Oil Company (Aramco) in Jeddah, Saudi Arabia, on an overseas contract assignment as a quality assurance consultant. His duties included full integration and system testing, and he served on the automated tool selection committee and made recommendations to management. He also created software testing standards and procedures.

In 1998 Lewis retired from IBM after 28 years. His jobs included 12 years as a curriculum/course developer and instructor, and numerous years as a system programmer/analyst and performance analyst. An overseas assignment included service in Seoul, Korea, where he was the software engineering curriculum manager for the Korean Advanced Institute of Science and

Technology (KAIST), which is considered the MIT of higher education in Korea. Another assignment was in Toronto, Canada, at IBM Canada's headquarters, where he was responsible for upgrading the corporate education program. He has also traveled throughout the U.S., Rome, Amsterdam, Southampton, Hong Kong, and Sydney, teaching software development and quality assurance classes with a specialty in software testing.

He has also taught at the university level for five years as an adjunct professor. While so engaged he published a five-book series on computer problem solving.

For further information about the training and consulting services provided by Software Testing Associates, Inc., contact:

Software Testing Associates, Inc.
2713 Millington Drive
Plano, Texas 75093
(972) 985-7546

Acknowledgments

I would like to express my sincere gratitude to my loving wife, Carol, for her infinite patience with me in the preparation of this work, and to my mother, Joyce, whom I will never forget.

I thank John Wyzalek, Senior Acquisitions Editor for Auerbach Publishers, for recognizing the importance and potential of this work, and Mike Terkel, a colleague and quality assurance analyst, for reviewing the book, providing invaluable suggestions, and contributing to Section IV, "Modern Testing Tools" and Section VI, "Modern Maintenance Tools."

Finally, I would like to thank the following software testing tool vendors for providing descriptions of their modern testing tools (in alphabetical order): AutoTester, Inc., McCabe and Associates, Mercury Interactive, Rational Software, Sun Microsystems, Inc., and Technology Builders, Inc.

Contents

Contents

Contents

Contents

EXHIBITS

Part 1

Part 2

Contents

Contents

Contents

Exhibits listed in italics are graphics.

Introduction

Numerous textbooks address software testing in a structured development environment. By "structured" is meant a well-defined development cycle in which discretely defined steps provide measurable outputs at each step. It is assumed that software testing activities are based on clearly defined requirements and software development standards, and that those standards are used to develop and implement a plan for testing. Unfortunately, this is often not the case. Typically, testing is performed against changing, or even wrong, requirements.

This text aims to provide a quality framework for the software testing process in the traditional structured as well as unstructured environments. The goal is to provide a continuous quality improvement approach to promote effective testing methods and provide tips, techniques, and alternatives from which the user can choose.

The basis of the continuous quality framework stems from Edward Deming's quality principles. Deming was the pioneer in quality improvement, which helped turn Japanese manufacturing around. Deming's principles are applied to software testing in the traditional "waterfall" and rapid application "spiral" development (RAD) environments. The waterfall approach is one in which predefined, sequential steps are followed with clearly defined requirements. In the spiral approach, these rigid sequential steps may, to varying degrees, be lacking or different.

Section I, "Software Quality in Perspective," reviews modern quality assurance principles and best practices. It provides the reader with a detailed overview of basic software testing techniques, and introduces Deming's concept of quality through a continuous improvement process. The Plan–Do–Check–Act (PDCA) quality wheel is applied to the software testing process.

The **Plan** step of the continuous improvement process starts with a definition of the test objectives, or what is to be accomplished as a result of testing. The elements of a test strategy and test plan are described. A test strategy is a concise statement of how to meet the goals of testing and precedes test plan development. The outline of a good test plan is provided, including an introduction, the overall plan, testing requirements, test procedures, and test plan details.

The **Do** step addresses how to design or execute the tests included in the test plan. A cookbook approach describes how to perform component, integration, and system acceptance testing in a spiral environment.

The **Check** step emphasizes the importance of metrics and test reporting. A test team must formally record the results of tests and relate them to the test plan and system objectives. A sample test report format is provided, along with several graphic techniques.

The **Act** step of the continuous improvement process provides guidelines for updating test cases and test scripts. In preparation for the next spiral, suggestions for improving the people, process, and technology dimensions are provided.

Section II, "Life Cycle Testing Review," reviews the waterfall development methodology and describes how continuous quality improvement can be applied to the phased approach through technical reviews and software testing. The requirements, logical design, physical design, program unit design, and coding phases are reviewed. The roles of technical reviews and software testing are applied to each. Finally, the psychology of software testing is discussed.

Section III, "Client/Server and Internet Testing Methodology," contrasts the waterfall development methodology to the rapid application (RAD) spiral environment from a technical and psychological point of view. A spiral testing approach is suggested when the requirements are rapidly changing. A spiral methodology is provided, broken down into parts, steps, and tasks, applying Deming's continuous quality improvement process in the context of the PDCA quality wheel.

Section IV, "Modern Testing Tools," provides an overview of tools and guidelines for when to consider a testing tool and when not to. It also provides a checklist for selecting testing tools, consisting of a series of questions and responses. Examples are given of some of the most popular products. Finally, a detailed methodology for evaluating testing tools is provided, ranging from the initial test goals through training and implementation.

Section V, "Testing in the Maintenance Environment," discusses the fundamental challenges of maintaining and improving existing systems. Software changes are described and contrasted. Strategies for managing the maintenance effort are presented, along with the psychology of the software maintenance activity. A maintenance testing methodology is then broken down into parts, steps, and tasks, applying Deming's continuous quality improvement process in the context of the PDCA quality wheel.

Section VI, "Modern Maintenance Tools," presents an overview of maintenance tools and provides guidelines for when to consider a maintenance testing tool and when not to. Using a question–response format, the section also provides a checklist for selecting maintenance testing tools. Samples of the most popular maintenance testing tools are included, ranging from code complexity tools to configuration/process management tools.

Section I
Software Quality in Perspective

Software quality is something everyone wants. Managers know that they want high quality; software developers know they want to produce a quality product; and users insist that software work consistently and be reliable.

Many organizations form software quality assurance groups to improve and evaluate their software applications. However, there is no commonly accepted practice for quality assurance. Thus the quality assurance groups in various organizations may perform different roles and may execute their planning using different procedures.

In some organizations, software testing is a responsibility of that group. In others, software testing is the responsibility of the development group or an independent organization.

Many software quality groups develop software quality assurance plans, which are similar to test plans. However, a software quality assurance plan may include a variety of activities beyond those included in a test plan.

The objectives of this section are to:

- Define quality and its cost
- Differentiate quality prevention from quality detection
- Differentiate verification from validation
- Outline the components of quality assurance
- Outline common testing techniques
- Describe how the continuous improvement process can be instrumental in achieving quality

Part 1
Quality Assurance Framework

WHAT IS QUALITY?

In *Webster's Dictionary*, quality is defined as "the essential character of something, an inherent or distinguishing character, degree or grade of excellence." If you look at the computer literature, you will see that there are two generally accepted meanings of quality. The first is that quality means "meeting requirements." With this definition, to have a quality product, the requirements must be measurable, and the product's requirements will either be met or not met. With this meaning, quality is a binary state, i.e., it is a quality product or it is not. The requirements may be very complete or they may be simple, but as long as they are measurable, it can be determined whether quality has or has not been met. This is the producer's view of quality as meeting the producer's requirements or specifications. Meeting the specifications becomes an end in itself.

Another definition of quality, the customer's, is the one we will use. With this definition, the customer defines quality as to whether or not the product or service does what the customer needs. Another way of wording it is "fit for use." There should also be a description of the purpose of the product, typically documented in a customer's "requirements specification" (see Appendix C, Requirements Specification, for more details). The requirements are the most important document, and the quality system revolves around it. In addition, quality *attributes* are described in the customer's requirements specification. Examples include usability, the relative ease with which a user communicates with the application, portability, the capability of the system to be executed across a diverse range of hardware architectures, and reusability, the ability to transfer software components constructed in one software system into another.

While everyone is committed to quality, the following are some confusions shared by many individuals, which inhibit achieving a quality commitment:

1. Quality requires a commitment, particularly from top management. Close cooperation of management and staff is required in order to make it happen.

3

2. Many individuals believe that defect-free products and services are impossible, and accept certain levels of defects are normal and acceptable.
3. Quality is frequently associated with cost, meaning that high quality equals high cost. This is a confusion between quality of design and quality of conformance.
4. Quality demands requirement specifications in enough detail that the products produced can be quantitatively measured against those specifications. Many organizations are not capable or willing to expend the effort to produce specifications at the level of detail required.
5. Technical personnel often believe that standards stifle their creativity, and thus do not abide by standards compliance. However, for quality to happen, well-defined standards and procedures must be followed.

PREVENTION VS. DETECTION

Quality cannot be achieved by assessing an already completed product. The aim, therefore, is to prevent quality defects or deficiencies in the first place, and to make the products assessable by quality assurance measures. Some quality assurance measures include: structuring the development process with a software development standard and supporting the development process with methods, techniques, and tools.

In addition to product assessments, process assessments are essential to a quality management program. Examples include documentation of coding standards, prescription and use of standards, methods, and tools, procedures for data backup, change management, defect documentation, and reconciliation.

Quality management decreases production costs because the sooner a defect is located and corrected, the less costly it will be in the long run. Although the initial investment can be substantial, the long-term result will be higher-quality products and reduced maintenance costs.

The total cost of effective quality management is the sum of four component costs — prevention, inspection, internal failure, and external failure. Prevention costs consist of actions taken to prevent defects from occurring in the first place. Inspection costs consist of measuring, evaluating, and auditing products or services for conformance to standards and specifications. Internal failure costs are those incurred in fixing defective products before they are delivered. External failure costs consist of the costs of defects discovered after the product has been released. The latter can be devastating because they may damage the organization's reputation or result in the loss of future sales.

The greatest payback is with prevention. Increasing the emphasis on prevention costs reduces the number of defects which go to the customer undetected, improves product quality, and reduces the cost of production and maintenance.

VERIFICATION VS. VALIDATION

Verification is proving that a product meets the requirements specified during previous activities carried out correctly throughout the development life cycle, while validation checks that the system meets the customer's requirements at the end of the life cycle. It is a proof that the product meets the expectations of the users, and it ensures that the executable system performs as specified. The creation of the test product is much more closely related to validation than to verification. Traditionally, software testing has been considered a validation process, i.e., a life cycle phase. After programming is completed, the system is validated or tested to determine its functional and operational performance.

When verification is incorporated into testing, testing occurs throughout the development life cycle. For best results, it is good practice to combine verification with validation in the testing process. Verification includes systematic procedures of review, analysis, and testing, employed throughout the software development life cycle, beginning with the software requirements phase and continuing through the coding phase. Verification ensures the quality of software production and maintenance. In addition, verification imposes such an organized, systematic development practice that the resulting program can be easily understood and evaluated by an independent party.

Verification emerged about 15 years ago as a result of the aerospace industry's need for extremely reliable software in systems in which an error in a program could cause mission failure and result in enormous time and financial setbacks, or even life-threatening situations. The concept of verification includes two fundamental criteria. First, the software must adequately and correctly perform all intended functions. Second, the software must not perform any function that either by itself or in combination with other functions can degrade the performance of the entire system. The overall goal of verification is to ensure that each software product developed throughout the software life cycle meets the customer's needs and objectives as specified in the software requirements document.

Verification also establishes tractability between the various sections of the software documentation and the associated parts of the requirements specification. A comprehensive verification effort ensures that all software performance and quality requirements in the specification are adequately tested and that the test results can be repeated after changes are installed. Verification is a "continuous improvement process" and has no definite termination. It should be used throughout the system life cycle to maintain configuration and operational integrity.

Verification ensures that the software functions as intended and has the required attributes, e.g., portability, and increases the chances that the software will contain few errors (i.e., an acceptable number in the final product). It provides a method for closely monitoring the software development project and provides management with a detailed status of the project at any point in time. When verification procedures are used, management can be assured that the developers follow a formal, sequential, traceable software development process, with a minimum set of activities to enhance the quality of the system.

One criticism of verification is that it increases software development costs considerably. When the cost of software throughout the total life cycle from inception to the final abandonment of the system is considered, however, verification actually reduces the overall cost of the software. With an effective verification program, there is typically a four-to-one reduction in defects in the installed system. Because error corrections can cost 20 to 100 times more during operations and maintenance than during design, overall savings far outweigh the initial extra expense.

SOFTWARE QUALITY ASSURANCE

A formal definition of software quality assurance is that it is "the systematic activities providing evidence of the fitness for use of the total software product." Software quality assurance is achieved through the use of established guidelines for quality control to ensure the integrity and prolonged life of software. The relationships between quality assurance, quality control, the auditing function, and software testing are often confused.

Quality assurance is the set of support activities needed to provide adequate confidence that processes are established and continuously improved in order to produce products that meet specifications and are fit for use. Quality control is the process by which product quality is compared with applicable standards and the action taken when nonconformance is detected. Auditing is the inspection/assessment activity that verifies compliance with plans, policies, and procedures.

Software quality assurance is a planned effort to ensure that a software product fulfills these criteria and has additional attributes specific to the project, e.g., portability, efficiency, reusability, and flexibility. It is the collection of activities and functions used to monitor and control a software project so that specific objectives are achieved with the desired level of confidence. It is not the sole responsibility of the software quality assurance group but is determined by the consensus of the project manager, project leader, project personnel, and users.

Quality assurance is the function responsible for managing quality. The word "assurance" means that if the processes are followed, management can be assured of product quality. Quality assurance is a catalytic function that should encourage quality attitudes and discipline on the part of management and workers. Successful quality assurance managers know how to make people quality conscious and to make them recognize the benefits of quality to themselves and to the organization.

The objectives of software quality are typically achieved by following a software quality assurance plan that states the methods the project will employ to ensure the documents or products produced and reviewed at each milestone are of high quality. Such an explicit approach ensures that all steps have been taken to achieve software quality and provides management with documentation of those actions. The plan states the criteria by which quality activities can be monitored rather than setting impossible goals, e.g., no software defects or 100% reliable software.

Software quality assurance is a strategy for risk management. It exists because software quality is typically costly and should be incorporated into the formal risk management of a project. Some examples of poor software quality include:

1. Delivered software frequently fails.
2. Unacceptable consequences of system failure, from financial to life-threatening scenarios.
3. Systems are often not available for their intended purpose.
4. System enhancements are often very costly.
5. Costs of detecting and removing defects are excessive.

Although most quality risks are related to defects, this only tells part of the story. A defect is a failure to comply with a requirement. If the requirements are inadequate or even incorrect, the risks of defects are more pervasive. The result is too many built-in defects and products that are not verifiable. Some risk management strategies and techniques include software testing, technical reviews, peer reviews, and compliance verification.

COMPONENTS OF QUALITY ASSURANCE

Most software quality assurance activities can be categorized into software testing, i.e., verification and validation, software configuration management, and quality control. But the success of a software quality assurance program also depends on a coherent collection of standards, practices, conventions, and specifications, as shown in Exhibit 1.

Software Testing

Software testing is a popular risk management strategy. It is used to verify that functional requirements were met. The limitation of this approach,

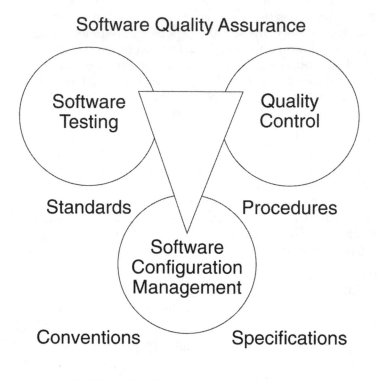

Exhibit 1. Quality Assurance Components

however, is that by the time testing occurs, it is too late to build quality into the product. Tests are only as good as the test cases, but they can be inspected to ensure that all the requirements are tested across all possible combinations of inputs and system states. However, not all defects are discovered during testing. Software testing includes the activities outlined in this text, including verification and validation activities. In many organizations, these activities, or their supervision, are included within the charter for the software quality assurance function. The extent to which personnel independent of design and coding should participate in software quality assurance activities is a matter of institutional, organizational, and project policy.

The major purpose of verification and validation activities is to ensure that software design, code, and documentation meet all the requirements imposed on them. Examples of requirements include user requirements, specifications derived from and designed to meet user requirements, code review and inspection criteria, test requirements at the modular, subsystem, and integrated software levels, and acceptance testing of the code after it has been fully integrated with hardware.

During software design and implementation, verification helps determine whether the products of one phase of the software development life cycle fulfill the requirements established during the previous phase. The verification effort takes less time and is less complex when conducted throughout the development process.

Quality Control

Quality control is defined as the processes and methods used to monitor work and observe whether requirements are met. It focuses on reviews and removal of defects before shipment of products. Quality control should be the responsibility of the organizational unit producing the product. It is possible to have the same group that builds the product perform the quality control function, or to establish a quality control group or department within the organizational unit that develops the product.

Quality control consists of well-defined checks on a product that are specified in the product quality assurance plan. For software products, quality control typically includes specification reviews, inspections of code and documents, and checks for user deliverables. Usually, document and product inspections are conducted at each life cycle milestone to demonstrate that the items produced are within the criteria specified by the software quality assurance plan. These criteria are normally provided in the requirements specifications, conceptual and detailed design documents, and test plans. The documents given to users are the requirement specifications, design documentation, results from the user acceptance test, the software code, user guide, and the operations and maintenance guide. Additional documents are specified in the software quality assurance plan.

Quality control can be provided by various sources. For small projects, the project personnel's peer group or the department's software quality coordinator can inspect the documents. On large projects, a configuration control board may be responsible for quality control. The board may include the users or a user representative, a member of the software quality assurance department, and the project leader.

Inspections are traditional functions of quality control, i.e., independent examinations to assess compliance with some stated criteria. Peers and subject matter experts review specifications and engineering work products to identify defects and suggest improvements. They are used to examine the software project for adherence to the written project rules at a project's milestones and at other times during the project's life cycle as deemed necessary by the project leader or the software quality assurance personnel. An inspection may be a detailed checklist for assessing compliance or a brief checklist to determine the existence of such deliverables as documentation. A report stating the purpose of the inspection and the deficiencies found goes to the project supervisor, project leader, and project personnel for action.

Responsibility for inspections is stated in the software quality assurance plan. For small projects, the project leader or the department's quality coordinator can perform the inspections. For large projects, a member of the software quality assurance group may lead an inspection performed by an audit team, which is similar to the configuration control board mentioned previously. Following the inspection, project personnel are assigned to correct the problems on a specific schedule.

Quality control is designed to detect and correct defects, while quality assurance is oriented toward preventing them. Detection implies flaws in the processes that are supposed to produce defect-free products and services. Quality assurance is a managerial function that prevents problems by heading them off, and by advising restraint and redirection.

Software Configuration Management

Software configuration management is concerned with labeling, tracking, and controlling changes in the software elements of a system. It controls the evolution of a software system by managing versions of its software components and their relationships.

The purpose of software configuration management is to identify all the interrelated components of software and to control their evolution throughout the various life cycle phases. Software configuration management is a discipline that can be applied to activities including software development, document control, problem tracking, change control, and maintenance. It can provide a high cost savings in software reusability because each software component and its relationship to other software components have been defined.

Software configuration management consists of activities that ensure that design and code are defined and cannot be changed without a review of the effect of the change itself and its documentation. The purpose of configuration management is to control code and its associated documentation so that final code and its description are consistent and represent those items that were actually reviewed and tested. Thus, spurious, last-minute software changes are eliminated.

For concurrent software development projects, software configuration management can have considerable benefits. It can organize the software under development and minimize the probability of inadvertent changes. Software configuration management has a stabilizing effect on all software when there is a great deal of change activity or a considerable risk of selecting the wrong software components.

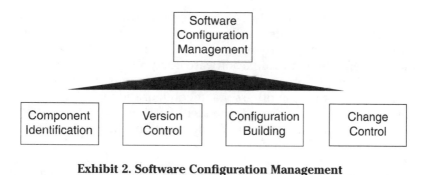

Exhibit 2. Software Configuration Management

ELEMENTS OF SOFTWARE CONFIGURATION MANAGEMENT

Software configuration management identifies a system configuration in order to systematically control changes, maintain integrity, and enforce tractability of the configuration throughout its life cycle. Components to be controlled include planning, analysis, and design documents, source code, executable code, utilities, job control language (JCL), test plans, test scripts, test cases, and development reports. The software configuration process typically consists of four elements — software component identification, software version control, configuration building, and software change control, as shown in Exhibit 2.

Component Identification

A basic software configuration management activity is the identification of the software components that make up a deliverable at each point of its development. Software configuration management provides guidelines to identify and name software baselines, software components, and software configurations.

Software components go through a series of changes. In order to manage the development process, one must establish methods and name standards for uniquely identifying each revision. A simple way to name component revisions is to use a series of discrete digits. The first integer could refer to a software component's external release number. The second integer could represent the internal software development release number. The transition from version number 2.9 to 3.1 would indicate that a new external release 3 has occurred. The software component version number is automatically incremented when the component is checked into the software library. Further levels of qualifiers could also be used as necessary, such as the date of a new version.

11

A software configuration is a collection of software elements that comprise a major business function. An example of a configuration is the set of program modules for an order system. Identifying a configuration is quite similar to identifying individual software components. Configurations can have a sequence of versions. Each configuration must be named in a way that distinguishes it from others. Each configuration version must be differentiated from other versions. The identification of a configuration must also include its approval status and a description of how the configuration was built.

A simple technique for identifying a configuration is to store all its software components in a single library or repository. The listing of all the components can also be documented.

Version Control

As an application evolves over time, many different versions of its software components are created, and there needs to be an organized process to manage changes in the software components and their relationships. In addition, there is usually the requirement to support parallel component development and maintenance.

Software is frequently changed as it evolves through a succession of temporary states called versions. A software configuration management facility for controlling versions is a software configuration management repository or library. Version control provides the tractability or history of each software change, including who did what, why, and when.

Within the software life cycle, software components evolve, and at a certain point each reaches a relatively stable state. But as defects are corrected and enhancement features are implemented, the changes result in new versions of the components. Maintaining control of these software component versions is called *versioning*.

A component is identified and labeled to differentiate it from all other software versions of the component. When a software component is modified, both the old and new versions should be separately identifiable. Therefore, each version, except for the initial one, has a predecessor. The succession of component versions is the component's history and tractability. Different versions also act as backups so that one can return to previous versions of the software.

Configuration Building

To build a software configuration one needs to identify the correct component versions and execute the component build procedures. This is often called *configuration building*.

A software configuration consists of a set of derived software components. An example is executable object programs derived from source programs. Derived software components are correctly associated with each source component to obtain an accurate derivation. The configuration build model defines how to control the way derived software components are put together.

The inputs and outputs required for a configuration build model include the primary inputs such as the source components, the version selection procedures, and the system model, which describes how the software components are related. The outputs are the target configuration and respectively derived software components.

Software configuration management environments use different approaches for selecting versions. The simplest approach to version selection is to maintain a list of component versions. Other approaches entail selecting the most recently tested component versions, or those modified on a particular date.

Change Control

Change control is the process by which a modification to a software component is proposed, evaluated, approved or rejected, scheduled, and tracked. Its basic foundation is a change control process, a component status reporting process, and an auditing process.

Software change control is a decision process used in controlling the changes made to software. Some proposed changes are accepted and implemented during this process. Others are rejected or postponed, and are not implemented. Change control also provides for impact analysis to determine the dependencies.

Modification of a configuration has at least four elements: a change request, an impact analysis of the change, a set of modifications and additions of new components, and a method for reliably installing the modifications as a new baseline (see Appendix D, Change Request Form, for more details).

A change often involves modifications to multiple software components. Therefore, a storage system that provides for multiple versions of a single file is usually not sufficient. A technique is required to identify the set of modifications as a single change. This is often called *delta storage*.

Every software component has a development life cycle. A life cycle consists of states and allowable transitions between those states. When a software component is changed, it should always be reviewed and frozen from further modifications until a new version is created. The reviewing authority must approve or reject the modified software component. A software library holds all software components as soon as they are frozen and also acts as a repository for approved components.

A derived component is linked to its source and has the same status as its source. In addition, a configuration cannot have a more complete status than any of its components, because it is meaningless to review a configuration when some of the associated components are not frozen.

All components controlled by software configuration management are stored in a software configuration library, including work products such as business data and process models, architecture groups, design units, tested application software, reusable software, and special test software. When a software component is to be modified, it is checked out of the repository into a private workspace. It evolves through many states which are temporarily out of the scope of configuration management control.

When a change is completed, the component is checked into the library and becomes a new software component version. The previous component version is also retained.

SOFTWARE QUALITY ASSURANCE PLAN

The software quality assurance (SQA) plan is an outline of quality measures to ensure quality levels within a software development effort. The plan is used as a baseline to compare the *actual* levels of quality during development with the *planned* levels of quality. If the levels of quality are not within the planned quality levels, management will respond appropriately as documented within the plan.

The plan provides the framework and guidelines for development of understandable and maintainable code. These ingredients help ensure the quality sought in a software project. A SQA plan also provides the procedures for ensuring that quality software will be produced or maintained in-house or under contract. These procedures affect planning, designing, writing, testing, documenting, storing, and maintaining computer software. It should be organized in this way because the plan ensures the quality of the software rather than describing specific procedures for developing and maintaining the software.

Steps to Develop and Implement a Software Quality Assurance Plan

Step 1. Document the Plan. The software quality assurance plan should include the sections below (see Appendix B, Software Quality Assurance Plan, which contains a template for the plan).

1. *Purpose Section*
   This section delineates the specific purpose and scope of the particular SQA plan. It should list the name(s) of the software items covered by the SQA plan and the intended use of the software. It states the portion of the software life cycle covered by the SQA plan for each software item specified.
2. *Reference Document Section*
   This section provides a complete list of documents referenced elsewhere in the text of the SQA plan.
3. *Management Section*
   This section describes the project's organizational structure, tasks, and responsibilities.
4. *Documentation Section*
   This section identifies the documentation governing the development, verification and validation, use, and maintenance of the software. It also states how the documents are to be checked for adequacy. This includes the criteria and the identification of the review or audit by which the adequacy of each document will be confirmed.
5. *Standards, Practices, Conventions, and Metrics Section*
   This section identifies the standards, practices, conventions, and metrics to be applied, and also states how compliance with these items is to be monitored and assured.
6. *Reviews and Inspections Section*
   This section defines the technical and managerial reviews, walk-throughs, and inspections to be conducted. It also states how the reviews, walkthroughs, and inspections, are to be accomplished including follow-up activities and approvals.
7. *Software Configuration Management Section*
   This section is addressed in detail in the project's software configuration management plan.
8. *Problem Reporting and Corrective Action Section*
   This section is addressed in detail in the project's software configuration management plan.
9. *Tools, Techniques, and Methodologies Section*
   This section identifies the special software tools, techniques, and methodologies that support SQA, states their purposes, and describes their use.
10. *Code Control Section*

This section defines the methods and facilities used to maintain, store, secure, and document the controlled versions of the identified software during all phases of development. This may be implemented in conjunction with a computer program library and/or may be provided as a part of the software configuration management plan.

11. *Media Control Section*

This section states the methods and facilities to be used to identify the media for each computer product and the documentation required to store the media, including the copy and restore process, and protects the computer program physical media from unauthorized access or inadvertent damage or degradation during all phases of development. This may be provided by the software configuration management plan.

12. *Supplier Control Section*

This section states the provisions for assuring that software provided by suppliers meets established requirements. In addition, it should state the methods that will be used to assure that the software supplier receives adequate and complete requirements. For previously developed software, this section will state the methods to be used to assure the suitability of the product for use with the software items covered by the SQA plan. For software to be developed, the supplier will be required to prepare and implement an SQA plan in accordance with this standard. This section will also state the methods to be employed to assure that the developers comply with the requirements of this standard.

13. *Records Collection, Maintenance, and Retention Section*

This section identifies the SQA documentation to be retained. It will state the methods and facilities to assemble, safeguard, and maintain this documentation, and will designate the retention period. The implementation of the SQA plan involves the necessary approvals for the plan as well as development of a plan for execution. The subsequent evaluation of the SQA plan will be performed as a result of its execution.

14. *Testing Methodology*

This section defines the testing approach, techniques, and automated tools that will be used.

Step 2. Obtain Management Acceptance. Management participation is necessary for the successful implementation of an SQA plan. Management is responsible both for ensuring the quality of a software project and for providing the resources needed for software development.

The level of management commitment required for implementing an SQA plan depends on the scope of the project. If a project spans organizational boundaries, approval should be obtained from all affected areas. Once approval has been obtained, the SQA plan is placed under configuration control.

In the management approval process, management relinquishes tight control over software quality to the SQA plan administrator in exchange for improved software quality. Software quality is often left to software developers. Quality is desirable, but management may express concern as to the cost of a formal SQA plan. Staff should be aware that management views the program as a means of ensuring software quality, and not as an end in itself.

To address management concerns, software life cycle costs should be formally estimated for projects implemented both with and without a formal SQA plan. In general, implementing a formal SQA plan makes economic and management sense.

Step 3. Obtain Development Acceptance. Since the software development and maintenance personnel are the primary users of an SQA plan, their approval and cooperation in implementing the plan are essential. The software project team members must adhere to the project SQA plan; everyone must accept it and follow it.

No SQA plan is successfully implemented without the involvement of the software team members and their managers in the development of the plan. Because project teams generally have only a few members, all team members should actively participate in writing the SQA plan. When projects become much larger (i.e., encompassing entire divisions or departments), representatives of project subgroups should provide input. Constant feedback from representatives to team members helps gain acceptance of the plan.

Step 4. Plan for Implementation of the SQA Plan. The process of planning, formulating, and drafting an SQA plan requires staff and word processing resources. The individual responsible for implementing an SQA plan must have access to these resources. In addition, the commitment of resources requires management approval and, consequently, management support. To facilitate resource allocation, management should be made aware of any project risks that may impede the implementation process (e.g., limited availability of staff or equipment). A schedule for drafting, reviewing, and approving the SQA plan should be developed.

Step 5. Execute the SQA Plan. The actual process of executing an SQA plan by the software development and maintenance team involves determining necessary audit points for monitoring it. The auditing function must be scheduled during the implementation phase of the software product so that the SQA plan will not be hurt by improper monitoring of the software project. Audit points should occur either periodically during development or at specific project milestones (e.g., at major reviews or when part of the project is delivered).

ISO9000 QUALITY STANDARDS

ISO9000 is a quality series and comprises a set of five documents developed in 1987 by the International Standards Organization (ISO). ISO9000 standards and certification are usually associated with non-IS manufacturing processes. However, application development organizations can benefit from these standards and position themselves for certification, if necessary. All the ISO9000 standards are guidelines and interpretive because of their lack of stringency and rules. ISO certification is becoming more and more important throughout Europe and the U.S. for the manufacture of hardware. Software suppliers will increasingly be required to have certification. ISO9000 is a definitive set of quality standards, but it represents quality standards as part of a total quality management (TQM) program. It consists of ISO9001, ISO9002, or ISO9003, and it provides the guidelines for selecting and implementing a quality assurance standard.

ISO9001 is a very comprehensive standard and defines all the quality elements required to demonstrate the supplier's ability to design and deliver a quality product. ISO9002 covers quality considerations for the supplier to control the design and development activities. ISO9003 demonstrates the supplier's ability to detect and control product nonconformity during inspection and testing. ISO9004 describes the quality standards associated with ISO9001, ISO9002, and ISO9003 and provides a comprehensive quality checklist.

Exhibit 3 shows the ISO9000 and companion international standards.

Exhibit 3. Companion ISO Standards

International	U.S.	Europe	U.K.
ISO9000	ANSI/ASQA	EN29000	BS5750 (Part 0.1)
ISO9001	ANSI/ASQC	EN29001	BS5750 (Part 1)
ISO9002	ANSI/ASQC	EN29002	BS5750 (Part 2)
ISO9003	ANSI/ASQC	EN29003	BS5750 (Part 3)
ISO9004	ANSI/ASQC	EN29004	BS5750 (Part 4)

Part 2
Overview of Testing Techniques

TEST CASE DESIGN

Ad hoc testing or error guessing is an informal testing technique that relies on inspiration, creative thinking, and brainstorming to design tests. While this technique is important and often very useful, there is no substitute for formal test techniques. Formal design techniques provide a higher probability of assuring test coverage and reliability. Test case design requires a specification that includes a description of the functionality, inputs, and outputs. Test case design becomes a part of the system documentation. Each test case must have a clear definition of the test objectives. Risk management may help define the test objectives, especially in areas of high risk. Following is a discussion of the leading test design approaches.

Black-Box Testing (functional)

Black-box or functional testing is one in which test conditions are developed based on the program or system's functionality, i.e., the tester requires information about the input data and observed output, but does not know how the program or system works. Just as one does not have to know how a car works internally to drive it, it is not necessary to know the internal structure of a program to execute it. The tester focuses on testing the program's functionality against the specification. With black-box testing, the tester views the program as a black-box and is completely unconcerned with the internal structure of the program or system. Some examples in this category include: decision tables, equivalence partitioning, range testing, boundary value testing, database integrity testing, cause-effect graphing, orthogonal array testing, array and table testing, exception testing, limit testing, and random testing.

A major advantage of black-box testing is that the tests are geared to what the program or system is supposed to do, and it is natural and understood by everyone. This should be verified with techniques such as structured walkthroughs, inspections, and JADs. A limitation is that exhaustive input testing is not achievable, because this requires that every possible input condition or combination be tested. Additionally, since there is no knowledge of the internal structure or logic, there could be errors or deliberate mischief on the part of a programmer, which may not be detectable with black-box testing. For example, suppose a payroll programmer wants to insert some job security into a payroll application he or she is developing. By inserting the following extra code into the application, if the employee were to be terminated, i.e., his or her employee ID no longer exists in the system, justice would sooner or later prevail.

```
if my employee ID exists
    deposit regular pay check into my bank account
else
    deposit an enormous amount of money into my bank account
    erase any possible financial audit trails
    erase this code
```

White-Box Testing (structural)

In white-box or structural testing test conditions are designed by examining paths of logic. The tester examines the internal structure of the program or system. Test data are driven by examining the logic of the program or system, without concern for the program or system requirements. The tester knows the internal program structure and logic, just as a car mechanic knows the inner workings of an automobile. Specific examples in this category include basis path analysis, statement coverage, branch coverage, condition coverage, and branch/condition coverage.

An advantage of white-box testing is that it is thorough and focuses on the produced code. Since there is knowledge of the internal structure or logic, errors or deliberate mischief on the part of a programmer have a higher probability of being detected.

One disadvantage of white-box testing is that it does not verify that the specifications are correct, i.e., it focuses only on the internal logic and does not verify the logic to the specification. Another disadvantage is that there is no way to detect missing paths and data-sensitive errors. For example, if the statement in a program should be coded "if $|a-b| < 10$" but is coded "if $(a-b) <1$," this would not be detectable without specification details. A final disadvantage is that white-box testing cannot execute all possible logic paths through a program because this would entail an astronomically large number of tests.

Gray-Box Testing (functional and structural)

Black-box testing focuses on the program's functionality against the specification. White-box testing focuses on the paths of logic. Gray-box testing is a combination of black- and white-box testing. The tester studies the requirements specifications and communicates with the developer to understand the internal structure of the system. The motivation is to clear up ambiguous specifications and "read between the lines" to design implied tests. One example of the use of gray-box testing is when it appears to the tester that a certain functionality seems to be reused throughout an application. If the tester communicates with the developer and understands the internal design and architecture, many tests will be eliminated, because it may be possible to test the functionality only once. Another example is when the syntax of a command consists of seven possible parameters that can be entered in any order, as follows:

Command parm1, parm2, parm3, parm4, parm5, parm6, parm7

In theory, a tester would have to create 7! or 5,040 tests. The problem is compounded further if some of the parameters are optional. If the tester uses gray-box testing, by talking with the developer and understanding the parser algorithm, if each parameter is independent, only seven tests may be required.

Manual vs. Automated Testing

The basis of the manual testing categorization is that it is not typically carried out by people and is not implemented on the computer. Examples include, structured walkthroughs, inspections, joint application designs (JADs), and desk checking.

The basis of the automated testing categorization is that it is implemented on the computer. Examples include boundary value testing, branch coverage testing, prototyping, and syntax testing. Syntax testing is performed by a language compiler, and the compiler is a program that executes on a computer.

Static vs. Dynamic Testing

Static testing approaches are time independent and are classified in this way because they do not necessarily involve either manual or automated execution of the product being tested. Examples include syntax checking, structured walkthroughs, and inspections. An inspection of a program occurs against a source code listing in which each code line is read line by line and discussed. An example of static testing using the computer is a static flow analysis tool, which investigates another program for errors without executing the program. It analyzes the other program's control and data flow to discover problems such as references to a variable that has not been initialized and unreachable code.

Dynamic testing techniques are time dependent and involve executing a specific sequence of instructions on paper or by the computer. Examples include structured walkthroughs, in which the program logic is simulated by walking through the code and verbally describing it. Boundary testing is a dynamic testing technique that requires the execution of test cases on the computer with a specific focus on the boundary values associated with the inputs or outputs of the program.

TAXONOMY OF SOFTWARE TESTING TECHNIQUES

A testing technique is a set of interrelated procedures which, together, produce a test deliverable. There are many possible classification schemes for software testing and Exhibit 1 describes one way. The exhibit reviews formal popular testing techniques and also classifies each per the above discussion as manual, automated, static, dynamic, functional (black-box), or structural (white-box). Exhibit 2 provides a description of each technique.

Exhibit 1. Testing Technique Categories

Technique	Manual	Automated	Static	Dynamic	Functional	Structural
Basis Path Testing		x		x		x
Black-Box Testing		x		x	x	
Bottom-Up Testing		x		x		x
Boundary Value Testing		x		x	x	
Branch/Condition Coverage		x		x		x
Branch Coverage Testing		x		x		x
Cause-Effect Graphing		x		x	x	
Condition Coverage Testing		x		x		x
CRUD Testing		x		x	x	
Database Testing		x		x		x
Decision Tables		x		x	x	
Desk Checking	x			x		x
Equivalence Partitioning		x		x		
Exception Testing		x		x	x	
Free Form Testing		x		x	x	

Exhibit 1. (Continued) Testing Technique Categories

Technique	Manual	Automated	Static	Dynamic	Functional	Structural
Gray-Box Testing		x		x	x	x
Histograms	x				x	
Inspections	x		x		x	x
JADs	x				x	x
Orthogonal Array Testing	x		x		x	
Pareto Analysis	x				x	
Positive and Negative Testing		x		x	x	
Prior Defect History Testing	x		x		x	
Prototyping		x		x	x	
Random Testing		x		x	x	
Range Testing		x		x	x	
Regression Testing				x	x	
Risk-Based Testing	x		x		x	
Run Charts	x		x		x	
Sandwich Testing		x		x		x
Statement Coverage Testing		x		x		x
State Transition Testing		x		x	x	
Statistical Profile Testing	x		x		x	
Structured Walkthroughs	x			x	x	x
Syntax Testing		x	x	x	x	
Table Testing		x		x		x
Thread Testing		x		x		x
Top-Down Testing		x		x	x	x
White-Box Testing		x		x		x

SOFTWARE QUALITY IN PERSPECTIVE

Exhibit 2. Testing Technique Descriptions

Technique	Brief Description
Basis Path Testing	Identifying tests based on flow and paths of a program or system
Black-Box Testing	Test cases generated based on the system's functionality
Bottom-Up Testing	Integrating modules or programs starting from the bottom
Boundary Value Testing	Test cases generated from boundary values of equivalence classes
Branch/Condition Coverage Testing	Verify each condition in a decision takes on all possible outcomes at least once
Branch Coverage Testing	Verify each branch has true and false outcomes at least once
Cause-Effect Graphing	Mapping multiple simultaneous inputs which may affect others to identify their conditions to test
Condition Coverage Testing	Verify that each condition in a decision takes on all possible outcomes at least once
CRUD Testing	Build CRUD matrix and test all object creations, reads, updates, and deletions
Database Testing	Check the integrity of database field values
Decision Tables	Table showing the decision criteria and the respective actions
Desk Checking	Developer reviews code for accuracy

Exhibit 2. (Continued) Testing Technique Descriptions

Technique	Brief Description
Equivalence Partitioning	Each input condition partitioned into two or more groups. Test cases are generated from representative valid and invalid classes
Exception Testing	Identify error messages and exception handling processes and conditions that trigger them
Free Form Testing	*Ad hoc* or brainstorming using intuition to define test cases
Gray-Box Testing	A combination of black-box and white-box testing to take advantage of both
Histograms	A graphical representation of measured values organized according to the frequency of occurrence used to pinpoint hot spots
Inspections	Formal peer review that uses checklists, entry criteria, and exit criteria
JADs	Technique that brings users and developers together to jointly design systems in facilitated sessions
Orthogonal Array Testing	Mathematical technique to determine which variations of parameters need to be tested
Pareto Analysis	Analyze defect patterns to identify causes and sources
Positive and Negative Testing	Test the positive and negative values for all inputs

Exhibit 2. (Continued) Testing Technique Descriptions

Technique	Brief Description
Prior Defect History Testing	Test cases are created or rerun for every defect found in prior tests of the system
Prototyping	General approach to gather data from users by building and demonstrating to them some part of a potential application
Random Testing	Technique involving random selection from a specific set of input values where any value is as likely as any other
Range Testing	For each input identifies the range over which the system behavior should be the same
Regression Testing	Tests a system in light of changes made during a development spiral, debugging, maintenance, or the development of a new release
Risk-Based Testing	Measure the degree of business risk in a system to improve testing
Run Charts	A graphical representation of how a quality characteristic varies with time
Sandwich Testing	Integrating modules or programs from the top and bottom simultaneously
Statement Coverage Testing	Every statement in a program is executed at least once

Exhibit 2. (Continued) Testing Technique Descriptions

Technique	Brief Description
State Transition Testing	Technique in which the states of a system are first identified and then test cases are written to test the triggers to cause a transition from one condition to another state
Statistical Profile Testing	Statistical techniques are used to develop a usage profile of the system that helps define transaction paths, conditions, functions, and data tables
Structured Walkthroughs	A technique for conducting a meeting at which project participants examine a work product for errors
Syntax Testing	Data-driven technique to test combinations of input syntax
Table Testing	Test access, security, and data integrity of table entries
Thread Testing	Combining individual units into threads of functionality which together accomplish a function or set of functions
Top-Down Testing	Integrating modules or programs starting from the top
White-Box Testing	Test cases are defined by examining the paths of logic of a system

Part 3
Quality Through a Continuous Improvement Process

CONTRIBUTION OF EDWARD DEMING

While Henry Ford and Fredrick Winslow Taylor made enormous contributions to factory production, Dr. Edward Deming has gone beyond them. He has influenced every facet of work in every industry, influencing government, schools, and hospitals. Deming has had a profound effect on how people think, how they see themselves, and how they relate to their customers, to one another, and to society.

In 1928 he earned his Ph.D. in physics and in the next four years published papers about the effect of electrons on the structure of materials. He started his career already at the frontiers of physics. In 1934 he began to move away from physics and physical chemistry and published his first paper in the field of statistics. In 1937 he wrote a paper on the statistical theory of errors.

The 1940 census. By law the federal government is required to take a population census every 10 years, and in 1940 Deming became involved with the Census Bureau of the Department of Commerce. The proper tool for this task was statistics, and so we find in his list of publications a series of 26 papers dealing almost solely with problems of sampling. One paper, published in 1944, during World War II, introduced Shewhart's methods of quality control to engineers. He took the lead in getting this subject into the wartime training of engineers, giving the first course himself at Stanford University. From around 1945 onward, people did not think of him as a physicist but as a statistician. It is not surprising, therefore, that when General MacArthur needed to make a population survey in Japan in 1948, he called upon Deming. In 1953 — three years after he started to work with Japanese managers — he started his crusade to bring quality management principles to American managers. In 1953 he published *Management's Responsibility for the Use of Statistical Techniques in Industry,* thus marking the start of a theme he would pursue for the next 40 years. He had begun to see the transformation in Japan.

ROLE OF STATISTICAL METHODS

Deming's quality method includes the use of statistical methods that he believed were essential to minimize the confusion when there is variation in a process. Statistics also helps us to understand the processes themselves, gain control, and improve them. This is brought home by the quote, "In God we trust. All others must use data." Particular attention is paid to locating a problem's major causes which, when removed, improve quality significantly. Deming points out that many statistical techniques are not difficult and require a strong background in mathematics. Education, however, is a very powerful tool and is required on all levels of an organization to make it work.

The following is an outline of some of the statistical methods which are further described and applied to software testing. More details are provided in Section III.

Cause-and-Effect Diagram. Often called the "fishbone" diagram, this method can be used in brainstorming sessions to locate factors that may influence a situation. This is a tool used to identify possible causes of a problem by representing the relationship between some effect and its possible cause.

Flow Chart. This is a graphical method of documenting a process. It is a diagram that shows the sequential steps of a process or of a work flow that goes into creating a product or service. The justification of flow charts is that in order to improve a process, one needs first to understand it.

Pareto Chart. This is a commonly used graphical technique in which events to be analyzed are named. The incidents are counted by name; the events are ranked by frequency in a bar chart in ascending sequence. Pareto analysis applies the 80/20 rule. An example of this is when 20% of an organization's customers account for 80% of the revenue, e.g., focus on the 20%.

Run Chart. A run chart is a graphical technique that graphs data points in chronological order to illustrate trends of a characteristic being measured in order to assign a potential cause rather than random variation.

Histogram. A histogram is a graphical description of measured values organized according to the frequency or relative frequency of occurrence. It also provides the average and variation.

Scatter Diagram. A scatter diagram is a graph designed to show where there is a relationship between two variables or changing factors.

Control Chart. A control chart is a statistical method for distinguishing between special and common variations exhibited by processes. It is a run chart with statistically determined upper and lower limits drawn on either side of the process averages.

DEMING'S 14 QUALITY PRINCIPLES

Deming outlined 14 quality principles, which must be used concurrently in order to achieve quality. While these principles were applied to industry, influencing government, schools, and hospitals, many are also applicable to achieving software quality from an information technology perspective. The following is a brief discuss of each point, followed by a description of how a quality assurance organization might apply each.

Point 1: Create Constancy of Purpose

Most companies tend to dwell on their immediate problems without adequate attention to the future. According to Deming, "It is easy to stay bound up in the tangled knots of the problems of today, becoming ever more and more efficient in the future, but no company without a plan for the future will stay in business." A constancy of purpose requires: innovation, e.g., long-term planning for it, investment in research and education, and continuous improvement of products and service.

To apply this point, an information technology quality assurance organization can:

1. Develop a quality assurance plan that provides a long-range quality direction
2. Require software testers to develop and maintain comprehensive test plans for each project
3. Encourage quality analysts and testers to come up with new and innovative ideas to maximize quality
4. Strive to continuously improve quality processes

Point 2: Adopt the New Philosophy

Quality must become the new religion. According to Deming, "The cost of living depends inversely on the goods and services that a given amount of money will buy, e.g., reliable service reduces costs. Delays and mistakes raise costs." Consumers of goods and services end up paying for delays and mistakes, which reduces their standard of living. Tolerance of acceptability levels and defects in systems is the roadblock between quality and productivity.

To apply this point, an information technology quality assurance organization can:

1. Educate the information technology organization on the need and value of quality
2. Promote the quality assurance department to the same level as any other department
3. Defuse the notion that quality assurance is negative and the "watch dogs"
4. Develop a risk management plan and not accept any anomalies outside the range of acceptable risk tolerance

Point 3: Cease Dependence on Mass Inspection

The old way of thinking is to inspect bad quality out. A better approach is that inspection should be used to see how we are doing, and not be left to the final product, when it is difficult to determine where in the process a defect took place. Quality should be built in without the dependence on mass inspections.

To apply this point, an information technology quality assurance organization can:

1. Promote and interject technical reviews, walkthroughs, and inspections as nondefensive techniques for achieving quality throughout the entire development cycle
2. Instill the need for the whole organization to be quality conscious and treat it as a tangible, measurable work product deliverable
3. Require statistical evidence of information technology quality

Point 4: End the Practice of Awarding Business on Price Tag Alone

"Two or more suppliers for the same item will multiply the evils that are necessarily inherent and bad enough with any one supplier." A buyer will serve his company best by developing a long-term relationship of loyalty and trust with a single vendor. Rather than using standards manuals by which vendors must qualify for business, a better approach is active involvement by the supplier's management with Deming's Fourteen Points.

To apply this point, an information technology quality assurance organization can:

1. Require software quality and test vendors to provide statistical evidence of their quality
2. Pick the best vendor for each quality assurance tool, testing tool, or service, and develop a working relationship consistent with the quality plan

Point 5: Improve Constantly and Forever the System of Production and Service

Improvement is not a one-time effort — management is obligated to improve quality continuously. "Putting out fires is not improvement. Finding a point out of control, finding the special cause and removing it, is only putting the process back to where it was in the first place. The obligation for improvement is a ceaseless process."

To apply this point, an information technology Quality Assurance organization can:

1. Constantly improve quality assurance and testing processes
2. Don't rely on judgment
3. Use statistical techniques such as root cause and effect analysis to uncover the sources of problems and test analysis

Point 6: Institute Training and Retraining

Often there is little or no training and workers do not know when they have done their jobs correctly. It is very difficult to erase improper training. Deming stresses that training should not end as long as performance is not in statistical control and there is something to be gained.

To apply this point, an information technology quality assurance organization can:

1. Institute modern training aids and practices
2. Encourage quality staff to constantly increase their knowledge of quality and testing techniques by attending seminars and classes
3. Reward staff for creating new seminars and special interest groups
4. Use statistical techniques to determine when training is needed and completed

Point 7: Institute Leadership

"There is no excuse to offer for putting people on a job that they know not how to do. Most so-called 'goofing off' — somebody seems to be lazy, doesn't seem to care — that person is almost always in the wrong job, or has very poor management." It is the responsibility of management to discover the inhibitors that prevent workers from taking pride in their jobs. From an information technology point of view, development often views the job of quality to be the QA department's responsibility. QA should be very aggressive as quality leaders and point out that quality is everyone's responsibility.

To apply this point, an information technology quality assurance organization can:

1. For example, if a developer has an excessive number of defects discovered by QA testing, take the time to train him or her on how to unit test his or her code effectively.
2. Improve supervision, which is the responsibility of management
3. Allow the project leader to have more time to help people on the job
4. Use statistical methods to indicate where there are faults

Point 8: Drive Out Fear

There is often no incentive for problem solving. Suggesting new ideas is too risky. People are afraid of losing their raises, promotions, or jobs. "Fear takes a horrible toll. Fear is all around, robbing people of their pride, hurting them, robbing them of a chance to contribute to the company. It is unbelievable what happens when you unloose fear." A common problem is the fear of inspections.

To apply this point, an information technology quality assurance organization can:

1. Promote the idea that quality is goodness and should be rewarded, and promote any new ideas to improve quality
2. Prior to a structured walkthrough, inspection, or JAD session, QA should make sure everyone understands the ground rules and promote an "egoless" environment
3. Periodically schedule a "Quality Day" in which quality improvement ideas are openly shared

Point 9: Break Down Barriers Between Staff Areas

There are numerous problems when departments have different goals and do not work as a team to solve problems, set policies, or define new directions. "People can work superbly in their respective departments, but if their goals are in conflict, they can ruin the company. It is better to have teamwork, working for the company."

To apply this point, an information technology quality assurance organization can:

1. Quality assurance and other departments (particularly development) need to work closely together; QA should be viewed as the "good guys" trying to make the software products the best in the world
2. Quality assurance should point out that a defect discovered before production is one that won't be discovered by the users

Point 10: Eliminate Slogans, Exhortations, and Targets for the Workforce

"Slogans never helped anybody do a good job. They generate frustration and resentment." Slogans such as "Zero Defects" or "Do it Right the First Time" are fine on the surface. The problem is that they are viewed as signals that management does not understand employees' problems, or care. There is a common practice of setting goals without describing how they are going to be accomplished.

To apply this point, an information technology quality assurance organization can:

1. Encourage management to avoid the use of slogans
2. Rather than generate slogans, the QA organization should develop and document quality standards, procedures, and processes which the rest of the organization can use to help them to maximize quality

Point 11: Eliminate Numerical Goals

"Quotas or other work standards, such as measured day work or rates, impede quality perhaps more than any other single working condition. As work standards are generally used, they guarantee inefficiency and high costs." A proper work standard would define what is and is not acceptable in terms of quality.

To apply this point, an information technology quality assurance organization can:

1. Look not just at the numbers but look carefully at the quality standards
2. Avoid formally publicizing defects rates by individual or department
3. Work with the development organization to define quality standards and procedures to improve quality
4. When there are specific quality issues, the QA and Development manager need to address them informally

Point 12: Remove Barriers to Pride of Workmanship

People are regarded as a commodity, to be used as needed. If not needed, they are returned to the market. Managers cope with many problems but tend to shy away from people problems. They often form "Quality Control Circles," but this is often a way for a manager to *pretend* to be doing something about a problem. Management seldom invests employees with any authority, nor does it act upon their recommendations.

To apply this point, an information technology quality assurance organization can:

1. Instill an image that quality is their deliverable and is a very valuable commodity

2. Delegate responsibility to the staff to seek out quality and do whatever it takes to accomplish it

Point 13: Institute a Vigorous Program of Education and Retraining

People must acquire new knowledge and skills. Education and retraining is an investment in people, which is required for long-term planning. Education and training must fit people into new jobs and responsibilities.

To apply this point, an information technology quality assurance organization can:

1. Encourage quality staff to constantly increase their knowledge of quality and testing techniques by attending seminars and classes
2. Reward staff for creating new seminars and special interest groups
3. Retrain individuals in new quality skills

Point 14: Take Action to Accomplish the Transformation

Top management needs to push these thirteen points. Every employee, including managers, should acquire a precise idea of how to improve quality continually, but the initiative must come from top management. The following discusses a process that can be used to apply Deming's point fourteen. It is also the process that will be constantly reinforced in this text to improve software testing processes.

CONTINUOUS IMPROVEMENT THROUGH THE PLAN, DO, CHECK, ACT PROCESS

The term control has various meanings, including to supervise, govern, regulate, or restrain. The *control* in quality control means defining the objective of the job, developing and carrying out a plan to meet that objective, and checking to determine if the anticipated results are achieved. If the anticipated results are not achieved, modifications are made in the work procedure to fulfill the plan.

One way to describe the above is with the "Deming Cycle" (or PDCA circle; see Exhibit 1), named after Deming in Japan because he introduced it there, although it was originated by Shewhart. It was the basis of the turnaround of the Japanese manufacturing industry, in addition to other Deming's management principles. The word management describes many different functions, encompassing policy management, human resources management, and safety control, as well as component control and management of materials, equipment, and daily schedules. In this text, the Deming model will be applied to software quality.

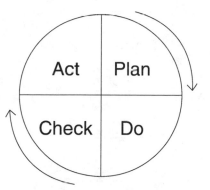

Exhibit 1. The Deming Quality Circle

In the **Plan** quadrant of the circle, one defines his or her objectives and determines the conditions and methods required to achieve them. It is crucial to clearly describe the goals and policies needed to achieve the objectives at this stage. A specific objective should be documented numerically, if possible. The procedures and conditions for the means and methods to achieve the objectives are described.

In the **Do** quadrant of the circle, the conditions are created and the necessary training to execute the plan is performed. It is paramount that everyone thoroughly understand the objectives and the plan. Workers need to be taught the procedures and skills they need to fulfill the plan and thoroughly understand the job. The work is then performed according to these procedures.

In the **Check** quadrant of the circle, one must check to determine whether work is progressing according to the plan and whether the expected results are obtained. The performance of the set procedures must be checked against changes in conditions, or abnormalities that may appear. As often as possible, the results of the work should be compared with the objectives. If a check detects an abnormality — that is, if the actual value differs from the target value — then a search for the cause of the abnormality must be initiated to prevent its recurrence. Sometimes it is necessary to retrain workers and revise procedures. It is important to make sure these changes are reflected and more fully developed in the next plan.

In the **Action** quadrant of the circle, if the checkup reveals that the work is not being performed according to plan or that results are not what was anticipated, measures must be devised for appropriate action.

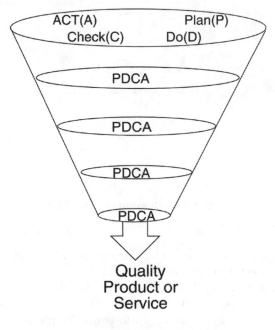

Exhibit 2. The Ascending Spiral

GOING AROUND THE PDCA CIRCLE

The above procedures not only ensure that the quality of the products meets expectations, but they also ensure that the anticipated price and delivery date are fulfilled. Sometimes our preoccupation with current concerns makes us unable to achieve optional results. By going around the PDCA circle, we can improve our working methods and obtain the desired results. Repeated use of PDCA makes it possible to improve the quality of the work, the work methods, and the results. Sometimes this concept is depicted as an ascending spiral as illustrated in Exhibit 2.

Section II
Life Cycle Testing Review

The life cycle development methodology consists of distinct phases from requirements to coding. Life cycle testing means that testing occurs in parallel with the development life cycle and is a continuous process. Deming's continuous improvement process is applied to software testing using the quality circle, principles, and statistical techniques.

The psychology of life cycle testing encourages testing to be performed outside the development organization. The motivation for this is that there are clearly defined requirements, and it is more efficient for a third party to verify these requirements.

The test plan is the bible of software testing and is a document prescribing the test objectives, scope, strategy approach and test details. There are specific guidelines for building a good test plan.

The two major quality assurance verification approaches for each life cycle phase are technical reviews and software testing. Technical reviews are more preventative, i.e., they aim to remove defects as soon as possible. Software testing verifies the actual code that has been produced.

The objectives of this section are to:

- Discuss how life cycle testing is a parallel activity
- Describe how Deming's process improvement is applied
- Discuss the psychology of life cycle development and testing
- Discuss the components of a good test
- List and describe how technical review and testing are verification techniques

Part 4
Overview

The following provides an overview of the "waterfall" life cycle development methodology and the associated testing activities. Deming's continuous quality improvement is applied with technical review and testing techniques.

WATERFALL DEVELOPMENT METHODOLOGY

The life cycle development or waterfall approach breaks the development cycle down into discrete phases, each with a rigid sequential begin and end (see Exhibit 1). Each phase is fully completed before the next is started. Once a phase is completed, in theory during development, one never goes back to change it.

In Exhibit 1 you can see that the first phase in the waterfall is user requirements. In this phase, the users are interviewed, their requirements are analyzed, and a document is produced detailing what the user's requirements are. Any reengineering or process redesign is incorporated into this phase.

In the next phase, entity relation diagrams, process decomposition diagrams, and data flow diagrams are created to allow the system to be broken into manageable components from a data and functional point of view. The outputs from the logical design phase are used to develop the physical design of the system. During the physical and program unit design phases, various structured design techniques, such as database schemas, Yourdon structure charts, and Warnier/Orr diagrams, are used to produce a design specification that will be used in the next phase.

In the program unit design phase, programmers develop the system according to the physical design produced in the previous phase. Once complete, the system enters the coding phase, where it will be written in a programming language, unit or component tested, integration tested, system tested, and finally user tested, often called acceptance testing.

Now the application is delivered to the users for the operation and maintenance phase, not shown on Exhibit 1. Defects introduced during the life cycle phases are detected, corrected, and new enhancements are incorporated into the application.

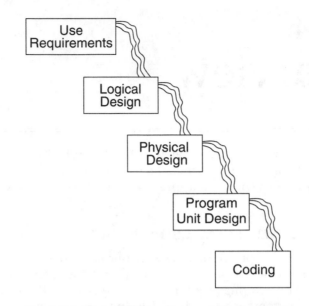

Exhibit 1. Waterfall Development Methodology

CONTINUOUS IMPROVEMENT "PHASED" APPROACH

Deming's continuous improvement process, which was discussed in the previous section, will be effectively applied to the waterfall development cycle using the Deming quality cycle, or PDCA, i.e., plan, do, check, and act. It is applied from two points of view: (1) software testing (2) quality control or technical reviews.

As defined in Section I, "Software Quality in Perspective," the three major components of quality assurance include software testing, quality control, and software configuration management. The purpose of software testing is to verify and validate the activities to ensure that the software design, code, and documentation meet all the requirements imposed on them. Software testing focuses on test planning, test design, test development, and test execution. Quality control is the process and methods used to monitor work and observe whether requirements are met. It focuses on structured walkthroughs and inspections to remove defects introduced during the software development life cycle.

PSYCHOLOGY OF LIFE CYCLE TESTING

In the waterfall development life cycle there is typically a concerted effort to keep the testing and development departments separate. This testing organization was typically separate from the development organization with a different reporting structure. The basis of this is that since requirements and design documents have been created at specific phases in the development life cycle, a separate quality assurance organization should be able to translate these documents into test plans, test cases, and test specifications. Underlying assumptions include the belief that (1) programmers should not test their own programs and (2) programming organizations should not test their own programs.

It is thought that software testing is a destructive process and that it would be very difficult for a programmer to suddenly change his or her perspective from developing a software product to trying to find defects, or breaking the software. It was believed that programmers cannot effectively test their own programs because they cannot bring themselves to attempt to expose errors.

Part of this argument was that there will be errors due to the programmer's misunderstanding of the requirements of the programs. Thus, a programmer testing his own code would have the same bias and would not be as effective testing it as someone else.

It is not impossible for a programmer to test his or her own programs, but testing is more effective when performed by someone who does not have a stake in it, as a programmer does. Since the development deliverables have been documented, why not let another individual verify them?

It is thought that a programming organization is measured by its ability to produce a program or system on time and economically. It is difficult for the programming organization to be objective, just as it is for an individual programmer. If a concerted effort were made to find as many defects as possible, it was believed that the project would probably be late and not cost effective. Less quality is the result.

From a practical point of view, an independent organization should be responsible for the quality of the software products. Such organizations as product test or quality assurance were created to serve as independent parties.

SOFTWARE TESTING AS A CONTINUOUS IMPROVEMENT PROCESS

Software life cycle testing means that testing occurs in parallel with the development cycle and is a continuous process (see Exhibit 2). The software testing process should start early in the application life cycle, not just in the traditional validation testing phase after the coding phase has been completed. Testing should be integrated into application development. In order to do so, there needs to be a commitment on the part of the development organization and close communication with the quality assurance function.

A test plan is started during the requirements phase. It is an organization of testing work. It is a document describing the approach to be taken

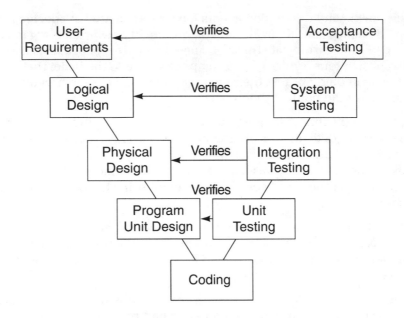

Exhibit 2. Development Phases vs. Testing Types

for the intended testing activities and includes the items to be tested, the types of tests to be performed, test schedules, human resources, reporting procedures, evaluation criteria, etc.

During logical, physical, and program unit design, the test plan is refined with more details. Test cases are also created. A test case is a specific set of test data and test scripts. A test script guides the tester through a test and ensures consistency among separate executions of the test. A test also includes the expected results to verify whether the test met the objective correctly. During the coding phase, test scripts and test data are generated. During application testing, the test scripts are executed and the results are analyzed.

Exhibit 2 shows a correspondence between application development and the testing activities. The application development cycle proceeds from user requirements and design until the code is completed. During test design and development, the acceptance test criteria was established in a test plan. As more details are refined, the system, integration, and unit testing requirements are established. There may or may not be a separate test plan for each test type, or one plan may be used.

During test execution, the process is reversed and starts with unit testing. Integration tests are performed which combine individual, unit tested pieces of code. Once this is completed, the system is tested from a total system point of view. This is known as system testing. System testing is a multifaceted test to evaluate the functionality, performance, and usability of the system. The final test is the acceptance test, which is a user-run test that verifies the ability of the system to meet the original user objectives and requirements. In some cases the system test serves as the acceptance test.

If you will recall, the PDCA approach, i.e., plan, do, check, and act, is a control mechanism used to control, supervise, govern, regulate, or restrain a system. The approach first defines the objectives of a process, develops and carries out the plan to meet those objectives, and checks to determine if the anticipated results are achieved. If they are not achieved, the plan is modified to fulfill the objectives. The PDCA quality cycle can be applied to software testing.

The **Plan** step of the continuous improvement process, when applied to software testing, starts with a definition of the test objectives, e.g., what is to be accomplished as a result of testing. Testing criteria do more than simply ensure that the software performs according to specifications. Objectives ensure that all responsible individuals contribute to the definition of the test criteria to maximize quality.

A major deliverable of this step is a software test plan. A test plan is the basis for accomplishing testing. The test plan should be considered an ongoing document. As the system changes, so does the plan. The test plan also becomes part of the system maintenance documentation after the application is delivered to the user. The outline of a good test plan includes an introduction, the overall plan, and testing requirements. As more detail is available, the business functions, test logs, problem and summary reports, test software, hardware, data, personnel requirements, test schedule, test entry criteria, and exit criteria are added.

The **Do** step of the continuous improvement process when applied to software testing describes how to design and execute the tests included in the test plan. The test design includes test cases, test procedures and scripts, expected results, function/test case matrix, test logs, etc. The more definitive a test plan is, the easier the test design will be. If the system changes between development of the test plan and when the tests are to be executed, the test plan should be updated accordingly, i.e., whenever the system changes, the test plan should change.

The test team is responsible for the execution of the tests and must ensure that the test is executed according to the plan. Elements of the **Do** step include selecting test tools, defining the resource requirements, defining the test setup conditions and environment, test requirements, and the actual testing of the application.

The **Check** step of the continuous improvement process when applied to software testing includes the evaluation of how the testing process is progressing. The credo for statisticians, "In God we trust. All others must use data," is crucial to the Deming method. It is important to base decisions as much as possible on accurate and timely data. Testing metrics such as the number and types of defects, the workload effort, and the schedule status are key.

It is also important to create test reports. Testing began with setting objectives, identifying functions, selecting tests to validate the test functions, creating test conditions, and executing the tests. To construct test reports, the test team must formally record the results and relate them to the test plan and system objectives. In this sense, the test report reverses all the previous testing tasks.

Summary and interim test reports should be written at the end of testing and at key testing checkpoints. The process used for report writing is the same whether it is an interim or a summary report, and, like other tasks in testing, report writing is also subject to quality control, i.e., it should be reviewed. A test report should at least include a record of defects discovered, data reduction techniques, root cause analysis, the development of findings, and recommendations to management to improve the testing process.

The **Act** step of the continuous improvement process when applied to software testing includes devising measures for appropriate actions relating to work that was not performed according to the plan or results that were not anticipated in the plan. This analysis is fed back to the plan. Examples include updating the test suites, test cases, test scripts, reevaluating the people, process, and technology dimensions of testing.

The Testing Bible: Software Test Plan

A test plan is a document describing the approach to be taken for intended testing activities and serves as a service level agreement between the quality assurance testing function and other interested parties, such as development. A test plan should be developed early in the development cycle and help improve the interactions of the analysis, design, and coding activities. A test plan defines the test objectives, scope, strategy and approach, test procedures, test environment, test completion criteria, test cases, items to be tested, the tests to be performed, the test schedules, personnel requirements, reporting procedures, assumptions, risks, and contingency planning.

While developing a test plan, one should be sure that it is simple, complete, current, and accessible by the appropriate individuals for feedback and approval. A good test plan flows logically and minimizes redundant testing, demonstrates full functional coverage, provides workable procedures for monitoring, tracking, and reporting test status, contains a clear definition of the roles and responsibilities of the parties involved, target delivery dates, and clearly documents the test results.

There are two ways of building a test plan. The first approach is a master test plan which provides an overview of each detailed test plan, i.e., a test plan of a test plan. A detailed test plan verifies a particular phase in the waterfall development life cycle. Test plan examples include unit, integration, system, acceptance. Other detailed test plans include application enhancements, regression testing, and package installation. Unit test plans are code oriented and very detailed but short because of their limited scope. System or acceptance test plans focus on the functional test or black-box view of the entire system, not just a software unit. See Appendix E-1, Unit Test Plan, and Appendix E-2, System/Acceptance Test Plan, for more details.

The second approach is one test plan. This approach includes all the test types in one test plan, often called the acceptance/system test plan, but covers unit, integration, system, and acceptance testing and all the planning considerations to complete the tests.

A major component of a test plan, often in the Test Procedure section, is a test case, as shown in Exhibit 3. (Also see Appendix E-8, Test Case.) A test case defines the step-by-step process whereby a test is executed. It includes the objectives and conditions of the test, the steps needed to set up the test, the data inputs, the expected results, and the actual results. Other information such as the software, environment, version, test ID, screen, and test type are also provided.

Major Steps to Develop a Test Plan

A test plan is the basis for accomplishing testing and should be considered a living document, i.e., as the application changes, the test plan should change.

A good test plan encourages the attitude of "quality before design and coding." It is able to demonstrate that it contains full functional coverage, and the test cases trace back to the functions being tested. It also contains workable mechanisms for monitoring and tracking discovered defects and report status. Appendix E-2 is a System/Acceptance Test Plan template which combines unit, integration, and system test plans into one. It will also be used in this section to describe how a test plan is built during the "waterfall" life cycle development methodology.

LIFE CYCLE TESTING REVIEW

Date: _____ Tested by: _____

System: _____ Environment: _____

Objective: _____ Test ID _____ Req ID _____

Function: _____ Screen: _____

Version: _____ Test Type: _____

(Unit, Integ., System, Accept.)

Condition to Test:

_____

_____

Data/Steps to Perform

_____

_____

Expected Results:

_____

_____

_____

Actual Results: Passed _____ Failed _____

_____

_____

_____

Exhibit 3. Test Case Form

_____

The following are the major steps that need to be completed to build a good test plan.

1. Define the Test Objectives. The first step for planning any test is to establish what is to be accomplished as a result of the testing. This step ensures that all responsible individuals contribute to the definition of the test criteria that will be used. The developer of a test plan determines what is going to be accomplished with the test, the specific tests to be performed, the test expectations, the critical success factors of the test, constraints, scope of the tests to be performed, the expected end products of the test, a final system summary report (see Appendix E-11, System Summary Report), and the final signatures and approvals. The test objectives are reviewed and approval for the objectives is obtained.

2. Develop the Test Approach. The test plan developer outlines the overall approach or how each test will be performed. This includes the testing techniques that will be used, test entry criteria, test exit criteria, procedures to coordinate testing activities with development, the test management approach, such as defect reporting and tracking, test progress tracking, status reporting, test resources and skills, risks, and a definition of the test basis (functional requirement specifications, etc.).

3. Define the Test Environment. The test plan developer examines the physical test facilities, defines the hardware, software, and networks, determines which automated test tools and support tools are required, defines the help desk support required, builds special software required for the test effort, and develops a plan to support the above.

4. Develop the Test Specifications. The developer of the test plan forms the test team to write the test specifications, develops test specification format standards, divides up the work tasks and work breakdown, assigns team members to tasks, and identifies features to be tested. The test team documents the test specifications for each feature and cross-references them to the functional specifications. It also identifies the interdependencies and work flow of the test specifications and reviews the test specifications.

5. Schedule the Test. The test plan developer develops a test schedule based on the resource availability and development schedule, compares the schedule with deadlines, balances resources and work load demands, defines major checkpoints, and develops contingency plans.

6. Review and Approve the Test Plan. The test plan developer or manager schedules a review meeting with the major players, reviews the plan in detail to ensure it is complete and workable, and obtains approval to proceed.

Components of a Test Plan

A system or acceptance test plan is based on the requirement specifications and is required in a very structured development and test environment. System testing evaluates the functionality and performance of the whole application and consists of a variety of tests including performance, usability, stress, documentation, security, volume, recovery, etc. Acceptance testing is a user-run test that demonstrates the application's ability to meet the original business objectives and system requirements and usually consists of a subset of system tests.

Exhibit 4 cross-references the sections of Appendix E-2, System/Acceptance Test Plan, against the "waterfall" life-cycle development phases. "Start" in the intersection indicates the recommended start time, or first-cut of a test activity. "Refine" indicates a refinement of the test activity started in a previous life cycle phase. "Complete" indicates the life cycle phase in which the test activity is completed.

TECHNICAL REVIEWS AS A CONTINUOUS IMPROVEMENT PROCESS

Quality control is a key *preventative* component of quality assurance. Defect removal via technical reviews during the development life cycle is an example of a quality control technique. The purpose of technical reviews is to increase the efficiency of the development life cycle and provide a method to measure the quality of the products. Technical reviews reduce the amount of rework, testing, and "quality escapes," i.e., undetected defects. They are the *missing links* to removing defects and can also be viewed as a testing technique, even though we have categorized testing as a separate quality assurance component.

Originally developed by Michael Fagan of IBM in the 1970s, inspections have several aliases. They are often referred to interchangeably as "peer reviews," "inspections," or "structured walkthroughs." Inspections are performed at each phase of the development life cycle from user requirements through coding. In the latter, code walkthroughs are performed in which the developer walks through the code for the reviewer.

Research demonstrates that technical reviews can be a lot more productive than automated testing techniques in which the application is executed and tested. A technical review is a form of testing, or manual testing, not involving program execution on the computer. Structured walkthroughs and inspections are a more efficient means of removing defects than software testing alone. They also remove defects earlier in the life cycle, thereby reducing defect-removal costs significantly. They represent a highly efficient, low-cost technique of defect removal and can potentially result in a reduction of defect-removal costs of greater than two-thirds when compared to dynamic software testing. A side benefit of inspections includes the ability to periodically analyze the defects recorded and remove the root causes early in the software development life cycle.

The purpose of the following section is to provide a framework for implementing software reviews. Discussed are the rationale for reviews, the roles of the participants, planning steps for effective reviews, scheduling, allocation, agenda definition, and review reports.

Exhibit 4. System/Acceptance Test Plan vs. Phase

Test Section	Requirements Phase	Logical Design Phase	Physical Design Phase	Program Unit Design Phase	Coding Phase
1. Introduction					
a. System Description	Start	Refine	Refine	Complete	
b. Objective	Start	Refine	Refine	Complete	
c. Assumptions	Start	Refine	Refine	Complete	
d. Risks	Start	Refine	Refine	Complete	
e. Contingencies	Start	Refine	Refine	Complete	
f. Constraints	Start	Refine	Refine	Complete	
g. Approval Signatures	Start	Refine	Refine	Complete	
2. Test Approach and Strategy					
a. Scope of Testing	Start	Refine	Refine	Complete	
b. Test Approach	Start	Refine	Refine	Complete	
c. Types of Tests	Start	Refine	Refine	Complete	
d. Logistics	Start	Refine	Refine	Complete	
e. Regression Policy	Start	Refine	Refine	Complete	
f. Test Facility		Start	Refine	Complete	
g. Test Procedures		Start	Refine	Complete	
h. Test Organization		Start	Refine	Complete	
i. Test Libraries		Start	Refine	Complete	
j. Test Tools		Start	Refine	Complete	
k. Version Control		Start	Refine	Complete	
l. Configuration Building		Start	Refine	Complete	
m. Change Control		Start	Refine	Complete	
3. Test Execution Setup					
a. System Test Process		Start	Refine	Complete	
b. Facility		Start	Refine	Complete	
c. Resources		Start	Refine	Complete	
d. Tool Plan		Start	Refine	Complete	
e. Test Organization		Start	Refine	Complete	
4. Test Specifications					
a. Functional Decomposition	Start	Refine	Refine	Complete	

Exhibit 4. (Continued) System/Acceptance Test Plan vs. Phase

Test Section	Requirements Phase	Logical Design Phase	Physical Design Phase	Program Unit Design Phase	Coding Phase
b. Functions Not to be Tested	Start	Refine	Refine	Complete	
c. Unit Test Cases				Start	Complete
d. Integration Test Cases			Start	Complete	
e. System Test Cases		Start	Refine	Complete	
f. Acceptance Test Cases	Start	Refine	Refine	Complete	
5. Test Procedures					
a. Test Case, Script, Data Development	Start	Refine	Refine	Refine	Complete
b. Test Execution	Start	Refine	Refine	Refine	Complete
c. Correction	Start	Refine	Refine	Refine	Complete
d. Version Control	Start	Refine	Refine	Refine	Complete
e. Maintaining Test Libraries	Start	Refine	Refine	Refine	Complete
f. Automated Test Tool Usage	Start	Refine	Refine	Refine	Complete
g. Project Management	Start	Refine	Refine	Refine	Complete
h. Monitoring and Status Reporting	Start	Refine	Refine	Refine	Complete
6. Test Tools					
a. Tools to Use		Start	Refine	Complete	
b. Installation and Setup		Start	Refine	Complete	
c. Support and Help		Start	Refine	Complete	
7. Personnel Resources					
a. Required Skills	Start	Refine	Refine	Complete	
b. Roles and Responsibilities	Start	Refine	Refine	Complete	
c. Numbers and Time Required	Start	Refine	Refine	Complete	
d. Training Needs	Start	Refine	Refine	Complete	
8. Test Schedule					
a. Development of Test Plan		Start	Refine	Refine	Complete
b. Design of Test Cases		Start	Refine	Refine	Complete

Exhibit 4. (Continued) System/Acceptance Test Plan vs. Phase

Test Section	Requirements Phase	Logical Design Phase	Physical Design Phase	Program Unit Design Phase	Coding Phase
c. Development of Test Cases		Start	Refine	Refine	Complete
d. Execution of Test Cases		Start	Refine	Refine	Complete
e. Reporting of Problems		Start	Refine	Refine	Complete
f. Developing Test Summary Report		Start	Refine	Refine	Complete
g. Documenting Test Summary Report		Start	Refine	Refine	Complete

Motivation for Technical Reviews

The motivation for a review is that it is impossible to test all software. Clearly, exhaustive testing of code is impractical. Technology also does not exist for testing a specification or high-level design. The idea of testing a software test plan is also bewildering. Testing also does not address quality issues or adherence to standards, which are possible with review processes.

There are a variety of software technical reviews available for a project, depending on the type of software product and the standards that affect the review processes. The types of reviews depend on the deliverables to be produced. For example, for a Department of Defense contract, there are certain stringent standards for reviews which must be followed. These requirements may not be required for in-house application development.

A review increases the quality of the software product, reduces rework and ambiguous efforts, reduces testing and defines test parameters, and is a repeatable and predictable process. It is an effective method in finding defects and discrepancies; it increases the reliability of the delivered product, impacts the schedule in a positive manner, and reduces development costs.

Early detection of errors reduces rework at later development stages, clarifies requirements and design, and identifies interfaces. It reduces the number of failures during testing, reduces the number of retests, identifies requirements testability, and helps identify missing or ambiguous requirements.

Types of Reviews

There are formal and informal reviews. Informal reviews occur spontaneously among peers, and the reviewers do not necessarily have any responsibility and do not have to produce a review report. Formal reviews are carefully planned meetings in which reviewers are held responsible for their participation and a review report is generated which contains action items.

The spectrum of review ranges from very informal peer reviews to extremely formal and structured inspections. The complexity of a review is usually correlated to the complexity of the project. As the complexity of a project increases, the need for more formal reviews increases.

Structured Walkthroughs

A structured walkthrough is a presentation review in which a review participant, usually the developer of the software being reviewed, narrates a description of the software, and the remainder of the group provides feedback throughout the presentation. Testing deliverables such as test plans, test cases, and test scripts can also be reviewed using the walkthrough technique. These are referred to as presentation reviews because the bulk of the feedback usually occurs only for the material actually presented.

Advanced preparation of the reviewers is not necessarily required. One potential disadvantage of a structured walkthrough is that, because of its informal structure, it may lead to disorganized and uncontrolled reviews. Walkthroughs may also be stressful if the developer is conducting the walkthrough.

Inspections

The inspection technique is a formally defined process for verification of the software product throughout its development. All software deliverables are examined at defined phases to assess the current status and quality effectiveness from the requirements to coding phase. One of the major decisions within an inspection is whether a software deliverable is eligible to proceed to the next development phase.

Software quality is achieved in a product during the early stages when the cost to remedy defects is 10 to 100 time less than it would be during testing or maintenance. It is, therefore, advantageous to find and correct defects as near to their point of origin as possible. Exit criteria are the standard against which inspections measure completion of the product at the end of a phase.

The advantages of inspections are that they are very systematic, controlled, and less stressful. The inspection process promotes the concept of egoless programming. If managed properly, it is a forum in which developers need not become emotionally protective of the work produced. An inspection requires an agenda to guide the review preparation and the meeting itself. Inspections have rigorous entry and exit requirements for the project work deliverables.

A major difference between structured walkthroughs and inspections is that inspections collect information to improve the development and review processes themselves. In this sense, an inspection is more of a quality assurance technique than walkthroughs.

Phased inspections apply the PDCA, (Plan, Do, Check, and Act) quality model. Each development phase has entrance requirements, e.g., how to qualify to enter an inspection and exit criteria, and how to know when to exit the inspection. In between the entry and exit are the project deliverables that are inspected. In Exhibit 5, the steps of a phased inspection and the corresponding PDCA steps are shown.

The **Plan** step of the continuous improvement process consists of inspection planning and preparing an education overview. The strategy of an inspection is to design and implement a review process that is timely, efficient, and effective. Specific products are designated, acceptable criteria, and meaningful metrics are defined to measure and maximize the efficiency of the process. Inspection materials must meet inspection entry criteria. The right participants are identified and scheduled. In addition, a suitable meeting place and time is arranged. The group of participants is educated on what is to be inspected and their roles.

The **Do** step includes individual preparation for the inspections and the inspection itself. Participants learn the material, prepare for their assigned roles, and the inspection proceeds. Each review is assigned one or more specific aspect of the product to be reviewed in terms of technical accuracy, standards and conventions, quality assurance, and readability.

Exhibit 5. PDCA Process and Inspections

Inspection Step	Description	Plan	Do	Check	Act
1. Planning	Identify participants, get materials together, schedule the overview	√			
2. Overview	Educate for the inspections	√			
3. Preparation	Individual preparation for the inspections		√		
4. Inspection	Actual inspection to identify defects		√	√	
5. Rework	Rework to correct any defects				√
6. Follow-up	Follow-up to ensure all defects are corrected				√

The **Check** step includes the identification and documentation of the defects uncovered. Defects are discovered during the inspection, but solution hunting and the discussion of design alternatives are discouraged. Inspections are a review process, not a solution session.

The **Act** step includes the rework and follow-up required to correct any defects. The author reworks all discovered defects. The team ensures that all the potential corrective actions are effective and no secondary defects are inadvertently introduced.

By going around the PDCA cycle for each development phase using inspections we verify and improve each phase deliverable at its origin and stop it dead in its tracks when defects are discovered (see Exhibit 6). The next phase cannot start until the discovered defects are corrected. The reason is that it is advantageous to find and correct defects as near to their point of origin as possible. Repeated application of the PDCA results in an ascending spiral to facilitate quality improvement at each phase. The end product is dramatically improved, and the bewildering task of software testing process will be minimized, e.g., a lot of the defects will have been identified and corrected by the time the testing team receives the code.

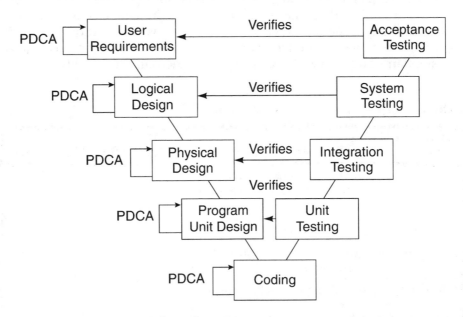

Exhibit 6. Phased Inspections as an Ascending Spiral

Participant Roles

Roles will depend on the specific review methodology being followed, i.e., structured walkthroughs or inspections. These roles are functional, which implies that it is possible in some reviews for a participant to execute more than one role. The role of the review participants after the review is especially important because many errors identified during a review may not be fixed correctly by the developer. This raises the issue of who should follow up on a review and whether or not another review is necessary.

The review leader is responsible for the review. This role requires scheduling the review, conducting an orderly review meeting, and preparing the review report. The review leader may also be responsible for ensuring that action items are properly handled after the review process. Review leaders must possess both technical and interpersonal management characteristics. The interpersonal management qualities include leadership ability, mediator skills, and organizational talents. The review leader must keep the review group focused at all times and prevent the meeting from becoming a problem-solving session. Material presented for review should not require the review leader to spend more than two hours for preparation.

The recorder role in the review process guarantees that all information necessary for an accurate review report is preserved. The recorder must digest complicated discussions and capture their essence in action items. The role of the recorder is clearly a technical function and one that cannot be performed by a nontechnical individual.

The reviewer role is to objectively analyze the software and be accountable for the review. An important guideline is that the reviewer must keep in mind that the software is being reviewed and *not* the producer of the software. This cannot be overstated. Also, the number of reviewers should be limited to six. If too many reviewers are involved, productivity will decrease.

In a technical review, the producer may actually lead the meeting in an organized discussion of the software. A degree of preparation and planning is needed in a technical review to present material at the proper level and pace. The attitude of the producer is also important, and it is essential that he or she does not take a defensive approach. This can be facilitated by the group leader's emphasizing that the purpose of the inspection is to uncover defects and produce the best product possible.

Steps for an Effective Review

1. Plan for the Review Process. Planning can be described at both the organizational level and the specific review level. Considerations at the organizational level include the number and types of reviews that are to be performed for the project. Project resources must be allocated for accomplishing these reviews.

At the specific review level, planning considerations include selecting participants and defining their respective roles, scheduling the review, and developing a review agenda. There are many issues involved in selecting of the review participants. It is a complex task normally performed by management, with technical input. When selecting review participants, care must be exercised to ensure that each aspect of the software under review can be addressed by at least some subset of the review team.

In order to minimize the stress and possible conflicts in review processes, it is important to discuss the role that a reviewer plays in the organization and the objectives of the review. Focus on the review objectives will lessen personality conflicts.

2. Schedule the Review. A review should ideally take place soon after a producer has completed the software but before additional effort is expended on work dependent on the software. The review leader must state the agenda based on a well thought out schedule. If all the inspection items have not been completed, another inspection should be scheduled.

The problem of allocating sufficient time to a review stems from the difficulty in estimating the time needed to perform the review. The approach that must be taken is the same as that for estimating the time to be allocated for any meeting; that is, an agenda must be formulated and time estimated for each agenda item. An effective technique is to estimate the time for each inspection item on a time line.

Another scheduling problem is the duration of the review when the review is too long. This requires that review processes be focused in terms of their objectives. Review participants must understand these review objectives and their implications in terms of actual review time, as well as preparation time, before committing to the review. The deliverable to be reviewed should meet a certain set of entry requirements before the review is scheduled. Exit requirements must also be defined.

3. Develop the Review Agenda. A review agenda must be developed by the review leader and the producer prior to the review. Although review agendas are specific to any particular product and the objective of its review, generic agendas should be produced for related types of products. These agendas may take the form of checklists (see Appendix F, Checklists, for more details).

4. Create a Review Report. The output of a review is a report. The format of the report is not important. The contents should address the management perspective, user perspective, developer perspective, and quality assurance perspective.

From a management perspective, the review report serves as a summary of the review that highlights what was reviewed, who did the reviewing, and their assessment. Management needs an estimate of when all action items will be resolved to successfully track the project.

The user may be interested in analyzing review reports for some of the same reasons as the manager. The user may also want to examine the quality of intermediate work products in an effort to monitor the development organization's progress.

From a developer's perspective, the critical information is contained in the action items. These may correspond to actual errors, possible problems, inconsistencies, or other considerations that the developer must address.

The quality assurance perspective of the review report is twofold. First, quality assurance must ensure that all action items in the review report are addressed. It should also be concerned with analyzing the data on the review forms and classifying defects to improve the software development and review process. For example, a high number of specification errors might suggest a lack of rigor or time in the requirements specifications phase of the project. Another example is a high number of defects reported, suggesting that the software has not been adequately unit tested.

Part 5
Verifying the Requirements Phase

The testing process should begin early in the application development life cycle, not just at the traditional testing phase at the end of coding. Testing should be integrated with the application development phases.

During the requirements phase of the software development life cycle, the business requirements are defined on a high level and are the basis of the subsequent phases and the final implementation. Testing in its broadest sense commences during the requirements phase (see Exhibit 1), which increases the probability of a quality system based on the user's expectations. The result is the requirements are verified as correct and complete. Unfortunately, more often than not, poor requirements are produced at the expense of the application. Poor requirements ripple down the waterfall and result in a product that does not meet the user's expectations. Some examples of poor requirements include:

- Partial set of functions defined
- Performance not considered
- Ambiguous requirements
- Security not defined
- Interfaces not documented
- Erroneous and redundant requirements
- Requirements too restrictive
- Contradictory requirements

The functionality is the most important part of the specification and should include a hierarchic decomposition of the functions. The reason for this is that it provides a description that is described in levels to enable all the reviewers to read as much detail as needed. Specifically, this will make the task of translating the specification to test requirements much easier.

Another important element of the requirements specification is the data description (see Appendix C, Requirements Specification, for more details). It should contain details such as whether the database is relational or hierarchical. If it is hierarchical, a good representation is with a data model or entity relationship diagram in terms of entities, attributes, and relationships.

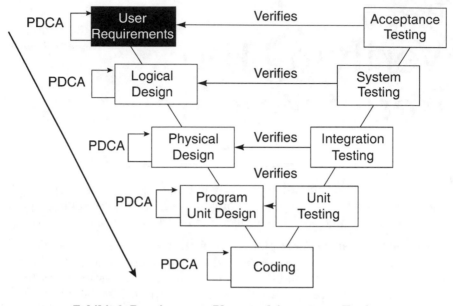

Exhibit 1. Requirements Phase and Acceptance Testing

Another section in the requirements should be a description of the interfaces between the system and external entities that interface with the system, such as users, external software, or external hardware. The human interaction should include a description of how the users will interact with the system. This would include the form of the interface and the technical capabilities of the users.

During the requirements phase, the testing organization needs to perform two functions simultaneously. It needs to build the system/acceptance test plan and also verify the requirements. The requirements verification entails ensuring the correctness and completeness of the documentation prepared by the development team.

TESTING THE REQUIREMENTS WITH TECHNICAL REVIEWS

Requirements definition is the result of creative thinking and is the basis for design. The requirements phase is verified with static techniques, i.e., nonexecution of the application since it does not yet exist. These techniques check the adherence to specification conventions, completeness, and language syntax, and includes the following (see Appendix H, Software Testing Techniques, for more details):

Inspections and Walkthroughs

These are formal techniques to evaluate the documentation form, interface requirements, and solution constraints as described in the previous section.

Checklists

These are orientated toward quality control and include questions to ensure the completeness of the requirements.

Methodology Checklist

This provides the methodology steps and tasks to ensure that the methodology is followed.

If the review is totally successful with no outstanding issues or defect discovered, the requirements specification is frozen, and any further refinements are monitored rigorously. If the review is not totally successful and there are minor issues, during the review, the author corrects them and it is reviewed by the moderator and signed off. On the other hand, if major issues and defects are discovered during the requirements review process, the defects are corrected and a new review occurs with the same review members at a later time.

Each defect uncovered during the requirements phase review should be documented. Requirement defect trouble reports are designed to assist in the proper recording of these defects. It includes the defect category and defect type. The description of each defect is recorded under the missing, wrong, or extra columns. At the conclusion of the requirements review, the defects are summarized and totaled. Exhibit 2 shows a partial requirements phase defect recording form (see Appendix F-1, Requirements Phase Defect Recording, for more details).

Requirements Traceability Matrix

A requirements traceability matrix is a document that traces user requirements from analysis through implementation. It can be used as a completeness check to verify that all requirements are present or that there are no unnecessary/extra features, and as a maintenance guide for new personnel. At each step in the development cycle, the requirements, code, and associated test cases are recorded to ensure that the user requirement is addressed in the final system. Both the user and developer have the ability to easily cross-reference the requirements to the design specifications, programming, and test cases. See Appendix E-3, Requirements Traceability Matrix, for more details.

Exhibit 2. Requirements Phase Defect Recording

Defect Category	Missing	Wrong	Extra	Total
1. Operating rules (or information) are inadequate or partially missing				
2. Performance criteria (or information) are inadequate or partially missing				
3. Environment information is inadequate or partially missing				
4. System mission information is inadequate or partially missing				
5. Requirements are incompatible				
6. Requirements are incomplete				
7. Requirements are missing				
8. Requirements are incorrect				
9. The accuracy specified does not conform to the actual need				
10. The data environment is inadequately described				

BUILDING THE SYSTEM/ACCEPTANCE TEST PLAN

Acceptance testing verifies that a system satisfies the user's acceptance criteria. The acceptance test plan is based on the requirement specifications and is required in a formal test environment. This test uses black-box techniques to test the system against its specifications and is generally tested by the end user. During acceptance testing, it is important for the project team to coordinate the testing process and update the acceptance criteria, as needed. Acceptance testing is often combined with the system-level test plan, which will be the case in this discussion.

The requirements phase is the first development phase that is completed before proceeding to the logical design, physical design, program unit design, and coding phases. During the requirements phase, it is not expected that all sections in the test plan will be completed, for not enough information is available.

In the *Introduction* section of the test plan (see Appendix E-2, System/Acceptance Test Plan), the documentation of "first-cut" test activities starts. Included are the system description, the overall system description, acceptance test objectives, assumptions, risks, contingencies, and constraints. At this point some thought about the appropriate authorities for the approval signatures begins.

Five key parts in the *Test Approach and Strategy* section include: (1) the scope of testing, (2) test approach, (3) types of tests, (4) logistics, and (5) the regression policy. The scope of testing defines the magnitude of the testing effort, e.g., whether to test the whole system or part. The testing approach documents the basis of the test design approach, e.g., black-box, white-box, gray-box testing, incremental integration, etc. The types of tests identifies the test types such as unit, integration, system, or acceptance, which will be performed within the testing scope. Details of the types of system-level tests may not be available at this point because of the lack of details but will be available during the next phase. Logistics documents the working relationship between the development and testing organizations and other interested parties. It defines such issues as how and when the testing group will receive the software, and how defects will be recorded, corrected, and verified. The regression policy determines whether previously tested system functions perform properly after changes are introduced.

A major difficulty in testing the requirements document is that testers have to determine whether the problem definition has been translated properly to the requirements document. This requires envisioning the final product and coming up with what would be tested to determine that the requirement solves the problem.

A useful technique to help analyze, review, and document the initial cut at the functional decomposition of the system in the *Test Specifications* section is the requirement/test matrix (see Exhibit 3). This matrix defines the scope of the testing for the project and ensures that tests are specified for each requirement as documented in the requirements specification. It also helps identify the functions to be tested as well as those not to be tested.

Some benefits of the requirements/test matrix are that it:

1. Correlates the tests and scripts with the requirements
2. Facilitates status of reviews
3. Acts as a traceability mechanism throughout the development cycle, including test design and execution.

The requirement/test matrix in Exhibit 3 documents each requirement and correlates it with the test cases and scripts to verify it. The requirements listed on the left side of the matrix can also aid in defining the types of system tests in the *Test Approach and Strategy* section.

It is unusual to come up with a unique test case for each requirement and, therefore, it takes several test cases to test a requirement thoroughly. This enables reusability of some test cases to other requirements. Once the requirement/test matrix has been built, it can be reviewed, and test case design and script building can commence.

The status column is used to track the status of each test case as it relates to a requirement. For example, "Q" in the status column can indicate that the requirement has been reviewed by QA; "U" can indicate that the

Test Requirement	Test Case									Comment
	1	2	3	4	5	6	7	8	9	
Functonal										
1										
2			Q					T		
3										
4		Q					Q			
Performance										
1										
2			T							
3		Q					Q	Q		
4										
Security										
1				U						
2										
3					Q					
4				U				T		

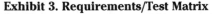

U — Users reviewed
Q — QA reviewed
T — Ready for testing

Exhibit 3. Requirements/Test Matrix

users had reviewed the requirement; and "T" can indicate that the test case specification has been reviewed and is ready.

In the *Test Specifications* section of the test plan, information about the acceptance tests is available and can be documented. These tests must be passed in order for the user to accept the system. A procedure is a series of related actions carried out using an operational mode, i.e., one which tells how to accomplish something. The following information can be documented in the *Test Procedures* section: test case, script, data development, test execution, correction, version control, maintaining test libraries, automated test tool usage, project management, monitoring, and status reporting.

It is not too early to start thinking about the testing personnel resources that will be needed. This includes the required testing skills, their roles and responsibilities, the numbers and time required, and the personnel training needs.

Part 6
Verifying the Logical Design Phase

The business requirements are defined during the requirements phase. The logical design phase refines the business requirements in preparation for system specification that can be used during physical design and coding. The logical design phase further refines the business requirements which were defined in the requirement phase from a functional and information model point of view.

DATA MODEL, PROCESS MODEL, AND THE LINKAGE

The logical design phase establishes a detailed system framework for building the application. Three major deliverables from this phase are the data model, also known as an entity relationship diagram, a process model, and the linkage between the two.

A data model is a representation of the information needed or data object types required by the application. It establishes the associations between people, places, and things of importance to the application and is used later in physical database design, which is part of the physical design phase. A data model is a graphical technique used to define the entities and the relationships. An entity is something about which we want to store data. It is a uniquely identifiable person, place, thing, or event of interest to the user, about which the application is to maintain and report data. Examples of entities are customers, orders, offices, and purchase orders.

Each entity is a table divided horizontally into rows and columns. Each row is a specific occurrence of each entity, much like records in a file. Each column is an attribute which helps describe the entity. Examples of attributes include size, date, value, and address. Each entity in a data model does not exist by itself and is linked to other entities by relationships. A relationship is an association between two or more entities of interest to the user, about which the application is to maintain and report data. There are three types of relationships. A one-to-one relationship links a single occurrence of an entity to zero or one occurrence of another entity. A one-to-many relationship links one occurrence of an entity to zero or more occurrences of an entity. A many-to-many relationship links many occurrences of an entity to many occurrences of an entity. The type of relationship defines the cardinality of the entity relationships. See Appendix H10, Database Testing, for more details about data modeling.

A process is a business activity and the associated inputs and outputs. Examples of processes are: accept order, update inventory, ship orders, schedule class. A process model is a graphical representation and should describe what the process does but not refer to why, how, or when the process is carried out. These are physical attributes of a process which are defined in the physical design phase.

A process model is a decomposition of the business. Process decomposition is the breakdown of the activities into successively more details. It starts at the top until elementary processes, the smallest unit of activity which has meaning to the user, are defined.

A process decomposition diagram is used to illustrate processes in a hierarchical structure showing successive levels of detail. The diagram is built iteratively as processes and nonelementary processes are decomposed. The root of a process is the starting point of the decomposition. A parent is the process at a higher level than lower levels. A child is the lower level that is joined to a higher level, or parent. A data flow diagram is often used to verify the process decomposition. It shows all the processes, data store accesses, and the incoming and outgoing data flows. It also shows the flows of data to and from entities external to the processes.

An association diagram, often called a CRUD matrix or process/data matrix, links data and process models (see Exhibit 1). It helps ensure that the data and processes are discovered and assessed. It identifies and resolves matrix omissions and conflicts and helps refine the data and process models, as necessary. It maps processes against entities showing which processes create, read, update, or delete the instances in an entity.

This is often called "entity life cycle analysis" and analyzes the birth and death of an entity and is performed by process against the entity. The analyst first verifies that there is an associated process to create instances in the entity. If there is an entity that has no associated process that creates it, a process is missing and must be defined. It is then verified that there are associated processes to update, read, or delete instances in an entity. If there is an entity that is never updated, read, or deleted, perhaps the entity may be eliminated. See Appendix H9, CRUD testing, for more details of how this can be applied to software testing.

TESTING THE LOGICAL DESIGN WITH TECHNICAL REVIEWS

The logical design phase is verified with static techniques, i.e., nonexecution of the application. As utilized in the requirements phase, these techniques check the adherence to specification conventions and completeness of the

Entity / Process	Entity Type									Comment
	1	2	3	4	5	6	7	8	9	
Planning	crud				cu			cu		
Selling		ud	c				c			
Scheduling	c				d	crud			d	
Compensation			cu	c	d		cu			
Shipping		crud	ud	u	c	crud				
Operations					crud		crud			
Maintenance		c			cu				cu	
Cost Planning	crud					crud				
Purchasing			ud					d		
Forecasting							c			
Receiving		c	c		c					
Ordering	d					d			cu	
Research			crud		c		crud			
• • •										

Exhibit 1. CRUD Matrix

models. The same static testing techniques used to verify the requirements are used in the logical design phase. The work products to be reviewed include the data model, the process model, and CRUD matrix.

Each defect discovered during the logical design review should be documented. A defect trouble report is designed to assist in the proper recording of these defects. It includes the defect category and defect type. The description of each defect is recorded under the missing, wrong, or extra columns. At the conclusion of the logical design review, the defects are summarized and totaled. Exhibit 2 shows a sample logical design phase defect recording form (see Appendix F2, Logical Design Phase Defect Recording, for more details).

Exhibit 2. Logical Design Phase Defect Recording

Defect Category	Missing	Wrong	Extra	Total
1. The data have not been adequately defined				
2. Entity definition is incomplete				
3. Entity cardinality is incorrect				
4. Entity attribute is incomplete				
5. Normalization is violated				
6. Incorrect primary key				
7. Incorrect foreign key				
8. Incorrect compound key				
9. Incorrect entity sub-type				
10. The process has not been adequately defined				

REFINING THE SYSTEM/ACCEPTANCE TEST PLAN

System testing is a multifaceted test that evaluates the functionality, performance, and fit of the whole application. It demonstrates whether the system satisfies the original objectives. During the requirements phase, enough detail was not available to define these types of tests. The logical design provides a great deal more information with data and process models. The scope of testing and types of tests in the *Test Approach and Strategy* section (see Appendix E2, System/Acceptance Test Plan) can now be refined to include details concerning the types of system-level tests to be performed. Examples of system-level tests to measure the fitness of use include functional, performance, security, usability, and compatibility. The testing approach, logistics, and regression policy are refined in this section. The rest of the items in this section, such as the test facility, test procedures, test organization, test libraries, and test tools, are started. Preliminary planning for the software configuration management elements, such as version and change control and configuration building, can begin. This includes acquiring a software configuration management tool if it does not already exist in the organization.

The *Test Execution Setup* section deals with those considerations for preparing for testing and includes the system test process, test facility, required testing resources, the testing tool plan, and test organization.

In the *Test Specifications* section more functional details are available from the data and process models and added in the requirements/test matrix. At this point, system-level test cases design is started. However, it is too early to complete detailed test development, e.g., test procedures, scripts, and the test case input/output data values associated with each test case. Acceptance test cases should be completed during this phase.

In the *Test Procedures* section, the items started in the previous phase are refined. Test items in the *Test Tools* and *Test Schedule* sections are started.

Part 7
Verifying the Physical Design Phase

The logical design phase translates the business requirements into system specifications that can be used by programmers during physical design and coding. The physical design phase determines how the requirements can be automated. During this phase a high-level design is created in which the basic procedural components and their interrelationships and major data representations are defined.

The physical design phase develops the architecture, or structural aspects, of the system. While logical design testing is functional, physical design testing is structural. This phase verifies that the design is structurally sound and accomplishes the intent of the documented requirements. It assumes that the requirements and logical design are correct and concentrates on the integrity of the design itself.

TESTING THE PHYSICAL DESIGN WITH TECHNICAL REVIEWS

The logical design phase is verified with static techniques, i.e., nonexecution of the application. As with the requirements and logical design phases, the static techniques check the adherence to specification conventions and completeness, with a focus on the architectural design. The basis for physical design verification is design representation schemes used to specify the design. Example design representation schemes include structure charts, Warnier-Orr diagrams, Jackson diagrams, data navigation diagrams, and relational database diagrams, which have been mapped from the logical design phase.

Design representation schemes provide mechanisms for specifying algorithms and their inputs and outputs to software modules. Various inconsistencies are possible in specifying the control flow of data objects through the modules. For example, a module may need a particular data item that another module creates but is not provided correctly. Static analysis can be applied to detect these types of control flow errors.

Other errors made during the physical design can also be detected. Design specifications are created by iteratively supplying detail. Although a

Exhibit 1. Physical Design Phase Defect Recording

Defect Category	Missing	Wrong	Extra	Total
1. Logic or sequencing is erroneous				
2. Processing is inaccurate				
3. Routine does not input or output required parameters				
4. Routine does not accept all data within the allowable range				
5. Limit and validity checks are made on input data				
6. Recovery procedures are not implemented or are not adequate				
7. Required processing is missing or inadequate				
8. Values are erroneous or ambiguous				
9. Data storage is erroneous or inadequate				
10. Variables are missing				

hierarchical specification structure is an excellent vehicle for expressing the design, it does not allow for inconsistencies between levels of detail. For example, coupling measures the degree of independence between modules. When there is little interaction between two modules, the modules are described as loosely coupled. When there is a great deal of interaction, they are tightly coupled. Loose coupling is considered a good design practice.

Examples of coupling include content, common, control, stamp, and data coupling. Content coupling occurs when one module refers to or changes the internals of another module. Data coupling occurs when two modules communicate via a variable or array (table) that is passed directly as a parameter between the two modules. Static analysis techniques can determine the presence or absence of coupling.

Static analysis of the design representations detects static errors and semantic errors. Semantic errors involve information or data decomposition, functional decomposition, and control flow. Each defect uncovered during the physical design review should be documented, categorized, recorded, presented to the design team for correction, and referenced to the specific document in which the defect was noted. Exhibit 1 shows a sample physical design phase defect recording form (see Appendix F3, Physical Design Phase Defect Recording, for more details).

CREATING INTEGRATION TEST CASES

Integration testing is designed to test the structure and the architecture of the software and determine whether all software components interface properly. It does not verify that the system is functionally correct, only that it performs as designed.

Integration testing is the process of identifying errors introduced by combining individual program unit tested modules. It should not begin until all units are known to perform according to the unit specifications. Integration testing can start with testing several logical units or can incorporate all units in a single integration test.

Because the primary concern in integration testing is that the units interface properly, the objective of this test is to ensure that they integrate, that parameters are passed, and the file processing is correct. Integration testing techniques include top-down, bottom-up, sandwich testing, and thread testing (see Appendix H, Software Testing Techniques, for more details).

Methodology for Integration Testing

The following describes a methodology for creating integration test cases.

Step 1: Identify Unit Interfaces. The developer of each program unit identifies and documents the unit's interfaces for the following unit operations:

- External inquiry (responding to queries from terminals for information)
- External input (managing transaction data entered for processing)
- External filing (obtaining, updating, or creating transactions on computer files)
- Internal filing (passing or receiving information from other logical processing units)
- External display (sending messages to terminals)
- External output (providing the results of processing to some output device or unit)

Step 2: Reconcile Interfaces for Completeness. The information needed for the integration test template is collected for all program units in the software being tested. Whenever one unit interfaces with another, those interfaces are reconciled. For example, if program unit A transmits data to program unit B, program unit B should indicate that it has received that input from program unit A. Interfaces not reconciled are examined before integration tests are executed.

Step 3: Create Integration Test Conditions. One or more test conditions are prepared for integrating each program unit. After the condition is created, the number of the test condition is documented in the test template.

Step 4: Evaluate the Completeness of Integration Test Conditions. The following list of questions will help guide evaluation of the completeness of integration test conditions recorded on the integration testing template. This list can also help determine whether test conditions created for the integration process are complete.

1. Is an integration test developed for each of the following external inquiries:
   a. Record test?
   b. File test?
   c. Search test?
   d. Match/merge test?
   e. Attributes test?
   f. Stress test?
   g. Control test?
2. Are all interfaces between modules validated so that the output of one is recorded as input to another?
3. If file test transactions are developed, do the modules interface with all those indicated files?
4. Is the processing of each unit validated before integration testing?
5. Do all unit developers agree that integration test conditions are adequate to test each unit's interfaces?
6. Are all software units included in integration testing?
7. Are all files used by the software being tested included in integration testing?
8. Are all business transactions associated with the software being tested included in integration testing?
9. Are all terminal functions incorporated in the software being tested included in integration testing?

The documentation of integration tests is started in the *Test Specifications* section (see Appendix E2, System/Acceptance Test Plan). Also in this section, the functional decomposition continues to be refined, but the system-level test cases should be completed during this phase.

Test items in the *Introduction* section are completed during this phase. Items in the *Test Approach and Strategy, Test Execution Setup, Test Procedures, Test Tool, Personnel Requirements,* and *Test Schedule* continue to be refined.

Part 8
Verifying the Program Unit Design Phase

The design phase develops the physical architecture, or structural aspects, of the system. The program unit design phase is refined to enable detailed design. The program unit design is the detailed design in which specific algorithmic and data structure choices are made. It is the specifying of the detailed flow of control that will make it easily translatable to program code with a programming language.

TESTING THE PROGRAM UNIT DESIGN WITH TECHNICAL REVIEWS

A good detailed program unit design is one that can easily be translated to many programming languages. It uses structured techniques such as while, for, repeat, if, and case constructs. These are examples of the constructs used in structured programming. The objective of structured programming is to produce programs with high quality at low cost. A structured program is one in which only three basic control constructs are used.

Sequence

Statements are executed one after another in the same order as they appear in the source listing. An example of a sequence is an assignment statement.

Selection

A condition is tested and, depending on whether the test is true or false, one or more alternative execution paths are executed. An example of a selection is an if-then-else. With this structure, the condition is tested, and if the condition is true, one set of instructions is executed. If the condition is false, another set of instructions is executed. Both sets join at a common point.

Exhibit 1. Program Unit Design Phase Defect Recording

Defect Category	Missing	Wrong	Extra	Total
1. Is the if-then-else construct used incorrectly?				
2. Is the dowhile construct used incorrectly?				
3. Is the dountil construct used incorrectly?				
4. Is the case construct used incorrectly?				
5. Are there infinite loops?				
6. Is it a proper program?				
7. Are there goto statements?				
8. Is the program readable?				
9. Is the program efficient?				
10. Does the case construct contain all the conditions?				

Iteration

Iteration is used to execute a set of instructions a number of times with a loop. Examples of iteration are dountil and dowhile. A dountil loop executes a set of instructions and then tests the loop termination condition. If it is true, the loop terminates and continues to the next construct. If it is false, the set of instructions is executed again until reaching the termination logic. A dowhile loop tests the termination condition. If it is true, control passes to the next construct. If it is false, a set of instructions is executed until control is unconditionally passed back to the condition logic.

Static analysis of the detailed design detects semantic errors involving information and logic control flow. Each defect uncovered during the program unit design review should be documented, categorized, recorded, presented to the design team for correction, and referenced to the specific document in which the defect was noted. Exhibit 1 shows a sample program unit design phase defect recording form (see Appendix F4, Program Unit Design Phase Defect Recording, for more details).

CREATING UNIT TEST CASES

Unit testing is the process of executing a functional subset of the software system to determine whether it performs its assigned function. It is oriented toward the checking of a function or a module. White-box test cases are created and documented to validate the unit logic and black-box test cases to test the unit against the specifications (see Appendix E8, Test Case, for a sample test case form). Unit testing, along with the version control necessary during correction and retesting, is typically performed by the developer. During unit test case development it is important to know which portions of the code have been subjected to test cases and which have not. By knowing this coverage, the developer can discover lines of code that are never executed or program functions that do not perform according to the specifications. When coverage is inadequate, implementing the system is risky because defects may be present in the untested portions of the code (see Appendix H, Software Testing Techniques for more unit test case development techniques). Unit test case specifications are started and documented in the *Test Specification* section (see Appendix E2, System/Acceptance Test Plan), but all other items in this section should have been completed.

All items in the *Introduction, Test Approach and Strategy, Test Execution Setup, Test Tools, Personnel Resources* should have been completed prior to this phase. Items in the *Test Procedures* section, however, continue to be refined. The functional decomposition, integration, system, and acceptance test cases should be completed during this section. Refinement continues for all items in the *Test Procedures* and *Test Schedule* sections.

Part 9
Verifying the Coding Phase

The program unit design is the detailed design in which specific algorithmic and data structure choices are made. Specifying the detailed flow of control will make it easily translatable to program code with a programming language. The coding phase is the translation of the detailed design to executable code using a programming language.

TESTING CODING WITH TECHNICAL REVIEWS

The coding phase produces executable source modules. The basis of good programming is programming standards that have been defined. Some good standards should include commenting, unsafe programming constructs, program layout, defensive programming, etc. Commenting refers to how a program should be commented and to what level or degree. Unsafe programming constructions are practices that can make the program hard to maintain. An example is goto statements. Program layout refers to how a standard program should be laid out on a page, indentation of control constructs, and initialization. A defensive programming practice describes the mandatory element of the programming defensive strategy. An example is error condition handling and control to a common error routine.

Static analysis techniques, such as structured walkthroughs and inspections, are used to ensure the proper form of the program code and documentation. This is accomplished by checking adherence to coding and documentation conventions and type checking.

Each defect uncovered during the coding phase review should be documented, categorized, recorded, presented to the design team for correction, and referenced to the specific document in which the defect was noted. Exhibit 1 shows a sample coding phase defect recording form (see Appendix F5, Coding Phase Defect Recording, for more details).

Exhibit 1. Coding Phase Defect Recording

Defect Category	Missing	Wrong	Extra	Total
1. Decision logic or sequencing is erroneous or inadequate				
2. Arithmetic computations are erroneous or inadequate				
3. Branching is erroneous				
4. Branching or other testing is performed incorrectly				
5. There are undefined loop terminations				
6. Programming language rules are violated				
7. Programming standards are violated				
8. The programmer misinterprets language constructs				
9. Typographical errors exist				
10. Main storage allocation errors exist				

EXECUTING THE TEST PLAN

By the end of this phase, all the items in each section of the test plan should have been completed. The actual testing of software is accomplished through the test data in the test plan developed during the requirements, logical design, physical design, and program unit design phases. Since results have been specified in the test cases and test procedures, the correctness of the executions is assured from a static test point of view, i.e., the tests have been reviewed manually.

Dynamic testing, or time dependent techniques, involves executing a specific sequence of instructions with the computer. These techniques are used to study the functional and computational correctness of the code.

Dynamic testing proceeds in the opposite order of the development life cycle. It starts with unit testing to verify each program unit independently and then proceeds to integration, system, and acceptance testing. After acceptance testing has been completed, the system is ready for operation and maintenance. Exhibit 2 briefly describes each testing type.

Unit Testing

Unit testing is the basic level of testing. Unit testing focuses on the smaller building blocks of a program or system separately. It is the process of

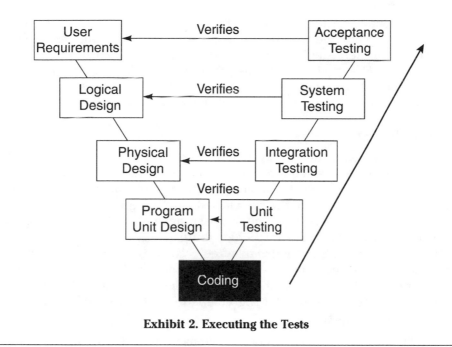

Exhibit 2. Executing the Tests

executing each module to confirm that each performs its assigned function. The advantage of unit testing is that it permits the testing and debugging of small units, thereby providing a better way to manage the integration of the units into larger units. In addition, testing a smaller unit of code makes it mathematically possible to fully test the code's logic with fewer tests. Unit testing also facilitates automated testing because the behavior of smaller units can be captured and played back with maximized reusability. A unit can be one of several types of application software. Examples include the module itself as a unit, GUI components such as windows, menus, and functions, batch programs, online programs, and stored procedures.

Integration Testing

After unit testing is completed, all modules must be integration tested. During integration testing, the system is slowly built up by adding one or more modules at a time to the core of already integrated modules. Groups of units are fully tested before system testing occurs. Since modules have been unit tested prior to integration testing, they can be treated as blackboxes, allowing integration testing to concentrate on module interfaces. The goals of integration testing are to verify that each module performs correctly within the control structure and that the module interfaces are correct.

Incremental testing is performed by combining modules in steps. At each step one module is added to the program structure, and testing concentrates on exercising this newly added module. When it has been demonstrated that a module performs properly with the program structure, another module is added, and testing continues. This process is repeated until all modules have been integrated and tested.

System Testing

After integration testing, the system is tested as a whole for functionality and fitness of use based on the system/acceptance test plan. Systems are fully tested in the computer operating environment before acceptance testing occurs. The source of the system tests are the quality attributes that were specified in the software quality assurance plan. System testing is a set of tests to verify these quality attributes and ensure that the acceptance test occurs relatively trouble-free. System testing verifies that the functions are carried out correctly. It also verifies that certain nonfunctional characteristics are present. Some examples include usability testing, performance testing, stress testing, compatibility testing, conversion testing, and document testing.

Black-box testing is a technique that focuses on testing a program's functionality against its specifications. White-box testing is a testing technique in which paths of logic are tested to determine how well they produce predictable results. Gray-box testing is a combination of these two approaches and is usually applied during system testing. It is a compromise between the two and is a well-balanced testing approach that is widely used during system testing.

Acceptance Testing

After systems testing, acceptance testing certifies that the software system satisfies the original requirements. This test should not be performed until the software has successfully completed systems testing. Acceptance testing is a user run test which uses black-box techniques to test the system against its specifications. The end-users are responsible for assuring that all relevant functionality has been tested.

The acceptance test plan defines the procedures for executing the acceptance tests and should be followed as closely as possible. Acceptance testing continues even when errors are found, unless an error itself prevents continuation. Some projects do not require formal acceptance testing. This is true when the customer or user is satisfied with the other system tests, when timing requirements demand it, or when end users have been involved continuously throughout the development cycle and have been implicitly applying acceptance testing as the system is developed.

Acceptance tests are often a subset of one or more system tests. Two other ways to measure acceptance testing is as follows:

1. Parallel Testing
   A business transaction level comparison with the existing system to ensure that adequate results are produced from the new system.
2. *Benchmarks*
   A static set of results produced either manually or from an existing system is used as expected results for the new system.

Defect Recording

Each defect discovered during the above tests is documented to assist in the proper recording of these defects. A problem report is generated when a test procedure gives rise to an event which cannot be explained by the tester. The problem report documents the details of the event and includes at least the following items (see Appendix E12, Defect Report, for more details):

- Problem Identification
- Author
- Release/Build #
- Open Date
- Close Date
- Problem Area
- Defect or Enhancement
- Test Environment
- Defect Type
- Who Detected
- How Detected
- Assigned to
- Priority
- Severity
- Status

Other test reports to communicate the testing progress and results include a test case log, test log summary report, and system summary report.

A test case log documents the test cases for a test type to be executed. It also records the results of the tests, which provides the detailed evidence for the test log summary report and enables reconstructing testing, if necessary. See Appendix E9, Test Case Log, for more information.

A test log summary report documents the test cases from the tester's logs in progress or completed for the status reporting and metric collection. See Appendix E10, Test Log Summary Report.

A system summary report should be prepared for every major testing event. Sometimes it summarizes all the tests. It typically includes the following major sections: general information (describing the test objectives, test environment, references), test results and findings (describing each test), software functions and findings), and analysis and test summary. See Appendix E11, System Summary Report, for more details.

Section III
Client/Server and Internet Testing Methodology

Spiral development methodologies are a reaction to the traditional "waterfall" systems development in which the product evolves in sequential phases. A common problem with the life cycle development model is that the elapsed time to deliver the product can be excessive with user involvement only at the very beginning and very end. As a result, the system that they are given is often not what they originally requested.

By contrast, spiral development expedites product delivery. A small but functioning initial system is built and quickly delivered, and then enhanced in a series of iterations. One advantage is that the users receive at least some functionality quickly. Another advantage is that the product can be shaped by iterative feedback, e.g., users do not have to define every feature correctly and in full detail at the beginning of the development cycle, but can react to each iteration.

Spiral testing is dynamic and may never be completed in the traditional sense of a delivered system's completeness. The term "spiral" refers to the fact that the traditional sequence of analysis-design-code-test phases are performed on a microscale within each spiral or cycle in a short period of time, and then the phases are repeated within each subsequent cycle.

The objectives of this section are to:

- Discuss the limitations of "waterfall" development
- Describe the complications of client/server
- Discuss the psychology of spiral testing
- Describe the iterative/spiral development environment
- Apply Deming's continuous improvement quality to a spiral development environment in terms of:
    - Information gathering
    - Test planning
    - Test case design

- Test development
- Test execution/evaluation
- Preparing for the next spiral
- System testing
- Acceptance testing
- Summarizing/reporting spiral test results

Part 10
Development Methodology Overview

LIMITATIONS OF LIFE CYCLE DEVELOPMENT

In Section II, "Life Cycle Testing Review," the waterfall development methodology was reviewed along with the associated testing activities. The life cycle development methodology consists of distinct phases from requirements to coding. Life cycle testing means that testing occurs in parallel with the development life cycle and is a continuous process. While the life cycle or waterfall development is very effective for many large applications requiring a lot of computer horse power, e.g., DOD, financial, security-based, etc., it has a number of shortcomings:

1. The end users of the system are only involved in the very beginning and the very end of the process. As a result, the system that they were given at the end of the development cycle is often not what they originally visualized or thought they requested.
2. The long development cycle and the shortening of business cycles leads to a gap between what is really needed and what is delivered.
3. End users are expected to describe in detail what they want in a system, before the coding phase. While this may seem logical to developers, there are end users who haven't used a computer system before and aren't really certain of its capabilities.
4. When the end of a development phase is reached, it is often not quite complete, but the methodology and project plans require that development press on regardless. In fact, a phase is rarely complete and there is always more work than can be completed. This results in the "rippling effect," where sooner or later, one must return to a phase to complete the work.
5. Often the waterfall development methodology is not strictly followed. In the haste to produce something quickly, critical parts of the methodology are not followed. The worst case is *ad hoc* development in which the analysis and design phases are bypassed and

the coding phase is the first major activity. This is an example of an unstructured development environment.

6. Software testing is often treated as a separate phase starting in the coding phase as a validation technique and is not integrated into the whole development life cycle.

The waterfall development approach can be woefully inadequate for many development projects, even if it were followed. An implemented software system is not worth very much if it is not the system the user wanted. If the requirements are incompletely documented, the system will not survive user validation procedures, i.e., it is the wrong system. Another variation is when the requirements are correct, but the design is inconsistent with the requirements. Once again, the completed product will probably fail the system validation procedures.

Due to the above, experts began to publish methodologies based on other approaches, such as prototyping.

THE CLIENT/SERVER CHALLENGE

The client/server architecture for application development allocates functionality between a client and server so that each performs its task independently. The client cooperates with the server to produce the required results.

The client is an intelligent workstation used as a single user, and since it has its own operating system it can run other applications such as spreadsheets, word processors, and file processors. Client/server application functions are processed cooperatively by the user and the server. The server can be a PC, minicomputer, local area network, or even a mainframe. The server receives requests from the clients and processes them. The hardware configuration is determined by the application's functional requirements.

Some advantages of client/server applications include reduced costs, improved accessibility of data, and flexibility. However, justifying a client/server approach and assuring quality is difficult and presents additional difficulties not necessarily found in mainframe applications. Some of these problems include:

1. The typical graphical user interface has more possible logic paths, and thus the large number of test cases in the mainframe environment is compounded.
2. Client/server technology is complicated and often new to the organization. Further, this technology often comes from multiple vendors and is used in multiple configurations and in multiple versions.
3. The fact that client/server applications are highly distributed results in a large number of failure sources and hardware/software configuration control problems.

4. A short- and long-term cost/benefit analysis must be performed to include the overall organizational costs and benefits to justify a client-server.
5. Successful migration to client/server depends on matching migration plans to the organization's readiness for client/server.
6. The effect of client/server technology on the user's business may be substantial.
7. Choosing which applications will be the best candidates for a client/server implementation is not straightforward.
8. An analysis needs to be performed of which development technologies and tools enable a client/server.
9. Availability of client/server skills and resources, which are expensive, needs to be considered.
10. Although the cost of client/server is more expensive than mainframe computing, cost is not the only issue. The function, business benefit, and the pressure from end users have to be balanced.

Integration testing in a client/server environment can be challenging. Client and server applications are built separately. When they are brought together, conflicts can arise no matter how clearly defined the interfaces are. When integrating applications, defect resolutions may have single or multiple solutions, and there must be open communication between quality assurance and development.

In some circles there exists a belief that mainframe is dead and the client/server prevails. The truth of the matter is that applications using a mainframe architecture are not dead, and client/server is not necessarily the panacea for all applications. The two will continue to coexist and complement each other in the future. Mainframes will not prosper as they have in the past but should certainly be part of any client/server strategy.

PSYCHOLOGY OF CLIENT/SERVER SPIRAL TESTING

The New School of Thought

The psychology of life cycle testing encourages testing by individuals outside the development organization. The motivation for this is that with the life cycle approach there typically exists clearly defined requirements, and it is more efficient for a third party to verify the requirements. Testing is often viewed as a destructive process designed to break development's work.

The psychology of spiral testing, on the other hand, encourages cooperation between quality assurance and the development organization. The basis of this argument is that, in a rapid application development environment, requirements may or may not be available, to varying degrees. Without this cooperation, the testing function would have a difficult task defining the test criteria. The only possible alternative is for testing and development to work together.

Testers can be powerful allies to development and, with a little effort, they can be transformed from adversaries into partners. This is possible because most testers want to be helpful; they just need a little consideration and support. In order to achieve this, however, an environment needs to be created to bring out the best of a tester's abilities. The test and development manager must set the stage for cooperation early in the development cycle and communicate throughout the development life cycle.

Tester/Developer Perceptions

To understand some of the inhibitors to a good relationship between the testing function and development, it is helpful to understand how each views his role and responsibilities.

Testing is a difficult effort. It is the task that's both infinite and indefinite. No matter what testers do, they can't be sure they will find all the problems, or even all the important ones.

Many testers are not really interested in testing and/or do not have the proper training in basic testing principles and techniques. Testing books or conferences typically treat the testing subject too rigorously and employ deep mathematical analysis. The insistence on formal requirement specifications as a prerequisite to effective testing is not realistic in the real world of a software development project.

It is hard to find individuals who are good at testing. It takes someone who is a critical thinker motivated to produce a quality software product, likes to evaluate software deliverables, and is not caught up in the assumption held by many developers that testing has a lesser job status than development. A good tester is a quick learner and eager to learn, is a good team player, and can effectively communicate both verbally and in written form.

The output from development is something that is real and tangible. A programmer can write code and display it to admiring customers who assume it is correct. From a developer's point of view, testing results in nothing more tangible than an accurate, useful, and all-too-fleeting perspective on quality. Given these perspectives, many developers and testers often work together in an uncooperative, if not hostile, manner.

In many ways the tester and developer roles are in conflict. A developer is committed to building something to be successful. A tester tries to minimize the risk of failure and tries to improve the software by detecting defects. Developers focus on technology, which takes a lot of time and energy when producing software. A good tester, on the other hand, is motivated to provide the user with the best software to solve a problem.

Testers are typically ignored until the end of the development cycle when the application is "completed." Testers are always interested in the progress of development and realize that quality is only achievable when they take a broad point of view and consider software quality from multiple dimensions.

Project Goal: Integrate QA and Development

The key to integrating the testing and developing activities is for testers to avoid giving the impression that they are out to "break the code" or destroy development's work. Ideally, testers are human meters of product quality and should examine a software product, evaluate it, and discover if the product satisfies the customer's requirements. They should not be out to embarrass or complain, but inform development how to make their product even better. The impression they should foster is that they are the "developer's eyes to improved quality."

Development needs to be truly motivated to quality and view the test team as an integral player on the development team. They need to realize that no matter how much work and effort has been expended by development, if the software does not have the correct level of quality, it is destined to fail. The testing manager needs to remind the project manager of this throughout the development cycle. The project manager needs to instill this perception in the development team.

Testers must coordinate with the project schedule and work in parallel with development. They need to be informed about what's going on in development and included in all planning and status meetings. This lessens the risk of introducing new bugs, known as "side-effects," near the end of the development cycle and also reduces the need for time-consuming regression testing.

Testers must be encouraged to communicate effectively with everyone on the development team. They should establish a good communication relationship with the software users, who can help them better understand acceptable standards of quality. In this way, testers can provide valuable feedback directly to development.

Testers should intensively review online help and printed manuals whenever they are available. It will relieve some of the communication burden to get writers and testers to share notes rather than burden development with the same information.

Testers need to know the objectives of the software product, how it is intended to work, how it actually works, the development schedule, any proposed changes, and the status of reported problems.

Developers need to know what problems were discovered, what part of the software is or is not working, how users perceive the software, what will be tested, the testing schedule, the testing resources available, what the testers need to know to test the system, and the current status of the testing effort.

When quality assurance starts working with a development team, the testing manager needs to interview the project manager and show an interest in working in a cooperative manner to produce the best software product possible. The next section describes how to accomplish this.

ITERATIVE/SPIRAL DEVELOPMENT METHODOLOGY

Spiral methodologies are a reaction to the traditional waterfall methodology of systems development, a sequential solution development approach. A common problem with the waterfall model is that the elapsed time for delivering the product can be excessive.

By contrast, spiral development expedites product delivery. A small but functioning initial system is built and quickly delivered, and then enhanced in a series of iterations. One advantage is that the clients receive at least some functionality quickly. Another is that the product can be shaped by iterative feedback, e.g., users do not have to define every feature correctly and in full detail at the beginning of the development cycle, but can react to each iteration.

With the spiral approach, the product evolves continually over time; it is not static and may never be completed in the traditional sense. The term "spiral" refers to the fact that the traditional sequence of analysis-design-code-test phases are performed on a microscale within each spiral or cycle, in a short period of time, and then the phases are repeated within each subsequent cycle. The spiral approach is often associated with prototyping and rapid application development.

Traditional requirements-based testing expects that the product definition will be finalized and even frozen prior to detailed test planning. With spiral development, the product definition and specifications continue to evolve indefinitely, i.e., there is no such thing as a frozen specification. A comprehensive requirements definition and system design probably never will be documented.

The only practical way to test in the spiral environment, therefore, is to "get inside the spiral." Quality assurance must have a good working relationship with development. The testers must be very close to the development effort, and test each new version as it becomes available. Each iteration of testing must be brief, in order not to disrupt the frequent delivery of the product iterations. The focus of each iterative test must be first

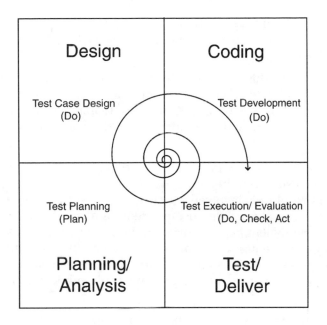

Design	Coding
Test Case Design (Do)	Test Development (Do)
Test Planning (Plan)	Test Execution/ Evaluation (Do, Check, Act
Planning/ Analysis	Test/ Deliver

Exhibit 1. Spiral Testing Process

to test only the enhanced and changed features. If time within the spiral allows, automated regression test also should be performed; this requires sufficient time and resources to update the automated regression tests within each spiral.

Clients typically demand very fast turnarounds on change requests; there may be no formal release nor a willingness to wait for the next release to obtain a new system feature. Ideally, there should be an efficient, automated regression test facility for the product, which can be used for at least a brief test prior to the release of the new product version (see Section IV, Modern Testing Tools, for more details).

Spiral testing is a process of working from a base and building a system incrementally. Upon reaching the end of each phase, developers reexamine the entire structure and revise it. The spiral approach is represented by drawing the four major phases of system development — planning/analysis, design, coding, and test/deliver — into quadrants, as shown in Exhibit 1. The respective testing phases are test planning, test case design, test development, and test execution/evaluation.

The spiral process begins with planning and requirements analysis to determine the functionality. Then a design is made for the base components of the system and the functionality determined in the first step. Next, the functionality is constructed and tested. This represents one complete iteration of the spiral.

Having completed this first spiral, the users are given the opportunity to examine the system and enhance its functionality. This begins the second iteration of the spiral. The process continues, looping around and around the spiral until the users and developers agree the system is complete and proceed to implementation.

The spiral approach, if followed systematically, can be effective for ensuring that the users' requirements are being adequately addressed and that the users are closely involved with the project. It can allow for the system to adapt to any changes in business requirements that occurred after the system development began. However, there is one major flaw with this methodology — there may never be any firm commitment to implement a working system. One can go around and around the quadrants, never actually bringing a system into production. This is often referred to as "spiral death."

While the waterfall development has often proved itself to be too inflexible, the spiral approach can produce the opposite problem. Unfortunately, the flexibility of the spiral methodology often results in the development team ignoring what the user really wants, and thus the product fails the user verification. This is where quality assurance is a key component to a spiral approach. It will make sure that user requirements are being satisfied.

A variation to the spiral methodology is the iterative methodology where the development team is forced to reach a point where the system will be implemented. The iterative methodology recognizes that the system is never truly complete, but is evolutionary. However, it also realizes that there is a point at which the system is close enough to complete to be of value to the end user.

The point of implementation is decided upon prior to the start of the system and a certain number of iterations will be specified with goals identified for each iteration. Upon completion of the final iteration, the system will be implemented whatever state it may be in.

Role of JADs

During the first spiral the major deliverables are the objectives, an initial functional decomposition diagram, and a functional specification. The functional specification also includes an external (user) design of the system. It has been shown that errors defining the requirements and external design are the most expensive to fix later in development. It is, therefore, imperative to get the design as correct as possible the first time.

A technique that helps accomplish this is joint application design (JAD) sessions (see Appendix H19, JADs, for more details). Studies show that JADs increase productivity over traditional design techniques. In JADs, users and IT professionals jointly design systems in facilitated group sessions. JADs go beyond the one-on-one interviews to collect information. They promote communication, cooperation, and teamwork among the participants by placing the users in the driver seat.

JADs are logically divided into phases: customization, session, and wrap-up. Regardless of what activity one is pursuing in development, these components will always exist. Each phase has its own objectives.

Role of Prototyping

Prototyping is an iterative approach often used to build systems that users are unable to describe precisely initially (see Appendix H24, Prototyping, for more details). The concept is made possible largely through the power of fourth-generation languages (4GLs) and application generators. Prototyping is, however, as prone to defects as any other development effort, maybe more so if not performed in a systematic manner. Prototypes need to be tested as thoroughly as any other system. Testing can be difficult unless a systematic process has been established for developing prototypes.

There are various types of software prototypes, ranging from simple printed descriptions of input, processes, and output to completely automated versions. An exact definition of a software prototype is impossible to find; the concept is made up of various components. Among the many characteristics identified by MIS professionals are the following:

- Comparatively inexpensive to build (i.e., less than 10% of the full system's development cost)
- Relatively quick development so that it can be evaluated early in the life cycle
- Provides users with a physical representation of key parts of the system before implementation

Prototypes:

- Do not eliminate or reduce the need for comprehensive analysis and specification of user requirements
- Do not necessarily represent the complete system
- Perform only a subset of the functions of the final product
- Lack the speed, geographical placement, or other physical characteristics of the final system

Basically, prototyping is the building of trial versions of a system. These early versions can be used as the basis for assessing ideas and making decisions about the complete and final system. Prototyping is based on the premise that, in certain problem domains (particularly in online interactive systems), users of the proposed application do not have a clear and comprehensive idea of what the application should do or how it should operate.

Often, errors or shortcomings overlooked during development appear after a system is operational. Applications prototyping seeks to overcome these problems by providing users and developers with an effective means of communicating ideas and requirements before a significant amount of development effort has been expended. The prototyping process results in a functional set of specifications that can be fully analyzed, understood, and used by users, developers, and management to decide whether an application is feasible and how it should be developed.

Fourth-generation languages have enabled many organizations to undertake projects based on prototyping techniques. They provide many of the capabilities necessary for prototype development, including user functions for defining and managing the user–system interface, data management functions for organizing and controlling access, and system functions for defining execution control and interfaces between the application and its physical environment.

In recent years, the benefits of prototyping have become increasingly recognized. Some include:

- Prototyping emphasizes active physical models. The prototype looks, feels, and acts like a real system.
- Prototyping is highly visible and accountable.
- The burden of attaining performance, optimum access strategies, and complete functioning is eliminated in prototyping.
- Issue of data, functions, and user–system interfaces can be readily addressed.
- Users are usually satisfied, because they get what they see.
- Many design considerations are highlighted and a high degree of design flexibility becomes apparent.
- Information requirements are easily validated.
- Changes and error corrections can be anticipated and in many cases made on the spur of the moment.
- Ambiguities and inconsistencies in requirements become visible and correctable.
- Useless functions and requirements can be quickly eliminated.

Methodology for Developing Prototypes

The following describes a methodology to reduce development time through reuse of the prototype and knowledge gained in developing and using the prototype. It also does not include how to test the prototype within spiral development. This is included in the next part.

1. Develop the Prototype. In the construction phase of spiral development, the external design and screen design are translated into real-world windows using a 4GL tool such as Visual Basic or Power Builder. The detailed business functionality is not built into the screen prototypes, but a "look and feel" of the user interface is produced so the user can imagine how the application will look.

Using a 4GL, the team constructs a prototype system consisting of data entry screens, printed reports, external file routines, specialized procedures, and procedure selection menus. These are based on the logical database structure developed in the JAD data modeling sessions. The sequence of events for performing the task of developing the prototype in a 4GL is iterative and is described as follows:

Define the basic database structures derived from logical data modeling. The data structures will be populated periodically with test data as required for specific tests.

Define printed report formats. These may initially consist of query commands saved in an executable procedure file on disk. The benefit of a query language is that most of the report formatting can be done automatically by the 4GL. The prototyping team need only define what data elements to print and what selection and ordering criteria to use for individual reports.

Define interactive data entry screens. Whether or not each screen is well designed is immaterial at this point. Obtaining the right information in the form of prompts, labels, HELP messages, and validation of input is more important. Initially, defaults should be used as often as possible.

Define external file routines to process data that is to be submitted in batches to the prototype or created by the prototype for processing by other systems. This can be done in parallel with other tasks.

Define algorithms and procedures to be implemented by the prototype and the finished system. These may include support routines solely for the use of the prototype.

Define procedure selection menus. The developers should concentrate on the functions as the user would see them. This may entail combining seemingly disparate procedures into single functions that can be executed with one command from the user.

Define test cases to ascertain that:

- Data entry validation is correct
- Procedures and algorithms produce expected results
- System execution is clearly defined throughout a complete cycle of operation

Reiterate this process by adding report and screen formatting options, corrections for errors discovered in testing, and instructions for the intended users. This process should end after the second or third iteration or when changes become predominantly cosmetic rather than functional.

At this point, the prototyping team should have a good understanding of the overall operation of the proposed system. If time permits, the team must now describe the operation and underlying structure of the prototype. This is most easily accomplished through the development of a draft user manual. A printed copy of each screen, report, query, database structure, selection menu, and cataloged procedure or algorithm must be included. Instructions for executing each procedure should include an illustration of the actual dialog.

2. Demonstrate Prototype to Management. The purpose of this demonstration is to give management the option of making strategic decisions about the application on the basis of the prototype's appearance and objectives. The demonstration consists primarily of a short description of each prototype component and its effects and a walkthrough of the typical use of each component. Every person in attendance at the demonstration should receive a copy of the draft user manual if one is available.

The team should emphasize the results of the prototype and its impact on development tasks still to be performed. At this stage, the prototype is not necessarily a functioning system, and management must be made aware of its limitations.

3. Demonstrate Prototype to Users. There are arguments for and against letting the prospective users actually use the prototype system. There is a risk that users' expectations will be raised to an unrealistic level with regard to delivery of the production system and that the prototype will be placed in production before it is ready. Some users have actually refused to give up the prototype when the production system was ready for delivery. This may not be a problem if the prototype meets the users' expectations and the environment can absorb the load of processing without affecting others. On the other hand, when users exercise the prototype, they can discover the problems in procedures and unacceptable system behavior very quickly.

The prototype should be demonstrated before a representative group of users. This demonstration should consist of a detailed description of the system operation, structure, data entry, report generation, and procedure execution. Above all, users must be made to understand that the prototype is not the final product, that it is flexible, and that it is being demonstrated to find errors from the users' perspective.

The results of the demonstration include requests for changes, correction of errors, and overall suggestions for enhancing the system. Once the demonstration has been held, the prototyping team reiterates the steps in the prototype process to make the changes, corrections, and enhancements deemed necessary through consensus of the prototyping team, the end users, and management.

For each iteration through prototype development, demonstrations should be held to show how the system has changed as a result of feedback from users and management. The demonstrations increase the users' sense of ownership, especially when they can see the results of their suggestions. The changes should therefore be developed and demonstrated quickly.

Requirements uncovered in the demonstration and use of the prototype may cause profound changes in the system scope and purpose, the conceptual model of the system, or the logical data model. Because these modifications occur in the requirements specification phase rather than in the design, code, or operational phases, they are much less expensive to implement.

4. Revise and Finalize Specifications. At this point, the prototype consists of data entry formats, report formats, file formats, a logical database structure, algorithms and procedures, selection menus, system operational flow, and possibly a draft user manual.

The deliverables from this phase consist of formal descriptions of the system requirements, listings of the 4GL command files for each object programmed (i.e., screens, reports, database structures), sample reports, sample data entry screens, the logical database structure, data dictionary listings, and a risk analysis. The risk analysis should include the problems and changes that could not be incorporated into the prototype and the probable impact that they would have on development of the full system and subsequent operation.

The prototyping team reviews each component for inconsistencies, ambiguities, and omissions. Corrections are made and the specifications are formally documented.

5. Develop the Production System. At this point, development can proceed in one of three directions:

- The project is suspended or canceled because the prototype has uncovered insurmountable problems or the environment is not ready to mesh with the proposed system.
- The prototype is discarded because it is no longer needed or because it is too inefficient for production or maintenance.

- Iterations of prototype development are continued, with each iteration adding more system functions and optimizing performance until the prototype evolves into the production system.

The decision on how to proceed is generally based on such factors as:

- The actual cost of the prototype.
- Problems uncovered during prototype development.
- The availability of maintenance resources.
- The availability of software technology in the organization.
- Political and organizational pressures.
- The amount of satisfaction with the prototype.
- The difficulty in changing the prototype into a production system.
- Hardware requirements.

CONTINUOUS IMPROVEMENT "SPIRAL" TESTING APPROACH

The purpose of software testing is to identify the differences between existing and expected conditions, i.e., to detect software defects. Testing identifies the requirements that have not been satisfied and the functions that have been impaired. The most commonly recognized test objective is to identify bugs, but this is a limited definition of the aim of testing. Not only must bugs be identified, but they must be put into a framework that enables testers to predict how the software will perform.

In the spiral and rapid application development testing environment there may be no final functional requirements for the system. They are probably informal and evolutionary. Also, the test plan may not be completed until the system is released for production. The relatively long lead time to create test plans based on a good set of requirement specifications may not be available. Testing is an ongoing improvement process that occurs frequently as the system changes. The product evolves over time and is not static.

The testing organization needs to get inside the development effort and work closely with development. Each new version needs to be tested as it becomes available. The approach is to first test the new enhancements or modified software to resolve defects reported in the previous spiral. If time permits, regression testing is then performed to assure that the rest of the system has not regressed.

In the spiral development environment, software testing is again described as a continuous improvement process that must be integrated into a rapid application development methodology. Testing as an integrated function prevents development from proceeding without testing. Deming's continuous improvement process using the PDCA model (see Exhibit 2) will again be applied to the software testing process.

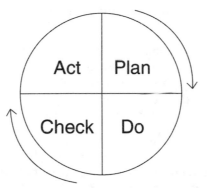

Exhibit 2. Spiral Testing and Continuous Improvement

Before the continuous improvement process begins, the testing function needs to perform a series of information-gathering planning steps to understand the development project objectives, current status, project plans, function specification, and risks.

Once this is completed, the formal **Plan** step of the continuous improvement process commences. A major step is to develop a software test plan. The test plan is the basis for accomplishing testing and should be considered an ongoing document, i.e., as the system changes, so does the plan. The outline of a good test plan includes an introduction, the overall plan, testing requirements, test procedures, and test plan details. These are further broken down into business functions, test scenarios and scripts, function/test matrix, expected results, test case checklists, discrepancy reports, required software, hardware, data, personnel, test schedule, test entry criteria, exit criteria, and summary reports.

The more definitive a test plan is, the easier the plan step will be. If the system changes between development of the test plan and when the tests are to be executed, the test plan should be updated accordingly.

The **Do** step of the continuous improvement process consists of test case design test development and test execution. This step describes how to design test cases and execute the tests included in the test plan. Design includes the functional tests, GUI tests, and fragment system and acceptance tests. Once an overall test design is completed, test development starts. This includes building test scripts and procedures to provide test case details.

The test team is responsible for executing the tests and must ensure that they are executed according to the test design. The do step also includes test setup, regression testing of old and new tests, and recording any defects discovered.

The **Check** step of the continuous improvement process includes metric measurements and analysis. As discussed in Section I, Part 3, "Quality Through a Continuous Improvement Process," crucial to the Deming method is the need to base decisions as much as possible on accurate and timely data. Metrics are key to verifying if the work effort and test schedule are on schedule, and to identify any new resource requirements.

During the check step it is important to publish intermediate test reports. This includes recording of the test results and relating them to the test plan and test objectives.

The **Act** step of the continuous improvement process involves preparation for the next spiral iteration. It entails refining the function/GUI tests, test suites, test cases, test scripts, and fragment system and acceptance tests, modifying the defect tracking system and the version and control system, if necessary. It also includes devising measures for appropriate actions relating to work that was not performed according to the plan or results that were not what was anticipated. Examples include a reevaluation of the test team, test procedures, and technology dimensions of testing. All the above is fed back to the test plan, which is updated.

Once several testing spirals have been completed and the application has been verified as functionally stable, full system and acceptance testing starts. These tests are often optional. Respective system and acceptance test plans are developed defining the test objects and the specific tests to be completed.

The final activity in the continuous improvement process is summarizing and reporting the spiral test results. A major test report should be written at the end of all testing. The process used for report writing is the same whether it is an interim or a final report, and, like other tasks in testing, report writing is also subject to quality control. However, the final test report should be much more comprehensive than interim test reports. For each type of test it should describe a record of defects discovered, data reduction techniques, root cause analysis, the development of findings, and follow-on recommendations for the current and/or future projects.

Exhibit 3 provides an overview of the spiral testing methodology by relating each step to the PDCA quality model. Appendix A, Spiral Testing Methodology, provides a detailed representation of each part of the methodology. The methodology provides a framework for testing in this environment. The major steps include information gathering, test planning, test design, test development, test execution/evaluation, and preparing for the next spiral. It includes a set of tasks associated with each step or a checklist

Continuous Process Improvement

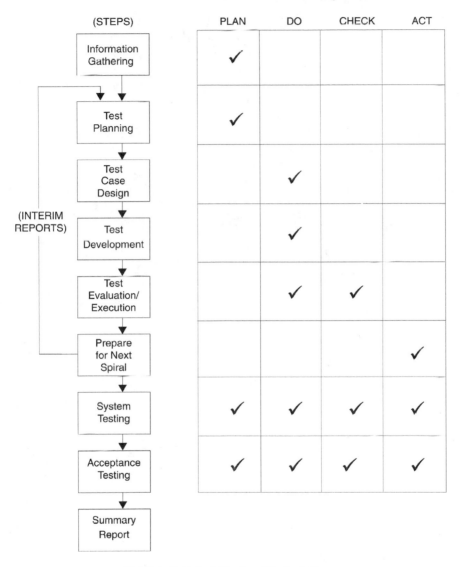

Exhibit 3. Spiral Testing Methodology

from which the testing organization can choose based on its needs. The spiral approach flushes out the system functionality. When this has been completed, it also provides for classical system testing, acceptance testing, and summary reports.

Part 11
Information Gathering (Plan)

If you will recall, in the spiral development environment, software testing is described as a continuous improvement process that must be integrated into a rapid application development methodology. Deming's continuous improvement process using the PDCA model (see Exhibit 1) is applied to the software testing process. We are now in the *Plan* part of the spiral model.

Exhibit 2 outlines the steps and tasks associated with information-gathering within the *Plan* part of spiral testing. Each step and task is described along with valuable tips and techniques.

The purpose of gathering information is to obtain information relevant to the software development project and organize it in order to understand the scope of the development project and start building a test plan. Other interviews may occur during the development project, as necessary.

Proper preparation is critical to the success of the interview. Before the interview, it is important to clearly identify the objectives of the interview to all parties, identify the quality assurance representative who will lead the interview and the scribe, schedule a time and place, prepare any required handouts, and communicate what is required from development.

While many interviews are unstructured, the interviewing steps and tasks shown in Exhibit 2 will be very helpful.

STEP 1: PREPARE FOR THE INTERVIEW

Task 1: Identify the Participants

It is recommended that there be no more than two interviewers representing quality assurance. It is helpful for one of these to assume the role of questioner while the other takes detailed notes. This will allow the interviewer to focus on soliciting information. Ideally the interviewer should be the manager responsible for the project testing activities. The scribe, or note taker, should be a test engineer or lead tester assigned to the project, who supports the interviewer and records each pertinent piece of information and lists the issues, the assumptions, and questions.

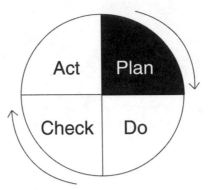

Exhibit 1. Spiral Testing and Continuous Improvement

The recommended development participants attending include the project sponsor, development manager, or a senior development team member. While members of the development team can take notes, this is the responsibility of the scribe. Having more than one scribe can result in confusion, because multiple sets of notes will eventually have to be consolidated. The most efficient approach is for the scribe to take notes and summarize at the end of the interview.

Task 2: Define the Agenda

The key factor for a successful interview is a well thought out agenda. It should be prepared by the interviewer ahead of time and agreed upon by the development leader. The agenda should include an introduction, specific points to cover, and a summary section. The main purpose of an agenda is to enable the testing manager to gather enough information to scope out the quality assurance activities and start a test plan. Exhibit 3 depicts a sample agenda (details are described in Step 2, "Conduct the Interview").

STEP 2: CONDUCT THE INTERVIEW

A good interview contains four elements. The first is defining what will be discussed, or "talking about what we are going to talk about." The second is discussing the details, or "talking about it." The third is summarizing, or "talking about what we talked about." The final element is timeliness. The interviewer should state up front the estimated duration of the interview and set the ground rule that if time expires before completing all items on the agenda, a follow-on interview will be scheduled. This is difficult, particularly when the interview is into the details, but nonetheless it should be followed.

Information Gathering

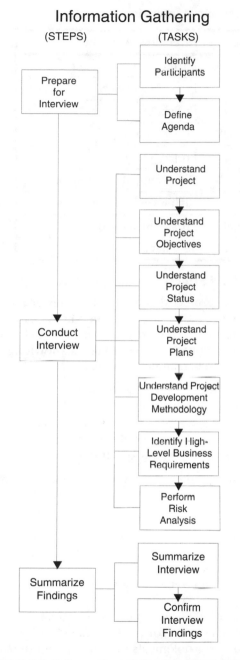

Exhibit 2. Information Gathering (Steps/Tasks)

Exhibit 3. Interview Agenda

Interview Agenda	
I.	Introductions
II.	Project Overview
III.	Project Objectives
IV.	Project Status
V.	Project Plans
VI.	Development Methodology
VII.	High-level Requirements
VIII.	Project Risks and Issues
IX.	Summary

Task 1: Understand the Project

Before getting into the project details the interviewer should state the objectives of the interview and present the agenda. As with any type of interview, he should indicate that only one individual should speak, no interruptions should occur until the speaker acknowledges a request, and focus should be on the material being presented.

He should then introduce himself and the scribe and ask each member on the development team to introduce themselves. Each should indicate name, title, specific roles and job responsibilities, as well as expectations of the interview. The interviewer should point out that the purpose of this task is to obtain general project background information.

The following general questions should be asked to solicit basic information:

- What is the name of the project?
- What are the high-level project objectives?
- What is the audience (users of the system) to be developed?
- When was the project started?
- When is it anticipated to be complete?
- Where is the project in developing the system?
- What is the projected effort in person-months?
- Is this a new, maintenance, or package development project?
- What are the major problems, issues, and concerns?
- Are there plans to address problems and issues?
- Is the budget on schedule?
- Is the budget too tight, too loose, or about right?
- What organizational units are participating in the project?

- Is there an established organization chart?
- What resources are assigned to each unit?
- What is the decision-making structure, i.e., who makes the decisions?
- What are the project roles and the responsibilities associated with each role?
- Who is the resource with whom the test team will communicate on a daily basis?
- Has a quality management plan been developed?
- Has a periodic review process been set up?
- Has there been a representative from the user community appointed to represent quality?

Task 2: Understand the Project Objectives

To develop a test plan for a development project it is important to understand the objectives of the project. The purpose of this task is to understand the scope, needs, and high-level requirements of this project.

The following questions should be asked to solicit basic information:

- Purpose
  - What type of system is being developed, e.g., payroll, order entry, inventory, accounts receivable/payable?
  - Why is the system being developed?
  - What subsystems are involved?
  - What are the subjective requirements, e.g., ease of use, efficiency, morale, flexibility?

- Scope
  - Who are the users of the system?
  - What are the users' job titles and roles?
  - What are the major and subfunctions of the system?
  - What functions will not be implemented?
  - What business procedures are within the scope of the system?
  - Are there analysis diagrams, such as business flow diagrams, data flow diagrams, or data models, to describe the system?
  - Have project deliverables been defined along with completeness criteria?

- Benefits
  - What are the anticipated benefits that will be provided to the user with this system:
    1. Increased productivity
    2. Improved quality
    3. Cost savings
    4. Increased revenue
    5. More competitive advantage, etc.

111

- Strategic
  - What are the strategic or competitive advantages?
  - What impact will the system have on the organization, customers, legal, government, etc.?

- Constraints
  - What are the financial, organizational, personnel, technological constraints, or limitations for the system?
  - What business functions and procedures are out of scope of the system?

Task 3: Understand the Project Status

The purpose of this task is to understand where the project is at this point, which will help define how to plan the testing effort. For example, if this is the first interview and the project is coding the application, the testing effort is already behind schedule. The following questions should be asked to solicit basic information:

- Has a detailed project work plan, including activities, tasks, dependencies, resource assignments, work effort estimates, and milestones, been developed?
- Is the project on schedule?
- Is the completion time too tight?
- Is the completion time too loose?
- Is the completion time about right?
- Have there been any major slips in the schedule that will impact the critical path?
- How far is the project from meeting its objectives?
- Are the user functionality and quality expectations realistic and being met?
- Are the project work effort hours trends on schedule?
- Are the project costs trends within the budget?
- What development deliverables have been delivered?

Task 4: Understand the Project Plans

Since the testing effort needs to track development, it is important to understand the project work plans. The following questions should be asked to solicit basic information:

- Work Break Down
  - Has a Microsoft Project (or other tool) plan been developed?
  - How detailed is the plan, e.g., how many major and bottom-level tasks have been identified?
  - What are the major project milestones (internal and external)?

- Assignments
  - Have appropriate resources been assigned to each work plan?
  - Is the work plan well balanced?
  - What is the plan to stage resources?

- Schedule
  - Is the project plan on schedule?
  - Is the project plan behind schedule?
  - Is the plan updated periodically?

Task 5: Understand the Project Development Methodology

The testing effort must integrate with the development methodology. If considered a separate function, it may not receive the appropriate resources and commitment. Testing as an integrated function should prevent development from proceeding without testing. Testing steps and tasks need to be integrated into the systems development methodology through addition or modification of tasks. Specifically, the testing function needs to know when in the development methodology test design can start. It also needs to know when the system will be available for execution and the recording and correction of defects.

The following questions should be asked to solicit basic information:

- What is the methodology?
  - What development and project management methodology does the development organization use?
  - How well does the development organization follow the development methodology?
  - Is there room for interpretation or flexibility?

- Standards
  - Are standards and practices documented?
  - Are the standards useful or do they hinder productivity?
  - How well does the development organization enforce standards?

Task 6: Identify the High-Level Business Requirements

A software requirements specification defines the functions of a particular software product in a specific environment. Depending on the development organization, it may vary from a loosely defined document with a generalized definition of what the application will do to a very detailed specification, as shown in Appendix C, "Requirements Specification." In either case, the testing manager must assess the scope of the development project in order to start a test plan.

The following questions should be asked to solicit basic information:

- What are high-level functions?

The functions at a high level should be enumerated. Examples include order processing, financial processing, reporting capability, financial planning, purchasing, inventory control, sales administration, shipping, cash flow analysis, payroll, cost accounting, recruiting. This list defines what the application is supposed to do and provides the testing manager an idea of the level of test design and implementation required. The interviewer should solicit as much detail as possible, including a detailed breakdown of each function. If this detail is not available during the interview, a request for a detailed functional decomposition should be made, and it should be pointed out that this information is essential for preparing a test plan.

- What are the system (minimum) requirements?
  A description of the operating system version (Windows, etc.) and minimum microprocessor, disk space, RAM, and communications hardware should be provided.
- What are the Windows or external interfaces?
  The specification should define how the application should behave from an external viewpoint, usually by defining the inputs and outputs. It also includes a description of any interfaces to other applications or subsystems.
- What are the performance requirements?
  This includes a description of the speed, availability, data volume throughput rate, response time, and recovery time of various functions, stress, etc. This serves as a basis for understanding the level of performance and stress testing that may be required.
- What other testing attributes are required?
  This includes such attributes as portability, maintainability, security, and usability. This serves as a basis for understanding the level of other system-level testing that may be required.
- Are there any design constraints?
  This includes a description of any limitation on the operating environment(s), database integrity, resource limits, implementation language standards, etc.

Task 7: Perform Risk Analysis

The purpose of this task is to measure the degree of business risk in an application system to improve testing. This is accomplished in two ways. First, high-risk applications can be identified and subjected to more extensive testing. Second, risk analysis can help identify the error-prone components of an individual application so that testing can be directed at those components. This task describes how to use risk assessment techniques to measure the risk of an application under testing.

Computer Risk Analysis

Risk analysis is a formal method for identifying vulnerabilities (i.e., areas of potential loss). Any area that could be misused, intentionally or accidentally, and result in a loss to the organization is a vulnerability. Identification of risks allows the testing process to measure the potential effect of those vulnerabilities (e.g., the maximum loss that could occur if the risk or vulnerability were exploited).

Risk has always been a testing consideration. Individuals naturally try to anticipate problems and then test to determine whether additional resources and attention need to be directed at those problems. Often, however, risk analysis methods are both informal and ineffective.

Through proper analysis, the test manager should be able to predict the probability of such unfavorable consequences as:

- Failure to obtain all, or even any, of the expected benefits.
- Cost and schedule overruns.
- An inadequate system of internal control.
- Technical performance of the resulting system that is significantly below the estimate.
- Incompatibility of the system with the selected hardware and software.

The following reviews the various methods used for risk analysis and the dimensions of computer risk and then describes the various approaches for assigning risk priorities. There are three methods of performing risk analysis.

Method 1 — Judgment and Instinct. This method of determining how much testing to perform enables the tester to compare the project with past projects to estimate the magnitude of the risk. Although this method can be effective, the knowledge and experience it relies on are not transferable but must be learned over time.

Method 2 — Dollar Estimation. Risk is the probability for loss. That probability is expressed through this formula:

(Frequency of occurrence) × (loss per occurrence) = (annual loss expectation)

Business risk based on this formula can be quantified in dollars. Often however, the concept, not the formula, is used to estimate how many dollars might be involved if problems were to occur. The disadvantages of projecting risks in dollars are that such numbers (i.e., frequency of occurrence and loss per occurrence) are difficult to estimate and the method implies a greater degree of precision than may be realistic.

Method 3 — Identifying and Weighting Risk Attributes. Experience has demonstrated that the major attributes causing potential risks are the project size, experience with the technology, and project structure. The larger the project is in dollar expense, staffing levels, elapsed time, and number of departments affected, the greater the risk.

Because of the greater likelihood of unexpected technical problems, project risk increases as the project team's familiarity with the hardware, operating systems, database, and application languages decreases. A project that has a slight risk for a leading-edge, large systems development department may have a very high risk for a smaller, less technically advanced group. The latter group, however, can reduce its risk by purchasing outside skills for an undertaking that involves a technology in general commercial use.

In highly structured projects, the nature of the task defines the output completely, from the beginning. Such output is fixed during the life of the project. These projects carry much less risk than those whose output is more subject to the manager's judgment and changes.

The relationship among these attributes can be determined through weighting, and the testing manger can use weighted scores to rank application systems according to their risk. For example, this method can show application A is a higher risk than application B.

Risk assessment is applied by first weighing the individual risk attributes. For example, if an attribute is twice as important as another it can be multiplied by the weight of two. The resulting score is compared with other scores developed for the same development organization and is used to determine a relative risk measurement among applications, but it is not used to determine an absolute measure.

Exhibit 4 compares three projects using the weighted risk attribute method. Project size has a 2 weight factor, experience with technology has a 3 weight factor, and project structure has a 1 weight factor. When the project scores are each multiplied by each of the three weight factors, it is clear that project A has the highest risk.

Information gathered during risk analysis can be used to allocate test resources to test application systems. For example, high-risk applications should receive extensive testing; medium-risk systems, less testing; and low-risk systems, minimal testing. The area of testing can be selected on the basis of high-risk characteristics. For example, if computer technology is a high-risk characteristic, the testing manager may want to spend more time testing how effectively the development team is using that technology.

Exhibit 4. Identifying and Weighting Risk Attributes

Weighting Factor	Project A (score × weight)	Project B (score × weight)	Project C (score × weight)
Project Size(2)	5 × 2 = 10	3 × 2 = 6	2 × 2 = 4
Experience with Technology(3)	7 × 3 = 21	1 × 3 = 3	5 × 3 = 15
Project Structure(1)	4 × 1 = 4	6 × 1 = 6	3 × 1 = 3
Total Score	35	15	22

STEP 3: SUMMARIZE THE FINDINGS

Task 1: Summarize the Interview

After the interview is completed, the interviewer should review the agenda and outline the main conclusions. If there is the need for a follow-up session, one should be scheduled at this point while the members are present.

Typically, during the interview, the notes are unstructured and hard to follow by anyone except the note taker. However, the notes should have at least followed the agenda. After the interview concludes, the notes should be formalized into a summary report. This should be performed by the scribe note taker. The goal is to make the results of the session as clear as possible for quality assurance and the development organization. However, the interview leader may have to embellish the material or expand in certain areas.

Task 2: Confirm the Interview Findings

The purpose of this task is to bring about agreement between the interviewer and the development organization to assure an understanding of the project. After the interview notes are formalized, it is important to distribute the summary report to the other members who attended the interview. A sincere invitation for their comments or suggestions should be communicated. The interviewer should then actively follow up interview agreements and disagreements. Any changes should then be implemented. Once there is full agreement, the interviewer should provide a copy of the summary report.

Part 12
Test Planning (Plan)

The purpose of test planning is to provide the basis for accomplishing testing in an organized manner. From a managerial point of view it is the most important document, because it helps manage the test project. If a test plan is comprehensive and carefully thought out, test execution and analysis should proceed smoothly.

The test plan is an ongoing document, particularly in the spiral environment since the system is constantly changing. As the system changes, so does it. A good test plan is one which:

- Has a good chance of detecting a majority of the defects
- Provides test coverage for most of the code
- Is flexible
- Is executed easily, repeatably, and automatically
- Defines the types of tests to be performed
- Clearly documents the expected results
- Provides for defect reconciliation when a defect is discovered
- Clearly defines the test objectives
- Clarifies the test strategy
- Clearly defines the test exit criteria
- Is not redundant
- Identifies the risks
- Documents the test requirements
- Defines the test deliverables

While there are many ways a test plan can be created, Exhibit 1 provides a framework that includes most of the essential planning considerations. It can be treated as a checklist of test items to consider. While some of the items, such as defining the test requirements and test team, are obviously required, others may not be. It depends on the nature of the project and the time constraints.

The planning test methodology includes three steps: building the test plan, defining the metrics, and reviewing/approving the test plan. Each of these is then broken down into its respective tasks, as shown in Exhibit 1.

Test Planning

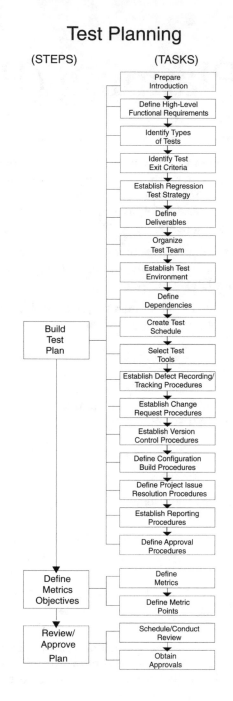

Exhibit 1. Test Planning (Steps/Tasks)

STEP 1: BUILD A TEST PLAN

Task 1: Prepare an Introduction

The first bit of test plan detail is a description of the problem(s) to be solved by the application of the associated opportunities. This defines the summary background describing the events or current status leading up to the decision to develop the application. Also, the application's risks, purpose, objectives, benefits, and the organization's critical success factors should be documented in the introduction. A critical success factor is a measurable item that will have a major influence on whether or not a key function meets its objectives. An objective is a measurable end state that the organization strives to achieve. Examples of objectives include:

- New product opportunity
- Improved efficiency (internal and external)
- Organizational image
- Growth (internal and external)
- Financial (revenue, cost profitability)
- Competitive position
- Market leadership

The introduction should also include an executive summary description. The executive sponsor (often called the project sponsor) is the individual who has ultimate authority over the project. This individual has a vested interest in the project in terms of funding, project results, resolving project conflicts, and is responsible for the success of the project. An executive summary describes the proposed application from an executive's point of view. It should describe the problems to be solved, the application goals, and the business opportunities. The objectives should indicate whether the application is a replacement of an old system and document the impact the application will have, if any, on the organization in terms of management, technology, etc.

Any available documentation should be listed and its status described. Examples include requirements specifications, functional specifications, project plan, design specification, prototypes, user manual, business model/flow diagrams, data models, and project risk assessments. In addition to project risks, which are the potential adverse effects on the development project, the risks relating to the testing effort should be documented. Examples include the lack of testing skills, scope of the testing effort, lack of automated testing tools, etc. See Appendix E4, Test Plan (Client/Server Spiral Testing), for more details.

Task 2: Define the High-Level Functional Requirements (In Scope)

A functional specification consists of the hierarchical functional decomposition, the functional window structure, the window standards, and the

Exhibit 2. High-Level Business Functions

Order Processing (ex. create new order, edit order, etc.)
Customer Processing (create new customer, edit customer, etc.)
Financial Processing (receive payment, deposit payment, etc.)
Inventory Processing (acquire products, adjust product price, etc.)
Reports (create order report, create account receivable report, etc.)

Exhibit 3. Functional Window Structure

The Main-Window (menu bar, customer order window, etc.)
The Customer-Order-Window (order summary list, etc.)
The Edit-Order-Window (create order, edit order, etc.)
The Menu Bar (File, Order, View, etc.)
The Tool Bar with icons (File→New, Order→Create)

minimum system requirements of the system to be developed. An example of windows standards is the Windows 95 GUI Standards. An example of a minimum system requirement could be Windows 95, a Pentium II microprocessor, 24 MB RAM, 3 gig-disk space, and a modem. At this point in development, a full functional specification may not have been defined. However, a list of at least the major business functions of the basic window structure should be available.

A basic functional list contains the main functions of the system with each function named and described with a verb–object paradigm. This list serves as the basis for structuring functional testing (see Exhibit 2).

A functional window structure describes how the functions will be implemented in the windows environment. At this point, a full functional window structure may not be available but a list of the major windows should be (see Exhibit 3).

Task 3: Identify Manual/Automated Test Types

The types of tests that need to be designed and executed depend totally on the objectives of the application, i.e., the measurable end state the organization strives to achieve. For example, if the application is a financial application used by a large number of individuals, special security and usability tests need to be performed. However, three types of tests which are nearly always required are: function, user interface, and regression testing. Function testing comprises the majority of the testing effort and is concerned with verifying that the functions work properly. It is a black-box-oriented activity in which the tester is completely unconcerned with the internal behavior and structure of the application. User interface testing, or GUI testing, checks the user's interaction or functional window structure. It ensures that object state dependencies function properly and provide useful navigation through the functions. Regression testing tests the application in light of changes made during debugging, maintenance, or the development of a new release.

Other types of tests that need to be considered include system and acceptance testing. System testing is the highest level of testing which evaluates the functionality as a total system, its performance and overall fitness of use. Acceptance testing is an optional user-run test which demonstrates the ability of the application to meet the user's requirements. This test may or may not be performed based on the formality of the project. Sometimes the system test suffices.

Finally, the tests that can be automated with a testing tool need to be identified. Automated tests provide three benefits: repeatability, leverage, and increased functionality. Repeatability enables automated tests to be executed more than once, consistently. Leverage comes from repeatability from tests previously captured and tests that can be programmed with the tool, which may not have been possible without automation. As applications evolve, more and more functionality is added. With automation, the functional coverage is maintained with the test library.

Task 4: Identify the Test Exit Criteria

One of the most difficult and political problems is deciding when to stop testing, since it is impossible to know when all the defects have been detected. There are at least four criteria for exiting testing:

- Scheduled testing time has expired
  This criteria is very weak, since it has nothing to do with verifying the quality of the application. This does not take into account that there may be an inadequate number of test cases or the fact that there may not be any more defects that are easily detectable.
- Some predefined number of defects discovered
  The problems with this is knowing the number of errors to detect and also overestimating the number of defects. If the number of defects is underestimated, testing will be incomplete. Potential solutions include experience with similar applications developed by the same development team, predictive models, and industry-wide averages. If the number of defects is overestimated, the test may never be completed within a reasonable time frame. A possible solution is to estimate completion time, plotting defects detected per unit of time. If the rate of

defect detection is decreasing dramatically, there may be "burnout," an indication that a majority of the defects have been discovered.

- All the formal tests execute without detecting any defects
  A major problem with this is that the tester is not motivated to design destructive test cases that force the tested program to its design limits, e.g., the tester's job is completed when the test program fields no more errors. The tester is motivated not to find errors and may subconsciously write test cases that show the program is error free. This criteria is only valid if there is a rigorous and totally comprehensive test case suite created which approaches 100% coverage. The problem with this is determining when there is a comprehensive suite of test cases. If it is felt that this is the case, a good strategy at this point is to continue with *ad hoc* testing. *Ad hoc* testing is a black-box testing technique in which the tester lets his or her mind run freely to enumerate as many test conditions as possible. Experience has shown that this technique can be a very powerful supplemental or add-on technique.
- Combination of the above
  Most testing projects utilize a combination of the above exit criteria. It is recommended that all the tests be executed, but any further *ad hoc* testing will be constrained by time.

Task 5: Establish Regression Test Strategy

Regression testing tests the application in light of changes made during a development spiral, debugging, maintenance, or the development of a new release. This test must be performed after functional improvements or repairs have been made to a system to confirm that the changes have no unintended side effects. Correction of errors relating to logic and control flow, computational errors, and interface errors are examples of conditions that necessitate regression testing. Cosmetic errors generally do not affect other capabilities and do not require regression testing.

It would be ideal if all the tests in the test suite were rerun for each new spiral, but due to time constraints, this is probably not realistic. A good regression strategy during spiral development is for some regression testing to be performed during each spiral to ensure that previously demonstrated capabilities are not adversely affected by later development spirals or error corrections. During system testing after the system is stable and the functionality has been verified, regression testing should consist of a subset of the system tests. Policies need to be created to decide which tests to include.

A retest matrix is an excellent tool that relates test cases to functions (or program units) as shown in Exhibit 4. A check entry in the matrix indicates that the test case is to be retested when the function (or program unit) has been modified due to an enhancement(s) or correction(s). No entry means that the test does not need to be retested. The retest matrix can be built before the first testing spiral but needs to be maintained during subsequent spirals. As functions (or program units) are modified during a development spiral, existing or new test cases need to be created and checked in the retest matrix in preparation for the next test spiral. Over time with subsequent spirals, some functions (or program units) may be stable with no recent modifications. Consideration to selectively remove their check entries should be undertaken between testing spirals. Also see Appendix E14, Retest Matrix.

Other considerations of regression testing:

- Regression tests are potential candidates for test automation when they are repeated over and over in every testing spiral.
- Regression testing needs to occur between releases after the initial release of the system.
- The test that uncovered an original defect should be rerun after it has been corrected.
- An in-depth effort should be made to ensure that the original defect was corrected and not just the symptoms.
- Regression tests that repeat other tests should be removed.
- Other test cases in the functional (or program unit) area where a defect is uncovered should be included in the regression test suite.
- Client-reported defects should have high priority and should be regression tested thoroughly.

Take 6: Define the Test Deliverables

Test deliverables result from test planning, test design, test development, and test defect documentation. Some spiral test deliverables from which you can choose include:

- Test plan: Defines the objectives, scope, strategy, types of tests, test environment, test procedures, exit criteria, etc. (see Appendix E-4, sample template).
- Test design: The tests for the application's functionality, performance, and appropriateness for use. The tests demonstrate that the original test objectives are satisfied.
- Change request: A documented request to modify the current software system, usually supplied by the user (see Appendix D, Change Request Form, for more details). It is typically different from a defect report which reports an anomaly in the system.
- Metrics: The measurable indication of some quantitative aspect of a system. Examples include the number of severe defects, the number of defects discovered as a function of the number of testers.

Exhibit 4. Retest Matrix

	Test Case				
	1	2	3	4	5
Business Function					
Order Processing					
Create New Order	√	√	√	√	
Fulfill Order					
Edit Order					
Delete Order	√			√	
Customer Processing					
Create New Customer					
Edit Customer					
Delete Customer		√			
Financial Processing					
Receive Customer Payment		√	√		√
Deposit Payment					
Pay Vendor					
Write a Check	√	√	√	√	√
Display Register					
Inventory Processing					
Acquire Vendor Products					
Maintain Stock					
Handle Back Orders	√	√	√	√	√
Audit Inventory					
Adjust Product Price					
Reports					
Create Order Report					
Create Account Receivables Report	√	√	√	√	√
Create Account Payables					
Create Inventory Report					

- Test case: A specific set of test data and associated procedures developed for a particular objective. It provides a detailed blueprint for conducting individual tests and includes specific input data values and the corresponding expected result(s). (see Appendix E8, Test Case for more details).
- Test log summary report: Specifies the test cases from the tester's individual test logs that are in progress or completed for status reporting and metric collection (see Appendix E10, Test Log Summary Report).
- Test case log: Specifies the test cases for a particular testing event to be executed during testing. It is also used to record the results of the test performed, to provide the detailed evidence for the summary of test results, and to provide a basis for reconstructing the testing event if necessary (see Appendix E9, Test Case Log).
- Interim test report: A report published between testing spirals indicating the status of the testing effort (see Part 16, Step 3, Publish Interim Report).
- System summary report: A comprehensive test report after all spiral testing that has been completed (see Appendix E11, System Summary Report).
- Defect report: Documents defect(s) discovered during spiral testing (see Appendix E12, Defect Report).

Task 7: Organize the Test Team

The people component includes human resource allocations and the required skill sets. The test team should comprise the highest-caliber personnel possible. They are usually extremely busy because their talents put them in great demand, and it therefore becomes vital to build the best case possible for using these individuals for test purposes. A test team leader and test team need to have the right skills and experience, and be motivated to work on the project. Ideally, they should be professional quality assurance specialists but can represent the executive sponsor, users, technical operations, database administration, computer center, independent parties, etc. The latter is particularly useful during final system and acceptance testing. In any event, they should not represent the development team, for they may not be as unbiased as an outside party. This is not to say that developers shouldn't test. For they should unit and function test their code extensively before handing it over to the test team.

There are two areas of responsibility in testing: testing the application, which is the responsibility of the test team, and the overall testing processes, which is handled by the test manager. The test manager directs one or more testers, is the interface between quality assurance and the development organization, and manages the overall testing effort. Responsibilities include:

- Setting up the test objectives
- Defining test resources
- Creating test procedures
- Developing and maintaining the test plan
- Designing test cases
- Designing and executing automated testing tool scripts
- Test case development
- Providing test status
- Writing reports
- Defining the roles of the team members
- Managing the test resources
- Defining standards and procedures
- Ensuring quality of the test process
- Training the team members
- Maintaining test statistics and metrics

The test team must be a set of team players and have the following responsibilities:

- Execute test cases according to the plan
- Evaluate the test results
- Report errors
- Design and execute automated testing tool scripts
- Recommend application improvements
- Record defects

The main function of a team member is to test the application and report defects to the development team by documenting them in a defect tracking system. Once the development team corrects the defects, the test team re-executes the tests which discovered the original defects.

It should be pointed out that the roles of the test manager and team members are not mutually exclusive. Some of the team leader's responsibilities are shared with the team member and visa versa.

The basis for allocating dedicated testing resources is the scope of the functionality and the development time frame, e.g., a medium development project will require more testing resources than a small one. If project A of medium complexity requires a testing team of 5, project B with twice the scope would require 10 testers (given the same resources).

Another rule of thumb is that the testing costs approach 25% of the total budget. Since the total project cost is known, the testing effort can be calculated and translated to tester headcount.

The best estimate is a combination of the project scope, test team skill levels, and project history. A good measure of required testing resources for a particular project is the histories of multiple projects, i.e., testing resource levels and performance compared to similar projects.

Task 8: Establish a Test Environment

The purpose of the test environment is to provide a physical framework for testing necessary for the testing activity. For this task, the test environment needs are established and reviewed before implementation.

The main components of the test environment include the physical test facility, technologies, and tools. The test facility component includes the physical setup. The technologies component includes the hardware platforms, physical network and all its components, operating system software, and other software such as utility software. The tools component includes any specialized testing software such as automated test tools, testing libraries, and support software.

The testing facility and workplace need to be established. This may range from an individual workplace configuration to a formal testing lab. In any event, it is important that the testers be together and in close proximity to the development team. This facilitates communication and the sense of a common goal. The testing tools which were acquired need to be installed.

The hardware and software technologies need to be set up. This includes the installation of test hardware and software, and coordination with vendors, users, and information technology personnel. It may be necessary to test the hardware and coordinate with hardware vendors. Communication networks need to be installed and tested.

Task 9: Define the Dependencies

A good source of information is previously produced test plans on other projects. If available, the sequence of tasks in the project work plans can be analyzed for activity and task dependencies that apply to this project.

Examples of test dependencies include:

- Code availability
- Tester availability (in a timely fashion)
- Test requirements (reasonably defined)
- Test tools availability
- Test group training
- Technical support
- Fix defects in a timely manner
- Adequate testing time
- Computers and other hardware
- Software and associated documentation
- System documentation (if available)

- Defined development methodology
- Test lab space availability
- Agreement with development (procedures and processes)

The support personnel need to be defined and committed to the project. This includes members of the development group, technical support staff, network support staff, and database administrator support staff.

Task 10: Create a Test Schedule

A test schedule should be produced that includes the testing steps (and perhaps tasks), target start and end dates, and responsibilities. It should also describe how it will be reviewed, tracked, and approved. A simple test schedule format, as shown in Exhibit 5, follows the spiral methodology.

Also, a project management tool such as Microsoft Project can format a Gantt Chart to emphasize the tests and group them into test steps. A Gantt Chart consists of a table of task information and a bar chart that graphically displays the test schedule. It also includes task time duration and links the task dependency relationships graphically. People resources can also be assigned to tasks for workload balancing. See Appendix E13, Test Schedule and Template file Gantt Spiral Testing Methodology Template.

Another way to schedule testing activities is with "relative scheduling" in which testing steps or tasks are defined by their sequence or precedence. It does not state a specific start or end date but does have a duration, such as days.

Exhibit 5. Test Schedule

Test Step	Begin Date	End Date	Responsible
First Spiral			
Information Gathering			
Prepare for Interview	6•1•98	6•2•98	Smith, Test Manager
Conduct Interview	6•3•98	6•3•98	Smith, Test Manager
Summarize Findings	6•4•98	6•5•98	Smith, Test Manager
Test Planning			
Build Test Plan	6•8•98	6•12•98	Smith, Test Manager
Define the Metric Objectives	6•15•98	6•17•98	Smith, Test Manager
Review/Approve Plan	6•18•98	6•18•98	Smith, Test Manager
Test Case Design			
Design Function Tests	6•19•98	6•23•98	Smith, Test Manager

Exhibit 5. (Continued) Test Schedule

Test Step	Begin Date	End Date	Responsible
Design GUI Tests	6•24•98	6•26•98	Smith, Test Manager
Define the System/Acceptance Tests	6•29•98	6•30•98	Smith, Test Manager
Review/Approve Design	7•3•98	7•3•98	Smith, Test Manager
Test Development			
Develop Test Scripts	7•6•98	7•16•98	Jones, Baker, Brown, Testers
Review/Approve Test Development	7•17•98	7•17•98	Jones, Baker, Brown, Testers
Test Execution/Evaluation			
Setup and Testing	7•20•98	7•24•98	Smith, Jones, Baker, Brown, Testers
Evaluation	7•27•98	7•29•98	Smith, Jones, Baker, Brown, Testers
Prepare for the Next Spiral			
Refine the Tests	8•3•98	8•5•98	Smith, Test Manager
Reassess Team, Procedures, and Test Environment	8•6•98	8•7•98	Smith, Test Manager
Publish Interim Report	8•10•98	8•11•98	Smith, Test Manager
•			
•			
•			
Last Spiral…			
Test Execution/Evaluation			
Setup and Testing	10•5•98	10•9•98	Jones, Baker, Brown, Testers
Evaluation	10•12•98	10•14•98	Smith, Test Manager
•			
•			
•			
Conduct System Testing			
Complete System Test Plan	10•19•98	10•21•98	Smith, Test Manager
Complete System Test Cases	10•22•98	10•23•98	Smith, Test Manager

Exhibit 5. (Continued) Test Schedule

Test Step	Begin Date	End Date	Responsible
Review/Approve System Tests	10•26•98	10•30•98	Jones, Baker, Brown, Testers
Execute the System Tests	11•2•98	11•6•98	Jones, Baker, Brown, Testers
Conduct Acceptance Testing			
Complete Acceptance Test Plan	11•9•98	11•10•98	Smith, Test Manager
Complete Acceptance Test Cases	11•11•98	11•12•98	Smith, Test Manager
Review/Approve Acceptance Test Plan	11•13•98	11•16•98	Jones, Baker, Brown, Testers
Execute the Acceptance Tests	11•17•98	11•20•98	
Summarize/Report Spiral Test Results			
Perform Data Reduction	11•23•98	11•26•98	Smith, Test Manager
Prepare Final Test Report	11•27•98	11•27•98	Smith, Test Manager
Review/Approve the Final Test Report	11•28•98	11•29•98	Smith, Test Manager Baylor, Sponsor

Exhibit 6. Project Milestones

Project Milestone	Due Date
Sponsorship approval	7•1•98
First prototype available	7•20•98
Project test plan	6•18•98
Test development complete	7•17•98
Test execution begins	7•20•98
Final spiral test summary report published	11•27•98
System ship date	12•1•98

It is also important to define major external and internal milestones. External milestones are events that are external to the project but may have a direct impact on the project. Examples include project sponsorship approval, corporate funding, and legal authorization. Internal milestones are derived for the schedule work plan and typically correspond to key deliverables which need to be reviewed and approved. Examples include test plan, design, and development completion approval by the project sponsor and the final spiral test summary report. Milestones can be documented in the test plan in table format as shown in Exhibit 6.

Task 11: Select the Test Tools

Test tools range from relatively simple to sophisticated software. New tools are being developed to help provide the high-quality software needed for today's applications.

Because test tools are critical to effective testing, those responsible for testing should be proficient in using them. The tools selected should be most effective for the environment in which the tester operates and the specific types of software being tested. The test plan needs to name specific test tools and their vendors. The individual who selects the test tool should also conduct the test and be familiar enough with the tool to use it effectively. The test team should review and approve the use of each test tool, because the tool selected must be consistent with the objectives of the test plan.

The selection of testing tools may be based on intuition or judgment. However, a more systematic approach should be taken. Section IV, Modern Testing Tools, provides a comprehensive methodology for acquiring testing tools. It also provides an overview of the types of modern testing tools available.

Task 12: Establish Defect Recording/Tracking Procedures

During the testing process, a defect is discovered. It needs to be recorded. A defect is related to individual tests that have been conducted, and the objective is to produce a complete record of those defects. The overall motivation for recording defects is to correct defects and record metric information about the application. Development should have access to the defects reports, which they can use to evaluate whether there is a defect and how to reconcile it. The defect form can either be manual or electronic, with the latter being preferred. Metric information such as the number of defects by type or open time for defects can be very useful to understand the status of the system.

Defect control procedures need to be established to control this process from initial identification to reconciliation. Exhibit 7 shows some possible defects states from open to closed with intermediate states. The testing department initially opens a defect report and also closes it. A "Yes" in a cell indicates a possible transition from one state to another. For example, an "Open" state can change to "Under Review," "Returned by Development," or "Deferred by Development." The transitions are initiated by either the testing department or development.

Exhibit 7. Defect States

	Open	Under Review	Returned by Development	Ready for Testing	Returned by QA	Deferred by Development	Closed
Open	—	Yes	Yes	—	—	Yes	—
Under Review	—	—	Yes	Yes	—	Yes	Yes
Returned by Development	—	—	—	—	Yes	—	Yes
Ready for Testing	—	—	—	—	Yes	—	Yes
Returned by QA	—	—	Yes	—	—	Yes	Yes
Deferred by Development	—	Yes	Yes	Yes	—	—	Yes
Closed	Yes	—	—	—	—	—	—

A defect report form also needs to be designed. The major fields of a defect form include (see Appendix E12, Defect Report for more details):

- Identification of the problem, e.g., functional area, problem type, etc.
- Nature of the problem, e.g., behavior
- Circumstances which led to the problem, e.g., inputs and steps
- Environment in which the problem occurred, e.g., platform, etc.
- Diagnostic information, e.g., error code, etc.
- Effect of the problem, e.g., consequence

It is quite possible that a defect report and change request form are the same. The advantage of this approach is that it is not always clear whether a change request is a defect or an enhancement request. The differentiation can be made with a form field that indicates whether it is a defect or enhancement request. On the other hand, a separate defect report can be very useful during the maintenance phase when the expected behavior of the software is well known and it is easier to distinguish between a defect and an enhancement.

Task 13: Establish Change Request Procedures

If it were a perfect world, a system would be built and there would be no future changes. Unfortunately, it is not a perfect world and after a system is deployed, there are change requests.

Some of the reasons for change are:

- The requirements change
- The design changes

- The specification is incomplete or ambiguous
- A defect is discovered that was not discovered during reviews
- The software environment changes, e.g., platform, hardware, etc.

Change control is the process by which a modification to a software component is proposed, evaluated, approved or rejected, scheduled, and tracked. It is a decision process used in controlling the changes made to software. Some proposed changes are accepted and implemented during this process. Others are rejected or postponed, and are not implemented. Change control also provides for impact analysis to determine the dependencies (see Appendix D, Change Request Form, for more details).

Each software component has a life cycle. A life cycle consists of states and allowable transitions between those states. Any time a software component is changed, it should always be reviewed. While being reviewed, it is frozen from further modifications and the only way to change it is to create a new version. The reviewing authority must approve the modified software component or reject it. A software library should hold all components as soon as they are frozen and also act as a repository for approved components.

The formal title of the organization to manage changes is a configuration control board, or CCB. The CCB is responsible for the approval of changes and for judging whether a proposed change is desirable. For a small project, the CCB can consist of a single person, such as a project manager. For a more formal development environment, it can consist of several members from development, users, quality assurance, management, etc.

All components controlled by software configuration management are stored in a software configuration library, including work products such as business data and process models, architecture groups, design units, tested application software, reusable software, and special test software. When a component is to be modified, it is checked out of the repository into a private workspace. It evolves through many states that are temporarily outside the scope of configuration management control.

When a change is completed, the component is checked in to the library and becomes a new component version. The previous component version is also retained.

Change control is based on the following major functions of a development process: requirements analysis, system design, program design, testing, and implementation. At least six control procedures are associated with these functions and need to be established for a change control system (see Appendix B, Software Quality Assurance Plan for more details):

1. Initiation Procedures
   This includes procedures for initiating a change request through a change request form, which serves as a communication vehicle. The

objective is to gain consistency in documenting the change request document and routing it for approval.

2. Technical Assessment Procedures

This includes procedures for assessing the technical feasibility, and technical risks, and scheduling a technical evaluation of a proposed change. The objectives are to ensure integration of the proposed change, the testing requirements, and the ability to install the change request.

3. Business Assessment Procedures

This includes procedures for assessing the business risk, effect, and installation requirements of the proposed change. The objectives are to ensure that the timing of the proposed change is not disruptive to the business goals.

4. Management Review Procedures

This includes procedures for evaluating the technical and business assessments through management review meetings. The objectives are to ensure that changes meet technical and business requirements and that adequate resources are allocated for testing and installation.

5. Test Tracking Procedures

This includes procedures for tracking and documenting test progress and communication, including steps for scheduling tests, documenting the test results, deferring change requests based on test results, and updating test logs. The objectives are to ensure that testing standards are utilized to verify the change, including test plans and test design, and that test results are communicated to all parties.

6. Installation Tracking Procedure

This includes procedures for tracking and documenting the installation progress of changes. It ensures that proper approvals have been completed, adequate time and skills have been allocated, installation and backup instructions have been defined, and proper communication has occurred. The objectives are to ensure that all approved changes have been made, including scheduled dates, test durations, and reports.

Task 14: Establish Version Control Procedures

A method for uniquely identifying each software component needs to be established via a labeling scheme. Every software component must have a unique name. Software components evolve through successive revisions, and each needs to be distinguished. A simple way to distinguish component revisions is with a pair of integers 1.1, 1.2 ..., which define the release number and level number. When a software component is first identified, it is revision 1 and subsequent major revisions are 2, 3, etc.

In a client/server environment it is highly recommended that the development environment be different from the test environment. This requires the application software components to be transferred from the development environment to the test environment. Procedures need to be set up.

Software needs to be placed under configuration control so that no changes are being made to the software while testing is being conducted. This includes source and executable components. Application software can be periodically migrated into the test environment. This process must be controlled to ensure that the latest version of software is tested. Versions will also help control the repetition of tests to ensure that previously discovered defects have been resolved.

For each release or interim change between versions of a system configuration, a version description document should be prepared to identify the software components.

Task 15: Define Configuration Build Procedures

Assembling a software system involves tools to transform the source components, or source code, into executable programs. Example of tools are compilers and linkage editors.

Configuration build procedures need to be defined to identify the correct component versions and execute the component build procedures. The configuration build model addresses the crucial question of how to control the way components are built.

A configuration typically consists of a set of derived software components. An example of derived software components is executable object programs derived from source programs. Derived components must be correctly associated with each source component to obtain an accurate derivation. The configuration build model addresses the crucial question of how to control the way derived components are built.

The inputs and outputs required for a configuration build model include primary inputs and primary outputs. The primary inputs are the source components, which are the raw materials from which the configuration is built, the version selection procedures, and the system model which describes the relationship between the components. The primary outputs are the target configuration and derived software components.

Different software configuration management environments use different approaches for selecting versions. The simplest approach to version selection is to maintain a list of component versions. Other automated approaches allow for the most recently tested component versions to be selected, or those updated on a specific date. Operating system facilities can

137

be used to define and build configurations including the directories and command files.

Task 16: Define Project Issue Resolution Procedures

Testing issues can arise at any point in the development process and must be resolved successfully. The primary responsibility of issue resolution is with the project manager who should work with the project sponsor to resolve them. Typically, the testing manager will document test issues which arise during the testing process. The project manager or project sponsor should screen every issue that arises. An issue can be rejected or deferred for further investigation but should be considered relative to its impact on the project. In any case, a form should be created that contains the essential information. Examples of testing issues include: lack of testing tools, lack of adequate time to test, inadequate knowledge of the requirements, etc.

Issue management procedures need to be defined before the project starts. The procedures should address how to:

- Submit an issue
- Report an issue
- Screen an issue (rejected, deferred, merged, or accepted)
- Investigate an issue
- Approve an issue
- Postpone an issue
- Reject an issue
- Close an issue

Task 17: Establish Reporting Procedures

Test reporting procedures are critical to manage the testing progress and manage the expectations of the project team members. This will keep the project manager and sponsor informed of the testing project progress and minimize the chance of unexpected surprises. The testing manager needs to define who needs the test information, what information they need, and how often the information is to be provided. The objectives of test status reporting are to report the progress of the testing toward its objectives and report test issues, problems, and concerns.

Two key reports that need to be published are:

- Interim Test Report
  An interim test report is a report published between testing spirals indicating the status of the testing effort.
- System Summary Report

  A test summary report is a comprehensive test report after all spiral testing has been completed.

Task 18: Define Approval Procedures

Approval procedures are critical in a testing project. They help provide the necessary agreement between members of the project team. The testing manager needs to define who needs to approve a test deliverable, when it will be approved, and what is the backup plan if an approval cannot be obtained. The approval procedure can vary from a formal signoff of a test document to an informal review with comments. Exhibit 8 shows test deliverables for which approvals are required or recommended, and by whom.

Exhibit 8. Deliverable Approvals

Test Deliverable	Approval Status	Suggested Approver
Test Plan	Required	Project Manager, Development Manager, Sponsor
Test Design	Required	Development Manager
Change Request	Required	Development Manager
Metrics	Recommended	Development Manager
Test Case	Required	Development Manager
Test Log Summary Report	Recommended	Development Manager
Test Log Summary Report	Recommended	Development Manager
Interim Test Report	Required	Project Manager, Development Manager
System Summary Report	Required	Project Manager, Development Manager, Sponsor
Defect Report	Required	Development Manager

STEP 2: DEFINE THE METRIC OBJECTIVES

"You can't control what you can't measure." This is a quote from Tom De-Marco's book, *Controlling Software Projects,* in which he describes how to organize and control a software project so it is measurable in the context of time and cost projections. Control is the extent to which a manager can ensure minimum surprises. Deviations from the plan should be signaled as early as possible in order to react. Another quote from DeMarco's book, "The only unforgivable failure is the failure to learn from past failure," stresses the importance of estimating and measurement. Measurement is a recording of past effects to quantitatively predict future effects.

Task 1: Define the Metrics

Software testing as a test development project has deliverables such as test plans, test design, test development and test execution. The objective of this task is to apply the principles of metrics to control the testing process. A metric is a measurable indication of some quantitative aspect of a system and has the following characteristics:

- Measurable
  A metric point must be measurable for it to be a metric, by definition. If the phenomenon can't be measured, there is no way to apply management methods to control it.
- Independent
  Metrics need to be independent of the human influence. There should be no way of changing the measurement other than changing the phenomenon that produced the metric.
- Accountable
  Any analytical interpretation of the raw metric data rests on the data itself, and it is, therefore, necessary to save the raw data and the methodical audit trail of the analytical process.
- Precise
  Precision is a function of accuracy. The key to precision is, therefore, that a metric is explicitly documented as part of the data collection process. If a metric varies, it can be measured as a range or tolerance.

A metric can be a "result," or a "predictor." A result metric measures a completed event or process. Examples include actual total elapsed time to process a business transaction or total test costs of a project. A predictor metric is an early warning metric that has a strong correlation to some later result. An example is the predicted response-time through statistical regression analysis when more terminals are added to a system when that many terminals have not yet been measured. A result or predictor metric can also be a derived metric. A derived metric is one that is derived from a calculation or graphical technique involving one or more metrics.

The motivation for collecting test metrics is to make the testing process more effective. This is achieved by carefully analyzing the metric data and taking the appropriate action to correct problems. The starting point is to define the metric objectives of interest. Some examples include:

- Defect analysis
  Every defect must be analyzed to answer such questions as the root causes, how detected, when detected, who detected, etc.
- Test effectiveness
  How well is testing doing, e.g., return on investment?
- Development effectiveness
  How well is development fixing defects?

- Test automation
  How much effort is expended on test automation?
- Test cost
  What are the resources and time spent on testing?
- Test status
  Another important metric is status tracking, or where are we in the testing process?
- User involvement

How much is the user involved in testing?

Task 2: Define the Metric Points

Exhibit 9 lists some metric points associated with the general metrics selected in the previous task and the corresponding actions to improve the testing process. Also shown is the source, or derivation, of the metric point.

STEP 3: REVIEW/APPROVE THE PLAN

Task 1: Schedule/Conduct the Review

The test plan review should be scheduled well in advance of the actual review and the participants should have the latest copy of the test plan.

As with any interview or review, it should contain four elements. The first is defining what will be discussed, or "talking about what we are going to talk about." The second is discussing the details, or "talking about it." The third is summarization, or "talking about what we talked about." The final element is timeliness. The reviewer should state up front the estimated duration of the review and set the ground rule that if time expires before completing all items on the agenda, a follow-on review will be scheduled.

The purpose of this task is for development and the project sponsor to agree and accept the test plan. If there any suggested changes to the test plan during the review, they should be incorporated into the test plan.

Task 2: Obtain Approvals

Approval is critical in a testing effort, for it helps provide the necessary agreements between testing, development, and the sponsor. The best approach is with a formal sign-off procedure of a test plan. If this is the case, use the management approval sign-off forms. However, if a formal agreement procedure is not in place, send a memo to each key participant, including at least the project manager, development manager, and sponsor. In the document attach the latest test plan and point out that all their feedback comments have been incorporated and that if you do not hear from them, it is assumed that they agree with the plan. Finally, indicate that in a spiral development environment, the test plan will evolve with each iteration but that you will include them in any modification.

Exhibit 9. Metric Points

Metric	Metric Point	Derivation
Defect analysis:	Distribution of defect causes	Histogram, Pareto
Defect analysis:	Number of defects by cause over time	Multi-line graph
Defect analysis:	Number of defects by how found over time	Multi-line graph
Defect analysis:	Distribution of defects by module	Histogram, Pareto
Defect analysis:	Distribution of defects by priority (critical, high, medium, low)	Histogram
Defect analysis:	Distribution of defects by functional area	Histogram
Defect analysis:	Distribution of defects by environment (platform)	Histogram, Pareto
Defect analysis:	Distribution of defects by type (architecture, connectivity, consistency, database integrity, documentation, GUI, installation, memory, performance, security, standards and conventions, stress, usability, bad fixes)	Histogram, Pareto
Defect analysis:	Distribution of defects by who detected (external customer, internal customer, development, QA, other)	Histogram, Pareto
Defect analysis:	Distribution by how detected (technical review, walkthroughs, JAD, prototyping, inspection, test execution)	Histogram, Pareto
Defect analysis:	Distribution of defects by severity (high, medium, low defects)	Histogram
Development effectiveness:	Average time for development to repair defect	Total repair time ÷ number of repaired defects

Exhibit 9. (Continued) Metric Points

Metric	Metric Point	Derivation
Test automation:	Percent of manual vs. automated testing	Cost of manual test effort ÷ total test cost
Test cost:	Distribution of cost by cause	Histogram, Pareto
Test cost:	Distribution of cost by application	Histogram, Pareto
Test cost:	Percent of costs for testing	Test testing cost ÷ total system cost
Test cost:	Total costs of testing over time	Line graph
Test cost:	Average cost of locating a defect	Total cost of testing ÷ number of defects detected
Test cost:	Anticipated costs of testing vs. actual cost	Comparison
Test cost:	Average cost of locating a requirements defect with requirements reviews	Requirements review costs ÷ number of defects uncovered during requirement reviews
Test cost:	Average cost of locating a design defect with design reviews	Design review costs ÷ number of defects uncovered during design reviews
Test cost:	Average cost of locating a code defect with reviews	Code review costs ÷ number of defects uncovered during code reviews
Test cost:	Average cost of locating a defect with test execution	Test execution costs ÷ number of defects uncovered during test execution
Test cost:	Number of testing resources over time	Line plot

Exhibit 9. (Continued) Metric Points

Metric	Metric Point	Derivation
Test effectiveness:	Percentage of defects discovered during maintenance	Number of defects discovered during maintenance ÷ total number of defects uncovered
Test effectiveness:	Percent of defects uncovered due to testing	Number of detected errors through testing ÷ total system defects
Test effectiveness:	Average effectiveness of a test	Number of tests ÷ total system defects
Test effectiveness:	Value returned while reviewing requirements	Number of defects uncovered during requirements review ÷ requirements test costs
Test effectiveness:	Value returned while reviewing design	Number of defects uncovered during design review ÷ design test costs
Test effectiveness:	Value returned while reviewing programs	Number of defects uncovered during program review ÷ program test costs
Test effectiveness:	Value returned during test execution	Number of defects uncovered during testing ÷ test costs
Test effectiveness:	Effect of testing changes	Number of tested changes ÷ problems attributable to the changes
Test effectiveness:	People's assessment of effectiveness of testing	Subjective scaling (1–10)
Test effectiveness:	Average time for QA to verify fix	Total QA verification time ÷ total number of defects to verify
Test effectiveness:	Number of defects over time	Line graph
Test effectiveness:	Cumulative number of defects over time	Line graph

Exhibit 9. (Continued) Metric Points

Metric	Metric Point	Derivation
Test effectiveness:	Number of application defects over time	Multi-line graph
Test extent:	Percent of statements executed	Number of statements executed ÷ total statements
Test extent:	Percent of logical paths executed	Number of logical paths ÷ total number of paths
Test extent:	Percent of acceptance criteria tested	Acceptance criteria tested ÷ total acceptance criteria
Test extent:	Number of requirements tested over time	Line plot
Test extent:	Number of statements executed over time	Line plot
Test extent:	Number of data elements exercised over time	Line plot
Test extent:	Number of decision statements executed over time	Line plot
Test status:	Number of tests ready to run over time	Line plot
Test status:	Number of tests runs over time	Line plot
Test status:	Number of tests run without defects uncovered	Line plot
Test status:	Number of defects corrected over time	Line plot
User involvement:	Percentage of user testing	User testing time ÷ total test time

Part 13
Test Case Design (Do)

If you will recall, in the spiral development environment, software testing is described as a continuous improvement process which must be integrated into a rapid application development methodology. Deming's continuous improvement process using the PDCA model is applied to the software testing process. We are now in the Do part of the spiral model (see Exhibit 1).

Exhibit 2 outlines the steps and tasks associated with the Do part of spiral testing. Each step and task is described along with valuable tips and techniques.

STEP 1: DESIGN FUNCTION TESTS

Task 1: Refine the Functional Test Requirements

At this point, the functional specification should have been completed. It consists of the hierarchical functional decomposition, the functional window structure, the window standards, and the minimum system requirements of the system to be developed. An example of windows standards are the Windows 95 GUI Standards. A minimum system requirement could consist of Windows 95, a Pentium II microprocessor, 24 MB RAM, 3 gig-disk space, and a modem.

A functional breakdown consists of a list of business functions, hierarchical listing, group of activities, or set of user profiles defining the basic functions of the system and how the user will use it. A business function is a discrete controllable aspect of the business and the smallest component of a system. Each should be named and described with a verb–object paradigm. The criteria used to determine the successful execution of each function should be stated. The functional hierarchy serves as the basis for function testing in which there will be at least one test case for each lowest level function. Examples of functions include: approve customer credit, handle order, create invoice, order components, receive revenue, pay bill, purchase items, etc. Taken together, the business functions constitute the total application including any interfaces. A good source of these

147

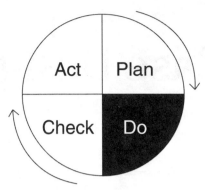

Exhibit 1. Spiral Testing and Continuous Improvement

functions (in addition to the interview itself) is a process decomposition and/or data flow diagram, or CRUD matrix which should be requested during the information-gathering interview.

A functional breakdown is used to illustrate the processes in a hierarchical structure showing successive levels of detail. It is built iteratively as processes and nonelementary processes are decomposed (see Exhibit 3).

A data flow diagram shows processes and the flow of data among these processes. It is used to define the overall data flow through a system and consists of external agents that interface with the system, processes, data flow, and stores depicting where the data is stored or retrieved. A data flow diagram should be reviewed, and each major and leveled function should be listed and organized into a hierarchical list.

A CRUD matrix, or association matrix, links data and process models. It identifies and resolves matrix omissions and conflicts and helps refine the data and process models, as necessary.

A functional window structure describes how the functions will be implemented in the windows environment. Exhibit 4 shows a sample functional window structure for order processing.

Task 2: Build a Function/Test Matrix

The function/test matrix cross-references the tests to the functions. This matrix provides proof of the completeness of the test strategies, illustrating in graphic format which tests exercise which functions. See Exhibit 5 and Appendix E5, Function/Test Matrix for more details.

It is used as a control sheet during testing and can also be used during maintenance. For example, if a function is to be changed, the maintenance

Test Case Design

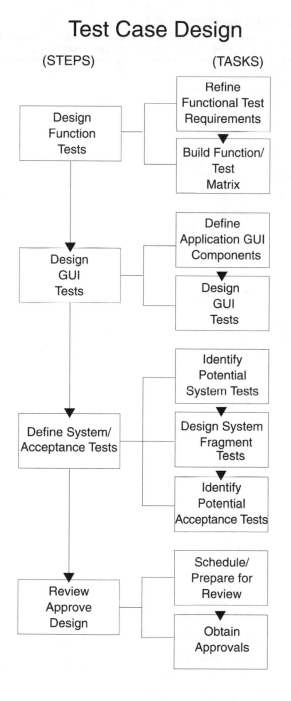

(STEPS)   (TASKS)

Exhibit 2. Test Design (Steps/Tasks)

Exhibit 3. Functional Breakdown

Functional Test Requirements (breakdown)
Order Processing
Create New Order
Fulfill Order
Edit Order
Delete Order
Customer Processing
Create New Customer
Edit Customer
Delete Customer
Financial Processing
Receive Customer Payment
Deposit Payment
Pay Vendor
Write a Check
Display Register
Inventory Processing
Acquire Vendor Products
Maintain Stock
Handle Back Orders
Audit Inventory
Adjust Product Price
Reports
Create Order Report
Create Account Receivable Report
Create Account Payable Report
Create Inventory Report

team can refer to the function/test matrix to determine which tests need to be run or changed. The business functions are listed vertically and the test cases are listed horizontally. The test case name is recorded on the matrix along with the number.

Exhibit 4. Functional Window Structure

The Main-Window

a. The top line of the main window has the standard title bar with Min/Max
    controls.
b. The next line contains the standard Windows menu bar.
c. The next line contains the standard Windows tool bar.
d. The rest of the Main-Application-Window is filled with the Customer-Order
    Window.

The Customer-Order-Window

a. This window shows a summary of each previously entered order.
b. Several orders will be shown at one time (sorted by order number and
    customer name). For each customer order, this window will show:
    1. Order Number
    2. Customer Name
    3. Customer Number
    4. Date
    5. Invoice Number
    6. Model Number
    7. Product Number
    8. Quantity Shipped
    9. Price
a. The scroll bar will be used to select which orders are to be viewed.
b. This window is read-only for viewing.
c. Double-clicking an order will display the Edit-Order Dialog where the order
    can be modified.

The Edit-Order-Window

a. This dialog is used to create new orders or for making changes to previously
    created orders.
b. This dialog will be centered over the Customer-Order-Window. The layout of
    this dialog will show the following:
    1. Order Number (automatically filled in)
    2. Edit field for: Customer Name
    3. Edit field for: Customer Number
    4. Date (initialized)
    5. Edit field for: Invoice Number
    6. Edit field for: Model Number
    7. Edit field for: Product Number
    8. Edit field for: Quantity Shipped
    9. Price (automatically filled in)
    10. Push buttons for: OK and Cancel

Exhibit 4. (Continued) Functional Window Structure

The Menu Bar will include the following menus:

File:

New:

Used to create a new order file

Open:

Used to open the order file.

Save:

Used to save the order file

Save As...:

Used to save the current order file under a new name

Exit:

Used to exit Windows

Order:

Create New Order:

Display Edit-Order-Window with blank fields (except date)

Fulfill Order:

This dialog will be used to verify that the order quantity is available in inventory stock   and validate customer credit.

The dialog will include:

1. Edit field for: Order Number
2. Edit field for: Customer Name
3. Edit field for: Customer Number
4. Date (initialized)
5. Invoice Number (initialized)
6. Model Number (initialized)
7. Product Number (initialized)
8. Quantity Shipped (initialized)
9. Price (initialized)
10. Push buttons for: OK and Cancel
    a. The quantity order is checked against the inventory stock level. If the order cannot be filled, a back order note is sent to purchasing.
    b. The customer history will be displayed (the scroll bar will be used to view the history information).
    c. An Accept button will fulfill the order and create an invoice for shipping.
    d. A Reject button deletes the order and creates a customer order rejection letter.

Edit an Order:

This dialog will be used to edit an existing order. The dialog will include:

1. Edit field for: Order Number
2. Edit field for: Customer Name
3. Edit field for: Customer Number
4. Push buttons for: OK and Cancel

Exhibit 4. (Continued) Functional Window Structure

Delete an Order:

This dialog will be used to delete an existing order. The dialog will include:

1. Edit field for: Order Number
2. Edit field for: Customer Name
3. Edit field for: Customer Number
4. Push buttons for: OK and Cancel
   a. A confirmation message will be displayed with Yes, No, or Cancel options.

Order Report:

This dialog will display one or more orders based upon order number or date ranges.

The layout of the dialog will include:

1. Radio buttons for: Order, Date
2. First Order Number (if report by Order)
3. Optional last Order Number (if report by Order)
4. First Date (if report by Date)
5. Optional last Date (if report by Date)

The user is prompted with the message "Would you like a hard copy printout?"

The user is prompted with the message "Would you like another report (Y/N)?" after each report.

View:

Toolbar:

Used to toggle the display of the toolbar on and off.

Status bar:

Used to toggle the display of the status bar on or off.

The Tool Bar with icons to execute the following menu commands:

File   → New
File   → Open
Order → Create
Order → Validate
Order → Edit
Order → Delete
File   → Exit

It is also important to differentiate those test cases that are manual and those that are automated. One way to accomplish this is to come up with a naming standard that will highlight an automated test case, e.g., first character of the name is "A."

Exhibit 5 shows an example of a function/test matrix.

Exhibit 5. Functional/Test Matrix

Business Function	Test Case				
	1	2	3	4	5
Order Processing					
Create New Order	CNO01	CNO02			
Fulfill Order	AO01				
Edit Order	EO01	EO02	EO03	EO04	
Delete Order	DO01	DO02	DO03	DO04	DO05
Customer Processing					
Create New Customer	ANC01	ANC02	ANC03		
Edit Customer	EC01	EC02	EC03	EC04	EC05
Delete Customer	DC01	DC02			
Financial Processing					
Receive Customer Payment	RCP01	RCP02	RCP03	RCP04	
Deposit Payment	AP01	AP02			
Pay Vendor	PV01	PV02	PV03	PV04	PV05
Write a Check	WC01	WC02			
Display Register	DR01	DR02			
Inventory Processing					
Acquire Vendor Products	AP01	AP02	AP03		
Maintain Stock	MS01	MS02	MS03	MS04	MS05
Handle Back Orders	HB01	HB02	HB03		
Audit Inventory	AI01	AI02	AI03	AI04	
Adjust Product Price	AC01	AC02	AC03		
Reports					
Create Order Report	CO01	CO02	CO03	CO04	CO05
Create Account Receivables Report	CA01	CA02	CA03		
Create Account Payables	AY01	AY02	AY03		
Create Inventory Report	CI01	CI02	CI03	CI04	

STEP 2: DESIGN GUI TESTS

The goal of a good GUI design should be consistent in "look and feel" for the users of the application. Good GUI design has two key components: interaction and appearance. Interaction relates to how the user interacts with the application. Appearance relates to how the interface looks to the user.

GUI testing involves the confirmation that the navigation is correct, e.g., when an ICON, menu choice, or ratio button is clicked, the desired response occurs. The following are some good GUI design principles the tester should look for while testing the application.

Ten Guidelines for Good GUI Design

1. Involve users
2. Understand the user's culture and experience
3. Prototype continuously to validate the requirements
4. Let the user's business workflow drive the design
5. Do not overuse or underuse GUI features
6. Create the GUI, help, and training concurrently
7. Do not expect users to remember secret commands or functions
8. Anticipate mistakes and don't penalize the user
9. Continually remind the user of the application status
10. Keep it simple

Task 1: Identify the Application GUI Components

Graphical User Interface (GUI) provides multiple channels of communication using words, pictures, animation, sound, and video. Five key foundation components of the user interface are windows, menus, forms, icons, and controls.

Windows. In a windowed environment, all user interaction with the application occurs through the windows. These include a primary window, along with any number of secondary windows generated from the primary one.

Menus. Menus come in a variety of styles and forms. Examples include action menus (push button, radio button), pull-down menus, pop-up menus, option menus, and cascading menus.

Forms. Forms are windows or screens into which the user can add information.

Icons. Icons, or "visual push buttons," are valuable for instant recognition, ease of learning, and ease of navigation through the application.

Controls. A control component appears on a screen that allows the user to interact with the application and is indicated by its corresponding

Exhibit 6. GUI Component Test Matrix

Name	GUI Type					P/F	Date	Tester
	Window	Menu	Form	ICON	Control			
Main-Window	✓							
Customer-Order Window	✓							
Edit-Order Window	✓							
Menu Bar		✓						
Tool Bar					✓			
•								
•								
•								

action. Controls include menu bars, pull-down menus, cascading menus, pop-up menus, push buttons, check boxes, radio buttons, list boxes, and drop-down list boxes.

A design approach to GUI test design is to first define and name each GUI component by name within the application as shown in Exhibit 6. In the next step, a GUI component checklist is developed that can be used to verify each component in the table above. (Also see Appendix E6, GUI Component Test Matrix.)

Task 2: Define the GUI Tests

In the previous task the application GUI components where defined, named, and categorized in the GUI component test matrix. In the present task, a checklist is developed against which each GUI component is verified. The list should cover all possible interactions and may or may not apply to a particular component. Exhibit 7 is a partial list of the items to check.

In addition to the GUI component checks above, if there is a GUI design standard, it should be verified as well. GUI standards are essential to ensure that the internal rules of construction are followed to achieve the desired level of consistency. Some of the typical GUI standards which should be verified include the following:

- Forms "enterable" and display-only formats
- Wording of prompts, error messages, and help features
- Use of color, highlight, and cursors
- Screen layouts

Exhibit 7. GUI Component Checklist

Access via double-click	Multiple windows open	Tabbing sequence
Access via menu	Ctrl menu (move)	Push buttons
Access via toolbar	Ctrl ı function keys	Pull-down menu and sub-menus options
Right-mouse options	Color	Dialog controls
Help links	Accelerators and hot keys	Labels
Context sensitive help	Cancel	Chevrons
Button bars	Close	Ellipses
Open by double-click	Apply	Gray out unavailability
Screen images and graphics	Exit	Check boxes
Open by menu	OK	Filters
Open by toolbar	Tile horizontal/vertical	Spin boxes
ICON access	Arrange icons	Sliders
Access to DOS	Toggling	Fonts
Access via single-click	Expand/contract tree	Drag/drop
Resize window panels	Function keys	Horizontal/vertical scrolling
Fields accept allowable values	Minimize the window Maximize the window	Cascade Window open
Fields handle invalid values	Tabbing Sequence	

- Function and shortcut keys, or "hot keys"
- Consistently locating screen elements on the screen
- Logical sequence of objects
- Consistent font usage
- Consistent color usage

It is also important to differentiate manual from automated GUI test cases. One way to accomplish this is to use an additional column in the GUI component matrix that indicates if the GUI test is manual or automated.

STEP 3: DEFINE THE SYSTEM/ACCEPTANCE TESTS

Task 1: Identify Potential System Tests

System testing is the highest level of testing which evaluates the functionality as a total system, its performance and overall fitness of use. This test is usually performed by the internal organization and is oriented to systems technical issues rather than acceptance, which is a more user-oriented test.

Systems testing consists of one or more tests that are based on the original objectives of the system which were defined during the project interview. The purpose of this task is to select the system tests that will be performed, not how to implement the tests. Some common system test types include:

- Performance Testing
  Verifies and validates that the performance requirements have been achieved; measures response times, transaction rates, and other time sensitive requirements.
- Security Testing
  Evaluates the presence and appropriate functioning of the security of the application to ensure the integrity and confidentiality of the data.
- Volume Testing
  Subjects the application to heavy volumes of data to determine if it can handle the volume of data.
- Stress Testing
  Investigates the behavior of the system under conditions that overload its resources. Of particular interest is the impact that this has on system processing time.
- Compatibility Testing
  Tests the compatibility of the application with other applications or systems.
- Conversion Testing
  Verifies the conversion of existing data and loads a new database.
- Usability Testing
  Determines how well the user will be able to use and understand the application.
- Documentation Testing
  Verifies that the user documentation is accurate and ensures that the manual procedures work correctly.
- Backup Testing
  Verifies the ability of the system to back up its data in the event of a software or hardware failure.
- Recovery Testing
  Verifies the system's ability to recover from a software or hardware failure.
- Installation Testing
  Verifies the ability to install the system successfully.

Task 2: Design System Fragment Tests

System fragment tests are sample subsets of full system tests that can be performed during each spiral loop. The objective of doing a fragment test is to provide early warning of pending problems which would arise in the full system test. Candidate fragment system tests include function, performance, security, usability, documentation, and procedure. Some of these fragment tests should have formal tests performed during each spiral, while others should be part of the overall testing strategy. Nonfragment system tests include installation, recovery, conversion, etc., which are probably going to be performed until the formal system test.

Function testing on a system level occurs during each spiral as the system is integrated. As new functionality is added, test cases need to be designed, implemented, and tested during each spiral.

Typically, security mechanisms are introduced fairly early in the development. Therefore, a set of security tests should be designed, implemented, and tested during each spiral as more features are added.

Usability is an ongoing informal test during each spiral and should always be part of the test strategy. When a usability issue arises, the tester should document it in the defect tracking system. A formal type of usability test is the end user's review of the prototype, which should occur during each spiral.

Documentation (such as online help) and procedures are also ongoing informal tests. These should be developed in parallel with formal system development during each spiral and not be put off until a formal system test. This will avoid last-minute surprises. As new features are added, documentation and procedure tests should be designed, implemented, and tested during each spiral.

Some performance testing should occur during each spiral at a noncontended unit level, i.e., one user. Baseline measurements should be performed on all key functions as they are added to the system. A baseline measurement is a measurement taken for the specific purpose of determining the initial value of the state or performance measurement. During subsequent spirals, the performance measurements can be repeated and compared to the baseline. Exhibit 8 provides an example of baseline performance measurements.

Task 3: Identify Potential Acceptance Tests

Acceptance testing is an optional user-run test which demonstrates the ability of the application to meet the user's requirements. The motivation for this test is to demonstrate rather than be destructive, i.e., to show that

Exhibit 8. Baseline Performance Measurements

Business Function	Baseline Seconds — Rel 1.0 (1/1/98)	Measure and Delta Seconds— Rel 1.1 (2/1/98)	Measure and Delta Seconds— Rel 1.2 (2/15/98)	Measure and Delta Seconds— Rel 1.3 (3/1/98)	Measure and Delta Seconds— Rel 1.4 (3/15/98)	Measure and Delta Seconds— Rel 1.5 (4/1/98)
Order Processing						
Create New Order	1.0	1.5/ (+50%)	1.3 (−13%)	1.0 (−23%)	.9 (−10%)	.75 (−17%)
Fulfill Order	2.5	2.0 (−20%)	1.5 (−25%)	1.0 (−33%)	1.0 (0%)	1.0 (0%)
Edit Order	1.76	2.0 (+14%)	2.5 (+25%)	1.7 (−32%)	1.5 (−12%)	1.2 (−20%)
Delete Order	1.1	1.1 (0%)	1.4 (+27%)	1.0 (−29%)	.8 (−20%)	.75 (−6%)
•	•	•	•	•	•	•
•	•	•	•	•	•	•
•	•	•	•	•	•	•
•	•	•	•	•	•	•
•	•	•	•	•	•	•
Reports						
Create Order Report	60	55 (−8%)	35 (−36%)	28 (−20%)	20 (−29%)	15 (−25%)
Create Account Receivables Report	55	65 (+18%)	55 (−15%)	35 (−36%)	25 (−29%)	20 (−20%)
Create Account Payables	120	90 (−25%)	65 (−28%)	45 (−31%)	65 (+44%)	25 (−62%)
Create Inventory Report	85	70 (−18%)	50 (−29%)	39 (−22%)	28 (−28%)	25 (−11%)

the system works. Less emphasis is placed on technical issues and more is placed on the question of whether the system is a good business fit for the end-user. The test is usually performed by users, if performed at all. Typically, 20% of the time this test is rolled into the system test. If performed, acceptance tests typically are a subset of the system tests. However, the users sometimes define "special tests," such as intensive stress or volume tests, to stretch the limits of the system even beyond what was testing during the system test.

STEP 4: REVIEW/APPROVE DESIGN

Task 1: Schedule/Prepare for Review

The test design review should be scheduled well in advance of the actual review, and the participants should have the latest copy of the test design.

As with any interview or review, it should contain four elements. The first is defining what will be discussed, or "talking about what we are going to talk about." The second is discussing the details, or "talking about it." The third is summarization, or "talking about what we talked about." The final element is timeliness. The reviewer should state up front the estimated duration of the review and set the ground rule that if time expires before completing all items on the agenda, a follow-on review will be scheduled.

The purpose of this task is for development and the project sponsor to agree and accept the test design. If there are any suggested changes to the test design during the review, they should be incorporated into the test design.

Task 2: Obtain Approvals

Approval is critical in a testing effort, because it helps provide the necessary agreements between testing, development, and the sponsor. The best approach is with a formal sign-off procedure of a test design. If this is the case, use the management approval sign-off forms. However, if a formal agreement procedure is not in place, send a memo to each key participant, including at least the project manager, development manager, and sponsor. In the document attach the latest test design and point out that all their feedback comments have been incorporated and that if you do not hear from them, it is assumed that they agree with the design. Finally, indicate that in a spiral development environment, the test design will evolve with each iteration but that you will include them in any modification.

Part 14
Test Development (Do)

Exhibit 1 outlines the steps and tasks associated with the Do part of spiral testing. Each step and task is described along with valuable tips and techniques.

STEP 1: DEVELOP TEST SCRIPTS

Task 1: Script the Manual/Automated GUI/Function Tests

In a previous step, a GUI/Function Test Matrix was built which cross-references the tests to the functions. The business functions are listed vertically, and the test cases are listed horizontally. The test case name is recorded on the matrix along with the number.

In the current task the functional test cases are documented and transformed into reusable test scripts with test data created. To aid in the development of the script of the test cases, the GUI-based Function Test Matrix template in Exhibit 2 can be used to document function test cases which are GUI-based (see Appendix E7, GUI-Based Function Test Matrix, for more details).

Consider the script in Exhibit 2, which uses the template to create a new customer order. The use of this template shows the function, the case number within the test case (a variation of a specific test), the requirement identification cross-reference, the test objective, the case steps, the expected results, the pass/fail status, the tester name, and the date the test was performed. Within a function, the current GUI component is also documented. In Exhibit 2, a new customer order is created by first invoking the menu bar to select the function, followed by the Edit-Order Window to enter the order number, customer number, model number, product number, and quantity.

Task 2: Script the Manual/Automated System Fragment Tests

In a previous task, the system fragment tests were designed. They are sample subsets of full system tests, which can be performed during each spiral loop.

Test Development

(STEPS)   (TASKS)

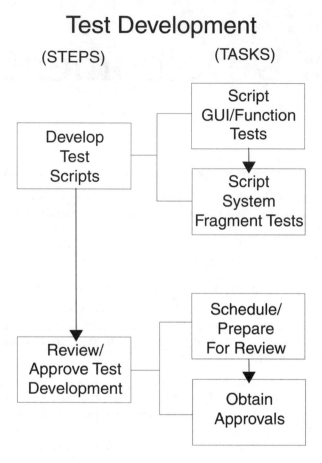

Exhibit 1. Test Development (Steps/Tasks)

In this task, the system fragment tests can be scripted using the GUI-Based Function Test Matrix discussed in the previous task. The test objective description is probably more broad than the Function/GUI tests, as they involve more global testing issues such as performance, security, usability, documentation, procedure, etc.

STEP 2: REVIEW/APPROVE TEST DEVELOPMENT

Task 1: Schedule/Prepare for Review

The test development review should be scheduled well in advance of the actual review and the participants should have the latest copy of the test design.

Exhibit 2. Function/GUI Test Script

Function (Create a New Customer Order)							
Case No.	REQ No.	Test Objective	Case Steps	Expected Results	(P/F)	Tester	Date
Menu Bar							
15	67	Create a Valid New Customer Order	Select File/Create Order from the menu bar	Edit-Order-Window appears	Passed	Jones	7/21/98
Edit-Order Window							
			1. Enter Order Number	Order Validated	Passed	Jones	7/21/98
			2. Enter Customer Number	Customer Validated	Passed	Jones	7/21/98
			3. Enter Model Number	Model Validated	Passed	Jones	7/21/98
			4. Enter Product Number	Product Validated	Passed	Jones	7/21/98
			5. Enter Quantity	Quantity Validated Date, Invoice Number, and Total Price Generated	Passed	Jones	7/21/98
			6. Select OK	Customer is Created Successfully	Passed	Jones	7/21/98

As with any interview or review, it should contain four elements. The first is defining what will be discussed, or "talking about what we are going to talk about." The second is discussing the details, or "talking about it." The third is summarization, or "talking about what we talked about." The final element is timeliness. The reviewer should state up front the estimated duration of the review and set the ground rule that if time expires before completing all items on the agenda, a follow-on review will be scheduled.

The purpose of this task is for development and the project sponsor to agree and accept the test development. If there are any suggested changes to the test development during the review, they should be incorporated into the test development.

Task 2: Obtain Approvals

Approval is critical in a testing effort, because it helps provide the necessary agreements between the testing, development, and the sponsor. The best approach is with a formal sign-off procedure of a test development. If this is the case, use the management approval sign-off forms. However, if a formal agreement procedure is not in place, send a memo to each key participant, including at least the project manager, development manager, and sponsor. In the document, attach the latest test development and point out that all their feedback comments have been incorporated and that if you do not hear from them, it is assumed that they agree with the development. Finally, indicate that in a spiral development environment, the test development will evolve with each iteration but that you will include them in any modification.

Part 15
Test Execution/ Evaluation (Do/Check)

If you will recall, in the spiral development environment, software testing is described as a continuous improvement process that must be integrated into a rapid application development methodology. Deming's continuous improvement process using the PDCA model is applied to the software testing process. We are now in the Do/Check part of the spiral model (see Exhibit 1).

Exhibit 2 outlines the steps and tasks associated with the Do/Check part of spiral testing. Each step and task is described along with valuable tips and techniques.

STEP 1: SETUP AND TESTING

Task 1: Regression Test the Manual/Automated Spiral Fixes

The purpose of this task is to retest the tests that discovered defects in the previous spiral. The technique used is regression testing. Regression testing is a technique that detects spurious errors caused by software modifications or corrections. See Appendix H27, Regression Testing, for more details.

A set of test cases must be maintained and available throughout the entire life of the software. The test cases should be complete enough so that all the software's functional capabilities are thoroughly tested. The question arises as to how to locate those test cases to test defects discovered during the previous test spiral. An excellent mechanism is the retest matrix.

As described earlier, a retest matrix relates test cases to functions (or program units). A check entry in the matrix indicates that the test case is to be retested when the function (or program unit) has been modified due to an enhancement(s) or correction(s). No entry means that the test does not need to be retested. The retest matrix can be built before the first testing spiral, but needs to be maintained during subsequent spirals. As

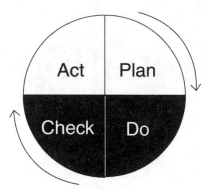

Exhibit 1. Spiral Testing and Continuous Improvement

Test Execution/Evaluation

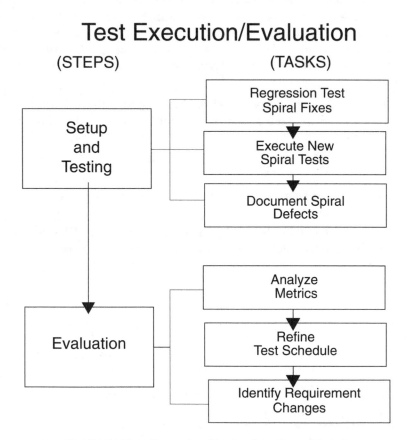

Exhibit 2. Test Execution/Evaluation (Steps/Tasks)

functions (or program units) are modified during a development spiral, existing or new test cases need to be created and checked in the retest matrix in preparation for the next test spiral. Over time with subsequent spirals, some functions (or program units) may be stable with no recent modifications. Consideration to selectively remove their check entries should be undertaken between testing spirals.

If a regression test passes, the status of the defect report should be changed to "closed."

Task 2: Execute the Manual/Automated New Spiral Tests

The purpose of this task is to execute new tests that were created at the end of the previous testing spiral. In the previous spiral, the testing team updated the test plan, GUI-based function test matrix, scripts, the GUI, the system fragment tests, and acceptance tests in preparation for the current testing spiral. During this task those tests are executed.

Task 3: Document the Spiral Test Defects

During spiral test execution, the results of the testing must be reported in the defect tracking database. These defects are typically related to individual tests that have been conducted. However, variations to the formal test cases often uncover other defects. The objective of this task is to produce a complete record of the defects. If the execution step has been recorded properly, the defects have already been recorded on the defect tracking database. If the defects are already recorded, the objective of this step becomes to collect and consolidate the defect information.

Tools can be used to consolidate and record defects depending on of the test execution methods. If the defects are recorded on paper, the consolidation involves collecting and organizing the papers. If the defects are recorded electronically, search features can easily locate duplicate defects.

STEP 2: EVALUATION

Task 1: Analyze the Metrics

Metrics are used so that we can help make decisions more effectively and support the development process. The objective of this task is to apply the principles of metrics to control the testing process.

In a previous task, the metrics and metric points were defined for each spiral to be measured. During the present task the metrics which were measured are analyzed. This involves quantifying the metrics and putting them into a graphical format.

The following is the key information a test manager needs to know at the end of a spiral:

- Test Case Execution Status
  How many test cases have been executed, how many not executed, and how many discovered defects. This provides an indication of the tester's productivity. If the test cases are not being executed in a timely manner, this raises a flag that more personnel may need to be assigned to the project.
- Defect Gap Analysis
  What is the gap between the number of defects that have been uncovered and the number that have been corrected. This provides an indication of development's ability to correct defects in a timely manner. If there is a relatively large gap, this raises the flag that perhaps more developers need to be assigned to the project.
- Defect Severity Status
  The distribution of the defect severity, e.g., critical, major, and minor, provides an indication of the quality of the system. If there is a large percentage of defects in the critical category, there probably exists a considerable number of design and architecture issues, which also raises a flag.
- Test Burnout Tracking
  Shows the cumulative and periodic number of defects being discovered. The cumulative number, e.g., the running total number of defects, and defects by time period help predict when fewer and fewer defects are being discovered. This is indicated when the cumulative curve "bends" and the defects by time period approaches zero. If the cumulative curve shows no indication of bending, it implies that defect discovery is still very robust and that many more still exist to be discovered in other spirals.

Graphical examples of the above metrics can be seen in Part 16, Prepare for the Next Spiral, Step 3, Publish Interim Report.

Task 2: Refine the Test Schedule

In a previous task, a test schedule was produced which includes the testing steps (and perhaps tasks), target start dates and end dates, and responsibilities. During the course of development, the testing schedule needs to be continually monitored. The objective of the current task is to update the test schedule to reflect the latest status. It is the responsibility of the test manager to:

- Compare the actual progress to the planned progress
- Evaluate the results to determine the testing status
- Take appropriate action based on the evaluation

If the testing progress is behind schedule, the test manager needs to determine the factors causing the slip. A typical cause is an underestimation of the test effort. Other factors could be that an inordinate number of defects are being discovered, causing a lot of the testing effort to be devoted to retesting old corrected defects. In either case, more testers may be needed and/or overtime may be required to compensate for the slippage.

Task 3: Identify Requirement Changes

In a previous task, the functional requirements were initially analyzed by the testing function, which consisted of the hierarchical functional decomposition, the functional window structure, the window standards, and the minimum system requirements of the system.

Between spirals new requirements may be introduced into the development process. It can consist of:

- New GUI interfaces or components
- New functions
- Modified functions
- Eliminated functions
- New system requirements, e.g., hardware
- Additional system requirements
- Additional acceptance requirements

Each new requirement needs to be identified, recorded, analyzed, and updated in the test plan, test design, and test scripts.

Part 16
Prepare for the Next Spiral (Act)

If you will recall, in the spiral development environment, software testing is described as a continuous improvement process which must be integrated into a rapid application development methodology. Deming's continuous improvement process using the PDCA model is applied to the software testing process. We are now in the Act part of the spiral model (see Exhibit 1), which prepares for the next spiral.

Exhibit 2 outlines the steps and tasks associated with the Act part of spiral testing. Each step and task is described along with valuable tips and techniques.

STEP 1: REFINE THE TESTS

Task 1: Update the Function/GUI Tests

The objective of this task is to update the test design to reflect the new functional requirements. The Test Change Function Test Matrix, which cross-references the tests to the functions, needs to be updated. The new functions are added in the vertical list and the respective test cases are added to the horizontal list. The test case name is recorded on the matrix along with the number. (See Appendix E5, Function/Test Matrix.)

Next, any new GUI/Function test cases in the matrix need to be documented or scripted. The conceptual test cases are then transformed into reusable test scripts with test data created. Also, any new GUI requirements are added to the GUI tests. (See Appendix E7, GUI-Based Function Test Matrix.)

Finally, the tests that can be automated with a testing tool need to be updated. Automated tests provide three benefits: repeatability, leverage, and increased functionality. Repeatability enables automated tests to be executed more than once, consistently. Leverage comes from repeatability from tests previously captured and tests that can be programmed with the tool, which might not have been possible without automation. As applications evolve, more and more functionality is added. With automation, the functional coverage is maintained with the test library.

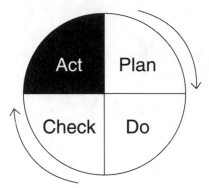

Exhibit 1. Spiral Testing and Continuous Improvement

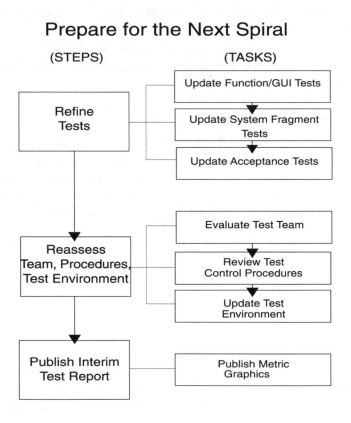

Exhibit 2. Prepare for the Next Spiral (Steps/Tasks)

Task 2: Update the System Fragment Tests

In a prior task, the system fragment tests were defined. System fragment tests are sample subsets of full system tests that can be performed during each spiral loop. The objective of doing a fragment test is to provide early warning of pending problems which would arise in the full system test.

Candidate fragment system tests include function, performance, security, usability, documentation, and procedure. Some of these fragment tests should have formal tests performed during each spiral, while others should be part of the overall testing strategy. The objective of the present task is to update the system fragment tests defined earlier based on new requirements. New baseline measurements are defined.

Finally, the fragment system tests which can be automated with a testing tool need to be updated.

Task 3: Update the Acceptance Tests

In a prior task, the initial list of acceptance tests was defined. Acceptance testing is an optional user-run test that demonstrates the ability of the application to meet the user's requirements. The motivation for this test is to demonstrate rather than be destructive, i.e., to show that the system works. If performed, acceptance tests typically are a subset of the system tests. However, the users sometimes define "special tests," such as intensive stress or volume tests, to stretch the limits of the system even beyond what was testing during the system test. The objective of the present task is to update the acceptance tests defined earlier based on new requirements.

Finally, the acceptance tests which can be automated with a testing tool need to be updated.

STEP 2: REASSESS THE TEAM, PROCEDURES, AND TEST ENVIRONMENT

Task 1: Evaluate the Test Team

Between each spiral, the performance of the test team needs to be evaluated in terms of its quality and productivity. The test team leader directs one of more testers to ensure that the right skill level is on the project. He or she makes sure that the test cases are being executed according to the plan, the defects are being reported and retested, and the test automation is successful. The basis for allocating dedicated testing resources is the scope of the functionality and the development time frame. If the testing is not being completed satisfactorily, the team leader needs to counsel one or more team members and/or request additional testers. On the other hand, if the test is coming to a conclusion, the testing manager needs to start thinking about reassigning testers to other projects.

Task 2: Review the Test Control Procedures

In a prior task, the test control procedures were set up before the first spiral. The objective of this task is to review those procedures and make appropriate modifications. The predefined procedures include the following:

- Defect Recording/Tracking Procedures
- Change Request Procedures
- Version Control Procedures
- Configuration Build Procedures
- Project Issue Resolution Procedures
- Reporting Procedures

The purpose of defect recording/tracking procedures is to record and correct defects and record metric information about the application. As the project progresses, these procedures may need tuning. Examples include new status codes or new fields in the defect tracking form, an expanded defect distribution list, and the addition of more verification checks.

The purpose of change request procedures is to allow new change requests to be communicated to the development and testing team. Examples include a new change control review board process, a new sponsor who has ideas of how the change request process should be implemented, a new change request database, and a new software configuration management tool.

The purpose of version control procedures is to uniquely identify each software component via a labeling scheme and allow for successive revisions. Examples include a new software configuration management tool with a new versioning scheme or new labeling standards.

The purpose of configuration build procedures is to provide an effective means to assemble a software system from the software source components into executable components. Examples include the addition of a new 4GL language, a new software configuration management tool, or a new delta build approach.

The purpose of project issue resolution procedures is to record and process testing issues that arise during the testing process. Examples include a new project manager who requests a Lotus Notes approach, a newly formed issue review committee, an updated issue priority categorization scheme, and a new issue submission process.

The purpose of reporting procedures is to facilitate the communication process and reporting. Examples include a new project manager who requires weekly testing status reports, a new interim test report structure, or an expanded reporting distribution.

Task 3: Update the Test Environment

In a prior task, the test environment was defined. A test environment provides a physical framework for testing necessary for the testing activity. During the present task, the test environment needs are reviewed and updated.

The main components of the test environment include the physical test facility, technologies, and tools. The test facility component includes the physical setup. The technologies component includes hardware platforms, physical network and all its components, operating system software, and other software, such as utility software. The tools component includes any specialized testing software, such as automated test tools, testing libraries, and support software. Examples of changes to the test environment include:

- Expanded test lab
- New testing tools required
- Additional test hardware required
- Additional network facilities
- Additional test database space required
- New Lotus Notes logons
- Additional software to support testing

STEP 3: PUBLISH INTERIM TEST REPORT

Task 1: Publish the Metric Graphics

Each spiral should produce an interim report to describe the status of testing. These tests are geared to the testing team, the test manager, and the development manager, which will help them make adjustments for the next spiral. The following minimal graphical reports are recommended between each spiral test.

Test Case Execution Status. The objective of Exhibit 3 is to show the status of testing and predict when the testing and development group will be ready for production. Test cases run with errors have not yet been corrected..

If there is a relatively large number of test cases that have not been run, the testing group needs to increase its productivity and/or resources. If there is a large number of test cases run with errors that have not been corrected, the development team also needs to be more productive.

Defect Gap Analysis. The objective of Exhibit 4 is to show the gap between the number of defects that have been uncovered compared to the number that have been corrected. A large gap indicates that development needs to increase effort and resources to correct defects more quickly.

Defect Severity Status. The objective of Exhibit 5 is to show the distribution of the three severity categories: critical, major, and minor. A large per-

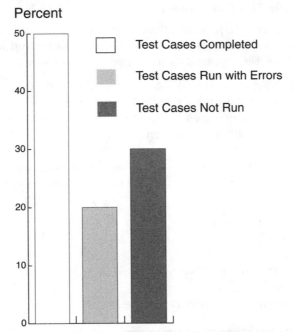

Exhibit 3. Test Execution Status

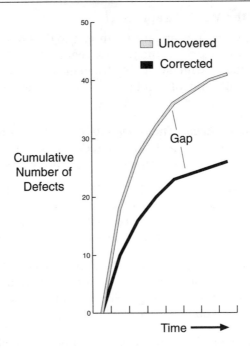

Exhibit 4. Defect Gap Analysis

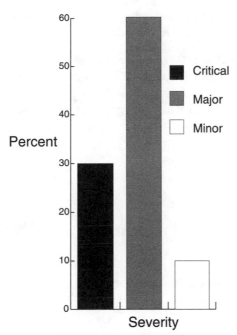

Exhibit 5. Defect Severity Status

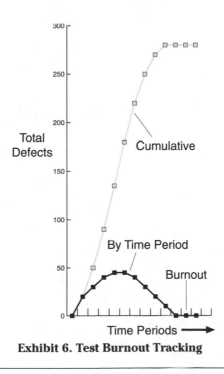

Exhibit 6. Test Burnout Tracking

centage of defects in the critical category indicates that a problem with the design or architecture of the application may exist.

Test Burnout Tracking. The objective of Exhibit 6 is to indicate the rate of uncovering defects. The cumulative, e.g., running total number of defects, and defects by time period help predict when fewer defects are being discovered. This is indicated when the cumulative curve "bend," and the defects by time period approach zero.

Part 17
Conduct the System Test

System testing evaluates the functionality and performance of the whole application and consists of a variety of tests including: performance, usability, stress, documentation, security, volume, recovery, etc. Exhibit 1 describes how to extend fragment system testing. It includes discussions of how to prepare for the system test, design and script them, execute them, and report anomalies discovered during the test.

STEP 1: COMPLETE SYSTEM TEST PLAN

Task 1: Finalize the System Test Types

In a previous task, a set of system fragment tests were selected and executed during each spiral. The purpose of the current task is to finalize the system test types which will be performed during system testing.

If you will recall, systems testing consists of one or more tests that are based on the original objectives of the system, which were defined during the project interview. The purpose of this task is to select the system tests to be performed, not to implement the tests. Our initial list consisted of the following system test types:

- Performance
- Security
- Volume
- Stress
- Compatibility
- Conversion
- Usability
- Documentation
- Backup
- Recovery
- Installation

The sequence of system test type execution should also be defined in this task. For example, related tests such as performance, stress, and volume, might be clustered together and performed early during system testing. Security, backup, and recovery are also logical groupings, etc.

Finally, the system tests that can be automated with a testing tool need to be finalized. Automated tests provide three benefits: repeatability, leverage, and increased functionality. Repeatability enables automated tests to be executed more than once, consistently. Leverage comes from repeatability from tests previously captured and tests that can be programmed with the tool, which might not have been possible without automation. As applications evolve, more and more functionality is added. With automation the functional coverage is maintained with the test library.

Task 2: Finalize System Test Schedule

In this task, the system test schedule should be finalized and includes the testing steps (and perhaps tasks), target start and target end dates, and responsibilities. It should also describe how it will be reviewed, tracked, and approved. A sample system test schedule is shown in Exhibit 2. (Also see the Gantt chart template, Gantt Spiral Testing Methodology Template.)

Task 3: Organize the System Test Team

With all testing types, the system test team needs to be organized. The system test team is responsible for designing and executing the tests, evaluating the results, and reporting any defects to development, using the defect tracking system. When development corrects defects, the test team retests the defects to ensure the correction.

The system test team is led by a test manager whose responsibilities include:

- Organizing the test team
- Establishing the test environment
- Organizing the testing policies, procedures, and standards
- Assurance test readiness
- Working the test plan and controlling the project
- Tracking test costs
- Assuring test documentation is accurate and timely
- Managing the team members

Task 4: Establish the System Test Environment

During this task, the system test environment is also finalized. The purpose of the test environment is to provide a physical framework for the testing activity. The test environment needs are established and reviewed before implementation.

The main components of the test environment include the physical test facility, technologies, and tools. The test facility component includes the

Conduct System Testing

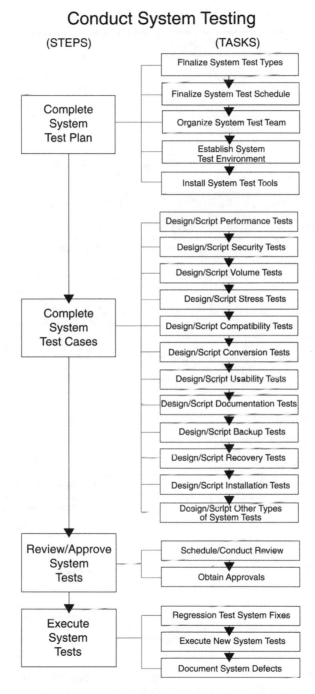

(STEPS)   (TASKS)

Complete System Test Plan
- Finalize System Test Types
- Finalize System Test Schedule
- Organize System Test Team
- Establish System Test Environment
- Install System Test Tools

Complete System Test Cases
- Design/Script Performance Tests
- Design/Script Security Tests
- Design/Script Volume Tests
- Design/Script Stress Tests
- Design/Script Compatibility Tests
- Design/Script Conversion Tests
- Design/Script Usability Tests
- Design/Script Documentation Tests
- Design/Script Backup Tests
- Design/Script Recovery Tests
- Design/Script Installation Tests
- Design/Script Other Types of System Tests

Review/Approve System Tests
- Schedule/Conduct Review
- Obtain Approvals

Execute System Tests
- Regression Test System Fixes
- Execute New System Tests
- Document System Defects

Exhibit 1. Conduct System Test (Steps/Tasks)

Exhibit 2. Final System Test Schedule

Test Step	Begin Date	End Date	Responsible
General Setup			
Organize the System Test Team	12•1•98	12•7•98	Smith, Test Manager
Establish the System Test Environment	12•1•98	12•7•98	Smith, Test Manager
Establish the System Test Tools	12•1•98	12•10•98	Jones, Tester
Performance Testing			
Design/Script the Tests	12•11•98	12•15•98	Jones, Tester
Test Review	12•16•98	12•16•98	Smith, Test Manager
Execute the Tests	12•17•98	12•22•98	Jones, Tester
Retest System Defects	12•23•98	12•25•98	Jones, Tester
Stress Testing			
Design/Script the Tests	12•26•98	12•30•98	Jones, Tester
Test Review	12•31•98	12•31•98	Smith, Test Manager
Execute the Tests	1•1•98	1•6•98	Jones, Tester
Retest System Defects	1•7•98	1•9•98	Jones, Tester
Volume Testing			
Design/Script the Tests	1•10•98	1•14•98	Jones, Tester
Test Review	1•15•98	1•15•98	Smith, Test Manager
Execute the Tests	1•16•98	1•21•98	Jones, Tester
Retest System Defects	1•22•98	1•24•98	Jones, Tester
Security Testing			
Design/Script the Tests	1•25•98	1•29•98	Jones, Tester
Test Review	1•30•98	1•31•98	Smith, Test Manager
Execute the Tests	2•1•98	2•6•98	Jones, Tester
Retest System Defects	2•7•98	2•9•98	Jones, Tester

Exhibit 2. (Continued) Final System Test Schedule

Test Step	Begin Date	End Date	Responsible
Backup Testing			
Design/Script the Tests	2•10•98	2•14•98	Jones, Tester
Test Review	2•15•98	2•15•98	Smith, Test Manager
Execute the Tests	2•16•98	1•21•98	Jones, Tester
Retest System Defects	2•22•98	2•24•98	Jones, Tester
Recovery Testing			
Design/Script the Tests	2•25•98	2•29•98	Jones, Tester
Test Review	2•30•98	2•31•98	Smith, Test Manager
Execute the Tests	3•1•98	3•6•98	Jones, Tester
Retest System Defects	3•7•98	3•9•98	Jones, Tester
Compatibility Testing			
Design/Script the Tests	3•10•98	3•14•98	Jones, Tester
Test Review	3•15•98	3•15•98	Smith, Test Manager
Execute the Tests	3•16•98	3•21•98	Jones, Tester
Retest System Defects	3•22•98	3•24•98	Jones, Tester
Conversion Testing			
Design/Script the Tests	4•10•98	4•14•98	Jones, Tester
Test Review	4•15•98	4•15•98	Smith, Test Manager
Execute the Tests	4•16•98	4•21•98	Jones, Tester
Retest System Defects	4•22•98	4•24•98	Jones, Tester
Usability Testing			
Design/Script the Tests	5•10•98	5•14•98	Jones, Tester
Test Review	5•15•98	5•15•98	Smith, Test Manager
Execute the Tests	5•16•98	5•21•98	Jones, Tester
Retest System Defects	5•22•98	5•24•98	Jones, Tester

Exhibit 2. (Continued) Final System Test Schedule

Test Step	Begin Date	End Date	Responsible
Documentation Testing			
Design/Script the Tests	6•10•98	6•14•98	Jones, Tester
Test Review	6•15•98	6•15•98	Smith, Test Manager
Execute the Tests	6•16•98	6•21•98	Jones, Tester
Retest System Defects	6•22•98	6•24•98	Jones, Tester
Installation Testing			
Design/Script the Tests	7•10•98	7•14•98	Jones, Tester
Test Review	7•15•98	7•15•98	Smith, Test Manager
Execute the Tests	7•16•98	7•21•98	Jones, Tester
Retest System Defects	7•22•98	7•24•98	Jones, Tester

physical setup. The technologies component includes the hardware platforms, physical network and all its components, operating system software, and other software. The tools component includes any specialized testing software, such as automated test tools, testing libraries, and support software.

The testing facility and workplace need to be established. These may range from an individual workplace configuration to a formal testing lab. In any event, it is important that the testers be together and near the development team. This facilitates communication and the sense of a common goal. The system testing tools need to be installed.

The hardware and software technologies need to be set up. This includes the installation of test hardware and software and coordination with vendors, users, and information technology personnel. It may be necessary to test the hardware and coordinate with hardware vendors. Communication networks need to be installed and tested.

Task 5: Install the System Test Tools

During this task the system test tools are installed and verified for readiness. A trial run of tool test cases and scripts should be performed to verify that the test tools are ready for the actual acceptance test. Some other tool readiness considerations include:

- Test team tool training
- Tool compatibility with operating environment

- Ample disk space for the tools
- Maximizing the tool potentials
- Vendor tool help hotline
- Test procedures modified to accommodate tools
- Installing the latest tool changes
- Assuring the vendor contractual provisions

STEP 2: COMPLETE SYSTEM TEST CASES

During this step the system test cases are designed and scripted. The conceptual system test cases are transformed into reusable test scripts with test data created.

To aid in developing script the test cases, the GUI-based Function Test Matrix template in the Appendix can be used to document system-level test cases with the "function" heading replaced with the system test name.

Task 1: Design/Script the Performance Tests

The objective of performance testing is to measure the system against predefined objectives. The required performance levels are compared against the actual performance levels and discrepancies are documented.

Performance testing is a combination of black-box and white-box testing. From a black-box point of view, the performance analyst does not have to know the internal workings of the system. Real workloads or benchmarks are used to compare one system version with another for performance improvements or degradation. From a white-box point of view, the performance analyst needs to know the internal workings of the system and define specific system resources to investigate, such as instructions, modules, and tasks.

Some of the performance information of interest includes the following:

- CPU utilization
- IO utilization
- Number of IOs per instruction
- Channel utilization
- Main storage memory utilization
- Secondary storage memory utilization
- Percent execution time per module
- Percent time a module is waiting for IO completion
- Percent of time module spent in main storage
- Instruction trace paths over time
- Number of times control is passed from one module to another
- Number of waits encountered for each group of instructions
- Number of pages-in and pages-out for each group of instructions
- System response time, e.g., last key until first key time

- System throughput, i.e., number of transactions per time unit
- Unit performance timings for all major functions

Baseline performance measurements should first be performed on all major functions in an noncontention mode, e.g., unit measurements of functions when a single task is in operation. This can be easily done with a simple stopwatch, as was done earlier for each spiral. The next set of measurements should be made in a system contended mode in which multiple tasks are operating and queuing results for demands on common resources such as CPU, memory, storage, channel, network, etc. Contended system execution time and resource utilization performance measurements are performed by monitoring the system to identify potential areas of inefficiency.

There are two approaches to gathering system execution time and resource utilization. With the first approach, samples are taken while the system is executing in its typical environment with the use of external probes, performance monitors, or stopwatch. With the second approach, probes are inserted into the system code, e.g., calls to a performance monitor program which gathers the performance information. The following is a discussion of each approach, followed by a discussion of test drivers, which are support techniques used to generate data for the performance study.

Monitoring Approach. This approach involves monitoring a system by determining its status at periodic time intervals and is controlled by an elapsed time facility in the testing tool or operating system. Samples taken during each time interval indicate the status of the performance criteria during the interval. The smaller the time interval, the more precise the sampling accuracy.

Statistics gathered by the monitoring are collected and summarized in performance.

Probe Approach. This approach involves inserting probes or program instructions into the system programs at various locations. To determine, for example, the CPU time necessary to execute a sequence of statements, a problem execution results in a call to the data collection routine that records the CPU clock at that instant. A second probe execution results in a second call to the data collection routine. Subtracting the first CPU time from the second yields the net CPU time used. Reports can be produced showing execution time breakdowns by statement, module, and statement type.

The value of these approaches is their use as performance requirements validation tools. However, formally defined performance requirements must be stated and the system should be designed so that the performance requirements can be traced to specific system modules.

Test Drivers. In many cases test drivers and test harnesses are required to make system performance measurements. A test driver provides the facilities needed to execute a system, e.g., inputs. The input data files for the system are loaded with data values representing the test situation to yield recorded data to evaluate against the expected results. Data are generated in an external form and presented to the system.

Performance test cases need to be defined, using one or more of the test templates located in the appendices, and test scripts need to be built. Before any performance test is conducted, however, the performance analyst must make sure that the target system is relatively bug-free. Otherwise, a lot of time will be spent documenting and fixing defects rather than analyzing the performance.

The following are the recommended steps for any performance study:

1. Document the performance objectives, e.g., exactly what the measurable performance criteria are must be verified.
2. Define the test driver or source of inputs to drive the system.
3. Define the performance methods or tools that will be used.
4. Define how the performance study will be conducted, e.g., what is the baseline, what are the variations, how can it be verified as repeatable, how does one know when the study is complete?
5. Define the reporting process, e.g., techniques and tools.

Task 2: Design/Script the Security Tests

The objective of security testing is to evaluate the presence and appropriate functioning of the security of the application to ensure the integrity and confidentiality of the data. Security tests should be designed to demonstrate how resources are protected.

A Security Design Strategy. A security strategy for designing security test cases is to focus on the following four security components: the assets, threats, exposures, and controls. In this manner, matrices and checklists will suggest ideas for security test cases.

Assets are the tangible and intangible resources of an entity. The evaluation approach is to list what should be protected. It is also useful to examine the attributes of assets, such as amount, value, use, and characteristics. Two useful analysis techniques are asset value and exploitation analysis. Asset value analysis determines how the value differs among users and potential attackers. Asset exploitation analysis examines different ways to use an asset for illicit gain.

Threats are events with the potential to cause loss or harm. The evaluation approach is to list the sources of potential threats. It is important to

189

distinguish between accidental, intentional, and natural threats, and threat frequencies.

Exposures are forms of possible loss or harm. The evaluation approach is to list what might happen to assets if a threat is realized. Exposures include disclosure violations, erroneous decision, and fraud. Exposure analysis focuses on identifying areas in which exposure is the greatest.

Security functions or controls are measures that protect against loss or harm. The evaluation approach is to list the security functions and tasks and focus on controls embodied in specific system functions or procedures. Security functions assess the protection against human errors and casual attempts to misuse the system. Some functional security questions include:

- Do the control features work properly?
- Are invalid and improbable parameters detected and properly handled?
- Are invalid or out-of-sequence commands detected and properly handled?
- Are errors and file accesses properly recorded?
- Do procedures for changing security tables work?
- Is it possible to login without a password?
- Are valid passwords accepted and invalid passwords rejected?
- Does the system respond properly to multiple invalid passwords?
- Does system-initialed authentication function properly?
- Are their security features for remote accessing?

It is important to assess the performance of the security mechanisms as well as the functions themselves. Some questions and issues concerning security performance include:

- Availability
  What portion of time is the application or control available to perform critical security functions? Security controls usually require higher availability than other portions of the system.
- Survivability
  How well does the system withstand major failures or natural disasters? This includes the support of emergency operations during failure, backup operations afterward, and recovery actions to return to regular operation.
- Accuracy
  How accurate is the security control? Accuracy encompasses the number, frequency, and significance of errors.
- Response time
  Are response times acceptable? Slow response times can tempt users to bypass security controls. Response time can also be critical for control management, as the dynamic modification of security tables.

- Throughput
  Does the security control support required use capacities? Capacity includes the peak and average loading of users and service requests.

A useful performance test is stress testing, which involves large numbers of users and requests to attain operational stress conditions. Stress testing is used to attempt to exhaust limits for such resources as buffers, queues, tables, and ports. This form of testing is useful in evaluating protection against service denial threats.

Task 3: Design/Script the Volume Tests

The objective of volume testing is to subject the system to heavy volumes of data to find if it can handle the volume of data. This test is often confused with stress testing. Stress testing subjects the system to heavy loads or stresses in terms of rates, such as throughputs over a short time period. Volume testing is data oriented, and its purpose is to show that the system can handle the volume of data specified in its objectives.

Some examples of volume testing are:

- Relative data comparisons when processing date-sensitive transactions
- A compiler is fed an extremely large source program to compile
- A linkage editor is fed a program containing thousands of modules
- An electronic-circuit simulator is given a circuit containing thousands of components
- An operation system's job queue is filled to maximum capacity
- Enough data is created to cause a system to span file
- A test-formating system is fed a massive document format
- The Internet is flooded with huge E-mail messages and files

Task 4: Design/Script the Stress Tests

The objective of stress testing is to investigate the behavior of the system under conditions that overload its resources. Of particular interest is the impact that this has on the system processing time. Stress testing is boundary testing. For example, test with the maximum number of terminals active and then add more terminals than specified in the requirements under different limit combinations. Some of the resources that stress testing subjects to heavy loads include:

- Buffers
- Controllers
- Display terminals
- Interrupt handlers
- Memory
- Networks

- Printers
- Spoolers
- Storage devices
- Transaction queues
- Transaction schedulers
- User of the system

Stress testing studies the system's response to peak bursts of activity in short periods of time and attempts to find defects in a system. It is often confused with volume testing, in which the system's capability of handling large amounts of data is the objective.

Stress testing should be performed early in development because it often uncovers major design flaws that can impact many areas. If stress testing is not performed early, subtle defects, which might have been more apparent earlier in development, may be difficult to uncover.

The following are the suggested steps for stress testing:

1. Perform simple multitask tests.
2. After the simple stress defects are corrected, stress the system to the breaking point.
3. Perform the stress tests repeatedly for every spiral.

Some stress testing examples include the following:

- Word processing response time for a fixed entry rate, such as 120 words per minute.
- Introduce a heavy volume of data in a very short period of time.
- Varying loads for interactive, real-time, and process control.
- Simultaneous introduction of a large number of transactions.
- Thousands of users signing on to the Internet within the same minute.

Task 5: Design/Script the Compatibility Tests

The objective of compatibility testing (sometimes called cohabitation testing) is to test the compatibility of the application with other applications or systems. This is a test that is often overlooked until the system is put into production and in which defects are often subtle and difficult to uncover. An example is when the system works perfectly in the testing lab in a controlled environment but does not work when it coexists with other applications. An example of compatibility is when two systems share the same data or data files or reside in the same memory at the same time. The system may satisfy the system requirements but not work in a shared environment and may interfere with other systems.

The following is a compatibility (cohabitation) testing strategy:

1. Update the compatibility objectives to note how the application has actually been developed and the actual environments in which it is to perform. Modify the objectives for any changes in the cohabiting systems or the configuration resources.
2. Update the compatibility test cases to make sure they are comprehensive. Make sure that the test cases in the other systems which can affect the target system are comprehensive. And ensure maximum coverage of instances in which one system could affect another.
3. Perform the compatibility tests and carefully monitor the results to ensure the expected results. Use a baseline approach, which is the system's operating characteristics before the addition of the target system into the shared environment. The baseline needs to be accurate and incorporate not only the functioning but the operational performance to ensure that it is not degraded in a cohabitation setting.
4. Document the results of the compatibility tests and note any deviations in the target system or the other cohabitation systems.
5. Regression test the compatibility tests after the defects have been resolved and record the tests in the retest matrix.

Task 6: Design/Script the Conversion Tests

The objective of conversion testing is to verify the conversion of existing data and load a new database. The most common conversion problem is between two versions of the same system. A new version may have a different data format but must include the data from the old system. Ample time needs to be set aside to carefully think of all the conversion issues that may arise.

Some key factors which need to be considered when designing conversion tests include:

- Auditability
  There needs to be a plan to perform before-and-after comparisons and analysis of the converted data to ensure it was converted successfully. Techniques to ensure auditability include file reports, comparison programs, and regression testing. Regression testing checks to verify that the converted data do not change the business requirements or cause the system to behave differently.
- Database Verification
  Prior to conversion, the new database needs to be reviewed to verify that it is designed properly, satisfies the business needs, and that the support center and database administrators are trained to support it.
- Data Clean-up
  Before the data is converted to the new system, the old data needs to be examined to verify that inaccuracies or discrepancies in the data are removed.

- Recovery Plan
  Roll-back procedures need to be in place before any conversion is attempted to restore the system to its previous state and undo the conversions.
- Synchronization
  It must be verified that the conversion process does not interfere with normal operations. Sensitive data, such as customer data, may be changing dynamically during conversions. One way to achieve this is to perform conversions during nonoperational hours.

Task 7: Design/Script the Usability Tests

The objective of usability testing is to determine how well the user will be able to use and understand the application. This includes the system functions, publications, help text, and procedures to ensure that the user comfortably interacts with the system. Usability testing should be performed as early as possible during development and should be designed into the system. Late usability testing might be impossible, because it is locked in and often requires a major redesign of the system to correct serious usability problems. This may make it economically infeasible.

Some of the usability problems the tester should look for include:

- Overly complex functions or instructions
- Difficult installation procedures
- Poor error messages, e.g., "syntax error"
- Difficult syntax to understand and use
- Nonstandardized GUI interfaces
- User forced to remember too much information
- Difficult login procedures
- Help text not context sensitive or not detailed enough
- Poor linkage to other systems
- Unclear defaults
- Interface too simple or too complex
- Inconsistency of syntax, format, and definitions
- User not provided with clear acknowledgment of all inputs

Task 8: Design/Script the Documentation Tests

The objective of documentation testing is to verify that the user documentation is accurate and ensure that the manual procedures work correctly. Documentation testing has several advantages, including improving the usability of the system, reliability, maintainability, and installability. In these cases, testing the document will help uncover deficiencies in the system and/or make the system more usable. Documentation testing also reduces customer support costs, as if customers can figure out their questions with the documentation, they are not forced to call the support desk.

The tester verifies the technical accuracy of the documentation to assure that it agrees with and describes the system accurately. He or she needs to assume the user's point of view and act out the actual behavior as described in the documentation.

Some tips and suggestions for the documentation tester include:

- Use documentation as a source of many test cases
- Use the system exactly as the documentation describes it
- Test every hint or suggestion
- Incorporate defects into the defect tracking database
- Test every online help hypertext link
- Test every statement of fact and don't take anything for granted
- Act like a technical editor rather than a passive reviewer
- Perform a general review of the whole document first and then a detailed review
- Check all the error messages
- Test every example provided in the document
- Make sure all index entries have documentation text
- Make sure documentation covers all key user functions
- Make sure the reading style is not too technical
- Look for areas that are weaker than others and need more explanation

Task 9: Design/Script the Backup Tests

The objective of backup testing is to verify the ability of the system to back up its data in the event of a software or hardware failure. This test is complementary to recovery testing and should be part of recovery test planning.

Some backup testing considerations include the following:

- Backup files and comparing the backup with the original
- Archiving files and data
- Complete system backup procedures
- Checkpoint backups
- Backup performance system degradation
- Effect of backup on manual processes
- Detection of "triggers" to backup system
- Security procedures during backup
- Maintaining transaction logs during backup procedures

Task 10: Design/Script the Recovery Tests

The objective of recovery testing is to verify the system's ability to recover from a software or hardware failure. This test verifies the contingency features of the system for handling interruptions and returning to specific points in the application's processing cycle. The key questions for designing recovery tests are:

1. Have the potentials for disasters and system failures been identified, and their respective damages? Fire drill brainstorming sessions can be an effective method of defining disaster scenarios.
2. Do the prevention and recovery procedures provide for adequate responses to failures? The plan procedures should be tested with technical reviews by subject matter experts and the system users.
3. Will the recovery procedures work properly when really needed? Simulated disasters need to be created with the actual system verifying the recovery procedures. This should involve the system users, the support organization, vendors, etc.

Some recovery testing examples include the following:

- Complete restoration of files which were backed up either during routine maintenance or error recovery
- Partial restoration of file backup to the last checkpoint
- Execution of recovery programs
- Archive retrieval of selected files and data
- Restoration when power supply is the problem
- Verification of manual recovery procedures
- Recovery by switching to parallel systems
- Restoration performance system degradation
- Security procedures during recovery
- Ability to recover transaction logs

Task 11: Design/Script the Installation Tests

The objective of installation testing is to verify the ability to install the system successfully. Customers have to install the product on their systems. Installation is often the developers' last activity and often receives the least amount of focus during development. Yet it is the first activity that the customer performs when using the new system. Therefore, clear and concise installation procedures are among the most important parts of the system documentation.

Reinstallation procedures need to be included to be able to reverse the installation process and validate the previous environmental condition. Also, the installation procedures need to document how the user can tune the system options and upgrade from a previous version.

Some key installation questions the tester needs to consider include:

- Who is the user installer, e.g., what technical capabilities are assumed?
- Is the installation process documented thoroughly with specific and concise installation steps?
- For which environments are the installation procedures supposed to work, e.g., platforms, software, hardware, networks, versions?

- Will the installation change the user's current environmental setup, e.g., config.sys etc.
- How does the installer know the system has been installed correctly, e.g., is there an installation test procedure in place?

Task 12: Design/Script Other System Test Types

In addition to the above system tests, the following system tests may also be required:

- API Testing
  Verify the system uses APIs correctly, e.g., operating system calls
- Communication Testing
  Verify the system's communications and networks
- Configuration Testing
  Verify the system works correctly in different system configurations, e.g., software, hardware, networks
- Database Testing
  Verify the database integrity, business rules, access, refresh capabilities
- Degraded System Testing
  Verify the system performs properly with less than full capabilities, e.g., line connections down, etc.
- Disaster Recovery Testing
  Verify the system recovery processes work correctly
- Embedded System Test
  Verify systems that operate on low-level devices, such as video chips
- Facility Testing
  Verify that each stated requirement facility is met
- Field Testing
  Verify the system works correctly in the real environment
- Middleware Testing
  Verify the middleware software works correctly, e.g., the common interfaces and accessibility among clients and servers
- Multimedia Testing
  Verify the multimedia system features, which use video, graphics and sound
- Online Help Testing
  Verify the system's online help features work properly
- Operability Testing
  Verify system will work correctly in the actual business environment
- Package Testing
  Verify installed software package works correctly
- Parallel Testing
  Verify system behaves the same in the old and new version

- Port Testing
  Verify system works correctly on different operating systems and computers
- Procedure Testing
  Verify nonautomated procedures work properly, e.g., operation, DBA, etc.
- Production Testing
  Verify the system will work correctly during actual ongoing production and not just in the test lab environment
- Real-time testing
  Verify systems in which time issues are critical and there are response time requirements
- Reliability Testing
  Verify the system works correctly within predefined expected failure duration, e.g., mean time to failure (MTF)
- Serviceability Testing
  Verify service facilities of the system work properly, e.g., mean time to debug a defect, maintenance procedures
- SQL Testing
  Verify the queries, data retrievals, and updates
- Storage Testing
  Verify that the system storage requirements are met, e.g., sizes of spill files, amount of main or secondary storage used
- Year 2000 Testing
  Verify the system works correctly after 1999

STEP 3: REVIEW/APPROVE SYSTEM TESTS

Task 1: Schedule/Conduct the Review

The system test plan review should be scheduled well in advance of the actual review, and the participants should have the latest copy of the test plan.

As with any interview or review, it should contain four elements. The first is defining what will be discussed; the second is discussing the details; and the third is summarization. The final element is timeliness. The reviewer should state up front the estimated duration of the review and set the ground rule that if time expires before completing all items on the agenda, a follow-on review will be scheduled.

The purpose of this task is for development and the project sponsor to agree and accept the system test plan. If there are any suggested changes to the test plan during the review, they should be incorporated into the test plan.

Task 2: Obtain Approvals

Approval is critical in a testing effort, because it helps provide the necessary agreement between testing, development, and the sponsor. The best approach is with a formal sign-off procedure of a system test plan. If this is the case, use the management approval sign-off forms. However, if a formal agreement procedure is not in place, send a memo to each key participant including at least the project manager, development manager, and sponsor. In the document attach the latest test plan and point out that all their feedback comments have been incorporated and that if you do not hear from them, it is assumed that they agree with the plan. Finally, indicate that in a spiral development environment, the system test plan will evolve with each iteration but that you will include them in any modification.

STEP 4: EXECUTE THE SYSTEM TESTS

Task 1: Regression Test the System Fixes

The purpose of this task is to retest the system tests which discovered defects in the previous system test cycle for this build. The technique used is regression testing. Regression testing is a technique that detects spurious errors caused by software modifications or corrections.

A set of test cases must be maintained and available throughout the entire life of the software. The test cases should be complete enough so that all the software's functional capabilities are thoroughly tested. The question arises as to how to locate those test cases to test defects discovered during the previous test spiral. An excellent mechanism is the retest matrix.

As described earlier, a retest matrix relates test cases to functions (or program units). A check entry in the matrix indicates that the test case is to be retested when the function (or program unit) has been modified due to an enhancement(s) or correction(s). No entry means that the test does not need to be retested. The retest matrix can be built before the first testing spiral but needs to be maintained during subsequent spirals. As functions (or program units) are modified during a development spiral, existing or new test cases need to be created and checked in the retest matrix in preparation for the next test spiral. Over time with subsequent spirals, some functions (or program units) may be stable with no recent modifications. Consideration to selectively remove their check entries should be undertaken between testing spirals.

Task 2: Execute the New System Tests

The purpose of this task is to execute new system tests that were created at the end of the previous system test cycle. In the previous spiral, the testing team updated the function/GUI, system fragment, and acceptance tests in preparation for the current testing spiral. During this task, those tests are executed.

Task 3: Document the System Defects

During system test execution, the results of the testing must be reported in the defect tracking database. These defects are typically related to individual tests that have been conducted. However, variations to the formal test cases often uncover other defects. The objective of this task is to produce a complete record of the defects. If the execution step has been recorded properly, the defects have already been recorded on the defect tracking database. If the defects are already recorded, the objective of this step becomes to collect and consolidate the defect information.

Tools can be used to consolidate and record defects depending on the test execution methods. If the defects are recorded on paper, the consolidation involves collecting and organizing the papers. If the defects are recorded electronically, search features can easily locate duplicate defects.

Part 18
Conduct Acceptance Testing

Acceptance testing is a user-run test that demonstrates the application's ability to meet the original business objectives and system requirements and usually consists of a subset of system tests (see Exhibit 1). It includes discussions on how to prepare for the acceptance test, design and script the acceptance tests, execute the acceptance tests, and report anomalies discovered during the test.

STEP 1: COMPLETE ACCEPTANCE TEST PLANNING

Task 1: Finalize the Acceptance Test Types

In this task the initial acceptance testing type list is refined and the actual tests to be performed are selected.

Acceptance testing is an optional user-run test that demonstrates the ability of the application to meet the user's requirements. The motivation for this test is to demonstrate rather than be destructive, i.e., to show that the system works. Less emphasis is placed on the technical issues and more on the question of whether the system is a good business fit for the end-user. The test is usually performed by users. However, the users sometimes define "special tests," such as intensive stress or volume tests to stretch the limits of the system even beyond what was tested during the system test.

Task 2: Finalize the Acceptance Test Schedule

In this task, the acceptance test schedule should be finalized and includes the testing steps (and perhaps tasks), target begin dates and target end dates, and responsibilities. It should also describe how it will be reviewed, tracked, and approved. For acceptance testing, the test team usually consists of user representatives. However, the team test environment and test tool are probably the same as used during system testing. A sample acceptance test schedule is shown in Exhibit 2.

Conduct Acceptance Testing

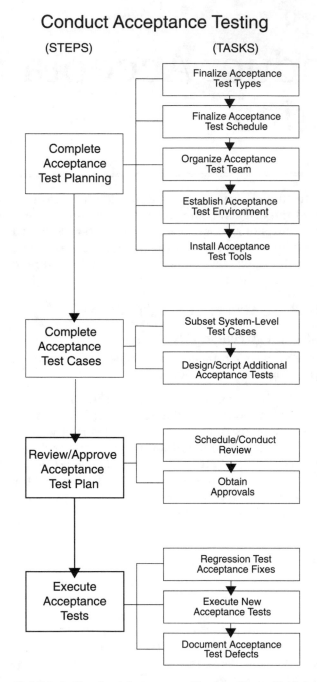

(STEPS)　　　　　　　　(TASKS)

Complete Acceptance Test Planning
- Finalize Acceptance Test Types
- Finalize Acceptance Test Schedule
- Organize Acceptance Test Team
- Establish Acceptance Test Environment
- Install Acceptance Test Tools

Complete Acceptance Test Cases
- Subset System-Level Test Cases
- Design/Script Additional Acceptance Tests

Review/Approve Acceptance Test Plan
- Schedule/Conduct Review
- Obtain Approvals

Execute Acceptance Tests
- Regression Test Acceptance Fixes
- Execute New Acceptance Tests
- Document Acceptance Test Defects

Exhibit 1. Conduct Acceptance Testing (Steps/Tasks)

Exhibit 2. Acceptance Test Schedule

Test Step	Begin Date	End Date	Responsible
General Setup			
Organize the Acceptance Test Team	8•1•98	8•7•98	Smith, Test Manager
Establish the Acceptance Test Environment	8•8•98	8•9•98	Smith, Test Manager
Establish the Acceptance Test Tools	8•10•98	8•10•98	Jones, Tester
Acceptance Testing			
Design/Script the Tests	12•11•98	12•15•98	Jones, Baker (user), Testers
Test Review	12•16•98	12•16•98	Smith, Test Manager
Execute the Tests	12•17•98	12•22•98	Jones, Baker (user), Tester
Retest Acceptance Defects	12•23•98	12•25•98	Jones, Baker (user), Tester

Task 3: Organize the Acceptance Test Team

The acceptance test team is responsible for designing and executing the tests, evaluating the test results, and reporting any defects to development, using the defect tracking system. When development corrects defects, the test team retests the defects to ensure the correction. The acceptance test team typically has representation from the user community, because this is their final opportunity to accept the system.

The acceptance test team is led by a test manager whose responsibilities include:

- Organizing the test team
- Establishing the test environment
- Organizing the testing policies, procedures, and standards
- Ensuring test readiness
- Working the test plan and controlling the project
- Tracking test costs
- Ensuring test documentation is accurate and timely
- Managing the team members

Task 4: Establish the Acceptance Test Environment

During this task, the acceptance test environment is finalized. Typically, the test environment for acceptance testing is the same as that for system testing. The purpose of the test environment is to provide the physical framework necessary for the testing activity. For this task, the test environment needs are established and reviewed before implementation.

The main components of the test environment include the physical test facility, technologies, and tools. The test facility component includes the physical setup. The technologies component includes the hardware platforms, physical network and all its components, operating system software, and other software, such as utility software. The tools component includes any specialized testing software — automated test tools, testing libraries, and support software.

The testing facility and workplace needs to be established. It may range from an individual workplace configuration to a formal testing lab. In any event, it is important that the testers be together and in close proximity to the development team. This facilitates communication and the sense of a common goal. The testing tools which were acquired need to be installed.

The hardware and software technologies need to be set up. This includes the installation of test hardware and software, and coordination with vendors, users, and information technology personnel. It may be necessary to test the hardware and coordinate with hardware vendors. Communication networks need to be installed and tested.

Task 5: Install Acceptance Test Tools

During this task, the acceptance test tools are installed and verified for readiness. A trial run of a sample tool test cases and scripts should be performed to verify that the test tools are ready for the actual acceptance test. Some other tool readiness considerations include:

- Test team tool training
- Tool compatibility with operating environment
- Ample disk space for the tools
- Maximizing the tool potentials
- Vendor tool help hotline
- Test procedures modified to accommodate tools
- Installing the latest tool changes
- Assuring the vendor contractual provisions

STEP 2: COMPLETE ACCEPTANCE TEST CASES

During this step, the acceptance test cases are designed and scripted. The conceptual acceptance test cases are transformed into reusable test scripts with test data created. To aid in the development of scripting the test cases, the GUI-based Function Test Matrix template in Appendix E7 can be used to document acceptance-level test cases, with the "function" heading replaced with acceptance test name.

Task 1: Subset the System-Level Test Cases

Acceptance test cases are typically (but not always) developed by the end-user and are not normally considered the responsibility of the development organization, because acceptance testing compares the system to its original requirements and the needs of the users. It is the final test for the end-users to accept or reject the system. The end-users supply the test resources and perform their own tests. They may or may not use the same test environment that was used during system testing. This depends on whether the test will be performed in the end-user's environment or not. The latter is the recommended approach.

Typically, the acceptance test consists of a subset of system tests which have already been designed during system testing. Therefore, the current task consists of identifying those system-level tests that will used during acceptance testing.

Task 2: Design/Script Additional Acceptance Tests

In addition to the system-level tests to be rerun during acceptance testing, they may be "tweaked" with special conditions to maximize the acceptability of the system. For example, the acceptance test might require that a certain throughput be sustained for a period of time with acceptable response time tolerance limits, e.g., 10,000 transactions per hour are processed with a mean response time of 3 seconds, with 90% less than or equal to 2 seconds. Another example might be that an independent user "off the street" sits down with the system and the document to verify that he or she can use the system effectively.

Other tests not designed during system testing might also be envisioned by the user. These may become more apparent to the user than they would have been to the developer because the user knows the business requirements and is intimately familiar with the business operations. He or she might uncover defects that only a user would see. This also helps the user to get ready for the real installation and production.

The acceptance test design might even include the use of live data, because the acceptance of test results will probably occur more readily if it looks real to the user. There are also unusual conditions that might not be defected unless live data is used.

STEP 3: REVIEW/APPROVE ACCEPTANCE TEST PLAN

Task 1: Schedule/Conduct the Review

The acceptance test plan review should be scheduled well in advance of the actual review and the participants should have the latest copy of the test plan.

As with any interview or review, it should contain four elements. The first defines what will be discussed; the second discusses the details; the third summarizes; and the final element is timeliness. The reviewer should state up front the estimated duration of the review and set the ground rule that if time expires before completing all items on the agenda, a follow-on review will be scheduled.

The purpose of this task is for development and the project sponsor to agree and accept the system test plan. If there are any suggested changes to the test plan during the review, they should be incorporated into the test plan.

Task 2: Obtain Approvals

Approval is critical in a testing effort, because it helps provide the necessary agreements between testing, development, and the sponsor. The best approach is with a formal sign-off procedure of an acceptance test plan. If this is the case, use the management approval sign-off forms. However, if a formal agreement procedure is not in place, send a memo to each key participant, including at least the project manager, development manager, and sponsor. Attach to the document the latest test plan and point out that all feedback comments have been incorporated and that if you do not hear from them, it is assumed they agree with the plan. Finally, indicate that in a spiral development environment, the system test plan will evolve with each iteration but that you will include them in any modification.

STEP 4: EXECUTE THE ACCEPTANCE TESTS

Task 1: Regression Test the Acceptance Fixes

The purpose of this task is to retest the tests which discovered defects in the previous acceptance test cycle for this build. The technique used is regression testing. Regression testing detects spurious errors caused by software modifications or corrections.

A set of test cases must be maintained and available throughout the entire life of the software. The test cases should be complete enough so that all the software's functional capabilities are thoroughly tested. The question arises as to how to locate those test cases to test defects discovered during the previous test spiral. An excellent mechanism is the retest matrix.

As described earlier, a retest matrix relates test cases to functions (or program units). A check entry in the matrix indicates that the test case is to be retested when the function (or program unit) has been modified due to an enhancement(s) or correction(s). No entry means that the test does not need to be retested. The retest matrix can be built before the first testing spiral but needs to be maintained during subsequent spirals. As functions (or program units) are modified during a development spiral, existing or new test cases need to be created and checked in the retest matrix in preparation for the next test spiral. Over time with subsequent spirals, some functions (or program units) may be stable with no recent modifications. Consideration to selectively remove their check entries should be undertaken between testing spirals.

Task 2: Execute the New Acceptance Tests

The purpose of this task is to execute new tests that were created at the end of the previous acceptance test cycle. In the previous spiral, the testing team updated the function/GUI, system fragment, and acceptance tests in preparation for the current testing spiral. During this task, those tests are executed.

Task 3: Document the Acceptance Defects

During acceptance test execution, the results of the testing must be reported in the defect tracking database. These defects are typically related to individual tests that have been conducted. However, variations to the formal test cases often uncover other defects. The objective of this task is to produce a complete record of the defects. If the execution step has been recorded properly, the defects have already been recorded on the defect tracking database. If the defects are already recorded, the objective of this step becomes to collect and consolidate the defect information.

Tools can be used to consolidate and record defects depending on the test execution methods. If the defects are recorded on paper, the consolidation involves collecting and organizing the papers. If the defects are recorded electronically, search features can easily locate duplicate defects.

Part 19
Summarize/Report Spiral Test Results

STEP 1: PERFORM DATA REDUCTION

Task 1: Ensure All Tests Were Executed/Resolved

During this task, the test plans and logs are examined by the test team to verify that all tests were executed (see Exhibit 1). The team can usually do this by ensuring that all the tests are recorded on the activity log and examining the log to confirm that the tests have been completed. When there are defects that are still open and not resolved, they need to be prioritized and deployment workarounds need to be established.

Task 2: Consolidate Test Defects by Test Number

During this task, the team examines the recorded test defects. If the tests have been properly performed, it is logical to assume that, unless a defect test document was reported, the correct or expected result was received. If that defect was not corrected, it would have been posted to the test defect log. The team can assume that all items are working except those recorded on the test log as having no corrective action or unsatisfactory corrective action. These defects should be consolidated by test number so that they can be posted to the appropriate matrix.

Task 3: Post Remaining Defects to a Matrix

During this task, the uncorrected or unsatisfactorily corrected defects should be posted to a special function test matrix. The matrix indicates which function was tested by which test by test number. The defect is recorded in the intersection between the test and the function for which that test occurred. All uncorrected defects should be posted to the function/test matrix intersection.

STEP 2: PREPARE FINAL TEST REPORT

The objective of the final spiral test report is to describe the results of the testing, including not only what works and what does not, from above, but the test team's evaluation regarding performance of the application when it is placed into production.

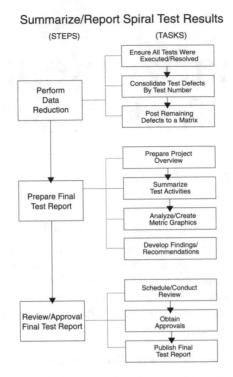

Exhibit 1. Summarize/Report Spiral Test Results

For some projects, informal reports are the practice, while in others very formal reports are required. The following is a compromise between the two extremes to provide essential information not requiring an inordinate amount of preparation (see Appendix E15, Spiral Testing Summary Report).

Task 1: Prepare the Project Overview

An objective of this task is to document an overview of the project in paragraph format. Some pertinent information contained in the introduction includes the project name, project objectives, the type of system, the target audience, the organizational units that participated in the project, why the system was developed, what subsystems are involved, the major and subfunctions of the system, and what functions are out of scope and will not be implemented.

Task 2: Summarize the Test Activities

The objective of this task is to describe the test activities for the project including such information as:

- Test Team
  The composition of the test team, e.g., test manager, test leader, testers, and the contribution of each, such as test planning, test design, test development, and test execution.
- Test Environment
  Physical test facility, technology, testing tools, software, hardware, networks, testing libraries, and support software.
- Types of Tests
  Spiral (how many spirals), system testing (types of tests and how many), acceptance testing (types of tests and how many)
- Test Schedule (major milestones)
  External and internal milestones. External milestones are those events external to the project but which may have a direct impact on it. Internal milestones are the events within the project to which some degree of control can be administered.
- Test Tools
  Which testing tools were used and for what purpose, e.g., path analysis, regression testing, load testing, etc.

Task 3: Analyze/Create Metric Graphics

During this task the defect and test management metrics measured during the project are gathered and analyzed. Hopefully, the defect tracking has been automated and will be used to make the work more productive. Reports are run and metric totals and trends are analyzed. This analysis will be instrumental in determining the quality of the system and its acceptability for use and also be useful for future testing endeavors. The final test report should include a series of metric graphics. Following are the suggested graphics.

Defects by Function. The objective of Exhibit 2 is to show the number and percentage of defects discovered for each function or group. This analysis will flag the functions that had the most defects. Typically, such functions had poor requirements or design. In the example below, the reports had 43% of the total defects, which suggests an area that should be examined for maintainability after it is released for production.

Defects by Tester. The objective of Exhibit 3 is to show the number and percentage of defects discovered for each tester during the project. This analysis flags those testers who documented fewer than the expected number of defects. These statistics, however, should be used with care. A tester may have recorded fewer defects because the functional area tested may have relatively fewer defects, e.g., tester Baker in Exhibit 3. On the other hand, a tester who records a higher percentage of defects could be more productive, e.g., tester Brown.

Exhibit 2. Defects Documented by Function

Function	Number of Defects	Percent of Total
Order Processing		
Create New Order	11	6
Fulfill Order	5	3
Edit Order	15	8
Delete Order	9	5
Subtotal	40	22
Customer Processing		
Create New Customer	6	3
Edit Customer	0	0
Delete Customer	10	6
Subtotal	16	9
Financial Processing		
Receive Customer Payment	0	0
Deposit Payment	5	3
Pay Vendor	9	5
Write a Check	4	2
Display Register	6	3
Subtotal	24	13
Inventory Processing		
Acquire Vendor Products	3	2
Maintain Stock	7	4
Handle Back Orders	9	5
Audit Inventory	0	0
Adjust Product Price	6	3
Subtotal	25	14

Exhibit 2. (Continued) Defects Documented by Function

Function	Number of Defects	Percent of Total
Reports		
Create Order Report	23	13
Create Account Receivable Report	19	11
Create Account Payable Report	35	19
Subtotal	77	43
Grand Totals	**182**	**100**

Exhibit 3. Defects Documented by Tester

Tester	Number of Defects	Percent of Total
Jones	51	28
Baker	19	11
Brown	112	61
Grand Totals	**182**	**100**

Defect Gap Analysis. The objective of Exhibit 4 is to show the gap between the number of defects that have been uncovered and the number that have been corrected during the entire project. At project completion these curves should coincide, indicating that the majority of the defects uncovered have been corrected and the system is ready for production.

Defect Severity Status. The objective of Exhibit 5 is to show the distribution of the three severity categories for the entire project, e.g., critical, major, and minor. A large percentage of defects in the critical category indicates that there existed a problem with the design or architecture of the application, which should be examined for maintainability after it is released for production.

Test Burnout Tracking. The objective of Exhibit 6 is to indicate the rate of uncovering defects for the entire project and is a valuable test completion indicator. The cumulative, e.g., running total number of defects, and defects by time period help predict when fewer and fewer defects are being

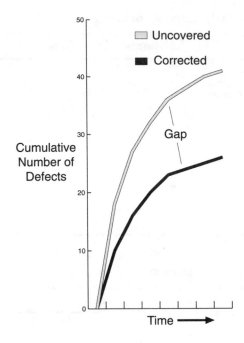

Exhibit 4. Defect Gap Analysis

---

discovered. This is indicated when the cumulative curve "bends" and the defects by time period approach zero.

Root Cause Analysis. The objective of Exhibit 7 is to show the source of the defects, e.g., architectural, functional, usability, etc. If the majority of the defects are architectural, this will pervade the whole system and require a great deal of redesign and rework. High percentage categories should be examined for maintainability after it is released for production.

Defects by How Found. The objective of Exhibit 8 is to show how the defects were discovered, e.g., by external customers, manual testing, etc. If a very low percentage of defects were discovered through inspections, walkthroughs, or JADs, this indicates that there may be too much emphasis on testing and too little on the review process. The percentage differences between manual and automated testing also illustrate the contribution of automated testing to the process.

Defects by Who Found. The objective of Exhibit 9 is to show who discovered the defects, e.g., external customers, development, quality assurance testing, etc. For most projects, quality assurance testing will discover most of the defects. However, if the majority of the defects were discovered by

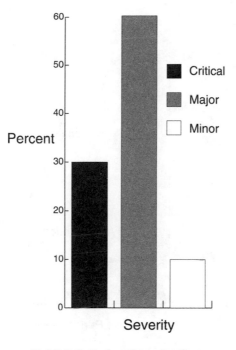

Exhibit 5. Defect Severity Status

external or internal customers, this indicates that quality assurance testing was lacking.

Functions Tested and Not. The objective of Exhibit 10 is to show the final status of testing and verify that all or most defects have been corrected and the system is ready for production. At the end of the project all test cases should have been completed and the percentage of test cases run with errors and/or not run should be zero. Exceptions should be evaluated by management and documented.

System Testing Defect Types. Systems testing consists of one or more tests which are based on the original objectives of the system. The objective of Exhibit 11 is to show a distribution of defects by system testing type. In the example, performance testing had the most defects, followed by compatibility and usability. An inordinate percentage of performance tests indicates a poorly designed system.

Acceptance Testing Defect Types. Acceptance testing is an optional user-run test that demonstrates the ability of the application to meet the user's requirements. The motivation for this test is to demonstrate rather than destroy, e.g., to show that the system works. Less emphasis is placed on

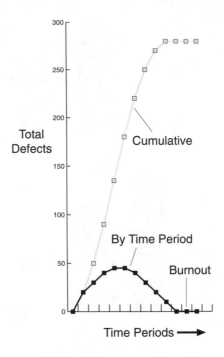

Exhibit 6. Test Burnout Tracking

---

the technical issues and more is placed on the question of whether the system is a good business fit for the end-user.

There should not be many defects discovered during acceptance testing, as most of them should have been corrected during system testing. In Exhibit 12, performance testing still had the most defects, followed by stress and volume testing.

Task 4: Develop Findings/Recommendations

A finding is a variance between what is and what should be. A recommendation is a suggestion on how to correct a defective situation or improve a system. Findings and recommendations from the test team constitute the majority of the test report.

The objective of this task is to develop the findings and recommendations from the testing process and document "lessons learned." Previously, data reduction has identified the findings, but they must be put in a format suitable for use by the project team and management.

The test team should make the recommendations to correct a situation. The project team should also confirm that the findings are correct and the

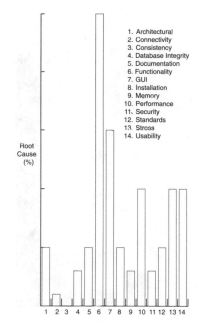

1. Architectural
2. Connectivity
3. Consistency
4. Database Integrity
5. Documentation
6. Functionality
7. GUI
8. Installation
9. Memory
10. Performance
11. Security
12. Standards
13. Stress
14. Usability

Exhibit 7. Root Cause Analysis

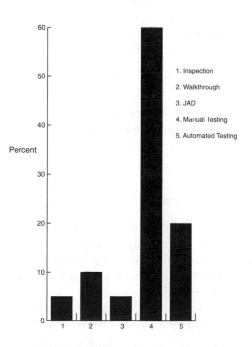

1. Inspection

2. Walkthrough

3. JAD

4. Manual Testing

5. Automated Testing

Exhibit 8. Defects by How Found

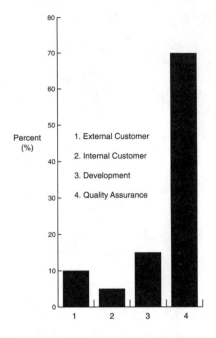

Exhibit 9. Defects by Who Found

---

recommendations reasonable. Each finding and recommendation can be documented in the Finding/Recommendation matrix depicted in Exhibit 13.

The following describes each column:

- Finding Description
  This includes a description of the problem found from the defect information recorded in the defect tracking database. It could also include test team, test procedures, or test environment findings and recommendations.
- Business Function
  Describes the business function that was involved and affected.
- Impact
  Describes the effect the finding will have on the operational system. The impact should be described only as major (the defect would cause the application system to produce incorrect results) or minor (the system is incorrect, but the results will be correct).
- Impact on Other Systems
  Describes where the finding will affect application systems other than the one being tested. If the finding affects other development

Percent

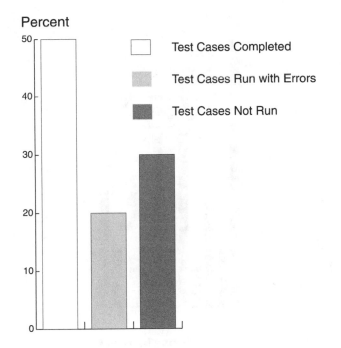

Exhibit 10. Functions Tested/Not Tested

---

teams, they should be involved in the decision on whether to correct the problem.

- Cost to Correct
  Management must know both the costs and the benefits before it can make a decision on whether to install the system without the problem being corrected.
- Recommendation
  Describes the recommendation from the test team on what action to take.

STEP 3: REVIEW/APPROVE THE FINAL TEST REPORT

Task 1: Schedule/Conduct the Review

The test summary report review should be scheduled well in advance of the actual review and the participants should have the latest copy of the test plan.

As with any interview or review, it should contain four elements. The first is defining what will be discussed; the second is discussing the details; the third is summarization; and the final element is timeliness. The review-

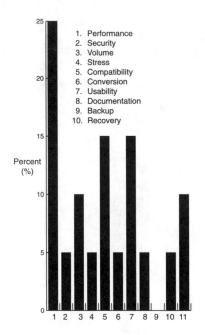

Exhibit 11. System Testing by Root Cause

er should state up front the estimated duration of the review and set the ground rule that if time expires before completing all items on the agenda, a follow-on review will be scheduled.

The purpose of this task is for development and the project sponsor to agree and accept the test report. If there are any suggested changes to the report during the review, they should be incorporated.

Task 2: Obtain Approvals

Approval is critical in a testing effort, because it helps provide the necessary agreement between testing, development, and the sponsor. The best approach is with a formal sign-off procedure of a test plan. If this is the case, use the management approval sign-off forms. However, if a formal agreement procedure is not in place, send a memo to each key participant, including at least the project manager, development manager, and sponsor. In the document attach the latest test plan and point out that all their feedback comments have been incorporated and that if you do not hear from them, it is assumed that they agree with the plan. Finally, indicate that in a spiral development environment, the test plan will evolve with each iteration but that you will include them in any modification.

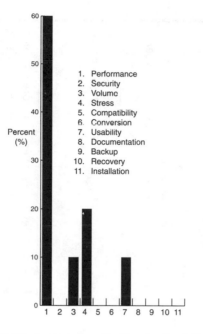

Percent
(%)

1. Performance
2. Security
3. Volume
4. Stress
5. Compatibility
6. Conversion
7. Usability
8. Documentation
9. Backup
10. Recovery
11. Installation

Exhibit 12. Acceptance Testing by Root Cause

Task 3: Publish the Final Test Report

The test report is finalized with the suggestions from the review and distributed to the appropriate parties. The purpose has short-term and long-term objectives.

The short-term objective is to provide information to the software user to determine if the system is ready for production. It also provides information about outstanding issues, including testing not completed or outstanding problems, and recommendations.

The long-term objectives are to provide information to the project regarding how it was managed and developed from a quality point of view. The project can use the report to trace problems if the system malfunctions in production, e.g., defect—prone functions that had the most errors and which ones were not corrected. The project and organization also have the opportunity to learn from the current project. A determination of which development, project management, and testing procedures worked, and which didn't work, or need improvement, can be invaluable to future projects.

Exhibit 13. Finding/Recommendations Matrix

Finding Description	Business Function	Impact	Impact on Other Systems	Costs to Correct	Recommendation
Not enough testers were initially assigned to the project	N/A	Caused the testing process to lag behind the original schedule	N/A	Contracted 5 additional testers from a contract agency	Spend more resource planning in future projects
Defect tracking was not monitored adequately by development	N/A	Number of outstanding defects grew significantly	N/A	Authorized overtime for development	QA needs to stress the importance of defect tracking on a daily basis in future projects
Automated testing tools did contribute significantly to regression testing	N/A	Increased testing productivity	N/A	N/A	Utilize testing tools as much as possible
Excessive number of defects in one functional area	Reports	Caused a lot of developer rework time	N/A	Excessive developer overtime	Perform more technical design reviews early in the project
Functional area not compatible with other systems	Order Processing	Re-work costs	Had to redesign the database	Contracted an Oracle database DBA	Perform more database design reviews early in the project

Exhibit 13. (Continued) Finding/Recommendations Matrix

Finding Description	Business Function	Impact	Impact on Other Systems	Costs to Correct	Recommendation
30% of defects had critical severity	N/A	Significantly impacted the development and testing effort	N/A	Hired additional development programmers	Perform more technical reviews early in the project and tighten up on the sign-off procedures
Function/GUI had the most defects	N/A	Required a lot of re-work	N/A	Testers authorized overtime	Perform more technical reviews early in the project and tighten up on the sign-off procedures
Two test cases could not be completed because performance load test tool did not work properly	Stress testing order entry with 1,000 terminals	Cannot guarantee system will perform adequately under extreme load conditions	N/A	Delay system delivery until new testing tool acquired (2 months delay at $85,000 loss in revenue, $10,000 for tool)	Loss of revenue overshadows risk. Ship system but acquire performance test tool and complete stress test

223

Section IV
Modern Testing Tools

Recent advances in client/server software tools enable developers to build applications quickly and with increased functionality. Quality assurance departments must cope with software that is dramatically improved, but increasingly complex. Testing tools have been developed to aid in the quality assurance process.

The objectives of this section are to:

- Describe when a testing tool is useful
- Describe when not to use a testing tool
- Provide a testing tool selection checklist
- Discuss types of testing tools
- Provide descriptions of modern and popular testing tools
- Describe a methodology to evaluate testing tools

Part 20
Introduction to Testing Tools

The objective of this section is to provide an overview of some popular test tools and demonstrate how they can improve the quality and productivity of a development effort.

JUSTIFYING TESTING TOOLS

There are numerous testing tools, each with specific capabilities and test objectives. The selection of the best testing tool for a particular development environment is a critical success factor for the testing activities. However, if the right testing tool is not selected and/or the organization is not positioned for a testing tool, it can easily become "shelfware," as testing tools require a learning curve, skills, standards, and must be integrated into the development methodology.

When to Consider Using a Testing Tool

A testing tool should be considered based on the test objectives. As a general guideline, one should investigate the appropriateness of a testing tool when the human manual process is inadequate. For example, if a system needs to be stress tested, a group of testers could simultaneously logon to the system and attempt to simulate peak loads using stopwatches. However, this approach has limitations. One cannot systematically measure the performance precisely or repeatably. For this case, a load testing tool can simulate several virtual users under controlled stress conditions.

A regression testing tool might be needed under the following circumstances:

- Tests need to be run at every build of an application, e.g., time consuming, unreliable and inconsistent use of human resources
- Tests are required using multiple data values for the same actions
- Tests require detailed information from system internals such as SQL, GUI attributes
- There is a need to stress a system to see how it performs

Testing tools have the following benefits:

- Speedy and much faster then their human counterpart
- Run unattended without human intervention
- Provide code coverage analysis after a test run
- Precisely repeatable
- Reusable, just as programming subroutines
- Programmable

When to *Not* Consider Using a Testing Tool

Contrary to popular belief, it is not always wise to purchase a testing tool. Some factors that limit a testing tool include:

- Cost
  A testing tool may not be affordable to the organization, e.g., the cost/performance tradeoff
- Culture
  The development culture may not be ready for a testing tool, because it requires the proper skills and commitment to long-term quality
- Usability testing
  There are no automated testing tools that can test usability
- One-time testing
  If the test is going to be performed only once, a testing tool may not be worth the required time and expense
- Time crunch
  If there is pressure to complete testing within a fixed time frame, a testing tool may not be feasible, because it takes time to learn, set up, and integrate a testing tool to the development methodology
- *Ad hoc* testing
  If there is no formal test design and test cases, a regression testing tool will be useless
- Predictable results
  If tests do not have predictable results, a regression testing tool will be useless
- Instability
  If the system is changing rapidly during each testing spiral, more time will be spent maintaining a regression testing tool than it is worth.

TESTING TOOL SELECTION CHECKLIST

Finding the appropriate tool can be difficult. Several questions need to be answered before selecting a tool. Exhibit 1 lists questions to help the QA team evaluate and select an automated testing tool. (See also Appendix F19, Testing Tool Selection Checklist.)

Exhibit 1. Testing Tool Selection Checklist

Item	Yes	No	N/A	Comments
1. How easy is the tool for your testers to use?				
2. Is it something that can be picked up quickly or is training going to be required?				
3. Do any of the team members already have experience using the tool?				
4. If training is necessary, are classes, books, or other forms of instruction available?				
5. Will the tool work effectively on the computer system currently in place?				
6. Or are more memory, faster processors, etc., going to be needed?				
7. Is the tool itself easy to use?				
8. Does it have a user-friendly interface?				
9. Is it prone to user error?				
10. Is the tool physically capable of testing your application? Many testing tools can only test in a GUI environment, while others test in non-GUI environments.				
11. Can the tool handle full project testing? That is, is it able to run hundreds if not thousands of test cases for extended periods of time?				
12. Can it run for long periods of time without crashing, or is the tool itself full of bugs?				

Exhibit 1. (Continued) Testing Tool Selection Checklist

Item	Yes	No	N/A	Comments
13. Talk to customers who currently or have previously used the tool. Did it meet their needs?				
14. How similar were their testing needs to yours and how well did the tool perform?				
15. Try to select a tool that is advanced enough so the costs of updating tests don't overwhelm any benefits of testing.				
16. If a demo version is available, try it out before you make any decisions.				
17. Does the price of the tool fit in the QA Department or company budget?				
18. Does the tool meet the requirements of the company testing methodology?				

TYPES OF TESTING TOOLS

Year 2000 Tools

Year 2000 tools help in date-sensitive testing which is critical to the YR2000 problem and also identify the scope and time dimensions of the applications through tools that automatically parse the source code.

Coverage and range-driven testing requirements will be greater than under normal regression scenarios. Absolutely essential are capture/playback tools which are "turned on" and record actual production transactions and data which has been modified to simulate the YR2000 scenarios. With several days' worth of such information, the results from these recording sessions can be sorted and categorized, yielding key information. (See Exhibit 2.)

Web Site Management Tools

Web site management tools are designed to help the Webmaster or business manager manage every aspect of a rapidly changing site. It helps detect and repair defects in the structural integrity of their sites, e.g., broken links, orphaned pages, potential performance problems on Web sites, etc. (See Exhibit 2.)

Requirements-Based Testing Tools

A requirements-based testing tool, or functional test case design tool, drives clarification of application requirements and uses the "requirements" as the basis for test design. Such tools validate requirements by identifying all functional variations and logical inconsistencies, and they determine the minimal number of test cases needed to maximize coverage of the functional requirements.

This allows project teams to review both the requirements and the test cases in a variety of formats to ensure that the requirements are correct, complete, fully understood, and testable. (See Exhibit 2.)

Test Management Tools

A test management tool keeps track of all the testing assets through a common repository of information and contains such information as test plans, test cases, and test scripts. It helps quality assurance plan, manage, and analyze the testing progress and enhances the communication of the development team, including testers, developers, project leaders, and QA managers. Using a test management tool, testers report defects and track progress, developers correct defects and update the defect status, project leaders extract information about the progress of the testing process. Quality assurance managers generate reports and create graphical analysis for management. (See Exhibit 2.)

Regression Testing Tools

Each code change, enhancement, bug fix, and platform port necessitates re-testing the entire application to ensure a quality release. Manual testing can no longer keep pace in this rapidly developing environment. A regression testing tool helps automate the testing process, from test development to execution. Reusable test scripts are created which test the system's functionality. Prior to a release, one can execute these tests in an unattended mode, which fosters the detection of defects and ensures quality deliverables. (See Exhibit 2.)

Coverage Analysis Tools

The purpose of coverage analysis tools is to monitor the system while a dynamic testing tool is executing. They are a form of white-box testing in which there is knowledge about the internal structure of the program of the system. Information is provided on how thorough the test was. Graphic analysis displays how much the system was covered during the test, such as the percent of code executed and in which locations. This will provide the tester with information on weaknesses in the test design, which can be solved with additional test cases.

Unit and integration coverage is provided with these tools. Unit coverage entails the coverage of the code and paths within a single program unit. Integration coverage comprises the interfaces between program units to determine the linkage between them. (See Exhibit 2.)

Dynamic Testing Tools

Dynamic testing techniques are time dependent and involve executing a specific sequence of instructions by the computer. The purpose of dynamic testing tools is to examine a program of systems behavior and performance while it is executing to verify whether it operated as expected. Examples include regression testing capture/playback and load/stress testing tools. (See Exhibit 2.)

Static Testing Tools

The purpose of static testing tools is to uncover defects by examining the software itself rather than executing it, as with dynamic testing. They are a form of white-box testing in which there is knowledge about the internal structure of the program of the system and can be thought of as automated code inspectors. (See Exhibit 2.)

Automated static testing tools typically operate on the program source code. There are two broad categories of this type of tool. The first type gathers and reports information about the program. Generally, this type of tool does not search for any particular type of error in a program. A symbol cross-reference generator and a consistency check with the specifications are examples. The other type of tool detects specific types of errors or anomalies in a program.

Typical defects reported by these tools include:

- Overly complex code
- Misspellings
- Incorrect punctuation
- Path analysis
- Improper statement sequencing
- Inconsistency of parameters
- Redundant code
- Unreachable code
- Overly complex system structure
- Faults
- Initialized variables
- Coding standard violations
- Inconsistent data attributes

Load Testing Tools

The purpose of load testing tools is to simulate a production environment to determine that normal or above-normal volumes of transactions can be completed successfully in an expected time frame. These tools test the availability and capacity of system resources, such as CPU, disk, memory, channel, and communication lines. (See Exhibit 2.)

Comparators

A comparator is a program used to compare two versions of source data to determine whether the two versions are identical or to specifically identify where any differences in the versions occur. Comparators are most effective during software testing and maintenance when periodic modifications to the software are anticipated.

Windows File Revision Feature. With Windows File Revision Feature one can compare two versions of a document. The two documents being compared must have different file names or the same file name in different folders. To use this feature under Windows 95:

1. Open the edited version of the document.
2. On the Tools menu, click Revisions.
3. Click Compare Versions.
4. Click the name of the original document, or type its name in the File Name box.
5. Accept or reject the revisions.

Exhibit 2 cross-references testing tool vendors with the testing tool types discussed above (in alphabetical order). Exhibit 3 gives contact information for the vendors.

VENDOR TOOL DESCRIPTIONS

The following is an overview of some of the major testing tool vendors. No one tool is favored over another.

McCabe's Visual 2000

Product Description. McCabe Visual 2000 offers testing capabilities coupled with analysis and assessment features that allow the user to prioritize, pinpoint, and manage high-risk areas.

McCabe Visual 2000 provides a date logic impact view of the system architecture based on date complexity, code quality, and visual impact diagrams. Project scope and prioritization strategies are based on date logic impacted instead of lines of code impacted. Year 2000 software remediation and testing strategy can be proposed based on quantifiable metrics.

Exhibit 2. Vendor vs. Testing Tool Type

Vendor Name	Y2000	Test Management	Requirements-Based Management	Web Site Management	Static	Dynamic	Load/ Performance	Coverage	Regression
Astra				x					
Load-Runner						x	x		
LoadTest						x	x		
PreVue						x	x		
Pure Coverage						x		x	
Purify					x	x			
Quantify						x	x		
Caliber–RBT			x						
SQA Manager		x							
SQA Robot	x					x			x
SQA SiteCheck				x					
Test Library Manager		x							

Exhibit 2. (Continued) Vendor vs. Testing Tool Type

Vendor Name	Y2000	Test Management	Requirements-Based Management	Web Site Management	Static	Dynamic	Load/ Performance	Coverage	Regression
Test Station	x					x			x
Test-Director		x							
Visual 2000	x								
Visual Quality ToolSet					x				
Visual Re-engineering ToolSet					x	x			
Visual Test	x				x	x			x
Visual Testing ToolSet					x			x	
Win-Runner	x					x			x
Xrunner	x					x			x

Exhibit 3. Vendor Information

Vendor Name	Address	Phone	Fax	Web Site	E-Mail
Technology Builders, Inc.	400 Interstate North Parkway, Suite 1090, Atlanta, GA 30339	(800) 937-0047	(770) 937-7901	www.tbi.com	marketing@tbi. com
Mercury Interactive	1325 Borregas Avenue, Sunnyvale, CA 94089	(408) 822-5200	(408) 822-5300	www.merc-int.com	info@merc.int.com
Rational Software Corporation	18880 Homestead Road, Cupertino, CA 95014	(800) 728-1212	(408) 863-4120	www.rational.com	product_info@ rational.com
McCabe & Associates	5501 Twin Knolls Road, Suite 111, Columbia, MD 21045	(800) 638-6316	(410) 995-1528	ww.mccabe.com	info@mccabe. com
AutoTester, Inc.	8150 N. Central Expressway, Suite 1300, Dallas, TX 75206	(214) 368-1196	(214) 750-9668	www.autotester.com	info@autotester. com
Sun Microsystems, Inc.	901 San Antonio Road, Palo Alto, CA 94303	(650) 960-1300	—	www.sun.com	—

McCabe Visual 2000 helps determine date testing requirements during the impact assessment and analysis phases. It identifies where to concentrate testing resources, what to test, how much to test, and when to stop testing. During validation, McCabe Visual 2000 monitors the test effort and ties testing results back to initial assessment information.

McCabe Visual 2000 provides a common methodology and interface across many languages with full language parsing technology that generates information on software characteristics, including flowgraphs and metrics.

Product Features.

- Comprehensive analysis, visual representation, and date-centric software testing to ensure improved project planning, architectural insight, and validation for Year 2000 compliance across numerous languages and platforms.
- An open API enabling the leverage of investments in existing tools (change and configuration management, editing, renovation, GUI testing, and even other Year 2000 assessment and remediation tools).
- A database of software characteristics including metrics and flowgraphs, used as a valuable resource for software development and testing efforts continuing into the next millennium.
- The "On-Screen Battlemap" renders a structure chart of a system and highlights modules/paragraphs containing date references. The highlight color is determined by the complexity of the code. Potential high-risk areas are easily detected.
- The "Scatterplot Diagrams" provide a view of the quality of the system and thoroughness of testing performed within a system. Modules are sorted by their ranking in user-specified metrics. Error prone or untested modules are effortlessly located.
- The "Unit-Level Slice" pinpoints date references and helps identify potential test paths for testing millennium bugs.

System Requirements.
   200 Mhz Pentium
   64 Mb RAM

Platforms Supported.

   SunOS 5.x (Solaris)
   Windows NT
   Windows 95
   Languages Supported: C, C++, Fortran, Visual Basic, COBOL, ASM370, Model204, Ada, Java

McCabe's Visual Testing ToolSet

Product Description. The McCabe Visual Testing ToolSet (VTT) employs robust tools and proven methodology. Based on software metrics widely accepted in the industry, VTT penetrates the complexity of modern systems. It graphically displays entire software systems and pinpoints where testing effort can be most effective.

The visual environment helps managers understand complex software projects and judge the resources needed to meet project goals. Developers use VTT to ensure that they have tested the code in the most thorough and efficient way. VTT calculates the cyclomatic complexity and identifies the relevant test paths necessary for structured testing. Unlike other testing methods, the number of tests is driven by the code's complexity. Studies have show that testing based on the cyclomatic complexity metric reduces the errors found in the delivered code.

Product Features.

- A visual environment that allows one to plan software testing resources in advance. Graphical displays of test paths and the number of tests required, visually identify the most complex areas to help focus testing efforts.
- Comprehensive software testing results that identify tested and untested paths and easily pinpoint problematic areas. Reports and graphical displays help testers quickly assess the need for additional tests.
- Multiple levels of code coverage including unit level, integration level, path coverage, branch coverage, and Boolean coverage.
- The Battlemap renders a structure chart of a system and color codes modules based on their testedness. Untested areas are easily detected.
- The Combined Coverage Metrics report ranks modules based on their testedness. Software metrics and code coverage information are also included.
- The Untested Graph/Listing calculates the remaining paths to be tested to complete structured testing. This can be very useful in creating new tests to complete a test suite.
- The Dependency Analyzer finds and helps one inspect data dependencies in code. With the dependency analyzer, one can determine whether a dependency is breakable with a careful selection of data or that the dependency is inherent in the code and the module can never be fully tested.
- Visual Testing ToolSet Reports provide testing statistics and indicate which specific tests remain. These include the Integration Coverage, Path Coverage, Branch Coverage, Code Coverage, Combined Coverage, and Boolean (MC/DC) Coverage reports.

- Visual Testing ToolSet provides a common methodology and interface across many languages with full language parsing technology that generates valuable information on software testing, including identifying untested areas and high complexity modules.

System Requirements.

166 Mhz Pentium
32 Mb RAM

Platforms Supported.

SunOS4.x (Motif)
SunOS 5.x (Solaris–Motif)
Windows NT
Windows 95
IBM RS6000, AIX 4.2
HP700, HP-UX 10.x
SGI, IRIX 5.x, 6.x
Languages Supported: C, C++, Fortran, Visual Basic, COBOL, ASM370, Model204, Ada83, Ada95, PL/1, Java

McCabe's Visual Quality ToolSet

Product Description. The Visual Quality ToolSet (VQT) answers the following questions: When is the quality acceptable or when will it be acceptable? How do you explain to developers and managers the basics of quality software? How do you establish an effective program that builds quality into the product? VQT combines graphical technology and objective standards of measurement, or metrics, to assess software quality and maintainability. The ToolSet computes over 100 metrics, including McCabe's ground-breaking cyclomatic complexity metric.

Product Features.

- Insight into software quality through module-by-module metric calculation. Metrics including cyclomatic complexity and essential complexity help identify where a program is more likely to contain errors. Metrics measurements are also traced over time to track program improvement.
- A visual environment for understanding software. Graphical displays represent the structure of code and the metrics rankings to provide assessment even of large systems.
- A database of software characteristics including metrics and flowgraphs, used as a resource for future software changes and upgrades.
- The Battlemap renders a structure chart of a system and color-codes modules based on their metrics. Potential high-risk areas are easily detected.

- The Scatterplot provides a view of the quality of the system. Modules are sorted by their ranking in user-specified metrics. Error prone or complex modules are located.
- The Metrics Trends report includes details of metrics calculations of individual modules over a period of time. This allows for tracking the quality of the code throughout the development life cycle.

System Requirements.

166 Mhz Pentium
32 Mb RAM

Platforms Supported.

SunOS4.x (Motif)
SunOS 5.x (Solaris–Motif)
Windows NT
Windows 95
IBM RS6000, AIX 4.2
HP700, HP-UX 10.x
SGI, IRIX 5.x, 6.x
Languages Supported: C, C++, Fortran, Visual Basic, COBOL, ASM370, Model204, Ada83, Ada95, PL/1, Java

McCabe's Visual Reengineering ToolSet

Product Description. Organizations today must respond to an avalanche of change in business conditions. Responding to change means that software must rapidly adapt to new needs. To be adapted, software must be understood. Yet due to a long history of evolution, lack of appropriate tools, and shifting personnel, legacy software is often neither understood nor well documented.

To meet these needs, the Visual Reengineering ToolSet (VRT) provides a rich graphical environment in which code can be analyzed, displayed, and understood. VRT serves well in any of these reengineering tasks: the ongoing maintenance of existing systems, their modification to add new functions or capabilities, or their migration to new hardware platforms or architectures such as client/server. 20 VRT can save time and resources during large reengineering projects.

Product Features.

- Analysis, visual representation, and metrics calculation to ensure improved project planning, architectural insight, and identification of complex code.
- Dynamic analysis of a program pinpoints code related to a specific functionality.

- Module comparison feature to locate redundant and reusable code which may be reengineered to reduce program size and complexity.
- The Slice report highlights executed code on the source code listing and the graphical flowgraph. This feature greatly assists in function extraction and reuse.
- The Module Comparison report identifies similar modules within the system. Modules are compared based on user-defined metrics or other criteria. Wasteful, redundant code can be removed.
- The Histogram report identifies modules that exceed user-defined metrics thresholds. Complex, unmaintainable code is easily pinpointed.
- Visual Reengineering ToolSet parses code and displays a picture of the structure of the software. Metrics indicate likely problems so one can focus efforts where they will have the most impact — on the modules of high complexity.
- The data dictionary tracks the use of data elements and highlights the associated modules on the Battlemap. With use of the data complexity metric, the data change can be visualized, the complexity of the data change quantified, and the related test paths generated.
- Visual Reengineering ToolSet provides a common methodology and interface across many languages and platforms with a language parsing technology that generates valuable information on software characteristics, including flowgraphs and metrics. This is especially useful in platform migration projects.

System Requirements.

166 Mhz Pentium
32 Mb RAM

Platforms Supported.

SunOS4.x
SunOS 5.x (Solaris)
Windows NT
Windows 95
SCO Open Desktop 3.0
SunOS 5.x, (Solaris x86)
IBM RS6000, AIX 3.2, AIX 4.x
HP700, HP-OX, 10.x
SGI, IRIX 5.x, 6.x
Languages Supported: C, C++, Fortran, Visual Basic, COBOL, ASM370, Model204, Ada83, Ada95, PL/1, Java

Rational's SQA Suite (Version 6.1)

Product Description. SQA Suite™ is an integrated product suite for the automated testing of Windows NT™, Windows® 95, and Windows 3.x client/server and Internet applications. SQA Suite includes a scalable, integrated, server-based test repository. It combines client/server and Internet testing power, management tools, and a formal methodology to set the standard for automated testing of cross-Windows client/server and Internet applications. SQA Suite is comprised of four products from Rational — SQA Robot™, SQA SiteCheck™, SQA Manager™, and SQA LoadTest™.

There are two versions of SQA Suite: TeamTest Edition and LoadTest Edition. SQA Suite: TeamTest Edition can be used to test code and determine if the software meets requirements and performs as expected and includes three components:

- SQA Robot
- SQA Manager (including WebEntry)
- SQA SiteCheck

SQA Suite: LoadTest Edition provides integrated testing of structure, function, and performance of Web-based applications and includes four components:

- SQA Robot
- SQA Manager (including WebEntry)
- SQA SiteCheck
- SQA LoadTest

Rational's SQA SiteCheck Tool

Tool Description. SQA SiteCheck is a Web site management tool for the Intranet or World Wide Web. It is designed to help the Webmaster or business manager keep up with every aspect of the rapidly changing site. The primary purpose of SQA SiteCheck is to detect broken links, orphaned pages, and potential performance problems on Web sites. SQA SiteCheck helps Webmasters and Web site administrators detect and repair defects in the structural integrity of their sites.

SQA SiteCheck includes many features that allow it to test Web sites that use the most current technology to present active content such as HTML forms and Java applets. It is also capable of testing secure sites making use of SSL, proxy servers, and multiple security realms to protect the data sent to and from the site. SQA SiteCheck's advanced level of integration with McAfee VirusScan enables one to detect infected documents on a site before visitors do.

Tool Features.

- A fully integrated internal browser and HTML editor
- Full support of the Secure Sockets Layer (SSL)

242

- Filters for Web-based forms, frames, Java, JavaScript, ActiveX, and VB-Script
- Automatic tracking of moved or orphan pages and broken links
- Fixes links without needing a separate editor
- Includes automatic virus scanning
- Pinpoints all slow pages and predicts performance time for all communication paths
- Can impersonate both Microsoft Internet Explorer and Netscape Navigator to see the different server responses to the different browsers
- Integration with SQA Suite: SQA Robot as the Web Site Test Case

System Requirements.

16 Mbytes, 32 Mbytes recommended for NT
10 Mbytes of disk space
PC with 486 processor, Pentium-class processor recommended

Platforms Supported.

Microsoft® Windows 95® or Windows NT 4.0 or later
ActiveScan View requires Microsoft Internet Explorer™ v3.0 or later

Rational's SQA Robot (Version 6.1)

Product Description. SQA Robot allows one to create, modify, and run automated tests on cross-Windows client/server applications. It offers reusability and portability of test recordings across Windows platforms to provide one recording that plays back on all Windows platforms. SQA Robot includes Object Testing™ of Object Properties and Data.

Product Features.

- Comprises an integrated product suite for testing Windows NT, Windows 95, and Windows 3.x client/server and Internet applications to deliver solutions for testing cross-Windows client/server and Internet applications
- Uses Object Testing to completely test 32- and 16-bit Windows objects and components, including ActiveX Controls, OLE Controls (OCXs), Visual Basic Controls (VBXs), Visual Basic® objects, PowerBuilder® objects, Oracle Developer/2000 objects, Delphi® objects, Win32 controls, etc.
- Delivers Rational's Object-Oriented Recording™ technology to provide a fast, intuitive test creation with a short learning curve
- Includes SQABasic™, an integrated, Visual Basic syntax-compatible scripting environment to deliver an integrated programming environment for script development

- Includes integrated Web site testing power with SQA SiteCheck™, to deliver Web site analysis, performance measurement, and repair technology
- Delivers seamless integration with the scalable, integrated network SQA Repository — test assets and results are centralized for easy analysis and improved communication among test team members

System Requirements.

Microsoft Windows 3.x
Windows 95
Windows NT
16 Mbytes; 24 Mbytes recommended for Windows NT and Windows 95, 8 Mbytes for Windows 3.x
40 Mbytes of disk space
PC with 486 processor, Pentium-class processor recommended

Platforms Supported.

Microsoft Visual Basic (versions 3, 4 & 5)
Sybase/Powersoft PowerBuilder (versions 4, 5 & 6)
Borland Delphi (versions 2.01 & 3.0)
PeopleSoft PeopleTools (versions 6 & 7)
Centura (version 1)
Microsoft Visual C++ (version 5 and later)

Rational's SQA Manager (Version 6.1)

Product Description. SQA Manager helps the entire test team run smoothly. It lets QA plan, manage, and analyze all aspects of cross-Windows client/server applications. SQA offers a viable way to ensure the client/server application is production-ready before deployment.

SQA Manager helps one keep track of all the test assets. Multiple test projects can be defined in the scalable SQA Repository, and larger projects can be broken into smaller projects. One can store data which is usable across projects on the network. Test cases (verification points) and test scripts can be stored and organized to ensure there is no duplication of effort and that the latest versions of a test are being run. Tight integration with SQA Robot™ means information about test creation and execution is updated automatically, and one can open an SQA Robot test script from SQA Manager.

SQA Manager is seamlessly integrated with the SQA Repository for a team-testing environment, ensuring effective communication. Every member of the development team benefits from access to the same up-to-date information about the testing projects. Testers can report defects and track their progress. Developers access the defect management system to

244

update the status of a defect, project leaders extract information about the progress of a testing project, and QA managers generate reports and graphs to measure progress and report to upper management. An administrator can assign and restrict access privileges for security and give team members different privileges to open, fix, verify, and resolve a defect.

SQA Manager WebEntry provides defect entry and tracking capabilities that are accessed via a web browser. This enables end users of an application to submit defects directly to an SQA Repository via a Web browser as well as list and display information about defects previously entered, giving one the ability to benefit from users' feedback at any stage of the release cycle.

SQA Manager delivers an automated test solution with an integrated, powerful report writer and graphing engine. The customizable report writer lets one create reports using any data in the SQA Repository through an intuitive drag-and-drop interface. One can also customize or use any of the more than 50 preformatted reports. The graphing engine offers a variety of customizable graphs to help analyze the progress of the testing project. Any information can be instantly sent via email.

Product Features.

- Delivers an advanced, integrated, email-enabled test planning, workflow tracking, and defect management for a comprehensive test management solution for cross-Windows client/server and Internet applications
- Provides a scalable, industrial-strength client/server test repository to integrate the testing process across all Windows platforms
- Imports RequisitePro requirements, Rational Rose Use Case/Use Case Scenarios, PowerBuilder Library (.PBLs) and ASCII text files for automatic generation of test requirements and test procedure names
- Provides graphical test planning to organize test plans based on the requirements of the application
- Tracks defects along a customizable, rules-based workflow for defect management and tracking
- Provides customizable reporting and graphing and a variety of standard reports and graphs for analysis of test progress and coverage
- Submits defects directly to the SQA Repository through SQA Manager WebEntry™, a browser-based defect entry and listing system, for Internet-based defect entry and viewing of defect status

System Requirements.

Microsoft Windows 3.x
Windows 95
Windows NT

16 Mbytes; 24 Mbytes recommended for Windows NT and Windows
95, 8 Mbytes for Windows 3.x
20 Mbytes
PC with 486 processor, Pentium-class processor recommended

Platforms Supported.

Windows NT
Windows 95
Windows 3.x

Rational's SQA LoadTest (Version 6.1)

Product Description. SQA LoadTest offers a method for load, stress, and
multiuser testing of Windows client/server applications. It is an automated
network testing tool for Windows that allows complete multimachine test
synchronization without programming. SQA LoadTest lets one test 32-bit
and 16-bit Windows NT and Windows 95 client/server applications and
16-bit Windows 3.x client/server applications.

With features such as virtual user testing, DataSmart™ Recording, Web-
Smart™ Playback, and HTTP Class Error Collection and Analysis, SQA
LoadTest provides a method of ensuring the quality of the HTTP Web servers. SQA LoadTest also provides a solution for complete cross-Windows
testing by enabling one to test 32-bit and 16-bit Windows NT and Windows
95 client/server applications, and 16-bit Windows 3.x applications.

Product Features.

- Provides DataSmart Recording™ which automatically creates data-
driven test scripts, enabling hundreds of virtual users to run the same
transaction with each user sending different data to the server, without programming
- Offers WebSmart™ Playback to enable playback of recorded HTTP
sessions by automatically handling changing Web page content
- Offers tracking and analysis of HTTP errors during load and stress
testing of Web-based applications
- Delivers HTTP/HTTPS virtual user testing to provide virtual user load
and stress testing for HTTP/HTTPS Web servers
- Supports distributed testing on 32- and 16-bit applications on Windows NT and Windows 95 and 16-bit applications on Windows 3.x cli-
ent/server machines for centralized control of multiple agent stations
from a single master station
- Delivers a 100% visual interface for creating client/server multimachine tests through a point-and-click interface — no programming is
required

- Provides an incremental loading option so one can start machines during test execution to vary the system load without programming
- Integrates with SQA Suite, including SQA Robot and SQA Manager, to deliver the one solution for testing cross-Windows client/server and Web applications

System Requirements (Master System).

Memory: 32 Mbytes
Disk Space: 100 Mbytes

System Requirements (Agent System).

PC with 486 processor; Pentium processor recommended
For GUI playback: Microsoft Windows 3.x, Windows NT, or Windows 95
For Web Virtual User recording playback: Windows NT 4.0
Networks: Native support for TCP/IP, IPX/SPX, NetBIOS/NetBEUI

Platforms Supported.

Windows NT 4.0
Windows 95

Rational's Visual Test (Version 4.0r)

Product Description. Visual Test is an automated testing tool that brings new levels of productivity to developers and testers and makes it easier for organizations to deploy mission-critical applications for the Microsoft Windows 95 and Windows NT operating systems and for the World Wide Web. Visual Test helps developers create tests for applications of virtually any size and created with any development tool. Visual Test is integrated with Microsoft Developer Studio, a desktop development environment, and has extensive integration with Microsoft Visual C++.

Product Features.

- Provides language independent testing of 32-bit Windows applications, components, and dynamically linked libraries
- Automates the repetitive tasks of regression testing
- Uses TestBasic, a powerful automated test programming language, which enables one to develop reusable, maintainable, and extendible test assets
- Includes the Suite Manager so that from a single point one can organize tests and collect test results
- Offers redistributable components so that the tests designed and developed by QA engineers are redistributable, providing maximum cost effectiveness

- Tests for control existence and location, retrieves property values, and allows updating of properties providing thorough testing of the application's OLE controls (OCXs) and ActiveX controls
- Supports special procedures that allow one to distribute and monitor testing tasks across a network
- Provides Microsoft Test 3.0 for testing of 16-bit Windows applications running in any Windows environment

System Requirements.

A CD-ROM drive
VGA or higher-resolution video adapter
Microsoft mouse or compatible pointing device
Optional: NetBIOS-compatible network
8 Mb of memory for Windows 95
12 Mb for Windows NT workstation (16 Mb recommended)
16 Mb for Windows NT workstation on RISC (20 Mb recommended)
15 Mb of available hard-disk space
Personal computer with a 386DX/25 or higher processor or a Digital
     Alpha running Microsoft Windows 95 or Windows NT workstation
     3.51 or later operating system

Platforms Supported.

Microsoft Windows 95
Windows NT

Rational's preVue Tool

Product Description. With preVue, Rational offers enterprise-wide testing solutions. Products and services are provided that reduce risk, lower costs, and increase user satisfaction when deploying applications for client/server, X Window, ASCII, and Web environments.

The newest release of the preVue product line, release 5.0, offers graphical analysis capabilities, client/server support for load testing, and the new preVue-Web extension. preVue-Web allows performance testing of the WW server with thousands of Web users.

preVue-C/S applies heavy user loads to database servers and application servers to give accurate performance and scalability data. Understanding system limitations and pinpointing potential breakpoints before they are seen by end users is only possible when a real-life user load is applied to a server.

preVue-Web records HTTP traffic, downloaded Java applets, user think-time, number of bytes received, connects and disconnects generated by any browser, running on any platform. By not requiring any recording software to be installed on the client browser or server machines, the traffic recorded can be used to generate heavy user loads against a Web server even as the environment changes. preVue-Web can record Internet and intranet application traffic from any Windows, Windows 95, Windows NT, MacOS, OS/2 or UNIX system. preVue-Web software is supported on all major UNIX platforms and Windows NT.

preVue-X automates both GUI regression testing and load testing for X Window applications and does not require special hooks into the application or X libraries.

The tool operates at the X protocol level, between the X server and the X client applications. It operates independently from the graphical user interface (Open Look, Motif, CDE, etc.), toolkits, and network.

preVue-ASCII (Version 5.0) is a remote terminal emulator (RTE) that replicates users running applications on a system under test (SUT). preVue-ASCII automates multiuser testing of the applications by replacing both users and physical devices with software scripts that deliver an accurate workload of user activity. It measures the quality and performance of the applications under large user loads.

Product Features.

(preVue-C/S Features)
- Emulates 2-tier and 3-tier network traffic
- SQL, HTTP, and Tuxedo traffic is captured and automatically turned into client-emulation scripts
- Supports testing of Oracle, Sybase, Informix, and SQL Server databases
- Presentation-quality data analysis tools
- Real-time test monitoring
- Server response time measured under varying user loads
- Integrated reporting with performance monitoring tools
- Easily varies the user workload during playback
- Tests are independent of client operating system and hardware environment

(preVue-Web Features)
- Measures Web server response times under large user loads
- Automatically captures and plays back HTTP traffic and downloading of Java applets
- Accurately emulates and time stamps concurrent responses to multiple HTTP requests
- Provides emulation of users of any Web browser, running on any client platform
- Supported on all major UNIX platforms and Windows NT
- Integrates with preVue-C/S to test both database and Web servers

(preVue-X Features)
- A single tool for both GUI and performance testing
- Nonintrusive approach lets one "test what you ship"
- Tests all versions of UNIX, X server, GUI tool kits, etc.
- Automatically generates test scripts reproducing user inputs and system responses

(preVue-ASCII Features)
- Cost-effectively and accurately emulates large user loads
- Tests any screen-based application in any operating system environment
- Measures the user's perception of performance–response times at the user's terminal
- Automatically generates test scripts reproducing user inputs and system responses
- Provides the realism of actual users, yet tests are reproducible
- Support on all major UNIX platforms
- Uncovers quality and performance problems with new software releases before the users see them
- Determines how the applications perform with new system hardware or software upgrades
- Verifies the quality of applications following Year 2000 code changes
- Tests the capacity of the current system as the number of users increases

System Requirements.

N/A

Platforms Supported.

UNIX
Windows NT

Rational's PureCoverage Tool

Product Description. PureCoverage is a code coverage analysis tool that helps developers and quality assurance engineers identify untested code. With patented Object Code Insertion technology (OCI), PureCoverage will check all parts of an application, including source code, third-party libraries and DLLs, shared or system libraries and DLLs, for code that has or has not been executed under test. PureCoverage provides accurate and complete code coverage information needed to evaluate tests and pinpoint parts of a program that are not being exercised in testing.

Product Features.

- Detects untested code with or without source code

- Detects untested code everywhere in UNIX applications
  - C and C++ source code
  - Third-party libraries
  - Shared or system libraries
- Detects untested code everywhere in Windows applications
  - C and C++, Visual Basic, and Java source code
  - ActiveX, DirectX, OLE, and COM components
  - Dynamic Link Libraries (DLLs)
  - Third-party DLLs
  - Windows operating system code
- Provides detailed coverage data per
  - Function
  - Line
  - Basic block
  - Application
  - File
  - Library
  - Directory
- Intuitive Displays
  - Outline view for efficient browsing of summary coverage information
  - Customizable views control data displayed and sorting criteria
  - Point-and-click access to line-by-line coverage data via an Annotated Source view
- Robust reporting mechanism includes ability to
  - Merge data over multiple runs and dynamically update coverage statistics
  - Merge data from multiple applications sharing common code
  - Generate difference reports between multiple runs or executables
  - Generate difference and low threshold reports
  - Email nightly coverage data to development and testing teams
  - Export data suitable for spreadsheets
- Integrated development solution with
  - Purify for run-time error detection in UNIX environments
  - ClearDDTS in UNIX environments for immediate coverage reporting with PureCoverage output
  - Microsoft Visual Studio in the Windows NT environment

Platforms Supported.

UNIX
- Sun SPARC workstations running SunOS 4.x, Solaris 2.3 - 2.6 HP9000 Series 700/800 workstations running HP-UX 9.0.x through 10.30
- Intel architecture only

Windows NT

- Windows NT 3.51 or above
- Visual C++ 2.2 or above
- Visual Basic 5.0 or above
- Java applications run through the Microsoft Virtual Machine for Java

Rational's Purify Tool

Product Description. Purify is a C and C++ run-time error and memory leak detection tool, using patented Object Code Insertion technology (OCI). It checks all application code, including source code, third-party libraries and DLLs, shared or system libraries and DLLs. Developers and quality assurance engineers can identify and eliminate run-time problems in all parts of their applications. Purify is available on both UNIX and Windows NT platforms.

Product Features.

- Pinpoints run-time errors with or without source code
- Detects errors everywhere in UNIX applications
  - C and C++ source code
  - Third-party libraries
  - Shared or system libraries
- Detects errors everywhere in Windows applications
  - C and C++ source code
  - ActiveX, DirectX, OLE, and COM components
  - Dynamic Link Libraries (DLLs)
  - Third-party DLLs
  - Windows operating system code
- Error checking categories include
  - Heap-related errors
  - Stack-related errors
  - Memory leaks
  - Windows handle leaks
  - Windows COM-related errors
  - Windows API errors
- Intuitive Display
  - Outline view for efficient error message browsing
  - Color support for identifying critical errors quickly
  - Detailed reports include stack trace and source line display
  - Point-and-click access to source code for editing
- Advanced Debugging Capabilities
  - Pinpoints bug origin by stack trace and source line number
  - Just-In-Time Debugging quickly isolates errors with the debugger
  - Filters and suppressions provide control over error-checking data
- Integrated development solution with:

- Most common UNIX debugging tools
- Microsoft Visual Studio development environment

Platforms Supported.

UNIX
- Sun SPARC workstations running SunOS 4.x, Solaris 2.3 - 2.6
- HP9000 Series 700/800 workstations running HP-UX 9.0.x through 10.30
- SGI workstations running IRIX 5.3, 6.2, 6.3 and 6.4

Windows NT
- Intel architecture only
- Windows NT 3.51 or above
- Visual C++ 2.2 or above

Rational's Quantify Tool

Product Description. Quantify is a performance analysis tool that gives developers a way to identify application performance bottlenecks. Using Rational's patented Object Code Insertion (OCI) technology, Quantify counts the individual machine instruction cycles it takes to execute an application and records the exact amount of time the application spends in any given block of code.

Product Features.

- Pinpoints performance bottlenecks in all parts of an application, including user functions, system calls, shared and third-party libraries
- Detects performance problems everywhere in UNIX applications
  - C and C++ source code
  - Third-party libraries
  - Shared or system libraries
- Detects performance problems everywhere in Windows applications:
  - C and C++, Visual Basic and Java source code
  - ActiveX, DirectX, OLE, and COM components
  - Dynamic Link Libraries (DLLs)
  - Third-party DLLs
  - Windows operating system code
- Presents performance data in graphical displays
- Offers multiple, complementary views of performance data
- Collects per-thread performance data
- Automatically compares runs for fast verification of performance improvements

Platforms Supported.

UNIX

253

- Sun SPARC workstations running SunOS 4.x, Solaris 2.3 - 2.6
- HP9000 Series 700/800 workstations running HP-UX 9.0.x through 10.30

Windows NT
- Intel architecture only
- Windows NT 3.51 or above
- Visual C++ 2.2 or above
- Visual Basic 5.0 or above
- Java applications run through the Microsoft Virtual Machine for Java

Technology Builders' Caliber–RBT

Product Description. Caliber–RBT is a software testing tool that validates requirements by identifying all functional variations and logical inconsistencies. It determines the necessary test cases by providing complete coverage of the functional requirements defined. It manages the test library by providing functional requirement coverage analysis and archiving both new and existing test definition libraries. It also aids in project management by providing quantitative measurements of the testing process.

The use of Caliber–RBT does not require that the user have good specifications. In the past, the company has analyzed only two projects that had good specs, and issues were found even in those. The use of Caliber–RBT and the supporting Requirements Based Testing (RBT) process drives the clarification of the application rules.

Typically, one is dealing with high-level (not testable) requirements and more detail in the design documents. However, the information in the design documents is not generally readable by the subject matter experts (SMEs). Caliber–RBT is used to clean up the wording. The SMEs review the test cases and the Caliber–RBT-generated Functional Specification. Since it is known that the set of tests generated by Caliber–RBT are mathematically equivalent to the original source material, any issue the SMEs find with the tests is really an issue with the specifications. Even where the specifications are fairly good, it has been found that the tests are easier to review than the specifications.

The algorithms used by Caliber–RBT are based on those used by engineers in testing integrated circuits. This lends strong, proven rigor to the test case design process. It also results in highly optimized test libraries — and more functional coverage for fewer test cases. In head-to-head comparisons, the tool generally covers twice as much function in half the test cases — a four-to-one reduction for equivalent coverage. Caliber–RBT also tells one where to insert diagnostic probe points in the code to ensure that one is receiving the right answer for the right reason.

The coverage facility in Caliber–RBT is the equivalent of a code coverage monitor. Code coverage monitors tell one the percent and number of statements and branches executed. The tool reports the percent of functions tested.

The functional coverage facility is used to plan the testing effort. If time is limited, it might not be possible to run all the tests prior to production startup. In such cases, one can determine which subsets provide the most coverage for the fewest tests. Of course, testing would continue after production starts. However, one can maximize the testing within the time and resource constraints.

A factor often overlooked in selecting testing tools is the synergy between them. For example, the best-selling test tools by far are the capture playback tools. However, they also represent the largest volume of "shelfware" once people realize how much work it is to build and maintain the test scripts. There are two issues to deal with. The first is that, as long as the specifications keep changing, one cannot finalize the scripts. Either this happens too late to code the scripts or the cost of scrap and rework is too great. Caliber–RBT and the RBT process stabilize the specifications in a timely manner. The second issue is the effort to code the scripts. It is normally estimated that playback scripting entails at least 3 to 5 times the effort spent on designing the test cases. Caliber–RBT significantly reduces the number of tests, resulting in major savings in the playback scripting effort.

Caliber–RBT also has a significant impact on the acceptability of code coverage monitors. Today, most applications go into production with less than half of the statements and branches having been executed. When people start using coverage monitors, their first pass numbers are usually around 30%, or even less. The tool gives them bad news. People do not like to use tools that give them bad news, especially bad news that managers will see. They stop using such tools quickly. The test cases generated by Caliber–RBT generally cover 70 to 95% of the code. In other words, people obtain good news from the coverage monitor and are thus more willing to use it.

Product Features.

(Validating Requirements Features)
- The system's functional requirements are defined by an analyst to Caliber–RBT via a series of Cause-Effect Graph statements. Caliber–RBT then translates the input Cause-Effect Graph statements into a set of "functional variations." It combines these functional variations into a suite of logical test cases. These functional variations and test cases can be reviewed by the analyst to verify the completeness and accuracy of the requirements specification vs. the Cause-Effect Graph input.

255

- The product provides feedback in the form of diagnostic messages associated with the functional variations. Further analysis of these diagnostics ensures the quality of the requirements specification in terms of logical consistency, completeness, and lack of ambiguity.

(Verifying the Design and Code Features)
- Caliber–RBT analyzes each individual relation defined by an analyst in order to identify the "functional variations." Functional variations describe all the expected actions of the system (i.e., effects) if it performs per the input specifications (i.e., causes). These functional variations are then reduced to the minimum set of variations necessary to detect a functional error in the software under test. The minimum set of variations are then logically combined into a suite of test case definitions such that each functional variation is covered by at least one of the test cases. This suite of test cases, then, may also be referred to as "the minimum set of tests necessary to detect a functional error in the software."

(Managing Test Cases Features)
- Produces a cross-reference showing which functional variations are covered by each test case. This information is useful in isolating failing functions and in subsetting the test library to test specific functions.
- Can also be used to evaluate the functional coverage achieved using previously existing test libraries. This will typically be used to demonstrate that Caliber–RBT will achieve more coverage using fewer tests.
- Can also be used to generate the supplemental tests necessary to bring a previously existing test library up to full functional coverage. This allows Caliber–RBT to specify what additional test cases are required when the previously existing test library was created without the benefit of Caliber–RBT usage, or when a functional change has been made to the specifications for a test library previously created by Caliber–RBT. In other words, one only needs to instrument the supplemental tests in order to update the test library instead of starting over from scratch.

(Project Management Features)
- Provides a quantifiable yardstick, via the functional variations, for measuring the status of the testing effort. For example, a test status report stating that testing is 92% finished is more meaningful than the wishful thinking or speculation that other reports often represent.
- Provides a cost-effective approach to testing. Studies have shown that 56% of all errors have their roots in poorly specified require-

ments. However, 82% of the total cost associated with system errors have their roots in these same requirements. The cost difference between detecting an error in the requirements at the time of writing them (call it x) vs. detecting an error after the system is in production has been measured at 270x.

- Allows the project manager the option of accelerating the project when faced with tight schedules. This is possible because the testing effort can be performed in parallel with the analysis, design, and coding efforts. Also, earlier detection of errors will minimize the costly and time-consuming rework effort associated with errors not detected until the end of the development cycle.

System Requirements.

The 16-bit version of Caliber–RBT Release 5.3 requires Microsoft Windows 3.1x running on a "386" (or, preferably, faster)-based machine.

The 32-bit version of Caliber–RBT Release 5.3 runs twice as fast as the 16-bit version and requires Microsoft Windows 9x or NT running on a "486" (or, preferably, much faster)-based machine.

Disk space — 6 megabytes (additional disk space will be required for user data files).

Platforms Supported.

Microsoft Windows 3.1x
Microsoft Windows 9x
Microsoft Windows NT
While a specific OS/2 version of the code is not available, clients do have Caliber–RBT under OS/2. A special install procedure has been put together to make this easier.

AutoTester's Test Library Manager

Product Description. Test Library Manager provides a long-term solution to the issues of analysis, management, and maintenance of an automated test library. Serving as a central repository on a network, Test Library Manager consolidates the application tests and results for simplified access and greater control. With Test Library Manager, one can preserve test integrity through centralized change and version control, perform global modifications to tests based on application changes, and accumulate results for effective test analysis.

Test Station and Test Library Manager work in tandem to give one an automated testing solution for a character-based PC, midrange, and mainframe applications. Test Station is an integrated environment that allows virtually anyone to develop, document, and execute a comprehensive automated test library. Test Library Manager is a central repository for your test library components which provides change and version control and global maintenance for tests across an entire application development life cycle.

Product Features.

- Change and Version Control — Through user access rights and standard change control procedures, one controls access to the test library and monitors any changes made and who makes them. Change control logs document all activity for a complete audit trail. For testing multiple releases of applications, Test Library Manager stores corresponding versions of test files for quick access.
- Simplified Maintenance — Centralized control means simplified maintenance. The inevitable modifications which need to be made to the test files are handled through Test Library Manager. Test library components can be modified using the Test Library Manager's built-in editors. Search and replace facilities provide global editing of data values across selected tests or your entire library.

  When tests must be modified due to changes in your application screens and fields, Test Library Manager automatically identifies the affected tests, thus eliminating time-consuming review of the test files.
- Analysis and Reporting — Test Library Manager's current and historical reporting capabilities give one quick access to consolidated test results whenever needed. For an analysis of testing over the life of an application, Test Library Manager stores cumulative results including: change logs for tracking all modifications made to the test library, test and error logs for assessing system failure rates over time, and host response logs for monitoring system performance over time
- Customized reporting options allow one to review and analyze only the data which is critical to the tester. In addition, test results can be exported for use with other tools including text editors, spreadsheets, or databases for further analysis.

System Requirements (Test Library Manager).

IBM PC 386 or 100% compatible machines
MS-DOS or PC-DOS 5.0 or higher
1.5 Megabytes minimum storage requirements

System Requirements.

(Windows 3.X)
IBM PC-386 or greater and 100% compatibles
4 Megabytes minimum memory plus Windows system requirements

10 Megabytes minimum disk storage

Supports Wall Data Rumba (DOS version only), DCA Irma, Attachmate Extra! and IBM (DOS version only) PC3270 terminal emulation

(Windows 95 and Windows NT)

IBM PC-486 or greater and 100% compatibles

4 Megabytes minimum memory plus Windows 95 or Windows NT
system requirements (V.4x only; V3.51 not supported)

8 Megabytes minimum disk storage per installed copy

(OS/2):

IBM PC-486 or greater and 100% compatibles

4 Megabytes minimum memory plus OS/2 system requirements

10 Megabytes minimum disk storage

Supports IBM OS/2 Communications Manager terminal emulation

Platforms Supported.

Windows 3.1x
Windows 95
Windows NT
OS/2 LAN MGr
Novell 3.12

AutoTester's Test Station Tool

Product Description. AutoTester Test Station is designed specifically to
help increase the quality of character-based PC and host applications. AutoTester provides capture/replay style test creation, yet stores the tests as
well-documented, easily maintainable, object-aware tests. The product includes an easy-to-use menu-driven interface as well as a powerful command set for advanced scripting needs.

Test Station and Test Library Manager work in tandem to provide automated testing solutions for character-based PCs, midrange, and mainframe
applications. Test Station is an integrated environment that allows virtually anyone to develop, document, and execute a comprehensive automated
test library. Test Library Manager is a central repository for the test library
components that provide change and version control and global maintenance for tests across an entire application development life cycle.

Product Features.

- Flexible Test Capture — Lets one build consistent, documented tests
  that can be used over the life of the application from tester to tester

and release to release. With Test Station, tests can be captured at any point in the software development process.

- Unattended Test Execution — Tests are intelligent scripts which provide dynamic verification of application responses against expected results, duplicating expectations and decision points. When unexpected application responses occur during test execution, the tests identify those responses and react accordingly. Recovery options log the details of application failures and then continue the testing process if possible. In addition, Test Station's playback synchronization provides proper test playback regardless of system performance.
- Reusability and Maintainability — Helps one develop an automated test library that can be easily modified to account for new or different application behavior over time. For ease of maintenance, tests can be edited while in the application and then executed immediately, or they can be edited off-line with Test Station or any text editor.
- Documentation and Reporting — Each step of every test is automatically documented in English for ease of understanding. Tests are identified with detailed descriptions, test case numbers, and test requirement identifiers for cross-reference purposes. After test execution, detailed results are available online or in report format for immediate review and analysis.
- Scripting — Includes the AutoTester Scripting Language. Designed to supplement the capabilities of Test Station, this language is a command set which can accommodate unique testing needs and provide general task automation functionality.

System Requirements.

(Test Station)
> IBM PC 386 or 100% compatible machines
> MS-DOS or PC-DOS 5.0 or higher
> 326K conventional memory or 30K with LIM 4.0 compliant expanded memory manager or DPMI 0.9 compliant extended memory manager
> 10 Megabytes minimum storage requirements
> Supports most network terminal emulation and communications protocols, including IBM 3270, IBM 5250 (AS400), Hewlett-Packard 2392, Tandem 6530 and Unisys

(Windows 3.X)
> IBM PC-386 or greater and 100% compatibles
> 4 Megabytes minimum memory plus Windows system requirements
> 10 Megabytes minimum disk storage

Supports Wall Data Rumba (Office 2.1A) and Attachmate Extra! V4.3A terminal emulation

(Windows 95 and Windows NT-16-BIT)
IBM PC-486 or greater and 100% compatibles
4 Megabytes minimum memory plus Windows 95 or Windows NT system requirements (V4.x, V3.51 not supported)
8 Megabytes minimum disk storage per installed copy

(OS/2): 2.11 and OS/2 warp
IBM PC-486 or greater and 100% compatibles
4 Megabytes minimum memory plus OS/2 system requirements
10 Megabytes minimum disk storage
Supports IBM OS/2 Communications Manager terminal emulation

Platforms Supported.

Windows 3.1x
Windows 95
Windows NT — V4.x local testing 16-BIT applications only. No emulation supported.

Mercury Interactive's TestDirector Test Management Tool

Product Description. TestDirector™ helps corporate IS personnel plan and organize the testing process. With TestDirector one can create a database of manual and automated tests, build test cycles, execute tests, and report and track bugs. One can also create reports and graphs to help review the progress of test planning, execution, and bug tracking before a software release.

When working with WinRunner, one has the option of creating tests and saving them directly in the TestDirector database. One can also execute tests in WinRunner and then use TestDirector to review the overall results of a test cycle.

TestDirector provides test management for planning, executing, and communicating quality control during the entire development process. TestDirector allows testers to translate business processes into a test plan that acts as a central point of control for all aspects of the test. With the flexibility to support both manual and automated testing, TestDirector is scalable to keep hundreds of users informed of project status.

Product Features.

(Test Planning Features)
• Intuitive user interface can be used easily by a broad range of users

261

- Both manual and automated tests are organized in the same visual, hierarchical tree
- Quick access folders allow for easy navigation through the test plan
- Test plan steps are converted automatically to WinRunner test templates
- Existing documents in other formats — Microsoft Word, Microsoft Excel, and others — can be included in TestDirector's repository
- Complete control over access privileges for both groups and individuals

(Scalable Architecture Features)
- Collaborative groupware provides access to all tests and defects with TestDirector's central repository
- Single repository for all test data supports industry-standard databases
- Complete control over access privileges

(Test Execution Features)
- Integration with WinRunner provides support for automated testing within the TestDirector environment
- Batch or individual tests are automatically launched from TestDirector; test results are then reported immediately back to TestDirector's repository
- All tests are clearly labeled as manual or automated
- Testers are guided step-by-step through manual tests, while allowing users to report actual behaviors, compare them to expected results, and report each step as passed or failed as they perform each test step
- Defect reports can be created at any point during test execution, importing information such as actual and expected results to the defect report
- Failures of automated tests show the exact place where the error occurred

(Defect Tracking Features)
- Defect reports include complete information, including the exact way to reproduce the problem, who in the development group has responsibility for correcting the problem, and where the defect occurred
- Remote Defect Reporter allows external users, such as off-site beta testers, to report defects using the same structure
- Remote users are automatically notified of changes in the status of relevant defect reports
- Defects are associated with the phase of the defect life cycle, the tests which produced them, and the application function where they occurred

Reporting and Analysis
- Fully-customizable reports using ReportSmith, Crystal Reports, Microsoft Excel, and other third-party reporting tools are supported
- Reports can be invoked at any stage of the testing process
- Extensive built-in reports can be filtered by subject, status, assignment, history, designer, and more

System Requirements.

Minimum 16 MB RAM
Minimum 40 MB disk space

Platforms Supported.

Oracle
Sybase
Microsoft SQL Server
Microsoft Access

Mercury Interactive's WinRunner Functional Testing Tool for Windows

Product Description. WinRunner® provides a way to test client/server GUI applications, and with WinRunner's RapidTest™ scripting, new testers can overcome the initial barriers to test automation by giving the test script development process instant momentum. Application testers and developers can now get high-quality software without compromising on-time deployment for Windows, Windows 95, and Windows NT.

RapidTest automatically creates a full suite of GUI tests from the application. RapidTest gets users started fast — instead of requiring users to create their first set of tests manually — they can use a Wizard to create test scripts directly from the application.

Today, test automation has successfully replaced manual test execution with automated test execution. But when it comes to building the automated tests, most conventional testing tools still rely exclusively on one-line-at-a-time scripting techniques like programming and object-oriented recording. These conventional tools merely transferred the burden from manual testing to manual test development.

Product Features.

(Visually Integrated Scripting Features)
- Visual testing for powerful, flexible test creation productivity
- Interpreted development workspace with test script interpreter and multiple document interface for simple management of script development

263

- Powerful script language to test everything needed to test
- Exception handling with built-in routines for automatic recovery
- Powerful script debugger to quickly "test" and fix scripts when problems occur
- Flexible verification to know exactly if the application is working or not
- New visual reporting that integrates high-level summary reports with detailed records for every test verification result, in a new, interactive reporting tool

(Script Mapping Features)
- Handles application changes automatically, using Script Mapping for Adaptable and Reusable Tests
- Learns the application hierarchy, organizing objects by window. It also handles independent GUI maps for separate applications simultaneously, and can invoke them automatically during testing.
- GUI map provides a single point of control for multiple tests by updating one attribute of an object in the map — its effect updates all scripts automatically.
- Includes an interactive editing tool for viewing or modifying the map file. Users can choose which attributes to track for which objects, and what to name the objects in the test script, affording flexibility for defining how WinRunner looks for and identifies application objects.

(Custom Control Features)
- Integrated object support for major development tools and industry-standard controls
- Open API for custom controls to enable users to define their own testing support for objects
- Analog recording and text recognition as an alternative for verification

(Powerful Client/Server GUI Test Automation)
- Provides a new, fully documented open testing API, enabling users to create full automated testing support for custom objects — capture, replay, and verification
- Supports point-to-point mouse movements, bitmap comparisons, or bitmapped test based on fixed window coordinates
- Can automate tests that depend on movement between fixed window coordinates, such as in graphical or drawing programs and programs that do not have GUI objects
- Text recognition makes it possible to read text displayed by these objects as alphanumeric data and provides the ability to perform key test operations when hooks are not available to retrieve text data from displayed objects.

System Requirements.

Minimum 16 MB RAM
Minimum 16 MB disk space

Platforms Supported.

Windows 95
Windows NT

Mercury Interactive's XRunner Functional Testing Tool for UNIX

Product Description. XRunner® offers a tool set for GUI test automation. Its fully integrated Visual Testing™ environment incorporates simplified test script management, point-and-click selection, interactive debugging, etc. To help one get started, XRunner's Script Wizard learns the application by navigating its way through all available UI paths to create a complex test script suite. With XRunner, one is guaranteed that GUI application testing is fast, reliable, and complete across all UNIX platforms.

XRunner extends a set of automated testing utilities to ensure GUI, reducing the time and expertise needed for creating, running, and maintaining automated tests. XRunner runs on all UNIX platforms and may be ported for testing across multiple environments such as Microsoft's Windows 3.x, Window 95, and Windows NT. One can develop a test once on one platform and replay it on another for added versatility.

Product Features.

(Automated GUI Regression Testing Features)
- XRunner runs on all UNIX platforms and may be ported for testing across multiple environments
- RapidTest™ Script Wizard automatically learns the entire application and generates tests for unattended regression testing
- Visual Testing environment for combining object-oriented recording
- Point-and-click test generation and test script logic into a single environment
- Flexible verification and replay options
- Sophisticated reporting tools
- Portability across multiple platforms and more

(Automatic Test Generation Features)
- A GUI regression test that captures a baseline checkpoint of GUI attributes for every window that opens
- A bitmap regression test that compares bitmaps between versions by creating a screen capture for every window that opens

265

- A user interface (UI) test that checks adherence to X Window UI conventions for every window that opens
- A template test that creates a test framework for future use

(Fully Integrated Scripting Environment Features)
- Provides flexibility to create test scripts as one uses the application and offers point-and-click, recording and programming
- Recording actions performed on a widget, such as selecting an item from a list or pressing a specific button, XRunner records a context-sensitive test script. XRunner is smart enough to select the item or press the button even when the UI changes.
- XRunner also supports analog test scripts when the tests are dependent upon movements between fixed window coordinates and do not have individual GUI objects. An analog test script will replay exact mouse movements or clicks and keystrokes, such as clicking the left mouse button.
- One can also use the programming method when enhancing tests created by recording, adding loops for flow control, setting and using variables, using conditional branching, filtering, and report messaging. XRunner's Test Script Language (TSL) is based on the C programming language with added testing functions. By implementing the programming test method, users can tailor their tests to meet specific functions.
- XRunner's test script interpreter provides test development power, since it supports simultaneous point-and-click test development, recording of user operations, and enhanced test script programming.
- To create the best possible script based on the testing requirements, XRunner fully supports mixing test script methods rather than requiring one to use them separately. It also provides an interactive debugger that enables one to "test the tests" for optimal performance.

(Flexible Verification Features)
- Using a point-and-click verification method of selecting the objects on the screen, one chooses the type of checkpoint to insert in the test script.
- Text recognition is a verification option exclusive to XRunner.
- XRunner is the only tool with a complete Optical Character Recognition (OCR) engine to recognize text, such as checking console windows for error messages.
- XRunner can also verify images, objects, files, and tables. For example, XRunner supports tables in Oracle Developer/2000 applications.
- Likewise, XRunner provides open systems extensions that will allow one to launch shell scripts, system utilities, and tools.

- XRunner can also verify Motif programs using WidgetLint, a set of verification functions used to test Motif applications. XRunner detects widget color and attachment problems, as well as any unmanaged widgets to help one effectively debug Motif applications. Its open API allows one to implement WidgetLint verification functions.

(Enhanced Replay Modes)
- XRunner provides several test script replay modes. Built-in automatic and custom synchronization allows one to run tests unattended to maximize the application development time.
- In addition, XRunner can run in background mode, freeing up the workstation during the day. One can continue writing code while XRunner executes test scripts.
- Provides exception handling to keep test execution on track. Exception handling offers automatic built-in recovery including
  - Overcoming unexpected conditions and resuming test execution without halting the test
  - Invoking a series of procedures to dismiss unexpected objects
  - Rewinding test script execution to a previous step
  - Navigating elsewhere in the application
  - Recording errors in the test log along with steps taken to resume testing
  - Exiting the test when encountering certain surprise conditions
- XRunner also enables one to define error recovery routines to ensure reliable replay and keep tests from coming to an abrupt halt.

(Interactive Reporting Tool Features)
- XRunner's interactive reporting tool combines a high-level view with detailed statistics about what bugs were found by the test and where.
- Includes the ability to drill down errors into greater detail, pinpointing the exact line in a test script. Both graphical and textual reports chart the testing results for further analysis.
- Interactive reporting identifies bugs that were found by the test, both in summary and in detail. A color-coded tree shows all executed tests along with their results.

(Script Mapping Features)
- XRunner handles application changes automatically, using Script Mapping for Adaptable, Reusable Tests (SMARTest), which automatically maintains object-specific data independent of individual scripts.
- XRunner's SMARTest monitors GUI application changes automatically so that the tests will run correctly.

- Automatically creates a SMARTest GUI map for the tested application. When SMARTest learns the application hierarchy, it captures key application attributes and organizes objects hierarchically, window by window. SMARTest guarantees test scripts will work correctly when the application changes without requiring rework.

(Portability Features)
- XRunner's TSL is designed to port tests across all UNIX and Microsoft Windows (Windows 3.x, Windows NT, Windows 95) platforms.
- It provides a scalable load testing solution for managing the risks of client/server systems.

System Requirements.

16MB minimum RAM
Approximately 100 MB disk space

Platforms Supported.

UNIX

Mercury Interactive's LoadRunner Load/Stress Testing Tool

Product Description. LoadRunner® is an integrated client, server, and Web load testing tool. It provides a scalable load testing solution for managing the risks of client/server systems. Using a minimum of hardware resources, LoadRunner provides consistent, repeatable, and measurable load to exercise a system. It exercises the client, server, and Web system just as real users do. It contains a single point of control for client, server, and Web load testing and supports hundreds or even thousands of virtual users.

By automating both client and server load testing from a single point of control, LoadRunner helps developers get an accurate view of system behavior and performance throughout the application development life cycle.

Product Features.

(Client Load Testing Features)
- Exercises the system, driving real applications through the virtual clients simultaneously from a single point of control
- Includes an integrated set of new load testing components: Virtual User Generator, ScenarioWizard, Visual Controller, and Load Analyzer
- Synchronizes all virtual users to create peak loads, pinpoint bottlenecks, and isolate problems
- Records test scripts automatically at GUI, SQL, Web, and terminal levels
- Aids in isolating problems at client, server, and network level

(Server Load Testing Features)
- Supports both two-tier and three-tier client/server architectures
- Generates an abstract data file of virtual users for nonprogrammers
- Generates a C code file of virtual users for programmers
- Verifies data retrieved from the server
- Supports multiple client/server protocols

(Data Analysis Features)
- Presents graphs and reports for analyzing load testing data
- Compares data across platform configurations and virtual users to help isolate and pinpoint problems
- Displays both code and GUI
- Measures performance "end-to-end" from client through application server and to the database
- Handles GUI changes automatically by maintaining scripts at object level

(Web Load Testing Features)
- Supports HTTP, HTML and Java applets
- Defines transactions automatically for individual and groups of HTTP messages
- Supports GET, POST, CGI messages
- Creates test scripts by recording the actions of a user or user groups surfing a Web site
- Determines the maximum number of concurrent users a Web site can handle

(RTE Load Testing Features)
- Records user interactions with character-based applications to create test scripts
- Inserts synchronization points automatically on unique text or cursor positions on the screen
- Generates a log file for debugging scripts and scenarios
- Replays RTE virtual user sessions just like a movie recording
- Verifies values as defined by row, column, or screen while server is under peak data conditions from the server visually with an online server monitor
- Exports data to standard formats (Microsoft Word, Microsoft Excel, Lotus 1-2-3, email, etc.)

System Requirements.

Controller
    32 MB RAM
    70 MB disk space
Virtual Users
    Minimum 2 MB per virtual user

256 MB/100 virtual users
Disk space: 10 MB each

Platforms Supported.

Windows 3.x
Windows NT
Windows 95
Sun OS, Solaris, HP-UX, IBM AIX, NCR

Client/Server Protocols Supported.

SQL: Oracle OCI, Oracle UPI, Sybase dbLib, Sybase CtLib, Informix
    I-NET
ODBC
TP Monitors: Tuxedo
Messaging: WinSocket
Web: HTTP, Java
Character-based: TTY, IBM 5250, IBM 3270
Applications: SAP R/3, Oracle Financials, PeopleSoft, Baan

Mercury Interactive's Astra Site Manager Web Site Management Tool

Product Description. Astra SiteManager™ is a comprehensive, visual Web site management tool designed to meet the challenges faced by Webmasters and business managers of rapidly growing Web sites with changing contents and shapes. Astra SiteManager scans the entire Web site, highlighting functional areas with color-coded links and URLs, to unfold a complete visual map of the site. It pinpoints broken links or access problems, compares maps as the site changes, identifies key usage patterns for improving Web site effectiveness, and validates dynamically generated pages.

Mercury Interactive's Astra SiteManager offers a single solution for gaining control of the Web site. From one page to the entire Web site, Astra SiteManager automatically scans and creates a visual map of the sites' URLs and their connections. This visual map includes all Web objects — Common Gateway Interface (CGI) scripts, Java applets, and HTML. Unlike other products which create complicated tree displays, Astra SiteManager maps the entire site in an easy-to-read format with map properties and helpful URL statistics. If one needs to focus on specific components, one can zoom in to find the information needed.

Product Features.

(Visual Web Display Features)
• View an entire Web site on screen

- Select from a variety of navigational options including zoom-in, zoom-out, window panning, instant focus, and moving viewpoint
- Invoke filters for hiding irrelevant URLs when trouble-shooting or creating what-if scenarios
- Print all Astra SiteManager map information for off-line work
- Choose textual view using split-screen display

(Action Tracking Features)
- Display usage patterns for instant analysis and Web site optimization
- Evaluate how users navigate the site using color-coded arrows and numerical statistics
- View hits per path

(Link Analysis Features)
- Detect broken links or pages quickly and easily
- Repair broken links instantly using any HTML editor, Netscape Navigator Gold or Notepad
- Select an updated link table to confirm that links are repaired
- Graphically compare previous Web site layouts to monitor all new, updated, deleted, or modified URLsDynamic

(Scanning Features)
- See and validate pages that are generated on the fly
- Map not only static links, but dynamically generated pages that represent information contained in a database or obtained in real-time
- Ensure new transactions are working properly and database connectivity is maintained for better customer service

(Plug-in API Features)
- Use Java, C++, or Visual Basic to create additional plug-in modules for specific Web management needs or authoring tool environments
- Integrate Astra SiteManager into the software applications

System Requirements.

486 or Pentium-based machine
6 MB RAM minimum
5 MB hard disk space
TCP/IP dial-up or LAN connection
Any Web browser (Netscape Navigator, Microsoft Internet Explorer, etc.)
Access to organization's Web site and one of its log files is preferred, but not required

Platforms Supported.

Windows 95
Windows NT 3.51 or 4.0

Part 21
Methodology to Evaluate Testing Tools

This part provides an outline of the steps involved in acquiring, implementing, and using testing tools. The management of any significant project requires that the work be divided into tasks for which completion criteria can be defined. The transition from one task to another occurs in steps; to permit the orderly progress of the activities, the scheduling of these steps must be determined in advance. A general outline for such a schedule is provided by the steps described. The actual time schedule depends on many factors that must be determined for each specific tool use.

STEP 1: DEFINE TEST GOALS

The goals to be accomplished should be identified in a format that permits later determination that they have been met (i.e., step 15). Typical goals include reducing the average processing time of C++ programs by one-fifth, achieving complete interchangeability of programs or data sets with another organization, and adhering to an established standard for documentation format. The statement of goals should also identify responsibilities, particularly the role that headquarters staff may have, and specify coordination requirements with other organizations. When a centralized management method is employed, the statement of goals may include a budget and a desired completion date. Once these constraints are specified, funding management may delegate the approval of the acquisition plan to a lower level.

STEP 2: SET TOOL OBJECTIVES

The goals generated in step 1 should be translated into desired tool features and requirements that arise from the development and operating environment identified. Constraints on tool cost and availability may also be added at this step. For example, a typical tool objective for a program format is to provide header identification, uniform indentation, and the facility to print listings and comments separately for all PASCAL programs. In addition, the program must be able to run on the organization's specific computer under its operating system. Only tools that have been in commercial use for at least one year and at no fewer than N sites should be considered. (The value of N is predetermined by the number of sites the organization has.)

STEP 3A: CONDUCT SELECTION ACTIVITIES FOR INFORMAL PROCUREMENT

The following tasks should be performed when an informal procurement plan is in effect.

Task 1: Develop the Acquisition Plan

The acquisition plan communicates the actions of software management both up and down the chain of command. The plan may also be combined with the statement of tool objectives (step 2). The acquisition plan includes the budgets and schedules for subsequent steps in the tool introduction, a justification of resource requirements in light of expected benefits, contributions to the introduction expected from other organizations (e.g., the tool itself, modification patches, or training materials), and the assignment of responsibility for subsequent events within the organization, particularly the identification of the software engineer. Minimum tool documentation requirements are also specified in the plan.

Task 2: Define Selection Criteria

The selection criteria include a ranked listing of attributes that should support effective tool use. Typical selection criteria include:

- The ability to accomplish specified tool objectives.
- Ease of use.
- Ease of installation.
- Minimum processing time.
- Compatibility with other tools.
- Low purchase or lease cost.

Most of these criteria must be considered further to permit objective evaluation, but this step may be left to the individual who does the scoring. Constraints that have been imposed by the preceding events or are generated at this step should be summarized together with the criteria.

Task 3: Identify Candidate Tools

This is the first step for which the software engineer is responsible. The starting point for preparing a list of candidate tools is a comprehensive tool catalog. Two lists are usually prepared, the first of which does not consider the constraints and contains all tools that meet the functional requirements. For the feasible candidates, literature should be requested from the developer and then examined for conformance with the given constraints. At this point, the second list is generated, which contains tools that meet both the functional requirements and the constraints. If this list is too short, some constraints may be relaxed.

Task 4: Conduct the Candidate Review

The user must review the list of candidate tools prepared by the software engineer. Because few users can be expected to be knowledgeable about software tools, specific questions should be raised by software management, including:

- Will this tool handle the present file format?
- Are tool commands consistent with those of the editor?
- How much training is required?

Adequate time should be allowed for this review, and a due date for responses should be indicated. Because users often view this as a low-priority, long-term task, considerable follow-up by line management is required. If possible, tools should be obtained for trial use, or a demonstration at another facility should be arranged.

Task 5: Score the Candidates

For each criterion identified in task 2, a numeric score should be generated on the basis of the information obtained from the vendor's literature, tool demonstrations, the user's review, observation in a working environment, or the comments of previous users. Once weighting factors for the criteria have been assigned, the score for each criterion is multiplied by the appropriate factor; the sum of the products represents the overall tool score. If the criteria are merely ranked, the scoring will consist of a ranking of each candidate under each criterion heading. Frequently during this process, a single tool will be recognized as clearly superior.

Task 6: Select the Tool

This decision is reserved for software managers: they can provide a review of the scoring and permit additional factors that are not expressed in the criteria to be considered. For example, a report from another agency may state that the selected vendor did not provide adequate service. If the selected tool did not receive the highest score, the software engineer must review the tool characteristics thoroughly to avoid unexpected installation difficulties. (Tool selection concludes the separate procedure for informal procurement. The overall procedure continues with step 4.)

STEP 3B: CONDUCT SELECTION ACTIVITIES FOR FORMAL PROCUREMENT

The following tasks should be performed when a formal tool procurement plan is in effect.

Task 1: Develop the Acquisition Plan

This plan must include all the elements mentioned for task 1 of step 3a, plus the constraints on the procurement process and the detailed responsibilities for all procurement documents (e.g., statement of work and technical and administrative provisions in the request for proposal).

Task 2: Create the Technical Requirements Document

The technical requirements document is an informal description of tool requirements and the constraints under which the tool must operate. It uses much of the material from the acquisition plan but should add enough detail to support a meaningful review by the tool user.

Task 3: Review Requirements

The user must review the technical requirements for the proposed procurement. As in the case of step 3a, task 4, the user may need to be prompted with pertinent questions, and there should be close management follow-up for a timely response.

Task 4: Generate the Request for Proposal

The technical portions of the request for proposal should be generated from the technical requirements document and any user comments on it. Technical considerations typically include:

- A specification of the tool as it should be delivered, including applicable documents, a definition of the operating environment, and the quality assurance provisions.
- A statement of work for which the tool is procured. This includes any applicable standards for the process by which the tool is generated (e.g., configuration management of the tool) and documentation or test reports to be furnished with the tool. Training and operational support requirements are also identified in the statement of work.
- Proposal evaluation criteria and format requirements. These criteria are listed in order of importance. Subfactors for each may be identified. Any restrictions on the proposal format (e.g., major headings, page count, or desired sample outputs) may be included.

Task 5: Solicit Proposals

This activity should be carried out by administrative personnel. Capability lists of potential sources are maintained by most purchasing organizations. When the software organization knows of potential bidders, those bidders' names should be submitted to the procurement office. Responses should be screened for compliance with major legal provisions of the request for proposal.

Task 6: Perform the Technical Evaluation

Each proposal received in response to the request for proposal should be evaluated in light of the previously established criteria. Failure to meet major technical requirements can lead to outright disqualification of a proposal. Those deemed to be in the competitive range are assigned point scores that are then considered together with cost and schedule factors, which are separately evaluated by administrative personnel.

Task 7: Select a Tool Source

On the basis of the combined cost, schedule, and technical factors, a source for the tool is selected. If this is not the highest-rated technical proposal, managers should require additional reviews by software management and the software engineer to determine whether the tool is acceptable. (Source selection concludes the separate procedure for formal procurement. The overall procedure continues with step 4.)

STEP 4: PROCURE THE TESTING TOOL

In addition to verifying that the cost of the selected tool is within the approved budget, the procurement process considers the adequacy of licensing and other contractual provisions and compliance with the fine print associated with all government procurements. The vendor must furnish the source program, meet specific test and performance requirements, and maintain the tool. In informal procurement, a trial period use may be considered if this has not already taken place under one of the previous steps.

If the acquisition plan indicates the need for outside training, the ability of the vendor to supply the training and any cost advantages from the combined procurement of the tool and the training should be investigated. If substantial savings can be realized through simultaneously purchasing the tool and training users, procurement may be held up until outside training requirements are defined (step 7).

STEP 5: CREATE THE EVALUATION PLAN

The evaluation plan is based on the goals identified in step 1 and the tool objectives derived in step 2. It describes how the attainment of these objectives should be evaluated for the specific tool selected. Typical items to be covered in the plan are milestones for installation and dates and performance levels for the initial operational capability and for subsequent enhancements. When improvements in throughput, response time, or turnaround time are expected, the reports for obtaining these data should be identified. Responsibility for tests, reports, and other actions must be assigned in the plan, and a topical outline of the evaluation report should be included.

The acceptance test procedure is part of the evaluation plan, although for a major tool procurement it may be a separate document. The procedure lists the detailed steps that are necessary to test the tool in accordance with the procurement provisions when it is received, to evaluate the interaction of the tool with the computer environment (e.g., adverse effects on throughput), and to generate an acceptance report.

STEP 6: CREATE THE TOOL MANAGER'S PLAN

The tool manager's plan describes how the tool manager is selected, the responsibilities for the adaptation of the tool, and the training that is required. The tool manager should be an experienced systems programmer who is familiar with the current operating system. Training in the operation and installation of the selected tool in the form of review of documentation, visits to the tool's current users, or training by the vendor must be arranged. The software engineer is responsible for the tool manager's plan, and the tool manager should work under the software engineer's direction. The tool manager's plan must be approved by software management.

STEP 7: CREATE THE TRAINING PLAN

The training plan should first consider the training that is automatically provided with the tool (e.g., documentation, test cases, and online diagnostics). These features may be supplemented by standard training aids supplied by the vendor for in-house training (e.g., audio- or videocassettes and lecturers). Because of the expense, training sessions at other locations should be considered only when nothing else is available. The personnel to receive formal training should also be specified in the plan, and adequacy of in-house facilities (e.g., number of terminals and computer time) should be addressed. If training by the tool vendor is desired, this should be identified as early as possible to permit training to be procured along with the tool (see step 4). Users must be involved in the preparation of the training plan; coordination with users is essential. The training plan must be prepared by the software engineer and approved by software management. Portions of the plan must be furnished to the procurement staff if outside personnel or facilities are used.

STEP 8: RECEIVE THE TOOL

The tool is turned over by the procuring organization to the software engineer.

STEP 9: PERFORM THE ACCEPTANCE TEST

The software engineer or staff should test the tool in an as-received condition with only those modifications made that are essential for bringing the tool up on the host computer. Once a report on the test has been issued and approved by the software manager, the tool is officially accepted.

STEP 10: CONDUCT ORIENTATION

When it has been determined that the tool has been received in a satisfactory condition, software management should hold an orientation meeting for all personnel involved in the use of the tool and tool products (e.g., reports or listings generated by the tool). The objectives of tool use (e.g., increased throughput or improved legibility of listings) should be directly communicated. Highlights of the evaluation plan should be presented, and any changes in duties associated with tool introduction should be described. Personnel should be reassured that allowances will be made for problems encountered during tool introduction and reminded that the tool's full benefits may not be realized for some time.

STEP 11: IMPLEMENT MODIFICATIONS

This step is carried out by the tool manager in accordance with the approved tool manager plan. It includes modifications of the tool, the documentation, and the operating system. In rare cases, some modification of the computer (e.g., channel assignments) may also be necessary. Typical tool modifications involve deletion of unused options, changes in prompts or diagnostics, and other adaptations made for efficient use in the current environment. In addition, the modifications must be thoroughly documented.

Vendor literature for the tool should be reviewed in detail and tailored to the current computer environment and to any tool modifications that have been made. Deleting sections that are not applicable is just as useful as adding material that is required for the specific programming environment. Unused options should be clearly marked or removed from the manuals. If the tool should not be used for some resident software (e.g., because of language incompatibility or conflicts in the operating system interface), warning notices should be inserted in the tool manual.

STEP 12: TRAIN TOOL USERS

Training is a joint responsibility of the software engineer and the tool users and should help promote tool use. The software engineer is responsible for the content (in accordance with the approved training plan), and the tool user controls the length and scheduling of sessions. The tool user should be able to terminate training steps that are not helpful and to extend portions that are helpful but need further explication. Retraining or training in the use of additional options may be necessary and can provide an opportunity for users to talk about problems associated with the tool.

STEP 13: USE THE TOOL IN THE OPERATING ENVIRONMENT

The first use of the tool in the operating environment should involve the most qualified user personnel and minimal use of options. This first use should not be on a project with tight schedule constraints. Resulting difficulties must be resolved before expanded service is initiated. If the first use is successful, use by additional personnel and use of further options may commence.

User comments on training, first use of the tool, and the use of extended capabilities should be prepared and furnished to the software engineer. Desired improvements in the user interface, in the speed or format of response, and in the use of computer resources are all appropriate topics. Formal comments may be solicited shortly after the initial use, after six months, and again after one year.

STEP 14: WRITE THE EVALUATION REPORT

Using the outline generated in step 5, the software engineer prepares the evaluation report. User comments and toolsmith observations provide important input to this document. Most of all, the document must discuss how the general goals and tool objectives were met. The report may also include observations on the installation and use of the tool, cooperation received from the vendor in installation or training, and any other lessons learned.

Tool and host computer modifications are also described in this report. It may contain a section of comments that are useful to future tool users. The report should be approved by software management and preferably by funding management as well.

STEP 15: DETERMINE WHETHER GOALS HAVE BEEN MET

Funding management receives the evaluation report and should determine whether the goals that were established in step 1 have been met. This written determination should address:

- Attainment of technical objectives.
- Adherence to budget and other resource constraints.
- Timeliness of the effort.
- Cooperation from other agencies.
- Recommendations for future tool acquisitions

Section V
Testing in the Maintenance Environment

Software maintenance encompasses all the changes, corrections, and enhancements that occur after an application system has been placed into production. Although the probability of making errors during maintenance is much greater than during maintenance development, maintenance testing often receives half or less of the resources spent on maintenance development testing.

The general approach to testing is similar whether an item to be tested is a new system or a change to an existing system. Test objectives must be set, a test plan developed, tests cases are designed and implemented, the test cases are executed in accordance with the test design, and the results analyzed and reported. If this process is cut short, an accurate prediction of how the application will perform in operation cannot be made, and users may be unhappily surprised by new defects in their application. Problems occur not only as a result of the items being changed but also because of unconsidered interfaces between the changed and unchanged parts of the system, often referred to as *regression*.

Regression testing is designed to confirm that unchanged portions of the system still work correctly. When regressing testing is employed correctly, all relevant parts of the system are tested every time a change is made. Regression testing tests the application in light of changes made during maintenance. This test must be performed after functional improvements or repairs have been made to a system to confirm that the changes have no unintended side effects. Correction of errors relating to logic and control flow, computational errors, and interface errors are examples of conditions that necessitate regression testing. Cosmetic errors generally do not affect other capabilities and do not require that regression testing be performed.

Testing maintenance changes can be difficult, particularly if the individuals changing the application are not well trained or not well trained in how the application operates, or if the documentation is inaccurate or incomplete.

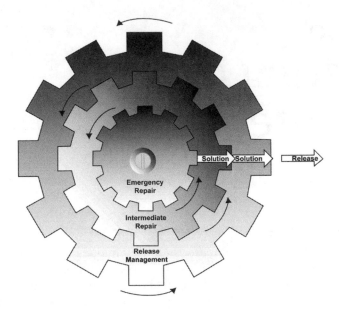

Solution Solution Release

Emergency
Repair

Intermediate
Repair

Release
Management

Exhibit 1. Release, Intermediate and Emergency Repair

This section explains some of the special test challenges during systems maintenance and proposes methods for dealing with them, including applying test methodologies to the adaptive and corrective environments.

The objectives of this section are to:

- Discuss the three conflicting factors in maintenance
- Describe software candidates for redesign
- Describe types of software changes
- Describe strategies to improve the maintenance function
- Discuss Deming's continuous improvement quality to the maintenance environment in terms of:
  - Enhancement/defect requirement analysis
  - Preliminary maintenance test planning
  - Enhancement prototype design
  - Completed maintenance test planning
  - Maintenance test case design
  - Maintenance test maintenance development
  - Maintenance test execution/evaluation
  - Preparing for the next test cycle
  - System testing
  - Acceptance testing
  - Summarizing/reporting maintenance test results
  - System installation

Part 22
Overview of Software Maintenance

BALANCING THREE CONFLICTING FORCES

The dilemma facing most software maintenance development organizations is the balance between three opposing forces: maintaining legacy systems, developing new systems, and a limited budget. Most of the budget is allocated to the maintenance of legacy systems because of numerous factors.

Maintenance intrinsically takes a lot of effort over a number of years before it is completed. There are continued demands for new enhancements to the application and the elimination of defects discovered after the application has been placed into production. The expenditure of money on maintenance is often justified, given that a great deal of money and resources have already been expended on the original maintenance development. New maintenance development is also a lot more risky than maintenance, and a lot of maintenance development managers are not willing to risk their jobs on high-risk maintenance development projects; i.e., it is easier to justify the maintenance of old systems. Maintenance development managers are hesitant to devote a great deal of money when the users of old systems are demanding enhancements and defect fixes.

It is necessary for management to periodically review their applications and sort out those that warrant continued maintenance over the long term and those in which maintenance should be limited or abandoned. Applications need to be judged in terms of how much they cost on an annual basis versus the costs to build a replacement using new technologies. These two factors can be quantified by creating a maintenance ratio of the annual maintenance cost to the cost to redevelop a system, i.e., dividing the annual maintenance cost by the cost to redevelop. A ratio of .10 can be considered acceptable, but one above .30 indicates the system is maintenance-intensive and is in question.

Legacy systems can then be evaluated on the basis of their maintenance ratios and their business importance by categorizing them into one of four categories:

1. *Poor*—Systems have little business value and high maintenance ratios.
2. *Low business/low maintenance ratios*—Systems have low business value and their maintenance ratios are acceptable.
3. *High business value/high maintenance ratios*—Systems have high business value but their maintenance ratios are high.
4. *Good*—Systems provide added business value and their maintenance ratios are acceptable.

IS managers can map applications into one of the following categories in the legacy tradeoff matrix shown in Exhibit 1, which clearly differentiates problem applications (high maintenance ratio and low business value) from those that are good (low maintenance ratio and high business importance). This will help maintenance planning to decide which applications should continue maintenance, which ones should be considered for redesign, and which applications should be phased out.

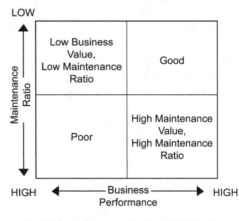

Exhibit 1. Legacy Trade-Off Matrix

SOFTWARE CANDIDATES FOR REDESIGN

Although maintenance is an ongoing process, serious consideration must eventually be given to redesigning a software system. A major concern is how to determine whether a system is hopelessly flawed or can be successfully maintained. As test groups work with software over time, they should observe the general condition of the software and, when necessary, recommend that the software be redesigned rather than continue to be maintained. The costs and benefits of the continued maintenance of software that has become error-prone, ineffective, and costly must be weighed against those of redesigning the system, even if redesign is not a popular recommendation.

A decision to redesign or to stop supporting a system can be implemented in several ways. Support can simply be removed and the system allowed to become obsolete; the minimum support needed to keep the system functioning may be provided while a new system is built; or the system may be rejuvenated section by section and given an extended life. How the redesign is effected depends on the individual circumstances of the system, its operating environment, and the needs of the organization it supports.

Although there are no absolute rules on when to redesign rather than maintain an existing system, some factors to consider are discussed in this section. The indication to redesign as opposed to continue to maintain is directly proportional to the number of characteristics listed in the following sections. The greater the number of characteristics, the greater the indication for redesign.

Frequent System Failures

An application that is in virtually constant need of corrective maintenance is a candidate for redesign. As systems age and additional maintenance is needed, they can become increasingly fragile and susceptible to changes. The older the code, the more likely that frequent modifications, new requirements, and enhancements can cause the system to break down.

Errors should be analyzed to determine whether the entire system is responsible for the failures or whether a few modules or sections of code are at fault. If the latter is found to be the case, then redesigning those parts of the system may suffice.

Code More Than Five Years Old

The estimated life cycle of a major application system is 3 to 5 years. Software deteriorates with age as a result of numerous fixes and patches. If a system is more than 5 years old, it is probably outdated and expensive to run—this is the state of much of the code now in use. After 5 years of maintenance, many systems have evolved to a point at which additional enhancements or fixes are very time-consuming. A substantial portion of the code is probably neither structured nor well written. Although the code was adequate and correct for the original environment, changes in technology and applications may have rendered it inefficient, difficult to revise, and in some cases obsolete.

If, however, the application was designed and developed in a systematic, maintainable manner and if maintenance was carefully performed and documented according to established standards and guidelines, it may be possible to run it efficiently and effectively for many more years.

Overly Complex Program Structure and Logic Flow

"Keep it simple" should be the golden rule of all programming standards and guidelines. Too often, programmers attempt to write a section of code using the fewest number of statements or the smallest amount of main storage possible. This approach to coding has resulted in complex, virtually incomprehensible code. Poor program structure contributes to complexity. If the system contains a great deal of this type of code and the documentation is also severely deficient, it is a candidate for redesign.

Complexity also refers to the level of decision making in the code. The greater the number of decision paths, the more complex the software is likely to be. Additionally, the greater the number of linearly independent control paths in a program (see Appendix H1: Basis Path Testing), the greater the program complexity. Programs with some or all of the following characteristics are usually very difficult to maintain and are candidates for redesign:

- Excessive use of DO loops
- Excessive use of IF statements
- Unnecessary GOTO statements
- Embedded constants and literals
- Unnecessary use of global variables
- Self-modifying code
- Multiple entry or exit modules
- Excessive interaction between modules
- Modules that perform the same or similar functions

Code Written for Previous Generation Hardware

Few industries have experienced as rapid a growth as the computer industry, particularly in the area of hardware. Not only have there been significant technological advances, but the cost of hardware has decreased tenfold during the last decade. This phenomenon has generated a variety of powerful hardware systems. Software written for earlier generations of hardware is often inefficient on newer systems. Attempts to modify the code superficially to take advantage of the newer hardware are generally ineffective, time-consuming, and expensive.

Systems Running in Emulation Mode

One technique used to keep a system running on newer hardware is to emulate the original hardware and operating system. Emulation is used when resources are not available to convert a system or the costs are prohibitive. For these systems, the line between usefulness and obsolescence is a fine one. One of the major difficulties in maintaining such a system is finding personnel who are familiar with the original hardware and are willing to maintain it. Because the hardware being emulated is outdated, the specific skills needed to maintain the system have little applicability elsewhere, and the career maintenance development potential of supporting such a system is not very promising.

Very Large Modules or Unit Subroutines

Mega-systems, which were written as one or several very large programs or subprograms (thousands or tens of thousands of lines of code per program), can be extremely difficult to maintain. The size of a module is usually directly proportional to the level of effort necessary to maintain it. If the large modules can be restructured and divided into smaller, functionally related sections, the maintainability of the system will be improved.

Excessive Resource Requirements

An application system that requires considerable CPU time, storage, or other system resources can place a very serious burden on all users. Such systems prevent other jobs from running and may not only require the addition of an extra shift but also degrade the service to all users. Questions that should be addressed concerning such a system include whether it is cheaper to add more computer power or to redesign and reimplement the system, and whether a redesign will reduce the resource requirements. If these requirements will not be reduced, there is no use in redesigning.

Hard-Coded Parameters That Are Subject to Change

Many older systems were designed with the values of parameters used in performing specific calculations hard-coded into the source code rather than stored in a table or read in from a data file. When changes in these values are necessary (e.g., to withholding rates), each program in the system must be examined, modified, and recompiled as necessary. This is a time-consuming, error-prone process that is costly in time and resources necessary to make the changes.

If possible, the programs should be modified to handle the input of parameters in a single module or to read the parameters from a central table of values. If this cannot be done, redesign of the system should be seriously considered.

Low-Level Language Support

Programs written in low-level languages, particularly Assembler, require an excessive amount of time and effort to maintain. Generally, such languages are not widely taught or known. Therefore, maintenance programmers who already know the language are increasingly difficult to find. Even if such programmers are found, their experience with low-level languages is probably dated.

Seriously Deficient Documentation

One of the most common software maintenance problems is the lack of adequate documentation. In most organizations, the documentation ranges from out of date to nonexistent. Even if the documentation is comprehensive when delivered, it will often steadily and rapidly deteriorate as the software is modified. In some cases, the documentation is up to date but still not useful (e.g., when the documentation is written by someone who does not understand the software).

Perhaps the worst documentation is that which is well structured and formatted but incorrect or outdated. If there is no documentation, the programmer is forced to analyze the code to understand the system. If the documentation is poor, the programmer may be skeptical of it and verify its accuracy. If it is apparently well done but is technically incorrect, however, the programmer may mistakenly believe it to be correct and accept what it contains. This results in serious problems in addition to those that necessitated the initial maintenance.

The maintenance group cannot rely on the documentation and may need to examine the code to determine how to make a change. This increases not only maintenance time but also the probability of introducing defects when the change is made.

Turnover of Personnel

Personnel added to a project during the maintenance phase must study the application and become familiar with the procedures used to process the data. Because of the long learning time for complex projects, some maintenance personnel have inadequate knowledge of how the application works; they may be able to implement a change but are not aware of its potential effects on the system. In addition, maintenance personnel may not understand the reasons for performing project activities in the manner in which they are performed.

Missing or Incomplete Design Specifications

Knowing how and why a system works is essential to proper maintenance. If the requirements and design specifications are missing or incomplete, the maintenance task is more difficult. If the specifications have always been missing or incomplete, the product has most likely not performed as intended and has been beset by requests for changes and enhancements.

Obsolete Technologies

Applications developed previously may use technologies that are now obsolete. Current systems technology will likewise be obsolete within a few years from now. Maintenance personnel must therefore be familiar with older technology. This can severely limit the personnel available to perform maintenance and may necessitate maintenance work by personnel unskilled in older technologies.

Extent of Testing vs. Size of Change

Many changes to application systems are minor (e.g., involving less than 1% of the program statements). To ensure that the application still functions as specified, however, the entire system must be tested. Testing 100% of the code when less than 1% is changed may not appear to be a cost-effective approach. When system testing is limited, however, the system is subject to regression defects (i.e., problems in the unchanged portion of the code caused by code that has been changed).

Inadequate Test Documentation

Programmers usually have adequate time and budget to make the needed change, create test conditions, and test that change but no time to create test conditions and approaches to test the entire application—especially if the test documentation is inaccurate or incomplete.

TYPES OF SOFTWARE CHANGES

Without control of software changes, testing cannot be controlled, e.g., it is impractical to design tests for software whose status is uncertain. Uncontrolled changes not only increase the cost of maintenance development and maintenance unnecessarily, but also make testing an extremely difficult and expensive part of system validation.

The control of changes to the software system should be addressed in the test plan and test strategy. The group developing the test criteria and test data must ensure that only the latest version of the requirements, specifications, code, or documentation is tested. The maintenance group must coordinate change control with the testing group.

There are three general categories of change: perfective, adaptive, and corrective (see Exhibit 2). These are briefly defined below, and some general guidelines for controlling change are provided. It is important that these concepts be incorporated into both the organization's change control procedures and software testing procedures.

Perfective Maintenance

Perfective maintenance refers to enhancements to software performance, maintainability, or understandability. It is generally performed as a result of new or changing requirements or to augment or fine-tune the software.

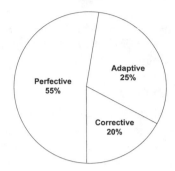

Exhibit 2. Perfective, Adaptive, and Corrective Maintenance

Activities designed to make the code easier to understand and to work with are considered perfective, as is optimizing code to make it run or use storage more efficiently.

Perfective maintenance is required as a result of both the successes and failures of the original system. If the system works well, the user usually requests additional features and capabilities. If the system works poorly, it must be fixed. As requirements change and the user becomes more sophisticated, changes are requested to make functions easier or clearer to use. Perfective maintenance is the method usually employed to keep the system up to date, responsive, and germane to the mission of the organization.

There *is* some disagreement as to whether the addition of new capabilities should be considered maintenance or additional maintenance development. Because it is an expansion of an existing system after it has been placed into operation and is usually performed by the same staff responsible for other forms of maintenance, it is appropriately classified as maintenance.

Fine-tuning existing systems to eliminate shortcomings and inefficiencies is often referred to as preventive maintenance. It can have dramatic effects on old, poorly written systems in terms of reducing resource requirements and making the system more maintainable and thus easier to change or enhance. Preventive maintenance may also include the study of a system before errors or problems occur. Fine-tuning is an excellent vehicle for introducing the programmer to the code while reducing the likelihood of serious errors in the future.

Controlling Perfective Maintenance. Perfective maintenance constitutes an estimated 55% of the total maintenance effort. It deals primarily with expanding, extending, and enhancing a system to increase its power, flexibility, or reliability or to give it additional capabilities. Requests for perfective maintenance are initiated by three groups: the user, senior management, and the maintenance staff.

The user is almost never completely satisfied with a system. Either it does not perform as expected or, as users gain confidence in the system, they perceive additional features that would enhance their work. This is the normal evolution of all software systems and must be planned for when budget requests and resource allocation schedules are developed.

Senior management initiates perfective maintenance tasks by requesting new features and enhancements that must be incorporated into the system. Again, this is a normal part of the functioning of any organization and must be planned for in the maintenance budget.

Finally, the maintenance staff itself makes changes. As a maintenance programmer works with a system, inefficiencies and potential problems are often found. These problems, although not requiring immediate attention, at some point could affect either the functioning of the system or the ability to maintain it. The "cleaning up" of code (often referred to as preventive maintenance) is an important perfective maintenance process that should be planned for and included in the resource allocation schedule. This type of maintenance can often prevent minor problems in a system from becoming major problems later.

Perfective maintenance is managed primarily by maintaining an orderly process in which all requests are formally submitted, reviewed, assigned a priority, and scheduled. This does not mean that unnecessary delays should be built into the process or that in small organizations these steps are not consolidated. It simply provides a structure for controlling many maintenance activities.

There should be a central coordination and approval point for all maintenance projects. This may be the maintenance project manager or, for larger systems and organizations, a review board. When a change or enhancement is needed, a formal written request should be submitted. Each request should be evaluated according to the following criteria:

- Resource requirements
- Time to complete the work
- Impact on the existing system and other maintenance efforts
- Justification of need

The centralized approval process enables one person or group to have knowledge of all the requested and actual work performed on the system. If this is not done, two or more independent changes to the system are likely to conflict with one another and, as a result, the system will not function properly. Additionally, different users often request the same enhancements to a system, but the details differ slightly. If these requests are coordinated, details can be combined and the total amount of resources required can be reduced.

If the system requires maintenance as a result of changes in policy or procedures in the organization, an evaluation of the cost and effects of the changes should be prepared for senior management. Ideally, this evaluation should be prepared before the decision to institute the changes; even if it is not, both management and users must be aware of the costs. Users often request an enhancement to a system because they feel it would be nice to have or because another system has a similar feature. These requested enhancements should be evaluated and the estimated costs reported to the user, regardless of whether users are responsible for funding the work. Doing so helps minimize the amount of unneeded or marginally needed enhancements to the system. This type of interchange with the user helps the maintenance manager evaluate and assign priorities to the work requests.

Many organizations have a significant backlog of maintenance requests. Users must understand the level of effort required to meet their requests and the relative priority of the work in relationship to other user requests. This can be accomplished only by involving all parties in the discussions and keeping everyone informed of the schedules and actual progress.

Adaptive Maintenance

Adaptive maintenance refers to modifications made to a system to accommodate changes in the processing environment. These environmental changes are usually beyond the control of the software maintainer. Adaptive maintenance is usually required under the conditions discussed in the following sections.

Changes to laws, regulations, and rules often require adaptive maintenance to a system. These changes must often be completed in a very short time frame to meet legally required dates. If rules and their actions are implemented modularly, the changes are relatively easy to install. Otherwise, they can be a nightmare.

Changes to hardware (e.g., new terminals, local printers) that supports the system are usually made to take advantage of new or improved features that will enhance system operation or response. These changes are usually performed on a scheduled basis. Changes to data formats and file structures may require extensive maintenance on a system if it was not properly designed and implemented. If reading or writing of data is isolated in specific modules, changes may have less effect. If a change must be made throughout the code, the effort can become very lengthy and costly.

Changes to operating system software (e.g., compilers, utilities) can have varying effects on the existing application systems. These effects can range from requiring little or no reprogramming to recompilation of all source code to the rewriting of code that contains features of a language no longer supported by the new system software.

Maintenance resulting from changes in the requirements specifications by the user, however, is considered to be perfective, not adaptive, maintenance.

Controlling Adaptive Maintenance. Adaptive maintenance is approximately 25% of the total maintenance effort. Changes to the operating system, system utilities, terminal devices, and the rules, laws, and regulations that the software must incorporate are the primary causes of adaptive maintenance, which usually does little to improve the system.

Although maintenance personnel cannot control changes to rules and legislation, such changes should be anticipated as much as possible and the code structured to facilitate making the needed changes. This type of adaptive maintenance usually must be performed whenever it is required; however, management should always be given feedback regarding the impact of any changes on the maintenance of a system, especially the cost. This feedback will improve the future decision-making process and may reduce the level of adaptive maintenance.

In many organizations, the application support group functions independently of the computer facility group. As a result, there is inadequate communication and understanding by each group regarding the impact of decisions and work on the other function. Changes may be made to the environment and announced to the user community before the application support function has an opportunity to analyze the impact of the changes and the effect on the application system. Similarly, changes or additions to an application system that increase the computer resource requirements may cause serious problems with the functioning of all applications using the computer. Therefore, it is extremely important that the facilities organization and the applications support organization work closely to minimize any adverse impact on each other's work. There are times when a choice simply does not exist, but usually, through adequate planning and evaluation, both organizations can accomplish their objectives with a net improvement for each.

The application support manager must know what changes to the environment are being planned and considered and keep management informed of their potential impact (negative and positive). This allows the total costs and implications of the changes to be reviewed by management. Decisions can then be made regarding which organization should bear the costs of adaptive maintenance.

Corrective Maintenance

Corrective maintenance is approximately 20% of the total maintenance effort. Corrective maintenance is primarily the identification and removal of any code defects that either reduce the effectiveness of the software or render it useless. The objective of such maintenance is to return the code to an operational state. By its nature, corrective maintenance is usually a reactive process related to the system not performing as originally intended. Often, errors must be fixed immediately.

Errors in the following categories indicate corrective maintenance.

Design Errors Resulting from Incomplete or Faulty Design. When a user gives incorrect, incomplete, or unclear descriptions of the system being requested or when the analyst or designer does not fully understand what the user is requesting, the resulting system often contains design errors.

Logic Errors. Logic errors result from such problems as invalid tests and conclusions, faulty logic flow, and incorrect implementation of the design specifications. Logic errors are usually attributable to the designer or previous maintenance employee. Often, the logic error occurs when unique or unusual combinations of data are encountered that were not tested during the maintenance development or previous maintenance phases.

Coding Errors. Coding errors result from either incorrect implementation of the detailed logic design or incorrect use of the source code. These errors are caused by the programmer. They are usually errors of negligence or carelessness and, though the most inexcusable, are usually the easiest to fix.

Computational Errors. Computational errors result from incorrect calculations, mixing data of incompatible types, or performing the correct computation on the wrong data.

Input/Output Errors. These errors result from I/O from/to the wrong record or file, format errors, and incorrect I/O protocols.

Data Handling Errors. Data handling errors result from the failure to initialize data, improper use of indexes, and edit errors.

Interface Errors. Interface errors result from mismatches of parameters passed among programs and incorrect subprogram calls.

Data Definition Errors. These errors result from incorrect type definitions, improper dimensioning of arrays, and using subscripts out of array bounds.

Controlling Corrective Maintenance. Most software maintenance is assumed to be the result of poor work during maintenance development and prior maintenance phases of the system. Although this is one cause, it is rare for even a "perfect" system not to require significant maintenance during its lifetime. Software can become nonfunctional or faulty because of changes in the environment in which it must operate, the size or sophistication of the user community, the amount of data it must process, or damage to code resulting from other maintenance efforts on other parts of the system. Corrective maintenance is necessitated by discovery of a flaw that has always existed in the system or was introduced during prior maintenance.

Difficulties encountered during corrective maintenance can be reduced significantly by the adoption and enforcement of appropriate standards and procedures during software maintenance development and maintenance. It is probably not possible to eliminate corrective maintenance, but the consistent and disciplined adherence to effective design and programming standards can and will significantly reduce the corrective maintenance burden.

STRATEGIES FOR MANAGING MAINTENANCE

The following strategies will help improve the efficiency of the maintenance activities.

Continue the Maintenance Development Test Strategies

The only true solution for effective maintenance testing is to create the test strategies during maintenance development and continue them into maintenance. Test plans and test execution documentation needs to be developed during maintenance development and used during maintenance. During each release, the test plan and test execution document should be updated to reflect the changes.

As functions are changed during maintenance, the tests required for those functions should be documented by using the appropriate test documents. These tests can be more extensively defined than in a new maintenance development test plan. They can include the actual test conditions and the correct results from processing those transactions. This process continues until all functions have been modified and a reasonable set of tests developed. This process may take many months, or even years, to develop. Even if the system is rewritten, however, this information is useful in testing the new system. Therefore, the time is not wasted.

The results of implementing the test plan should be recorded using test execution documents. As these test execution results are built up, it becomes easier to perform more extensive testing before the implementation of each release. A test report should be documented to explain what works and what does not and describes the expected performance of the application. Although these reports may be extensive for large new systems, the entire report may not exceed a single page for software releases during maintenance. It is important to formally document the results of testing so that defects noted in production can be checked against the reports. If the defects were not properly identified during testing, that indicates a potential weakness in the testing process. Therefore, the test report information and the actual operational results (i.e., defects uncovered in operation) become the basis for improving the test process.

Establish Automated Regression Testing Approach

Regression testing involves the selective retesting of an application to detect possible defects introduced during maintenance. Capture/playback automated testing tools (see Section VI — Modern Maintenance Tools) capture inputs and outputs while the target system is functioning in the background. During playback the captured script repeats the same sequence of actions and compares the actual responses from the captured results. Any differences are reported as errors.

For capture/playback to be successful, there should exist only one script per requirement. This has the advantage of allowing the script to be used by multiple testers. Another major advantage is that if the level is granularity of the script is isolated to one requirement, when there is a change to the requirement, the associated script is known and will not be played back until it is modified to reflect the change. This allows a tester to focus on specific part of the system and simplifies later maintenance.

Scripts can also be packaged together into similar test scenarios such as at the beginning or end of the application. Depending on the testing tool, they can also be called from other test scripts, just as with maintenance development software modules. A master test script can be used to generate a series of calls to individual scripts to perform a larger set of functions.

Establish a Change Request System

It is imperative that a comprehensive method for tracking change requests be developed. The maintenance team must know what changes have been requested, who requested them, and why they were requested. The change tracking system will also related change requests for similarity and duplication. If several change requests are submitted for improved performance during an on-line session, the application must be fine tuned using a perfective approach.

A change request tracking method will help identify conflicting change requests. These conflicts will have to be resolved before maintenance can start. Mutually exclusive change requests may indicate that a group of adaptive evolution projects is required. The tracking system will identify changes which must be reengineered because of a negative impact or because the change was made incorrectly. Change priorities must also be taken into account by the change tracking system.

The change tracking system should implement a clear categorization scheme for change requests (e.g., corrective, perfective, etc.). Corrective changes are also categorized as to whether emergency repair is required or not. Adaptive changes are typically included in a project, while perfective changes are included in new releases.

Establish a Software Configuration Management System

A good software configuration management (SCM) system is just as important as with original development. An SCM will provide a method for recording all of the component parts of an application and their associations. This identifies all the software components that may be affected by the changes to be made and is essential to make changes safely among a complex set of multiple software components. It is also important to know where proposed changes will affect components that are not part of the application to avoid adverse impacts.

An SCM ensures that the correct version of a software component will be included in the testing and eventual reimplementation. It may be necessary to maintain a number of different versions of the same software component, and it is necessary to be able to recreate previous software versions of the application.

An effective SCM will enable the maintenance to secure, manage, and control the maintenance development process and the delivery process. This is becoming more and more a requirement as more and more applications are developed in a client/server approach and as these applications are delivered to multiple locations.

Establish a Maintenance "Triage Approach"

A triage system is designed to produce the greatest benefit from limited treatment facilities for battlefield casualties by giving full treatment to those who may survive and not to those who have no chance of survival and those who will survive without it.

The same approach can be applied to the software maintenance effort. Depending on the type of change request or defect discovered and the immediacy of the change, the maintenance activity can be handled in one of three approaches as discussed below. (See also Exhibit 3.)

Release Management Approach. For non-emergency corrective, perfective, and adaptive projects, a formal release management process should be established. Well-developed test strategies are ineffectual when changes are installed on a daily or weekly basis. There is no time to test correctly when all maintenance development resources are consumed with the repetitive tasks of documenting, analyzing, and changing code and recompiling and installing those changes. The most common outcome is poor testing that permits the release of many defects into production.

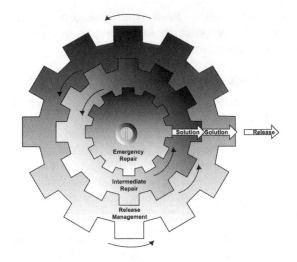

Exhibit 3. Release, Intermediate, and Emergency Repair

Maintenance releases should be no more frequent than monthly, and preferably quarterly. Although many maintenance development organizations do not believe the release concept is practical, the advantages are so great that most users want to adapt the procedure once the options have been explained. Prioritization schemes need to be developed and applied.

Time will never be available to reconstruct testing unless that time can be freed up from other existing activities. Only the adoption of the release mode can free the time from other activities to bring the older systems to the current test standards.

When maintenance moves to the release mode, the repetitive process of recompilation and testing is significantly reduced because more changes are installed at a single time. For example, in many instances, a second change can be implemented along with another in only a little more time than would have been required to install the first change. Without the release mode, the time would be doubled.

Develop and maintain a permanent testing capability and when possible, implement the automated testing strategies. Manual testing will remain a significant resource requirement until test automation is fully completed. Consider automating software configuration and version issues, even though this will require extensive manual management in the absence of a repository of automated test scripts.

Emergency and Intermediate Repair Approaches. Some corrective defects need to be corrected before the next release but may not need to be corrected immediately. For example, such repairs can be made in a week or so.

300

These fall under the category of intermediate repairs. For emergency corrective defects, institute an emergency repair approach to handle problems that need immediate attention, i.e., which cannot wait for a release or even an intermediate repair.

Additional support technology for emergency repairs needs to be developed to improve the capability to analyze, assess, and test applications that need rapid repair. A library of test cases, test plans, and test results should be developed, as repairs will often center around a relatively small proportion of application. A comprehensive log of emergency repair work should be maintained so that the initial assessment can be updated and refined.

The following approach can be applied to the emergency repair situation to react swiftly:

1. Develop a problem fix.
2. Test the fix in a programmer library with a focus on the change.
3. Test the fix against the acceptance library and test the change in the larger setting (if tests are available).
4. Apply the fix to the production library on an emergency basis.
5. The next day move the fix to the integration library (installation approval) and follow the full testing process.

PSYCHOLOGY OF MAINTENANCE TESTING

Typically, the same psychological factors that played a part in a phased waterfall maintenance development life cycle or RAD maintenance development apply to the maintenance environment.

An additional negative factor in the maintenance environment is the common misconception that maintenance has a lower "status" than original development. This is ironic, since maintenance comprises most of the development costs and requires a great deal of skill and knowledge about the system. The maintenance developers and maintenance testers may feel that they are "second-class citizens" as compared to the new development and may strive to be involved with new development projects rather than maintenance. Maintenance management should be sensitive to this and promote the maintenance activity as one that is as desirable as (or even more than) new development.

Phased Life Cycle Maintenance. In a phased maintenance approach there is typically a concerted effort to keep the maintenance testing and development activities separate. Underlying assumptions include the belief that (1) maintenance programmers should not test their own programs and (2) the maintenance programming organization should not test their own programs.

It is thought that software testing is a destructive process and that it is very difficult for a maintenance programmer to suddenly change his perspective from maintaining a software component to try to locate defects or break the software. It was believed that maintenance programmers cannot effectively test their own programs because they cannot bring themselves to attempt to expose errors.

It is possible for maintenance programmers to test their own programs, but that testing is more effective when performed by someone who did not have a stake in it as a maintenance programmer does.

The psychology of life cycle testing encourages testing be performed by individuals outside the maintenance organization. The motivation for this is that with the life cycle approach there typically exist clearly defined requirements and it is more efficient for a third party to verify the requirements. Testing is often viewed as a destructive process to break maintenance development's work.

RAD Maintenance. The psychology of maintenance testing in a RAD environment, on the other hand, encourages cooperation between the maintenance testers and maintenance developers. The basis of this argument is that in a rapid application maintenance environment, requirements may or may not be available, to varying degrees. Without this cooperation, the testing function would have a very difficult task of defining the test criteria. The only workable alternative is for testing and maintenance development to work closely together.

Testers can be powerful allies to maintenance development, and with a little effort, testers can be transformed from adversaries into partners. This is possible because most testers want to be helpful; they just need a little consideration and support. In order to foster this, however, an environment needs to be created to bring out the best of testers' abilities. The test and maintenance development manager must set the stage for cooperation early in the maintenance development cycle and communicate throughout the maintenance development life cycle.

In many ways the maintenance tester and developer roles are in conflict. A maintenance developer is committed to building or fixing something to be successful. A tester tries to minimize the risk of failure and tries to improve the software by detecting defects. Maintenance developers are focused on technology, which takes a lot of time and energy to produce software. A good tester, on the other hand, is motivated to provide the user with the best software to solve a problem.

The key to integrating the testing and developing maintenance activities is for testers to avoid giving the perception that they are out to "break the code" or destroy maintenance development's work. Ideally, testers are human meters of product quality and should examine a software product, evaluate it, and discover if the product satisfies customer requirements. They should not be out to embarrass or complain, but to inform maintenance development how to make their work product even better. The impression they should strive to exhibit is that they are the "developer's eyes to improved quality."

Maintenance development needs to be truly motivated to quality and view the maintenance test team as an integral players on the maintenance development team. They need to realize that no matter how much work and effort has been expended by maintenance development, if the software does not possess the correct level of quality, it is destined to failure. The maintenance testing manager needs to remind the project manager of this throughout the maintenance development cycle. The project manager needs to instill this perception in the maintenance development team.

Testers must coordinate with the project schedule and work in parallel with maintenance development. They need to be informed about what's going on in the maintenance effort and should be included in all planning and status meetings. This lessens the risk of introducing new bugs, known as "side-effects," near the end of the maintenance development cycle and lessens the need for time-consuming regression testing.

Testers must be encouraged to communicate effectively with everyone on the maintenance development team. They should establish a good communication relationship with the software users, who can help them better understand acceptable standards of quality. In this way, testers can provide valuable feedback directly to maintenance development.

Testers should intensively review online help and printed manuals whenever they are available. Getting writers and testers to share notes rather than burdening both with the task of finding the same information will relieve some of the communication burden.

Testers need to know the objectives of the software product being modified, how it is intended to work, how it actually works, the maintenance development schedule, any proposed changes, and the status of reported problems.

Maintenance developers need to know what problems were discovered, what part of the software is or is not working, how users perceive the software, what will be tested, the testing schedule, the testing resources available, what the testers need to know to test the system, and the current status of the testing effort.

When quality assurance starts working with a maintenance development team, the maintenance testing manager needs to interview the project manager and show an interest in working in a cooperative manner to improve the software product as much as possible. The next part describes how to accomplish this. (See Part 23 — Enhancement/Defect Requirements Analysis [Plan].)

A CONTINUOUS IMPROVEMENT MAINTENANCE APPROACH

The purpose of maintenance software testing is to identify the differences between existing and expected conditions of a system being enhanced or modified, i.e., to detect software defects. Testing identifies the new requirements that have not been satisfied and the functions that have been impaired due to regression. The most commonly recognized test objective is to identify bugs, but this is a limited definition of the aim of testing. Not only must bugs be identified, but they must be put into a framework that enables maintenance testers to predict how the software will perform.

The maintenance testing organization needs to get inside the maintenance development effort and work closely with development. Each new maintenance version needs to be tested as it becomes available. The approach is to first test the new enhancements or modified software to resolve defects reported previously. Regression testing is then performed to assure that the rest of the system has not regressed.

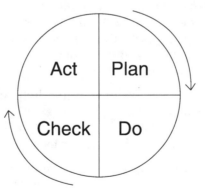

Exhibit 4. Maintenance Testing and Continuous Improvement

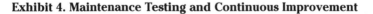

In the maintenance environment, software testing is again described as a continuous improvement process that must be integrated into a release or emergency situations. Testing as an integrated function prevents maintenance development from proceeding without testing. Deming's continuous improvement process using the PDCA model (see Exhibit 4) will again be applied to the maintenance testing process.

Before the continuous improvement process begins, the testing function needs to be involved in a series of enhancement definition/ analysis steps to understand the scope of the original system to be enhanced or corrected.

The **Plan** step of the maintenance continuous improvement process commences. A major step is to develop a preliminary software test plan (see Part 24—Preliminary Maintenance Test Planning). This test plan sets the stage for accomplishing testing and should be considered an ongoing document, i.e., as the system changes, so does the plan. Later this plan will be finalized. The outline of the preliminary test plan includes an introduction, the overall plan, high-level requirement changes, maintenance test deliverables, defect recording, change requests, version control, configuration building, project issue management, reporting and approval procedures.

The next major planning step is for the maintenance development team to design an enhancement prototype (see Part 25 — Enhancement Prototype Design), which includes the functional, data, and GUI interface changes.

The final planning step is the completion of the test plan (see Part 26—Completed Maintenance Test Planning), in which additional details are added to the preliminary test plan. It includes manual/automated test types, exit test criteria, regression test strategy, test team organization, test environment, dependencies, schedule, tools, metric objectives and points.

The **Do** step of the continuous improvement process consists of test case design and test execution (see Part 27—Maintenance Test Case Design). This step describes how to design maintenance test cases and execute the tests included in the test plan. Design includes the functional tests, GUI tests, and fragment system and acceptance tests. Once an overall maintenance test design is completed, test maintenance development starts. This includes building maintenance test scripts and procedures to provide test case details (see Part 28—Maintenance Test Development).

The test team is responsible for executing the tests and must ensure that they are executed according to the test design. The Do step also includes test setup, regression testing of old and new tests, and recording any defects discovered.

The **Check** step of the continuous improvement process includes metric measurements and analysis used during maintenance test cycles (see Part 29—Maintenance Test Execution/Evaluation). Crucial to the Deming method is the need to base decisions as much as possible on accurate and timely data. Metrics are key to verifying if the maintenance work effort and test schedule are on schedule, to identify any new resource requirements, and predict when the all defects will be uncovered. During the Check step it is important to publish intermediate maintenance test reports. This includes recording of the test results and relating them to the test plan and test objectives.

The **Act** step of the continuous improvement process involves preparation for the next maintenance test cycle iteration (see Part 30 — Prepare for the Next Test Cycle). A test cycle is a collection of test cases that are executed in sequence. The Act step entails refining the function/GUI tests, test suites, test cases, test scripts, and fragment system and acceptance tests, modifying the defect tracking system and the version and control system, if necessary. It also includes devising measures for appropriate actions relating to work that was not performed according to the plan or results that were not what was anticipated. Examples include a reevaluation of the test team, test procedures, technology dimensions of testing, and anticipating when testing will be completed. All the above is fed back to the completed test plan, which is updated.

Once several maintenance test cycles have been completed and the application has been verified as functionally stable, full system and acceptance testing starts (see Part 31—Maintenance System Testing, and Part 32—Maintenance Acceptance Testing). These tests are often optional. Respective system and acceptance test plans are developed defining the test objects and the specific tests to be completed.

A major test report should be written at the end of all testing. A summary report (see Part 33—Maintenance Summary Test Report) and test cycle results are prepared and published. The process used for report writing is the same whether it is an interim or a final report and, like other tasks in testing, report writing is also subject to quality control. However, the final test report should be much more comprehensive than interim test reports. For each type of test it should describe a record of defects discovered, data reduction techniques, root cause analysis, the maintenance development of findings, and follow-on recommendations for the current and/or future projects.

The final step in the continuous improvement maintenance process is system installation (see Part 34—System Installation), which describes how to verify the ability to install the system at the right time and successfully. The intent is to make sure the system operates correctly and take appropriate actions to resolve problems.

Going around the PDCA Circle

The above procedures not only ensure that the quality of maintenance deliveries meets expectations, but they also ensure that the anticipated price and delivery date are fulfilled. Sometimes our preoccupation with current concerns makes us unable to achieve optional results. By going around the PDCA circle either for a particular maintenance release or through several releases, we can improve our working methods and obtain the desired results for the overall product. Repeated use of PDCA makes it possible to improve the quality of the work methods, and the results.

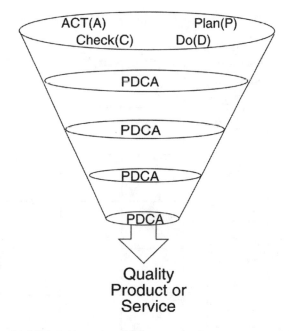

Exhibit 5. Iterative Maintenance Improvements

Maintenance Testing Methodology

Exhibit 6 provides a framework for testing in the maintenance environment. It provides a maintenance testing methodology and relates each step to the PDCA quality wheel. The major steps include enhancement requirements gathering, preliminary test planning, enhancement prototype design, completed test planning, test design, test maintenance development, test execution/evaluation, and preparing for the next test cycle. It includes a set of tasks associated with each step or a checklist from which the maintenance testing organization can choose based on its needs. The above approach flushes out the system functionality to be maintained. When this has been completed, it also provides for system testing, acceptance testing, maintenance summary reporting, and maintenance system installation.

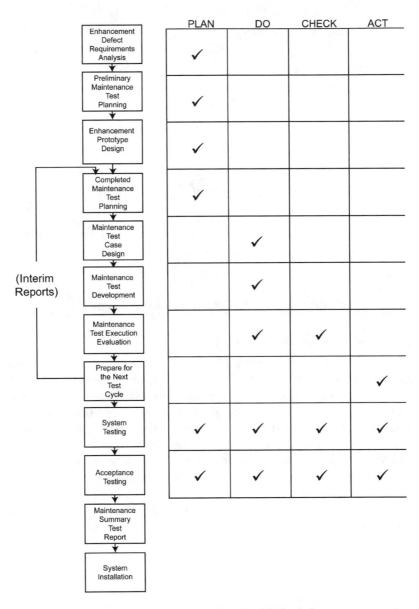

Exhibit 6. Maintenance Testing Methodology

Part 23

Enhancement/Defect Requirements Analysis (Plan)

In the maintenance development environment, software testing is described as a continuous improvement process that must be integrated into maintenance development. Deming's continuous improvement process using the PDCA model (Exhibit 1) is applied to the software testing process. We are now in the **Plan** part of the model.

Exhibit 2 outlines the steps and tasks associated with the **Plan** part of the maintenance testing methodology. Each step and task is described along with valuable tips and techniques.

The purpose of enhancement/defect requirement analysis is to obtain information that is relevant to the maintenance development project to understand the requirements of the maintenance project and for the testing manager to start building a preliminary maintenance test plan. Other interviews may occur during the maintenance project, as necessary.

Proper preparation is critical to the success of the maintenance interview if it is to be a carefully organized event. Before the interview, it is important to clearly identify the objectives of the interview to all parties, identify the maintenance development and testing representatives, identify who will lead the interview and the scribe, schedule the meeting with a time and place, prepare any required handouts, and communicate what is required from maintenance development.

While many interviews are unstructured, the interviewing steps and tasks shown in Exhibit 2 will be very helpful.

STEP 1: PREPARE FOR THE MAINTENANCE REVIEW

Task 1: Identify the Participants

It is recommended that there be no more than two interviewers representing software testing. It is helpful for one of these to ask questions while the

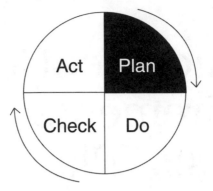

Exhibit 1. Maintenance Testing and Continuous Improvement

other takes detailed notes from a testing perspective. This will allow the interviewer to focus on soliciting information. Ideally the interviewer should be the manager responsible for the maintenance development activities. The scribe, or notetaker representing the testing organization, should be a test engineer or lead tester assigned to the project, who supports the interviewer and records each pertinent piece of information and lists the issues, the assumptions, and questions.

The recommended maintenance development participants attending include the project sponsor, maintenance development manager, or a senior maintenance development team member. While members of the maintenance development team can take notes, it is the responsibility of the maintenance development scribe. Having more than one scribe can result in confusion, because multiple sets of notes will eventually have to be consolidated. The most efficient approach is for the scribe to take notes and summarize at the end of the interview.

Task 2: Define the Agenda

The key factor for a successful maintenance interview is a well thought out agenda. It should be prepared by the interviewer ahead of time and agreed upon by the maintenance development leader. The agenda should include an introduction, specific points to cover, and a summary section. The main purpose of an agenda from a testing point of view is to enable the testing manager to gather enough information to scope out the quality assurance activities and start a test plan. Exhibit 3 depicts a sample agenda (details are described in Step 2: Conduct the Maintenance Interview below).

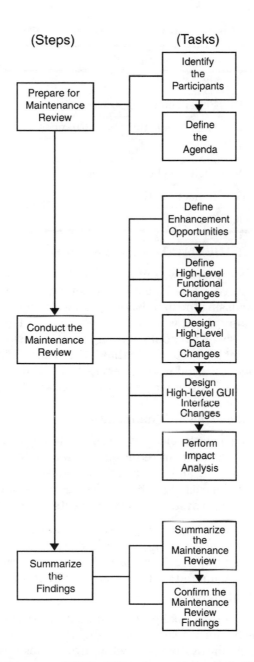

Exhibit 2. Enhancement/Defect Requirement Analysis (Steps/Tasks)

Exhibit 3. Maintenance Interview Agenda

Interview Agenda	
I.	Introductions
II.	Enhancement Opportunities
III.	High-Level Functional Changes
IV.	High-Level Data Changes
V.	High-Level GUI Changes
VI.	Impact Analysis
VII.	Summary

STEP 2: CONDUCT THE MAINTENANCE REVIEW

A good maintenance interview contains four elements. The first is defining what will be discussed, or "talking about what we are going to talk about." The second is discussing the details, or "talking about it." The third is summarizing, or "talking about what we talked about." The final element is timeliness. The interviewer should state up front the estimated duration of the interview and set the ground rule that if time expires before completing all items on the agenda, a follow-on interview will be scheduled. This is difficult, particularly when the interview is detailed, but it should be followed.

Task 1: Define Enhancement Opportunities

During this task, the maintenance development and testing team gather and define the system enhancement requirements and potential improvements to existing functions, data, and user interfaces. It also focuses on pending defects discovered in the existing software. The sources of the enhancement opportunities come from system change requests and the defect log.

Change requests consist of a formal description of the request to make a change on the existing system and are typically initiated by a system user to describe the need to perfect or adapt the existing system. Each system change request is evaluated and approved prior to be accepted and applied to the existing system.

Some key questions to ask include which processes drive the requirement, what is the business reason for changing the system and what value is added to the existing system, and what are the business rules, information requirements, performance requirements, operational requirements, and additional security access controls.

In addition to new system enhancements, the resolution of documented defects recorded in the error log must be evaluated. Examples of defects include coding, computation, input/output, data handling, interface, data definition errors, business rule violations, and performance problems during data transfer. The defect log contains all defects documented since the last release. Since there may be many documented defects, they need to be prioritized.

During the process of evaluating enhancement and defect improvements, the impact on the organization needs to be considered. Organizations need time to adjust from the current state to future state enhancements. The information about a change or defect removal, the reason for the change, and the impact on the organization needs to be clearly documented and shared with the user. Exhibits 4, 5, 6, and 7 help focus on the key areas.

Exhibit 4, Defects by Priority, provides defect priorities by percentage for all defects. This defines the overall scope of the rework priorities. If there are a great percentage of critical and high defects, the defect removal efforts will likely overshadow new enhancement development.

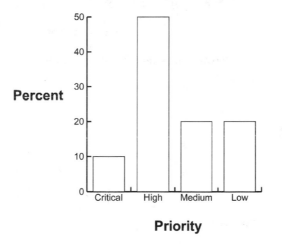

Priority

Exhibit 4. Defects by Priority

Exhibit 5, Defects by Defect Type, helps identify the types of defects. If a majority of the defects are performance related, this will indicate that there may be some major design flaws and more effort needs to be focused to improve performance.

Exhibit 6, Defects by Module/Program, highlights those modules or programs that have an excessive number of defects. This requires a close reevaluation of their detailed design and perhaps a redesign. A redesign effort may be warranted if there are frequent program failures, if there is an

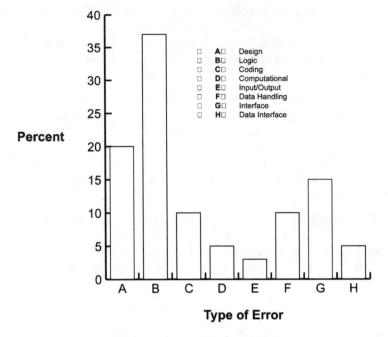

Type of Error

Exhibit 5. Defects by Defect Type

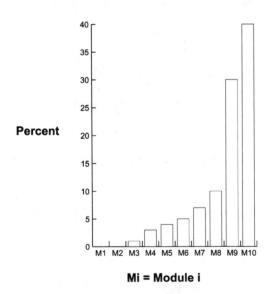

Mi = Module i

Exhibit 6. Defects by Module/Program

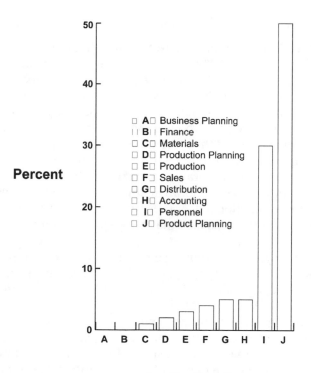

Application Area

Exhibit 7. Defects by Application Area

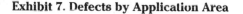

overlay complex program structure and logic flow, if the program is very large, there are excessive resource requirements, or if deficient design and test documentation is lacking.

Exhibit 7, Defects by Application Area, helps identify those application areas that are prone to more defects than others. The evaluation is, of course, weighed against the relative importance of the application area.

In all the above cases, the 80/20 rule applies, i.e., it is often the case that 20% of the factors account for 80% of the effects. If there is a resource or time constraint, one should focus on the 20%.

Task 2: Define High-Level Functional Changes

During enhancement/defect requirement analysis, the new high-level functions or modifications need to be identified. This enables the maintenance development manager to assess the scope of the maintenance project. With this information the testing manager can start a test plan.

The following questions should be asked to solicit the basic information:

- What high-level functions are to be added/modified? The functions at a high level that should be considered are listed. Examples include order processing, financial processing, reporting capability, financial planning, purchasing, inventory control, sales administration, shipping, cash flow analysis, payroll, cost accounting, recruiting. This list defines what the application is supposed to do and provides the testing manager an idea of the level of test design, implementation, and rework required. The interviewer should solicit as much detail as possible, including a detailed breakdown of each new or modified function. If this detail is not available during the interview, a request for a detailed functional decomposition should be made and it should be pointed out that this information is essential for preparing the test plan.
- What are the new or modified (minimum) system requirements? A description of the operating system version (Windows, etc.) and minimum microprocessor, disk space, RAM, and communications hardware should be provided.
- What are the new or modified Windows or external interfaces? The new requirements should define how the application should behave from an external viewpoint, usually by defining the inputs and outputs. It also includes a description of any interfaces to other applications or subsystems.
- What are the additional performance requirements? This includes a description of the speed, availability, data volume throughput rate, response time, and recovery time of various functions, stress, etc. This serves as a basis for understanding the level of maintenance performance and stress testing which may be required.
- What new testing attributes are required? This includes such attributes as portability, maintainability, security and usability, and serves as a basis for understanding the level of other system-level testing that may be required.
- Are there any new or modified design constraints? This includes a description of any limitation on the operating environment(s), database integrity, resource limits, implementation language standards, etc.

Task 3: Define High-Level Data Changes

New or modified data requirements need to be identified from a structural, data element, or distribution point of view. Examples include the need to store additional information, the development of new databases, the need for additional data elements, the modification of the format of existing data, providing additional users access to existing data, and installing databases in other geographical locations.

Referential integrity involves the actions taken by a system to maintain the integrity of the data relationships as represented in a data model. Any new requirements need to be evaluated, e.g., new create and delete access operation, modified create and delete accesses.

Task 4: Define High-Level GUI Interface Changes

Graphical User Interface (GUI) provides multiple channels of communication using words, pictures, animation, sound, and video. Five key foundation components of the user interface are windows, menus, forms, icons, and controls.

During enhancement analysis/defect analysis, changes to the GUI design of the system need to be identified. Examples include the addition of new screens, improvement of screen navigation and flow, new function keys or accelerators, additional or modified help text, additional or modified information on screens, new or modified reports to display additional information or modifications.

The information gathered during this task will be instrumental when GUI tests are later designed, implemented, or modified. During the test design process the GUI components are defined, named, and categorized in the GUI component test matrix. A checklist is developed against each GUI component that describes how all interactions which may or may not apply to a GUI component.

Task 5: Perform Impact Analysis

Analysis of the direct and indirect impacts to the system due to the proposed enhancements and corrections needs to be performed. Impacts are related to the major functions, data, and user interface changes. Examples of impacts include the impact on business processes, functions, procedures, databases, the screen navigation flow.

Also, the consequence of the impacts are addressed, including any user interfacing with the system, the user environment (technology, organization, procedures), maintenance development organization (technology, procedures), the existing system software, or related software systems. Examples of the latter include other applications sharing the target software, hardware, or databases. The following steps are performed during impact analysis:

1. **Identify the Problem to be Addressed.** Verify that the problem to be solved by the enhancement or defect removal is defined clearly in terms of its nature, the time frame the problem existed, any constraints, and the priority to make a change.
2. **Define the Problem's Causes and Effects.** Document the effect of each event (or cause) to categorize the effect(s) that will occur.

317

3. **Analyze Application Problem's Causes and Effects.** Identify how the current system causes a problem and identify the missing elements needed to solve it. Causes may be major and may also consist of a set of minor causes. Effects are the result of the cause and are usually logically associated with the cause. An example of a cause–effect relationship is, when there is not enough memory, the effect is poor performance because the system has to perform more data accesses.

4. **Document the Problem.** Define which existing elements of the system are causing the problem and what is inhibited by the problem, e.g., functionality, performance, usability, etc. Relate the causes and effects to the problem and identify the initial solution(s).

5. **Prioritize the Problems.** Prioritize all the problems that were discovered. This will provide a focus on those problems which are more important than others. Make sure the users are involved, for they are the benefactors or the improvement efforts and will be the most directly affected.

6. **Build an Impact/Consequence Matrix.** An impact/consequence matrix consists of the Impact Area, Impact Description, Impact Rating (high, medium, low), Consequence Description, and Consequence Rating fields (high, medium, low), as shown in Exhibit 8. Impact change areas are divided into the three impact change types: function, data, and user interface. The following procedure is used to document the impact/consequences matrix:

- List each major impact area in the Impact Area field.
- Describe each impact in the Impact Description field.
- Rate each impact as either high, medium, or low in the Impact Rating field.
- Describe the consequence of the impact in the Consequences Description field, e.g., the implications.
- Rate the consequences associated either high, medium, or low in the Consequence Rating field.
- Sort the impact areas by priority rating.

The impact/consequence matrix in Exhibit 8 serves as the basis for choosing new enhancements and/or improving the existing system. Impact and consequence with high ratings stand out.

STEP 3: SUMMARIZE THE FINDINGS

Task 1: Summarize the Maintenance Review

After the maintenance interview is completed, the interviewer should review the agenda and outline the main conclusions. The impact/consequence matrix should be reviewed and finalized. If there is the need for a

Exhibit 8. Impact/Consequence Matrix

Impact Area	Impact Description	Impact Rating (H,M,L)	Consequence Description	Consequence Rating (H,M,L)
Major Function Changes 1. 2. 3.				
Major Data Changes 1. 2. 3.				
Major User Interface Changes 1. 2. 3.				

follow-up session, one should be scheduled at this point while the members are present.

Typically during the interview, the notes are unstructured and hard to follow by anyone except the note taker. However, the notes should have at least followed the agenda. After the interview concludes, the notes should be formalized into a summary report. This should be performed by the scribe note taker. The goal is to make the results of the session as clear as possible for quality assurance and maintenance development. However, the interview leader may have to embellish the material or expand in certain areas.

Task 2: Confirm the Maintenance Review Findings

The purpose of this task is to come to an agreement between the interviewer and the maintenance review members to assure an understanding of the scope of the enhancements and defects to be in scope for the maintenance project.

After the interview notes are formalized, it is important to distribute the maintenance summary report to the other members who attended the interview. A sincere invitation for their comments or suggestions should be communicated. The interviewer should then actively follow up interview agreements and disagreements. Any changes should then be implemented. Once completed and there is full agreement, the interviewer should provide a copy of the maintenance summary report.

Part 24
Preliminary Maintenance Test Planning (Plan)

During this activity, a preliminary test plan is created that covers most of the setup, organizational, and infrastructure points. After this and enhancement prototype design activities, the test plan is finalized.

The purpose of the test planning is to provide the basis for accomplishing testing in an organized manner. From a managerial point of view it is the most important document, for it helps manage the test project. If a test plan is comprehensive and carefully thought out, test execution and analysis should proceed smoothly.

While there are many ways a test plan can be created, Exhibit 1 below provides a framework which includes most of the setup considerations. It can be treated as a checklist of test items to consider. While some of the items such as defining the test requirement and test team are obviously required, others may not be. It depends on the nature of the project and the time constraints.

Preliminary maintenance test planning consists of the following two steps: (1) build the preliminary maintenance test plan, (2) review the preliminary maintenance test plan. Each step is then broken down into its respective tasks.

STEP 1: BUILD PRELIMINARY MAINTENANCE TEST PLAN

The purpose of test planning is to provide the basis for accomplishing testing in an organized manner. From a managerial point of view it is the most important document, because it helps manage the test project. If a test plan is comprehensive and carefully thought out, test execution and analysis should proceed smoothly.

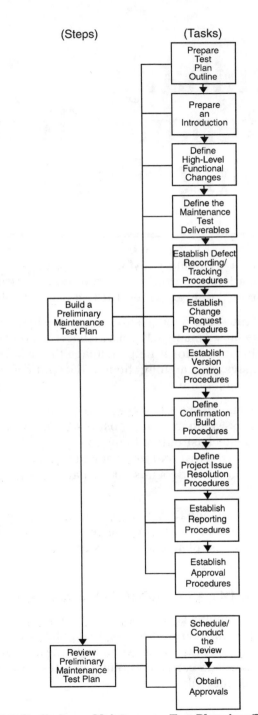

(Steps)　　　　　　(Tasks)

Exhibit 1. Preliminary Maintenance Test Planning (Steps/Tasks)

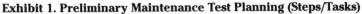

The test plan is an ongoing document, particularly in the rapid maintenance environment, since the system is constantly changing. As the system changes, so does it. A good test plan is one that:

- Has a good chance of detecting a majority of the defects
- Provides test coverage for most of the code
- Is flexible
- Is executed easily, repeatably, and automatically
- Defines the types of tests to be performed
- Clearly documents the expected results
- Provides for defect reconciliation when a defect is discovered
- Clearly defines the test objectives
- Clarifies the test strategy
- Clearly defines the test exit criteria
- Is not redundant
- Identifies the risks
- Documents the test requirements
- Defines the test deliverables

Task 1: Prepare Test Plan Outline

The key factor for a successful maintenance test plan is a well thought out outline. It should be prepared by the test manager and be consistent with the goals of the maintenance project. Exhibit 2 depicts a preliminary test plan outline.

Exhibit 2. Preliminary Maintenance Test Plan Outline

Test Plan Outline
I.   Introductions
II.   High-Level Functional Changes
III. Maintenance Test Deliverables
IV. Defect Recording/Tracking
V.   Change Requests
VI. Version Control
VII. Configuration Builds
VIII. Issue Resolution
IX. Reporting
X.   Approvals

Task 2: Prepare an Introduction

The first bit of test plan detail is a description of the problem(s) to be solved by the maintenance project and the associated improvement opportunities. This defines the summary background describing the events or current status leading up to the decision to improve the application. Also, the maintenance risks, purpose, objectives, benefits, and the organization's critical success factors should be documented in the introduction. A critical success factor is a measurable item that will have a major influence on whether or not a key function improvement meets its objectives. An objective is a measurable end state that the organization strives to achieve. Examples of objectives include

- New product opportunity
- Improved efficiency (internal and external)
- Organizational image to improve system
- Growth (internal and external)
- Financial (revenue, cost profitability) with new enhancements
- Competitive position
- Market leadership

The introduction should also include an executive summary description. The executive sponsor (often called the project sponsor) is the individual who has ultimate authority over the maintenance project. This individual has a vested interest in the project in terms of funding, project results, resolving project conflicts, and is responsible for the success of the project. An executive summary describes the proposed application improvements from an executive's point of view. It should describe the problems to be solved, the application goals, and the business opportunities. The objectives should indicate whether the application improvements is a replacement of an old system and document the impact and consequences the application will have, if any, on the organization in terms of management, technology, etc.

Any available documentation should be listed and its status described. Examples include enhancement requirements specifications, functional specifications, project plan, design specification, prototypes, user manual, business model/flow diagrams, data models, and project risk assessments. In addition to project risks, which are the potential adverse effects on the maintenance project, the risks relating to the testing effort should be documented. Examples include the lack of testing skills, scope of the maintenance testing effort, lack of automated testing tools, etc.

Task 3: Define the High-Level Functional Changes

A functional maintenance specification consists of the hierarchical functional decomposition, the functional window structure, the window standards, and the minimum system requirements of the system to be improved. An example of window standards is the Windows 95 GUI Standards. An example of a minimum system requirement could be Windows 95, a Pentium II microprocessor, 24 MB RAM, 3 gig disk space, and a modem.

At this point in the maintenance effort, a full functional specification reflecting the existing system probably exists. A list of at least the major business functions of the basic window structure and enhancements should be available. A basic functional list contains the main functions of the system with each function named and described with a verb–object paradigm. This list serves as the basis for structuring maintenance functional testing (see Exhibit 3). A functional window structure describes how the functions will be implemented in the windows environment. At this point, a full functional window structure may not be available, but a list of the major windows should be (see Exhibit 4).

Exhibit 3. High-Level Business Functions

Order Processing (create new order, edit order, etc.)
Customer Processing (create new customer, edit customer, etc.)
Financial Processing (receive payment, deposit payment, etc.)
Inventory Processing (acquire products, adjust product price, etc.)
Reports (create order report, create account receivable report, etc.)

Exhibit 4. Functional Window Structure

The Main Window (menu bar, customer order window, etc.)
The Customer-Order Window (order summary list, etc.)
The Edit-Order Window (create order, edit order, etc.)
The Menu Bar (File, Order, View, etc.)
The Tool Bar with icons (File→New, Order→Create)

Task 4: Define the Maintenance Test Deliverables

Test deliverables result from maintenance test planning, design, maintenance development, and defect documentation. Some maintenance test deliverables from which you can choose include the following:

- *Test plan:* Defines the objectives, scope, strategy, types of tests, test environment, test procedures, exit criteria, etc. (see Appendix E4, Sample Template).

- *Test design:* The tests for the application's functionality, performance, and appropriateness for use. The tests demonstrate that the original test objectives are satisfied.
- *Change request:* A documented request to modify the current software system, usually supplied by the user (see Appendix D: Change Request Form, for more details). It is typically different from a defect report, which reports an anomaly in the system.
- *Metrics:* The measurable indication of some quantitative aspect of a system. Examples include the number of severe defects, the number of defects discovered as a function of the number of testers.
- *Test case:* A specific set of test data and associated procedures developed for a particular objective. It provides a detailed blueprint for conducting individual tests and includes specific input data values and the corresponding expected result(s). (see Appendix E8: Test Case for more details).
- *Test log summary report:* Specifies the test cases from the tester's individual test logs that are in progress or completed for status reporting and metric collection (see Appendix E10: Test Log Summary Report).
- *Test case log:* Specifies the test cases for a particular testing event to be executed during testing. It is also used to record the results of the test performed, to provide the detailed evidence for the summary of test results, and to provide a basis for reconstructing the testing event if necessary (see Appendix E9: Test Case Log).
- *Interim test report:* A report published between testing cycles indicating the status of the testing effort (see Part 16, Step 3, Publish Interim Report).
- *System summary report:* A comprehensive test report after all test cycles that have been completed (see Appendix E11: System Summary Report).
- *Defect report:* Documents defect(s) discovered during the test cycles (see Appendix E12: Defect Report).

Task 5: Establish Defect Recording/Tracking Procedures

During the maintenance testing process, a defect is discovered. It needs to be recorded. A defect is related to individual tests that have been conducted, and the objective is to produce a complete record of those defects. The overall motivation for recording defects is to correct defects and record metric information about the application. Maintenance development should have access to the defects reports, which they can use to evaluate whether there is a defect and how to reconcile it. The defect form can either be manual or electronic, with the latter being preferred. Metric information such as the number of defects by type or open time for defects can be very useful to understand the status of the system.

Exhibit 5. Maintenance Defect States

	Open	Under Review	Returned by Development	Ready for Testing	Returned by QA	Deferred by Development	Closed
Open	—	Yes	Yes	—	—	Yes	—
Under Review	—	—	Yes	Yes	—	Yes	Yes
Returned by Development	—	—	—	—	Yes	—	Yes
Ready for Testing	—	—	—	—	Yes	—	Yes
Returned by QA	—	—	Yes	—	—	Yes	Yes
Deferred by Development	—	Yes	Yes	Yes	—	—	Yes
Closed	Yes	—	—	—	—	—	—

Defect control procedures need to be established to control this process from initial identification to reconciliation. Exhibit 5 shows some possible defects states from open to closed with intermediate states. The maintenance testing department initially opens a defect report and also closes it. A "Yes" in a cell indicates a possible transition from one state to another. For example, an "Open" state can change to "Under Review," "Returned by Maintenance Development," or "Deferred by Maintenance Development." The transitions are initiated by either the testing department or maintenance development.

A defect report form also needs to be designed. The major fields of a defect form include (see Appendix E12: Defect Report for more details):

- Identification of the problem, e.g., functional area, problem type, etc.
- Nature of the problem, e.g., behavior
- Circumstances that led to the problem, e.g., inputs and steps
- Environment in which the problem occurred, e.g., platform, etc.
- Diagnostic information, e.g., error code, etc.
- Effect of the problem, i.e., consequence

It is quite possible for a defect report and change request form to be the same. The disadvantage of this approach is that it is not always clear whether a change request is a defect or an enhancement request. The differentiation can be made with a form field that indicates whether it is a defect or enhancement request. On the other hand, a separate defect report can be very useful during the maintenance phase when the expected behavior of the software is well known and it is easier to distinguish between a defect and an enhancement.

Task 6: Establish Change Request Procedures

If it were a perfect world, a system would be built and there would be no future changes. Unfortunately, it is not a perfect world and after enhancement and defect analysis has occurred, there are change requests within the maintenance effort.

Some of the reasons for change are that

- The requirements change
- The design changes
- The maintenance specification is incomplete or ambiguous
- A defect is discovered that was not discovered during previous releases
- The software environment changes, e.g., platform, hardware, etc.

Change control is the process by which a modification to a software component is proposed, evaluated, rejected or approved, scheduled, and tracked. It is a decision process used in controlling the changes made to software. Some proposed changes are accepted and implemented during this process. Others are rejected or postponed, and are not implemented. Change control also provides for impact analysis to determine the dependencies (see Appendix D: Change Request Form for more details).

Each software component has a life cycle. A life cycle consists of states and allowable transitions between those states. Any time a software component is changed, it should always be reviewed. While being reviewed, it is frozen from further modifications, and the only way to change it is to create a new version. The reviewing authority must approve the modified software component or reject it. A software library should hold all components as soon as they are frozen and also act as a repository for approved components.

The formal title of the organization to manage changes is a configuration control board, or CCB. The CCB is responsible for the approval of changes and for judging whether a proposed change is desirable. For a small project, the CCB can consist of a single person, such as a project manager. For a more formal maintenance development environment, it can consist of several members from maintenance development, users, quality assurance, management, etc.

All components controlled by software configuration management are stored in a software configuration library, including work products such as business data and process models, architecture groups, design units, tested application software, reusable software, and special test software. When a component is to be modified, it is checked out of the repository into a private workspace. It evolves through many states that are temporarily outside the scope of configuration management control. When a change is completed, the component is checked in to the library and becomes a new component version. The previous component version is also retained. Change control is based on the following major functions of a maintenance development process: requirements analysis, system design, program design, testing, and implementation. At least six control procedures are associated with these functions and need to be established for a change control system (see Appendix B: Software Quality Assurance Plan for more details):

1. *Initiation Procedures*—This includes procedures for initiating a maintenance change request through a change request form, which serves as a communication vehicle. The objective is to gain consistency in documenting the change request document and routing it for approval.
2. *Technical Assessment Procedures*—This includes procedures for assessing the technical feasibility and technical risks, and scheduling a technical evaluation of a proposed maintenance change. The objectives are to ensure integration of the proposed change, the testing requirements, and the ability to install the change request.
3. *Business Assessment Procedures*—This includes procedures for assessing the business risk, effect, and installation requirements of the proposed maintenance change. The objectives are to ensure that the timing of the proposed change is not disruptive to the business goals.
4. *Management Review Procedures*—This includes procedures for evaluating the technical and business assessments through management review meetings. The objectives are to ensure that changes meet technical and business requirements and that adequate resources are allocated for testing and installation.
5. *Test Tracking Procedures*—This includes procedures for tracking and documenting test progress and communication, including steps for scheduling tests, documenting the test results, deferring change requests based on test results, and updating test logs. The objectives are to ensure that testing standards are utilized to verify the change, including test plans and test design, and that test results are communicated to all parties.
6. *Installation Tracking Procedure*—This includes procedures for tracking and documenting the installation progress of changes. It ensures that proper approvals have been completed, adequate time and skills have been allocated, installation and backup instructions have been defined, and proper communication has occurred. The objectives are to ensure that all approved changes have been made, including scheduled dates, test durations, and reports.

Task 7: Establish Version Control Procedures

In the maintenance environment, a method for uniquely identifying each software component is critical. These version control procedures are particularly important during maintenance, as some software components are changed while others are not. Every software component must have a unique name. Software components evolve through successive revisions, and each needs to be distinguished. A simple way to distinguish component revisions is with a pair of integers 1.1, 1.2, . . . , which define the release number and level number. When a software component is first identified, it is revision 1 and subsequent major revisions are 2, 3, etc.

In a client–server environment it is highly recommended that the maintenance development environment be different from the test environment. This requires the application software components to be transferred from the maintenance development environment to the test environment. Procedures need to be set up. Software needs to be placed under configuration control so that no changes are being made to the software while testing is being conducted. This includes source and executable components. Application software can be periodically migrated into the test environment. This process must be controlled to ensure that the latest version of software is tested. Versions will also help control the repetition of tests to ensure that previously discovered defects have been resolved.

For each release or interim change between versions of a system configuration, a version description document should be prepared to identify the software components.

Task 8: Define Configuration Build Procedures

Assembling a software system in an maintenance environment involves tools to transform the source components, or source code, into executable programs. Examples of tools are compilers and linkage editors.

Configuration build procedures need to be defined to identify the correct component versions and execute the component build procedures. The configuration build model addresses the crucial question of how to control the way components are built.

A configuration typically consists of a set of derived software components. An example of derived software components is executable object programs derived from source programs. Derived components must be correctly associated with each source component to obtain an accurate derivation. The configuration build model addresses the crucial question of how to control the way derived components are built.

The inputs and outputs required for a configuration build model include primary inputs and primary outputs. The primary inputs are the source components, which are the raw materials from which the configuration is

330

built, the version selection procedures, and the system model which describes the relationship between the components. The primary outputs are the target configuration and derived software components.

Different software configuration management environments use different approaches for selecting versions. The simplest approach to version selection is to maintain a list of component versions. Other automated approaches allow for the most recently tested component versions to be selected, or those updated on a specific date. Operating system facilities can be used to define and build configurations including the directories and command files.

Task 9: Define Project Issue Resolution Procedures

Testing issues can arise at any point in the maintenance effort and must be resolved successfully. The primary responsibility of issue resolution is with the maintenance project manager who should work with the project sponsor to resolve them. Typically, the testing manager will document test issues that arise during the testing process. The project manager or project sponsor should screen every issue that arises. An issue can be rejected or deferred for further investigation but should be considered relative to its impact on the project. In any case, a form should be created that contains the essential information. Examples of testing issues include lack of testing tools, lack of adequate time to test, inadequate knowledge of the requirements, etc.

Issue management procedures need to be defined before the project starts. The procedures should address how to

- Submit a maintenance issue
- Report a maintenance issue
- Screen a maintenance issue (rejected, deferred, merged, or accepted)
- Investigate a maintenance issue
- Approve a maintenance issue
- Postpone a maintenance issue
- Reject a maintenance issue
- Close a maintenance issue

Task 10: Establish Reporting Procedures

Test reporting procedures are critical to manage the maintenance testing progress and manage the expectations of the project team members. This will keep the project manager and sponsor informed of the maintenance testing project progress and minimize the chance of unexpected surprises. The testing manager needs to define who needs the test information, what information they need, and how often the information is to be provided. The objectives of test status reporting are to report the progress of the testing toward its objectives and report test issues, problems, and concerns.

Two key reports that need to be published are

- *Interim Maintenance Test Report*—A report published between testing cycles indicating the status of the testing effort.
- *Maintenance System Summary Report*—A comprehensive test report after all test cycles have been completed.

Task 11: Establish Approval Procedures

Approval procedures are critical in a maintenance testing project. They help provide the necessary agreement between members of the project team. The testing manager needs to define who needs to approve a maintenance test deliverable, when it will be approved, and what is the backup plan if an approval cannot be obtained. The approval procedure can vary from a formal sign-off of a test document to an informal review with comments. Exhibit 6 shows maintenance test deliverables for which approvals are required or recommended, and by whom.

Exhibit 6. Maintenance Deliverable Approvals

Test Deliverable	Approval Status	Suggested Approver
Test Plan	Required	Project Manager, Development Manager, Sponsor
Test Design	Required	Development Manager
Change Request	Required	Development Manager
Metrics	Recommended	Development Manager
Test Case	Required	Development Manager
Test Log Summary Report	Recommended	Development Manager
Test Log Summary Report	Recommended	Development Manager
Interim Test Report	Required	Project Manager, Development Manager
System Summary Report	Required	Project Manager, Development Manager, Sponsor
Defect Report	Required	Development Manager

STEP 2: REVIEW THE PRELIMINARY MAINTENANCE TEST PLAN

Task 1: Schedule/Conduct the Review

The preliminary test plan review should be scheduled well in advance of the actual review and the participants should have the latest copy of the test plan.

As with any interview or review, it should contain four elements. The first is defining what will be discussed, or "talking about what we are going to talk about." The second is discussing the details, or "talking about it." The third is summarization, or "talking about what we talked about." The final element is timeliness. The reviewer should state up front the estimated duration of the review and set the ground rule that if time expires before completing all items on the agenda, a follow-on review will be scheduled.

The purpose of this task is for maintenance development and the project sponsor to agree and accept the preliminary test plan. If there any suggested changes to the test plan during the review, they should be incorporated into the plan.

Task 2: Obtain Approvals

Approval is critical in a maintenance testing effort, for it helps provide the necessary agreements between the testing, maintenance development, and the sponsor. The best approach is with a formal sign-off procedure of the preliminary test plan. If this is the case, use the management approval sign-off forms. However, if a formal agreement procedure is not in place, send a memo to each key participant including at least the project manager, maintenance development manager, and sponsor. In the document attach the latest preliminary test plan and point out that all their feedback comments have been incorporated and that it you do not hear from them, it is assumed that they agree with the plan. Finally, indicate that in a maintenance development environment, the test plan will evolve with each iteration but that you will include them on any modification.

Part 25
Enhancement Prototype Design (Plan)

Previously the enhancement and defects requirements were evaluated and documented. Then the preliminary test plan was built. Now, during enhancement prototype design, enhancements are made and defects are corrected. Design review sessions are conducted to reflect the new functions, business transactions, data and user interface changes.

Exhibit 1 outlines the steps and tasks associated with this **Plan** part of the maintenance testing methodology. Each step and task is described along with valuable tips and techniques.

STEP 1: PREPARE FOR THE DESIGN SESSION

Task 1: Identify the Design Participants

It is recommended that during a maintenance design session there be no more than two interviewers representing quality assurance. It is helpful for one of these to assume the role of questioner while the other takes detailed notes. This will allow the interviewer to focus on soliciting information. Ideally the interviewer should be the manager responsible for the project testing activities. The scribe, or note taker, should be a test engineer or lead tester assigned to the project, who supports the interviewer and records each pertinent piece of information and lists the issues, the assumptions, and questions.

The recommended maintenance development participants attending include the project sponsor, maintenance development manager, or a senior maintenance development team member. While members of the maintenance development team can take notes, this is the responsibility of the scribe. Having more than one scribe can result in confusion, because multiple sets of notes will eventually have to be consolidated. The most efficient approach is for the scribe to take notes and summarize at the end of the interview.

(Steps)   (Tasks)

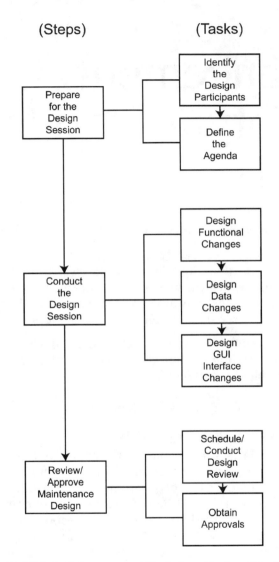

Exhibit 1. Enhancement Prototype Design (Plan)

Task 2: Define the Agenda

The key factor for a successful maintenance design session is a well-thought-out agenda. It should be prepared by the interviewer ahead of time and agreed upon by the maintenance development leader. The agenda should include an introduction, specific points to cover, and a summary section. The main purpose of an agenda is to enable the testing manager to gather enough information to scope out the quality assurance activities

**Exhibit 2. Maintenance Design
Session Agenda**

Design Session Agenda
I.   Functional Design Changes
II.   Data Design Changes
III.   GUI Design Changes
IV.   Summary

and complete the test plan. Exhibit 2 depicts a sample agenda (details are described in Step 2, "Conduct the Design Session").

STEP 2: CONDUCT THE DESIGN SESSION

Task 1: Design Functional Changes

During this task new and modified business functional changes defined during Enhancement/Defect Requirements Analysis are designed. A business function is a discrete controllable aspect of the business and the smallest component of a system. Each is named and described with a verb–object paradigm.

Each function requires an expert from that area to help define or modify existing functions and how they should be measured. For example, for an order function, a staff member experienced in order management should be part of the maintenance design.

In an online application a function consists of one or more business transactions. A business transaction consists of a set of automated and manual activities needed to satisfy one or more business events. Order processing is an example business transaction. The activities associated with taking an order might include taking an order, fulfilling the order, editing the order, and deleting an order. A business event that triggers order handling is the arrival of a new order from a customer.

The first step in designing the functional changes is to describe the normal flow of activities within a business transaction. Once this is completed, exception handling activities need to be addressed which less common circumstances from the normal flow. When an incorrect order information is input from the user, the transaction must handle this.

Task 2: Design Data Changes

During this task databases and files affected by new data requirements and data changes are designed. The data access requirements, data access models, and data integrity requirements are reviewed in light of the changes.

A good starting point for understanding the changes to databases is a data model. It is a logical representation of the information needed or data object types required by the application, may need to be modified. It establishes the associations between people, places, and things of importance to the application and is used later in physical database design which is part of physical design phase. A data model is a graphical technique used to define the entities and the relationships of the real database. An entity is something about which we want to store data. It is a uniquely identifiable person, place, thing, or event of interest to the user, about which the application is to maintain and report data. Examples of entities are customers, orders, offices, purchase orders. Data attributes and/or relationships may also need to also be added or modified as part of the enhancement/defect analysis. The logical database also needs to be refined and tuned for design considerations and in some cases needs to be denormalized because of performance requirements.

All locations where data is physically stored in the real database need to be reviewed to determine what changes need to be made for each location including additional locations. The data traffic levels at all locations need to be reevaluated to take into consideration new performance requirements.

Task 3: Design GUI Interface Changes

During this task the user GUI interface components are enhanced and modified by building a working prototype of the applications' on-line activities. All new GUI changes need to be prototyped. Screen flow diagrams and templates are used to model the functionality and screen behavior and navigation.

Each screen panel is redesigned to suit the purpose of the business transaction activity, within the format of the standard screen templates. Attention should also be paid to the time for a user to learn the new enhancement features, the speed to perform the new functions, and the ease of remembering transaction sequences. The number of keystrokes and mouse movements should be optimized and minimized for usability. Performance problems associated with new enhancements or changes can be avoided by minimizing the number of different record types to be accessed.

As the GUI design evolves and is improved, a CRUD matrix should also be modified. A CRUD matrix links data and processes or functions and helps ensure that the data and processes are discovered and assessed in the GUI design. It identifies and resolves matrix omissions and conflicts and helps refine the data and processes, as necessary. It maps processes against entities to show which processes create, read, update, or delete the instances in an entity.

Entity \ Process	Entity Type									Comment
	1	2	3	4	5	6	7	8	9	
Planning	crud				cu			cu		
Selling		ud	c			c				
Scheduling	c				d	crud		d		
Compensation			cu	c	d		cu			
Shipping		crud	ud	u	c	crud				
Operations					crud		crud			
Maintenance		c			cu			cu		
Cost Planning	crud					crud				
Purchasing			ud				d			
Forecasting							c			
Receiving		c	c		c					
Ordering	d					d		cu		
Research			crud		c		crud			
• • •										

Exhibit 3. CRUD Matrix

This will later enable CRUD testing (see Appendix H9: CRUD Testing), a testing technique that verifies the life cycle of all business objects. In the exhibit below, each CRUD cell object is tested. As shown in Exhibit 3, when an object does not have full life cycle operations a "–" can be placed in a cell. A variation of this is to also make unit performance measurements for each operation.

STEP 3: REVIEW/APPROVE MAINTENANCE DESIGN

Task 1: Schedule/Conduct Design Review

The design review should be scheduled well in advance of the actual review, and the participants should have the latest copy of the preliminary test plan.

As with any interview or review, it should contain four elements. The first is defining what will be discussed, or "talking about what we are going to talk about." The second is discussing the details, or "talking about it." The third is summarization, or "talking about what we talked about." The final element is timeliness. The reviewer should state up front the estimated duration of the review and set the ground rule that if time expires before completing all items on the agenda, a follow-on review will be scheduled.

The purpose of this task is for maintenance development and the project sponsor to agree and accept the test plan. If there are any suggested changes to the test plan during the review, they should be incorporated into the test plan.

Task 2: Obtain Approvals

Approval is critical in a maintenance testing effort, for it helps provide the necessary agreements between the testing, maintenance development, and the sponsor. The best approach is with a formal sign-off procedure of a test plan. If this is the case, use the management approval sign-off forms. However, if a formal agreement procedure is not in place, send a memo to each key participant including at least the project manager, maintenance development manager, and sponsor. In the document attach the latest test plan and point out that all their feedback comments have been incorporated and that it you do not hear from them, it is assumed that they agree with the plan. Finally, indicate that in a maintenance development environment, the test plan will evolve with each iteration but that you will include them on any modification.

Part 26
Completed Maintenance Test Planning (Plan)

Previously the preliminary test plan was documented, which included a description of the high-level functional changes, maintenance test deliverables, defect recording/tracking, change request, version control, configuration build, issue resolution, reporting, and approval procedures.

During completed maintenance test planning, the preliminary test plan is expanded to include more details, including

- Manual versus automated testing
- Test exit criteria
- Regression test strategy
- Test team
- Test environment
- Test dependencies
- Test schedule
- Test tools
- Test metrics and metric points

Exhibit 1 outlines the steps and tasks associated with this Plan part of the maintenance testing methodology. Each step and task is described along with valuable tips and techniques.

STEP 1: FINALIZE THE MAINTENANCE TEST PLAN

Task 1: Identify Manual/Automated Test Types

The types of tests that need to be designed and executed depend totally on the maintenance objectives, i.e., the measurable end state the organization strives to achieve. For example, if the application is an enhanced financial application used by a large number of individuals, special security and

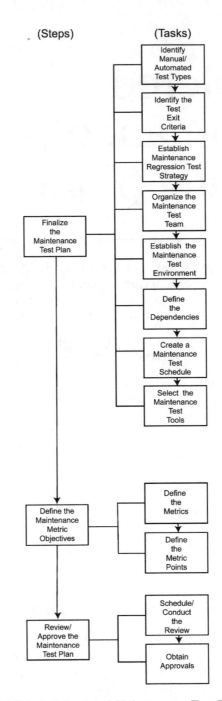

Exhibit 1. Completed Maintenance Test Plan

usability tests need to be performed. However, three types of tests which are nearly always required are

- Function
- User interface
- Regression testing

Function testing comprises the majority of the testing effort and is concerned with verifying that the functions work properly. It is a black-box-oriented activity (see Appendix H2: Black Box Testing) in which the tester is completely unconcerned with the internal behavior and structure of the application. User interface testing, or GUI testing, checks the user's interaction or functional window structure. It ensures that object state dependencies function properly and provide useful navigation through the functions. Regression testing (see Appendix H27: Regression Testing) tests the application in light of changes made during debugging, maintenance, or the maintenance development of a new release.

Other types of tests that need to be considered include system and acceptance testing. System testing is the highest level of testing, evaluating the functionality as a total system, its performance and overall fitness of use. Acceptance testing is an optional user-run test that demonstrates the ability of the application to meet the user's requirements. This test may or may not be performed, based on the formality of the project. Sometimes the system test suffices.

Finally, the tests that can be automated with a testing tool need to be identified. Automated tests provide three benefits: repeatability, leverage, and increased functionality. Repeatability is essential in the maintenance environment and enables automated tests to be executed more than once, consistently. Leverage comes from repeatability from tests previously captured and tests that can be programmed with the tool, which may not have been possible without automation. As applications evolve, more and more functionality is added. With automation, the functional coverage is maintained with the test library.

Task 2: Identify the Test Exit Criteria

Even in the maintenance environment, one of the most difficult and politically charged problems is deciding when to stop testing, since it is impossible to know when all the defects have been detected. There are at least four criteria for exiting testing:

- *Scheduled testing time has expired.* This criteria is very weak, since it has nothing to do with verifying the quality of the application. This does not take into account that there may be an inadequate number of test cases or the fact that there may not be any more defects that are easily detectable.

- *Some predefined number of defects discovered.* The problems with this are knowing the number of errors to detect and also overestimating the number of defects. If the number of defects is underestimated, testing will be incomplete. Potential solutions include experience with similar applications developed by the same maintenance development team, predictive models, and industry-wide averages. If the number of defects is overestimated, the test may never be completed within a reasonable time frame. A possible solution is to estimate completion time, plotting defects detected per unit of time. If the rate of defect detection is decreasing dramatically, there may be "burnout," an indication that a majority of the defects have been discovered.

- *Predicted number of total defects.* By measuring the percentage of requirements tested or test cases executed versus the number of uncovered defects, one can extrapolate the number of remaining defects given the remaining number of requirements or test cases. A straight line is curve-fitted to the real number of requirements or test cases. The line is stretched to the vertical axis representing the total number of requirements or test cases. At this point, a horizontal line is drawn to the left-hand side number of defects uncovered. The crossover point represents a gross predication of the number of total defects.

- *All the formal tests execute without detecting any defects.* A major problem with this is that the tester is not motivated to design destructive test cases that force the tested program to its design limits, e.g., the tester's job is completed when the test program fields no more errors. The tester is motivated not to find errors and may subconsciously write test cases that show the program is error free. This criteria is only valid if there is a rigorous and totally comprehensive test case suite created that approaches 100% coverage. The problem with this is determining when there is a comprehensive suite of test cases. If it is felt that this is the case, a good strategy at this point is to continue with *ad hoc* testing. *Ad hoc* testing is a black-box testing technique in which the tester lets his or her mind run freely to enumerate as many test conditions as possible. Experience has shown that this technique can be a very powerful supplemental or add-on technique.

- *Combination of the above.* Most testing projects utilize a combination of the above exit criteria. It is recommended that all the tests be executed, but any further *ad hoc* testing will be constrained by time.

Task 3: Establish Maintenance Regression Test Strategy

Regression testing tests the application in light of changes made during maintenance for a new release, intermediate fixes, and emergency repairs. This test must be performed after functional improvements or repairs have been made to a system to confirm that the changes have no unintended side effects. Correction of errors relating to logic and control flow, computational errors, and interface errors are examples of conditions that necessitate regression testing. Cosmetic errors generally do not affect other capabilities and do not require regression testing.

It would be ideal if all the tests in the test suite were rerun for each new test cycle, but due to time constraints this is probably not realistic. A good regression strategy during maintenance development is for some regression testing to be performed during each iteration to ensure that previously demonstrated capabilities are not adversely affected by later maintenance development iterations or error corrections. During system testing, after the system is stable and the functionality has been verified, regression testing should consist of a subset of the system tests. Policies need to be created to decide which tests to include.

A retest matrix is an excellent tool that relates test cases to functions (or program units), as shown in Exhibit 2. A check entry in the matrix indicates that the test case is to be retested when the function (or program unit) has been modified due to an enhancement(s) or correction(s). No entry means that the test does not need to be retested. The retest matrix can be built before the first testing cycle but needs to be maintained during subsequent iterations. As functions (or program units) are modified during a maintenance development iteration, existing or new test cases need to be created and checked in the retest matrix in preparation for the next test cycle. Over time with subsequent iterations, some functions (or program units) may be stable with no recent modifications. Consideration to selectively remove their check entries should be undertaken between testing cycles. Also see Appendix E14, Retest Matrix.

Other considerations of regression testing follow:

- Regression tests are potential candidates for test automation when they are repeated over and over in every testing life cycle.
- Regression testing needs to occur between releases after the initial release of the system.
- The test that uncovered an original defect should be rerun after it has been corrected.
- An in-depth effort should be made to ensure that the original defect was corrected and not just the symptoms.

Exhibit 2. Retest Matrix

	Test Case				
	1	2	3	4	5
Business Function					
Order Processing					
Create New Order	√	√	√	√	
Fulfill Order					
Edit Order					
Delete Order	√			√	
Customer Processing					
Create New Customer					
Edit Customer					
Delete Customer		√			
Financial Processing					
Receive Customer Payment		√	√		√
Deposit Payment					
Pay Vendor					
Write a Check	√	√	√	√	√
Display Register					
Inventory Processing					
Acquire Vendor Products					
Maintain Stock					
Handle Back Orders	√	√	√	√	√
Audit Inventory					
Adjust Product Price					
Reports					
Create Order Report					
Create Account Receivables Report	√	√	√	√	√
Create Account Payables					
Create Inventory Report					

- Regression tests that repeat other tests should be removed. Other test cases in the functional (or program unit) area where a defect is uncovered should be included in the regression test suite.
- Client-reported defects should have high priority and should be regression tested thoroughly.

Task 4: Organize the Maintenance Test Team

The people component includes human maintenance resource allocations and the required skill sets. The test team should comprise the highest-caliber maintenance personnel possible. They are usually extremely busy because their talents put them in great demand, and it therefore becomes vital to build the best case possible for using these individuals for test purposes. A test team leader and test team need to have the right skills and experience, and be motivated to work on the project. Ideally, they should be professional quality assurance specialists but can represent the executive sponsor, users, technical operations, database administration, computer center, independent parties, etc. The latter is particularly useful during final system and acceptance testing. In any event, they should not represent the maintenance development team, for they may not be as unbiased as an outside party. This is not to say that developers shouldn't test. For they should unit and function test their code extensively before handing it over to the test team.

There are two areas of responsibility in testing: testing the application under maintenance development, which is the responsibility of the test team; and the overall testing process, which is handled by the test manager. The test manager directs one or more testers, is the interface between quality assurance and the maintenance development organization, and manages the overall testing effort. Responsibilities include

- Setting up the test objectives
- Defining maintenance test resources
- Creating maintenance test procedures
- Developing and maintaining the maintenance test plan
- Designing maintenance test cases
- Designing and executing automated testing tool scripts
- Test case maintenance development
- Providing test status
- Writing reports
- Defining the roles of the team members
- Managing the test resources
- Defining standards and procedures
- Ensuring quality of the test process

- Training the team members
- Maintaining test statistics and metrics

The maintenance test team must be a set of team players and have the following responsibilities:

- Execute maintenance test cases according to the plan
- Evaluate the test results
- Report errors
- Design and execute automated testing tool scripts
- Recommend application improvements
- Record defects

The main function of a team member is to test the application and report defects to the maintenance development team by documenting them in a defect tracking system. Once the maintenance development team corrects the defects, the test team reexecutes the tests that discovered the original defects. It should be pointed out that the roles of the test manager and team members are not mutually exclusive. Some of the team leader's responsibilities are shared with the team member and visa versa.

The basis for allocating dedicated testing resources is the scope of the functionality and the maintenance time frame, e.g., a medium maintenance project will require more testing resources than a small one. If project A of medium complexity requires a testing team of 5, project B with twice the scope would require 10 testers (given the same resources). Another rule of thumb is that the testing costs approach 25% of the total budget. Since the total project cost is known, the testing effort can be calculated and translated to tester headcount.

The best estimate is a combination of the project scope, test team skill levels, and project history. A good measure of required testing resources for a particular project is the histories of multiple projects, i.e., testing resource levels and performance compared to similar projects.

Task 5: Establish the Maintenance Test Environment

The purpose of the maintenance test environment is to provide a physical framework for testing necessary for the testing activity. For this task, the test environment needs are established and reviewed before implementation.

The main components of the test environment include the physical test facility, technologies, and tools. The test facility component includes the physical setup. The technologies component includes the hardware platforms, physical network and all its components, operating system software, and other software such as utility software. The tools component includes any specialized testing software such as automated test tools, testing libraries, and support software.

The testing facility and workplace need to be established. This may range from an individual workplace configuration to a formal testing lab. In any event, it is important that the testers be together and in close proximity to the maintenance development team. This facilitates communication and the sense of a common goal. The testing tools that were acquired need to be installed.

The hardware and software technologies need to be set up. This includes the installation of test hardware and software, and coordination with vendors, users, and information technology personnel. It may be necessary to test the hardware and coordinate with hardware vendors. Communication networks need to be installed and tested.

Task 6: Define the Dependencies

A good source of information is previously produced test plans on other projects. If available, the sequence of tasks in the project work plans can be analyzed for activity and task dependencies that apply to this project. Examples of test dependencies include

- Previous release notes
- Previous release defect log
- Code availability
- Tester availability (in a timely fashion)
- Test requirements (reasonably defined)
- Test tools availability
- Test group training
- Technical support
- Fix defects in a timely manner
- Adequate testing time
- Computers and other hardware
- Software and associated documentation
- System documentation (if available)
- Defined maintenance development methodology
- Test lab space availability
- Agreement with maintenance development (procedures and processes)

The support personnel need to be defined and committed to the project. This includes members of the maintenance development group, technical support staff, network support staff, and database administrator support staff.

Task 7: Create a Maintenance Test Schedule

A maintenance test schedule should be produced that includes the testing steps (and perhaps tasks), target start and end dates, and responsibilities. It should also describe how these will be reviewed, tracked, and approved.

Exhibit 3. Test Schedule

Test Step	Begin Date	End Date	Responsible
First Spiral			
Information Gathering			
Prepare for Interview	6•1•98	6•2•98	Smith, Test Manager
Conduct Interview	6•3•98	6•3•98	Smith, Test Manager
Summarize Findings	6•4•98	6•5•98	Smith, Test Manager
Test Planning			
Build Test Plan	6•8•98	6•12•98	Smith, Test Manager
Define the Metric Objectives	6•15•98	6•17•98	Smith, Test Manager
Review/Approve Plan	6•18•98	6•18•98	Smith, Test Manager
Test Case Design			
Design Function Tests	6•19•98	6•23•98	Smith, Test Manager
Design GUI Tests	6•24•98	6•26•98	Smith, Test Manager
Define the System/Acceptance Tests	6•29•98	6•30•98	Smith, Test Manager
Review/Approve Design	7•3•98	7•3•98	Smith, Test Manager
Test Development			
Develop Test Scripts	7•6•98	7•16•98	Jones, Baker, Brown, Testers
Review/Approve Test Development	7•17•98	7•17•98	Jones, Baker, Brown, Testers
Test Execution/Evaluation			
Setup and Testing	7•20•98	7•24•98	Smith, Jones, Baker, Brown, Testers
Evaluation	7•27•98	7•29•98	Smith, Jones, Baker, Brown, Testers
Prepare for the Next spiral			
Refine the Tests	8•3•98	8•5•98	Smith, Test Manager
Reassess Team, Procedures, and Test Environment	8•6•98	8•7•98	Smith, Test Manager
Publish Interim Report	8•10•98	8•11•98	Smith, Test Manager
•			
•			
•			

Exhibit 3. (Continued) Test Schedule

Test Step	Begin Date	End Date	Responsible
Last Spiral…			
Test Execution/Evaluation			
Setup and Testing	10•5•98	10•9•98	Jones, Baker, Brown, Testers
Evaluation	10•12•98	10•14•98	Smith, Test Manager
•			
•			
•			
Conduct System Testing			
Complete System Test Plan	10•19•98	10•21•98	Smith, Test Manager
Complete System Test Cases	10•22•98	10•23•98	Smith, Test Manager
Review/Approve System Tests	10•26•98	10•30•98	Jones, Baker, Brown, Testers
Execute the System Tests	11•2•98	11•6•98	Jones, Baker, Brown, Testers
Conduct Acceptance Testing			
Complete Acceptance Test Plan	11•9•98	11•10•98	Smith, Test Manager
Complete Acceptance Test Cases	11•11•98	11•12•98	Smith, Test Manager
Review/Approve Acceptance Test Plan	11•13•98	11•16•98	Jones, Baker, Brown, Testers
Execute the Acceptance Tests	11•17•98	11•20•98	
Summarize/Report Spiral Test Results			
Perform Data Reduction	11•23•98	11•26•98	Smith, Test Manager
Prepare Final Test Report	11•27•98	11•27•98	Smith, Test Manager
Review/Approve the Final Test Report	11•28•98	11•29•98	Smith, Test Manager Baylor, Sponsor

A simple test schedule format, as shown in Exhibit 3, follows the maintenance methodology. Also, a project management tool such as Microsoft Project can format a Gantt chart to emphasize the tests and group them into test steps. A Gantt chart consists of a table of task information and a bar chart that graphically displays the test schedule. It also includes task time duration and links the task dependency relationships graphically. People resources can also be assigned to tasks for workload balancing. See

Appendix E13, Test Schedule. Another way to schedule testing activities is with "relative scheduling" in which testing steps or tasks are defined by their sequence or precedence. It does not state a specific start or end date but does have a duration, such as days.

It is also important to define major external and internal milestones. External milestones are events that are external to the project but may have a direct impact on the project. Examples include project sponsorship approval, corporate funding, and legal authorization. Internal milestones are derived for the schedule work plan and typically correspond to key deliverables which need to be reviewed and approved. Examples include test plan, design, and maintenance development completion approval by the project sponsor and the final maintenance test summary report. Maintenance milestones can be documented in the test plan in table format, as shown in Exhibit 4.

Exhibit 4. Maintenance Milestones

Project Milestone	Due Date
Sponsorship approval	7•1•98
First prototype available	7•20•98
Project test plan	6•18•98
Test development complete	7•17•98
Test execution begins	7•20•98
Final spiral test summary report published	11•27•98
System ship date	12•1•98

Task 8: Select the Maintenance Test Tools

Maintenance test tools range from relatively simple to sophisticated software. New tools are being developed to help provide the high-quality software needed for today's applications. Because test tools are critical to effective testing, those responsible for testing should be proficient in using them. The tools selected should be most effective for the environment in which the tester operates and the specific types of software being tested. The test plan needs to name specific test tools and their vendors. The individual who selects the test tool should also conduct the test and be familiar enough with the tool to use it effectively. The test team should review and approve the use of each test tool, because the tool selected must be consistent with the objectives of the test plan.

The selection of testing tools may be based on intuition or judgment. However, a more systematic approach should be taken. Section VI, Modern Maintenance Tools, provides a comprehensive methodology for acquiring testing tools. It also provides an overview of the types of modern maintenance tools available.

STEP 2: DEFINE THE MAINTENANCE METRIC OBJECTIVES

"You can't control what you can't measure." This is a quote from Tom De-Marco's book, *Controlling Software Projects*, in which he describes how to organize and control software project so they are measurable in the context of time and cost projections. Control is the extent to which a manager can ensure minimum surprises. Deviations to the plan should be signaled as early as possible in order to react. Another quote from DeMarco's book is "the only unforgivable failure is the failure to learn from past failure," which stresses the importance of estimating and measurement. Measurement is a recording of past effects to quantitatively predict future effects.

Task 1: Define the Metrics

Software testing as a test maintenance development project has deliverables such as test plans, test design, test maintenance development and test execution. The objective of this task is to apply the principles of metrics to control the testing process. A metric is a measurable indication of some quantitative aspect of a system and has the following characteristics:

- *Measurable*—A metric point must be measured for it to be a metric, by definition. If the phenomenon can't be measured, there is no way to apply management methods to control it.
- *Independent*—Metrics need to be independent of the human influence. There should be no way of changing the measurement other than changing the phenomenon that produced the metric.
- *Accountable*—Any analytical interpretation of the raw metric data rests on the data itself and it is, therefore, necessary to save the raw data and the methodical audit trail of the analytical process.
- *Precise*—Precision is a function of accuracy. The key to precision is, therefore, that a metric is explicitly documented as part of the data collection process. If a metric varies, it can be measured as a range or tolerance.

A metric can be a "result," or "predictor." A result metric measures a completed event or process. Examples include actual total elapsed time to process a business transaction or total test costs of a project. A predictor metric is an early warning metric that has a strong correlation to some later result. An example is the predicated response-time through statistical regression analysis when more terminals are add to a system when that many terminals have not yet been measured. A result or predictor metric can also be a derived metric. A derived metric is one that is derived from a calculation or graphical technique involving one or more metrics.

The motivation for collecting test metrics is to make the maintenance testing process more effective. This is achieved by carefully analyzing the metric data and taking the appropriate action to correct problems. The starting point is to define the metric objectives which are of interest. Some examples include

- *Defect analysis*—Every defect must be analyzed to answer such questions as the root causes, how detected, when detected, who detected, how long to fix, etc.
- *Test effectiveness*—How well is testing doing, e.g., return on investment?
- *Maintenance development effectiveness*—How well is maintenance development fixing defects?
- *Test automation*—How much effort is expended on test automation?
- *Test cost*—What are the resources and time spent on testing?
- *Test status*—Another important metric is status tracking, or where are we in the testing process? How much function has been tested, etc?
- *User involvement*—How much is the user involved in testing?
- *Installation effectiveness*—How well is installation going?

Task 2: Define the Metric Points

Exhibit 5 lists some metric points associated with the general metrics selected in the previous task and the corresponding actions to improve the testing process.

STEP 3: REVIEW/APPROVE THE MAINTENANCE TEST PLAN

Task 1: Schedule/Conduct the Review

The completed maintenance test plan review should be scheduled well in advance of the actual review, and the participants should have the latest copy of the test design.

As with any interview or review, it should contain four elements. The first is defining what will be discussed, or "talking about what we are going to talk about." The second is discussing the details, or "talking about it." The third is summarization, or "talking about what we talked about." The final element is timeliness. The reviewer should state up front the estimated duration of the review and set the ground rule that if time expires before completing all items on the agenda, a follow-on review will be scheduled.

Exhibit 5. Test Schedule

Metric	Metric Point	Derivation
Defect analysis:	Distribution of defect causes	Histogram, Pareto
Defect analysis:	Number of defects by cause over time	Multi-line graph
Defect analysis:	Number of defects by how found over time	Multi-line graph
Defect analysis:	Distribution of defects by module	Histogram, Pareto
Defect analysis:	Distribution of defects by priority (critical, high, medium, low)	Histogram
Defect analysis:	Distribution of defects by functional area	Histogram
Defect analysis:	Distribution of defects by environment (platform)	Histogram, Pareto
Defect analysis:	Distribution of defects by type (architecture, connectivity, consistency, database integrity, documentation, GUI, installation, memory, performance, security, standards and conventions, stress, usability, bad fixes)	Histogram, Pareto
Defect analysis:	Distribution of defects by who detected (external customer, internal customer, development, QA, other)	Histogram, Pareto
Defect analysis:	Distribution by how detected (technical review, walkthroughs, JAD, prototyping, inspection, test execution)	Histogram, Pareto
Defect analysis:	Distribution of defects by severity (high, medium, low defects)	Histogram
Defect analysis:	Average fix rate	Total fix rate times/number of fixes

Exhibit 5. (Continued) Test Schedule

Metric	Metric Point	Derivation
Defect analysis:	Recurrence ration	Number fixes that fail to correct defect/number of fixes
Defect analysis:	Post-release defects	Count
Defect analysis:	Defect prevention	Determining within maintenance development defect could have been detected
Development effectiveness:	Average time for development to repair defect	Total repair time ÷ number of repaired defects
Installation effectiveness:	Number of software changes installed	Count
Installation effectiveness:	Number of software changes installed by application	Histogram
Installation effectiveness:	Number of old software versions deleted	Count
Installation effectiveness:	Number of new software versions installed	Count
Installation effectiveness:	Number of installation conditions monitored	Count
Installation effectiveness:	Number of software changes not installed on time	Count
Test automation:	Percent of manual vs. automated testing	Cost of manual test effort ÷ total test cost
Test cost:	Distribution of cost by cause	Histogram, Pareto
Test cost:	Distribution of cost by application	Histogram, Pareto
Test cost:	Percent of costs for testing	Test testing cost ÷ total system cost
Test cost:	Total costs of testing over time	Line graph

Exhibit 5. (Continued) Test Schedule

Metric	Metric Point	Derivation
Test cost:	Average cost of locating a defect	Total cost of testing ÷ number of defects detected
Test cost:	Anticipated costs of testing vs. actual cost	Comparison
Test cost:	Average cost of locating a requirements defect with requirements reviews	Requirements review costs ÷ number of defects uncovered during requirement reviews
Test cost:	Average cost of locating a design defect with design reviews	Design review costs ÷ number of defects uncovered during design reviews
Test cost:	Average cost of locating a code defect with reviews	Code review costs ÷ number of defects uncovered during code reviews
Test cost:	Average cost of locating a defect with test execution	Test execution costs ÷ number of defects uncovered during test execution
Test cost:	Number of testing resources over time	Line plot
Test effectiveness:	Percentage of defects discovered during maintenance	Number of defects discovered during maintenance ÷ total number of defects uncovered
Test effectiveness:	Percent of defects uncovered due to testing	Number of detected errors through testing ÷ total system defects
Test effectiveness:	Average effectiveness of a test	Number of tests ÷ total system defects

Exhibit 5. (Continued) Test Schedule

Metric	Metric Point	Derivation
Test effectiveness:	Value returned while reviewing requirements	Number of defects uncovered during requirements review ÷ requirements test costs
Test effectiveness:	Value returned while reviewing design	Number of defects uncovered during design review ÷ design test costs
Test effectiveness:	Value returned while reviewing programs	Number of defects uncovered during program review ÷ program test costs
Test effectiveness:	Value returned during test execution	Number of defects uncovered during testing ÷ test costs
Test effectiveness:	Effect of testing changes	Number of tested changes ÷ problems attributable to the changes
Test effectiveness:	People's assessment of effectiveness of testing	Subjective scaling (1–10)
Test effectiveness:	Average time for QA to verify fix	Total QA verification time ÷ total number of defects to verify
Test effectiveness:	Number of defects over time	Line graph
Test effectiveness:	Cumulative number of defects over time	Line graph
Test effectiveness:	Number of application defects over time	Multi-line graph
Test effectiveness:	Number of problems discovered during installation	Count
Test extent:	Percent of statements executed	Number of statements executed ÷ total statements

Exhibit 5. (Continued) Test Schedule

Metric	Metric Point	Derivation
Test extent:	Percent of logical paths executed	Number of logical paths ÷ total number of paths
Test extent:	Percent of acceptance criteria tested	Acceptance criteria tested ÷ total acceptance criteria
Test extent:	Number of requirements tested over time	Line plot
Test extent:	Number of statements executed over time	Line plot
Test extent:	Number of data elements exercised over time	Line plot
Test extent:	Number of decision statements executed over time	Line plot
Test extent:	Code average	Number statements/ total number of statements
Test extent:	Requirements coverage	Number of requirements tested/ total number of requirements
Test extent:	Remaining number of defects	Line graph extrapolation
Test extent:	Requirements satisfied	Number of requirements tests passed/number of requirement tests
Test extent:	Requirements priority coverage	Number of requirements tested (by priority)/total number of requirements (by priority)
Test status:	Number of tests ready to run over time	Line plot

Exhibit 5. (Continued) Test Schedule

Metric	Metric Point	Derivation
Test status:	Number of tests runs over time	Line plot
Test status:	Number of tests run without defects uncovered	Line plot
Test status:	Number of defects corrected over time	Line plot
User involvement:	Percentage of user testing	User testing time ÷ total test time

The purpose of this task is for maintenance development and the project sponsor to agree and accept the test design. If there are any suggested changes to the test design during the review, they should be incorporated into the test design.

Task 2: Obtain Approvals

Approval is critical in a maintenance testing effort, for it helps provide the necessary agreements between the testing, maintenance development, and the sponsor. The best approach is with a formal sign-off procedure of a test design. If this is the case, use the management approval sign-off forms. However, if a formal agreement procedure is not in place, send a memo to each key participant including at least the project manager, maintenance development manager, and sponsor. In the document attach the latest test design and point out that all their feedback comments have been incorporated and that it you do not hear from them, it is assumed that they agree with the design. Finally, indicate that in a rapid spiral maintenance development environment, the test design will evolve with each iteration but that you will include them on any modification.

Part 27
Maintenance Test Case Design (Do)

If you will recall, in a maintenance improvement environment, software testing is described as a continuous improvement process that must be integrated into an application maintenance development methodology. We are now in the Do part of the model. Deming's continuous improvement process using the PDCA model (Exhibit 1) is applied to the software testing process.

Exhibit 2 below outlines the steps and tasks associated with the Do part of maintenance testing. Each step and task is described below, along with valuable tips and techniques.

STEP 1: DESIGN FUNCTION TESTS

Task 1: Refine the Functional Test Requirements

At this point, the functional specification should have been modified to reflect the maintenance changes. It consists of the hierarchical functional decomposition, the functional window structure, the window standards, and the minimum system requirements of the system to be developed. An example of a window standard is the Windows 95 GUI Standards. A minimum system requirement could consist of Windows 95, a Pentium II microprocessor, 24 MB RAM, 3 GB disk space, and a modem.

A functional breakdown consists of a list of business functions, hierarchical listing, group of activities, or set of user profiles defining the basic functions of the system and how the user will use it. A business function is a discrete controllable aspect of the business and the smallest component of a system. Each should be named and described with a verb–object paradigm. The criteria used to determine the successful execution of each function should be stated. The functional hierarchy serves as the basis for function testing in which there will be at least one test case for each lowest level function. Examples of functions include the following: approve customer credit, handle order, create invoice, order components, receive revenue, pay bill, purchase items, etc. Taken together, the business functions

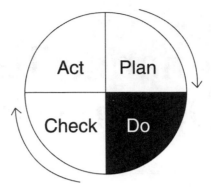

Exhibit 1. Maintenance Testing and Continuous Improvement

constitute the total application including any interfaces. A good source of these functions (in addition to the interview itself) is a process decomposition and/or data flow diagram, or CRUD matrix, which should be requested during the interview.

A functional breakdown is used to illustrate the processes in a hierarchical structure showing successive levels of detail. It is built iteratively as processes and nonelementary processes are decomposed (see Exhibit 3).

A data flow diagram shows processes and the flow of data among these processes. It is used to define the overall data flow through a system and consists of external agents which interface with the system, processes, data flow, and stores depicting where the data is stored or retrieved. A data flow diagram should be reviewed and each major function should be listed and organized into a hierarchical list.

A CRUD matrix, or association matrix, links data and process models. It identifies and resolves matrix omissions and conflicts and helps refine the data and process models, as necessary.

A functional window structure describes how the functions will be implemented in the windows environment. Exhibit 4 shows a sample functional window structure for order processing.

Task 2: Build/Modify Function/Test Matrix

The function/test matrix cross references the tests to the functions. This matrix provides proof of the completeness of the maintenance test

Test Case Design

(STEPS)   (TASKS)

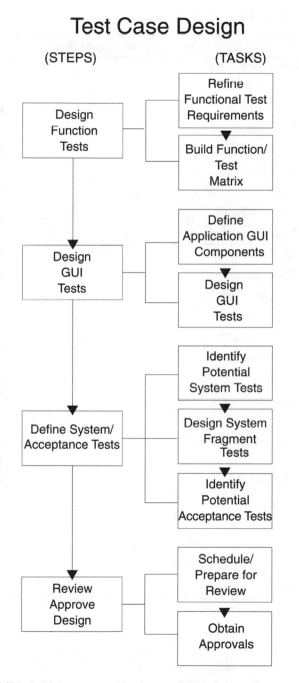

Exhibit 2. Maintenance Testing and Continuous Improvement

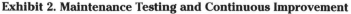

Exhibit 3. Functional Breakdown

Functional Test Requirements (breakdown)
Order Processing
Create New Order
Fulfill Order
Edit Order
Delete Order
Customer Processing
Create New Customer
Edit Customer
Delete Customer
Financial Processing
Receive Customer Payment
Deposit Payment
Pay Vendor
Write a Check
Display Register
Inventory Processing
Acquire Vendor Products
Maintain Stock
Handle Back Orders
Audit Inventory
Adjust Product Price
Reports
Create Order Report
Create Account Receivable Report
Create Account Payable Report
Create Inventory Report

strategies and illustrates in graphic format which tests exercise which functions. See Exhibit 5 and Appendix E5, Function/Test Matrix for more details.

Exhibit 4. Functional Window Structure

The Main-Window

a. The top line of the main window has the standard title bar with Min/Max controls.
b. The next line contains the standard Windows menu bar.
c. The next line contains the standard Windows tool bar.
d. The rest of the Main-Application-Window is filled with the Customer-Order Window.

The Customer-Order-Window

a. This window shows a summary of each previously entered order.
b. Several orders will be shown at one time (sorted by order number and customer name). For each customer order, this window will show:
   1. Order Number
   2. Customer Name
   3. Customer Number
   4. Date
   5. Invoice Number
   6. Model Number
   7. Product Number
   8. Quantity Shipped
   9. Price
a. The scroll bar will be used to select which orders are to be viewed.
b. This window is read-only for viewing.
c. Double-clicking an order will display the Edit-Order Dialog where the order can be modified.

The Edit-Order-Window

a. This dialog is used to create new orders or for making changes to previously created orders.
b. This dialog will be centered over the Customer-Order-Window. The layout of this dialog will show the following:
   1. Order Number (automatically filled in)
   2. Edit field for: Customer Name
   3. Edit field for: Customer Number
   4. Date (initialized)
   5. Edit field for: Invoice Number
   6. Edit field for: Model Number
   7. Edit field for: Product Number
   8. Edit field for: Quantity Shipped
   9. Price (automatically filled in)
   10. Push buttons for: OK and Cancel

Exhibit 4. (Continued) Functional Window Structure

The Menu Bar will include the following menus:

File:

New:

Used to create a new order file

Open:

Used to open the order file.

Save:

Used to save the order file

Save As...:

Used to save the current order file under a new name

Exit:

Used to exit Windows

Order:

Create New Order:

Display Edit-Order-Window with blank fields (except date)

Fulfill Order:

This dialog will be used to verify that the order quantity is available in inventory stock   and validate customer credit.

The dialog will include:

1. Edit field for: Order Number
2. Edit field for: Customer Name
3. Edit field for: Customer Number
4. Date (initialized)
5. Invoice Number (initialized)
6. Model Number (initialized)
7. Product Number (initialized)
8. Quantity Shipped (initialized)
9. Price (initialized)
10. Push buttons for: OK and Cancel
    a. The quantity order is checked against the inventory stock level. If the order cannot be filled, a back order note is sent to purchasing.
    b. The customer history will be displayed (the scroll bar will be used to view the history information).
    c. An Accept button will fulfill the order and create an invoice for shipping.
    d. A Reject button deletes the order and creates a customer order rejection letter.

Edit an Order:

This dialog will be used to edit an existing order. The dialog will include:

1. Edit field for: Order Number
2. Edit field for: Customer Name
3. Edit field for: Customer Number
4. Push buttons for: OK and Cancel

Exhibit 4. (Continued) Functional Window Structure

Delete an Order:

This dialog will be used to delete an existing order. The dialog will include:

1. Edit field for: Order Number
2. Edit field for: Customer Name
3. Edit field for: Customer Number
4. Push buttons for: OK and Cancel
    a. A confirmation message will be displayed with Yes, No, or Cancel options.

Order Report:

This dialog will display one or more orders based upon order number or date ranges.

The layout of the dialog will include:

1. Radio buttons for: Order, Date
2. First Order Number (if report by Order)
3. Optional last Order Number (if report by Order)
4. First Date (if report by Date)
5. Optional last Date (if report by Date)

The user is prompted with the message "Would you like a hard copy printout?"

The user is prompted with the message "Would you like another report (Y/N)?" after each report.

View:

Toolbar:

Used to toggle the display of the toolbar on and off.

Status bar:

Used to toggle the display of the status bar on or off.

The Tool Bar with icons to execute the following menu commands:

File → New
File → Open
Order → Create
Order → Validate
Order → Edit
File → Exit

The matrix is used as a control sheet during testing and can also be used during maintenance. For example, if a function is to be changed, the maintenance team can refer to the function/test matrix to determine which tests need to be run or changed. The business functions are listed vertically and

Exhibit 5. Functional/Test Matrix

Business Function	Test Case				
	1	2	3	4	5
Order Processing					
Create New Order	CNO01	CNO02			
Fulfill Order	AO01				
Edit Order	EO01	EO02	EO03	EO04	
Delete Order	DO01	DO02	DO03	DO04	DO05
Customer Processing					
Create New Customer	ANC01	ANC02	ANC03		
Edit Customer	EC01	EC02	EC03	EC04	EC05
Delete Customer	DC01	DC02			
Financial Processing					
Receive Customer Payment	RCP01	RCP02	RCP03	RCP04	
Deposit Payment	AP01	AP02			
Pay Vendor	PV01	PV02	PV03	PV04	PV05
Write a Check	WC01	WC02			
Display Register	DR01	DR02			
Inventory Processing					
Acquire Vendor Products	AP01	AP02	AP03		
Maintain Stock	MS01	MS02	MS03	MS04	MS05
Handle Back Orders	HB01	HB02	HB03		
Audit Inventory	AI01	AI02	AI03	AI04	
Adjust Product Price	AC01	AC02	AC03		
Reports					
Create Order Report	CO01	CO02	CO03	CO04	CO05
Create Account Receivables Report	CA01	CA02	CA03		
Create Account Payables	AY01	AY02	AY03		
Create Inventory Report	CI01	CI02	CI03	CI04	

the test cases are listed horizontally. The test case name is recorded on the matrix along with the number.

It is also important to differentiate those test cases that are manual and those that are automated. One way to accomplish this is to come up with a naming standard that will highlight an automated test case, e.g., first character of the name is "A."

Exhibit 5 shows an example of a function/test matrix.

STEP 2: DESIGN GUI TESTS

In the maintenance environment, GUI may have to be designed or updated to reflected change requests and defects discovered.

The goal of a good GUI design should be consistent in "look and feel" for the users of the application. Good GUI design has two key components: interaction and appearance. Interaction relates to how the user interacts with the application. Appearance relates to how the interface looks to the user.

GUI testing involves the confirmation that the navigation is correct, e.g., when an ICON, menu choice, or ratio button is clicked, the desired response occurs. The following are some good GUI design principles that the tester should look for while testing the application.

Ten Guidelines for Good GUI Design

1. Involve users.
2. Understand the user's culture and experience.
3. Prototype continuously to validate the requirements.
4. Let the user's business workflow drive the design.
5. Do not overuse or underuse GUI features.
6. Create the GUI, help, and training concurrently.
7. Do not expect user to remember secret commands or functions.
8. Anticipate mistakes and don't penalize the user.
9. Continually remind the user of the application status.
10. Keep it simple.

Task 1: Define the Application GUI Components

Graphical User Interface (GUI) provides multiple channels of communication using words, pictures, animation, sound, and video.

Five key foundation components of the user interface are windows, menus, forms, icons, and controls.

Windows. In a windowed environment, all user interaction with the application occurs through the windows. These include a primary window, along with any number of secondary windows generated from the primary one.

Menus. Menus come in a variety of styles and forms. Examples include Action Menus (push button, radio button), Pull-Down Menus, Pop-Up Menus, Option Menus, and Cascading Menus.

Forms. Forms are windows or screens into which the user can add information.

Icons. Icons, or "visual push buttons," are valuable for instant recognition, ease of learning, and ease of navigation through the application.

Controls. A control component appears on a screen that allows the user to interact with the application and is indicated by its corresponding action. Controls include Menu Bars, Pull-Down Menus, Cascading Menus, Pop-Up Menus, Push Buttons, Check Boxes, Radio Buttons, List Boxes, and Drop-Down List Boxes.

A design approach to GUI test design is to first define and name each GUI component by name within the application, as shown in Exhibit 6. In the next step a GUI component checklist is developed that can be used to verify each component in the table. (Also see Appendix E6, GUI Component Test Matrix).

Exhibit 6. GUI Component Test Matrix

	GUI Type							
Name	**Window**	**Menu**	**Form**	**ICON**	**Control**	**P/F**	**Date**	**Tester**
Main-Window	√							
Customer-Order Window	√							
Edit-Order Window	√							
Menu Bar		√						
Tool Bar					√			
•								
•								
•								

Task 2: Define the GUI Tests

In the previous task the application GUI components were defined or modified, named, and categorized in the GUI component test matrix. In the present task, a checklist is developed against which each GUI component

Exhibit 7. GUI Component Checklist

Access via double-click	Multiple windows open	Tabbing sequence
Access via menu	Ctrl menu (move)	Push buttons
Access via toolbar	Ctrl + function keys	Pull-down menu and sub-menus options
Right-mouse options	Color	Dialog controls
Help links	Accelerators and hot keys	Labels
Context sensitive help	Cancel	Chevrons
Button bars	Close	Ellipses
Open by double-click	Apply	Gray out unavailability
Screen images and graphics	Exit	Check boxes
Open by menu	OK	Filters
Open by toolbar	Tile horizontal/vertical	Spin boxes
ICON access	Arrange icons	Sliders
Access to DOS	Toggling	Fonts
Access via single-click	Expand/contract tree	Drag/drop
Resize window panels	Function keys	Horizontal/vertical scrolling
Fields accept allowable values	Minimize the window Maximize the window	Cascade Window open
Fields handle invalid values	Tabbing Sequence	

is verified. The list should cover all possible interactions and may or may not apply to a particular component. Exhibit 7 is a partial list of the items to check.

In addition to the GUI component checks above, if there is a GUI design standard, it should be verified as well. GUI standards are essential to ensure that the internal rules of construction are followed to achieve the desired level of consistency. Some of the typical GUI standards which should be verified, include the following:

- Forms "enterable" and display-only formats
- Wording of prompts, error messages, and help features
- Use of color, highlight, and cursors
- Screen layouts

- Function and shortcut keys, or "hot keys"
- Consistently locating screen elements on the screen
- Logical sequence of objects
- Consistent font usage
- Consistent color usage

It is also important to differentiate manual from automated GUI test cases. One way to accomplish this is to use an additional column in the GUI component matrix that indicates if the GUI test is manual or automated.

STEP 3: DEFINE THE SYSTEM/ACCEPTANCE TESTS

Task 1: Identify Potential System Tests

In a maintenance environment, system testing is the highest level of testing that evaluates the functionality as a total system, e.g., its performance and overall fitness of use. This test is usually performed by the internal organization and is orientated to systems technical issues rather than acceptance, which is a more user-orientated test.

Systems testing consists of one or more tests that are based upon the original objectives of the system, which were defined during the project interview (see Part 23, Enhancement/Defect Requirements Analysis). The purpose of this task is to select the system tests that will be performed, not how to implement the tests. Some common system test types include

- *Performance Testing*—Verifies and validates that the performance maintenance requirements have been achieved; measures response times, transaction rates, and other time-sensitive requirements.
- *Security Testing*—Evaluates the presence and appropriate functioning of the security of the application to ensure the integrity and confidentiality of the data.
- *Volume Testing*—Subjects the application to heavy volumes of data to show if it can handle the volume of data.
- *Stress Testing*—Investigates the behavior of the system under conditions that overload its resources. Of particular interest is the impact that this has on the system processing time.
- *Compatibility Testing*—Tests the compatibility of the application with other applications or systems.
- *Conversion Testing*—Verifies the conversion of existing data and loads a new database.
- *Usability Testing*—Determines how well the user will be able to use and understand the application.
- *Documentation Testing*—Verifies that the user documentation is accurate and assures that the manual procedures work correctly.
- *Backup Testing*—Verifies the ability of the system to back up its data in the event of a software or hardware failure.

- *Recovery Testing*—Verifies the system's ability to recover from a software or hardware failure.
- *Installation Testing*—Verifies the ability to install the system successfully.

Task 2: Design System Fragment Tests

System fragment tests are sample subsets of full system tests that can be performed during each test cycle. The objective of doing a fragment test during maintenance is to provide early warning of pending problems that might arise in the full system test. Candidate fragment system tests include function, performance, security, usability, documentation, and procedure. Some of these fragment tests should have formal tests performed during each test cycle, while others should be part of the overall testing strategy. Nonfragment system tests include installation, recovery, conversion, etc., which are probably going to be performed until the formal system test.

Function testing on a system level occurs during each test cycle as the system is integrated. As new functionality is added, test cases need to be designed, implemented, and tested during each test cycle.

Typically, security mechanisms are introduced fairly early in the maintenance development. Therefore, a set of security tests should be designed, implemented, and tested during each test cycle as more features are added.

Usability is an ongoing informal test during each test cycle and should always be part of the test strategy. When a usability issue arises, the tester should document it in the defect tracking system. A formal type of usability test is the end user's review of prototype, which should occur during each test cycle.

Documentation (such as online help) and procedures are also ongoing informal tests. These should be developed in parallel with formal system maintenance development during each test cycle and not wait until a formal system test. This will avoid last minute surprises. As new features are added, documentation and procedure tests should be designed, implemented, and tested during each test cycle.

Some performance testing should occur during each test cycle at non-contended unit level, e.g., one user. Baseline measurements should be performed on all key functions as they are added to the system. A baseline measurement is a measurement taken for the specific purpose of determining the initial value of the state or performance measurement. During subsequent test cycles, the performance measurements can be repeated and compared to the baseline. Exhibit 8 provides an example of baseline performance measurements.

Exhibit 8. Baseline Performance Measurements

Business Function	Baseline Seconds — Rel 1.0 (1/1/98)	Measure and Delta Seconds— Rel 1.1 (2/1/98)	Measure and Delta Seconds— Rel 1.2 (2/15/98)	Measure and Delta Seconds— Rel 1.3 (3/1/98)	Measure and Delta Seconds— Rel 1.4 (3/15/98)	Measure and Delta Seconds— Rel 1.5 (4/1/98)
Order Processing						
Create New Order	1.0	1.5/ (+50%)	1.3 (–13%)	1.0 (–23%)	.9 (–10%)	.75 (–17%)
Fulfill Order	2.5	2.0 (–20%)	1.5 (–25%)	1.0 (–33%)	1.0 (0%)	1.0 (0%)
Edit Order	1.76	2.0 (+14%)	2.5 (+25%)	1.7 (–32%)	1.5 (–12%)	1.2 (–20%)
Delete Order	1.1	1.1 (0%)	1.4 (+27%)	1.0 (–29%)	.8 (–20%)	.75 (–6%)
•	•	•	•	•	•	•
•	•	•	•	•	•	•
•	•	•	•	•	•	•
•	•	•	•	•	•	•
•	•	•	•	•	•	•
Reports						
Create Order Report	60	55 (–8%)	35 (–36%)	28 (–20%)	20 (–29%)	15 (–25%)
Create Account Receivables Report	55	65 (+18%)	55 (–15%)	35 (–36%)	25 (–29%)	20 (–20%)
Create Account Payables	120	90 (–25%)	65 (–28%)	45 (–31%)	65 (+44%)	25 (–62%)
Create Inventory Report	85	70 (–18%)	50 (–29%)	39 (–22%)	28 (–28%)	25 (–11%)

Task 3: Identify Potential Acceptance Tests

In a maintenance environment, acceptance testing is an optional user-run test that demonstrates the ability of the application to meet the user's maintenance requirements. The motivation for this test is to demonstrate rather than be destructive, e.g., showing that the system works. Less emphasis is on the technical issues and more is placed on the question of whether the system is a good business fit for the end-user. The test is usually performed by users, if performed. Typically 20% of the time this test is rolled into the system test. If performed, acceptance tests typically are a subset of the system tests. However, the users sometimes define "special tests" such as intensive stress or volume tests to stretch the limits of the system even beyond what was tested during the system test.

STEP 4: REVIEW/APPROVE DESIGN

Task 1: Schedule/Prepare for Review

The maintenance test design review should be scheduled well in advance of the actual review, and the participants should have the latest copy of the test design.

As with any interview or review, it should contain four elements. The first is defining what will be discussed, or "talking about what we are going to talk about." The second is discussing the details, or "talking about it." The third is summarization, or "talking about what we talked about." The final element is timeliness. The reviewer should state up front the estimated duration of the review and set the ground rule that if time expires before completing all items on the agenda, a follow-on review will be scheduled.

The purpose of this task is for maintenance development and the project sponsor to agree and accept the test design. If there are any suggested changes to the test design during the review, they should be incorporated into the test design.

Task 2: Obtain Approvals

Approval is critical in a maintenance testing effort, for it helps provide the necessary agreements between the testing, maintenance development, and the sponsor. The best approach is with a formal sign-off procedure of a test design. If this is the case, use the management approval sign-off forms. However, if a formal agreement procedure is not in place, send a memo to each key participant, including at least the project manager, maintenance development manager, and sponsor. In the document attach the latest test design and point out that all their feedback comments have been incorporated and that if you do not hear from them, it is assumed that they agree with the design. Finally, indicate that in a maintenance development environment, the test design will evolve with each iteration but that you will include them on any modification.

Part 28
Maintenance Test Development (Do)

Exhibit 1 outlines the steps and tasks associated with the Do/Check part of maintenance testing. Each step and task is described, along with valuable tips and techniques.

STEP 1: DEVELOP TEST SCRIPTS

Task 1: Script the Manual/Automated GUI Function Tests

In a previous step, a GUI function/test matrix was built that cross references the maintenance tests to the functions. The business functions are listed vertically and the test cases are listed horizontally. The test case name is recorded on the matrix along with the number. During this task the GUI test cases defined in the GUI function/test matrix are documented or scripted. The conceptual test cases are transformed into reusable test scripts with test data created.

To aid in the maintenance development of scripting the test cases, the GUI-based function test matrix template shown in Exhibit 2 can be used to document GUI-based test cases. Consider the following script using the template to create a new customer order. The use of this template shows the function, the case number within the test case, the requirement cross reference, the test objective, current GUI component to perform the function, the steps, the expected results, a pass/fail status, the tester, and the date the test was performed.

Task 2: Script the System Fragment Tests

In a previous task the maintenance system fragment tests were designed. They are sample subsets of full system tests that can be performed during each test loop.

Test Development

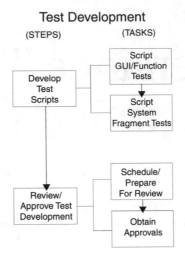

Exhibit 1. Maintenance Test Development (Steps/Tasks)

Exhibit 2. Function/GUI Test Script

Function (Create a New Customer Order)							
Case No.	REQ No.	Test Objective	Case Steps	Expected Results	(P/F)	Tester	Date
Menu Bar							
15	67	Create a Valid New Customer Order	Select File/Create Order from the menu bar	Edit-Order-Window appears	Passed	Jones	7/21/98
Edit-Order Window							
			1. Enter Order Number	Order Validated	Passed	Jones	7/21/98
			2. Enter Customer Number	Customer Validated	Passed	Jones	7/21/98
			3. Enter Model Number	Model Validated	Passed	Jones	7/21/98
			4. Enter Product Number	Product Validated	Passed	Jones	7/21/98
			5. Enter Quantity	Quantity Validated Date, Invoice Number, and Total Price Generated	Passed	Jones	7/21/98
			6. Select OK	Customer is Created Successfully	Passed	Jones	7/21/98

In this task the system fragment tests are scripted using the GUI/Function/Test Matrix discussed in Task 1. The test objective description is more broad than the Function/GUI tests, as they involve more global testing issues such as performance, security, usability, documentation, procedure, etc.

STEP 2: REVIEW/APPROVE TEST MAINTENANCE DEVELOPMENT

Task 1: Schedule/Prepare for Review

The test maintenance development review should be scheduled well in advance of the actual review and the participants should have the latest copy of the test design.

As with any interview or review, it should contain four elements. The first is defining what will be discussed, or "talking about what we are going to talk about." The second is discussing the details, or "talking about it." The third is summarization, or "talking about what we talked about." The final element is timeliness. The reviewer should state up front the estimated duration of the review and set the ground rule that if time expires before completing all items on the agenda, a follow-on review will be scheduled.

The purpose of this task is for maintenance development and the project sponsor to agree and accept the test maintenance development. If there are any suggested changes to the test maintenance development during the review, they should be incorporated into the test maintenance development.

Task 2: Obtain Approvals

Approval is critical in a testing effort, for it helps provide the necessary agreements between the testing, maintenance development, and the sponsor. The best approach is with a formal sign-off procedure of a test maintenance development. If this is the case, use the management approval sign-off forms. However, if a formal agreement procedure is not in place, send a memo to each key participant, including at least the project manager, maintenance development manager, and sponsor. In the document attach the latest test maintenance development and point out that all their feedback comments have been incorporated and that if you do not hear from them, it is assumed that they agree with the maintenance development. Finally, indicate that in a maintenance development environment, the test maintenance development will evolve with each iteration but that you will include them on any modification.

Part 29
Maintenance Test Execution/ Evaluation (Do/Check)

Recall that in a maintenance improvement environment, software testing is described as a continuous improvement process that must be integrated into an application maintenance methodology. We are now in the Check part of the model. Deming's continuous improvement process using the PDCA model (Exhibit 1) is applied to the software testing process.

Exhibit 2 below outlines the steps and tasks associated with the Do/Check part of maintenance testing. Each step and task is described, along with valuable tips and techniques.

STEP 1: SETUP AND TESTING

Task 1: Regression Test the Maintenance Fixes

The purpose of this task is to retest the tests that discovered defects in the previous maintenance test cycle. The technique used is regression testing. Regression testing is a technique that detects spurious errors caused by software modifications or corrections.

A set of test cases must be maintained and available throughout the entire life of the software. The test cases should be complete enough so that all the software's functional capabilities are thoroughly tested. The question arises as to how to locate those test cases to test defects discovered during the previous test cycle. An excellent mechanism is the retest matrix.

As described earlier, a retest matrix relates test cases to functions (or program units). A check entry in the matrix indicates that the test case is to be retested when the function (or program unit) has been modified due

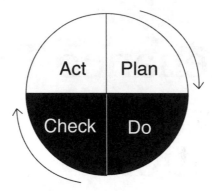

Exhibit 1. Maintenance Testing and Continuous Improvement

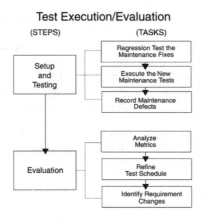

Exhibit 2. Maintenance Test Execution/Evaluation (Tasks/Steps)

to an enhancement(s) or correction(s). No entry means that the test does not need to be retested. The retest matrix can be built before the first testing cycle but needs to be maintained during subsequent iterations. As functions (or program units) are modified during a maintenance development, existing or new test cases need to be created and checked in the retest matrix in preparation for the next test cycle. Over time with subsequent test cycles, some functions (or program units) may be stable with no recent modifications. Consideration to selectively remove their check entries should be undertaken between testing cycles.

If a regression test passes, the status of the defect report should be changed to a "closed" status.

Task 2: Execute the New Maintenance Tests

The purpose of this task is to execute new maintenance tests that were created at the end of the previous testing cycle. In the previous test cycle, the testing team updated the function/GUI, system fragment, and acceptance tests in preparation for the current testing cycle. During this task those tests are executed.

Task 3: Record the Maintenance Defects

During maintenance test execution, the results of the testing must be reported in the defect tracking database. These defects are typically related to individual tests that have been conducted. However, variations to the formal test cases often uncover other defects. The objective of this task is to produce a complete record of the defects. If the execution step has been recorded properly, the defects have already been recorded on the defect tracking database. If the defects are already recorded, the objective of this step becomes to collect and consolidate the defect information.

Tools that can be used to consolidate and record defects depend on the test execution methods. If the defects are recorded on paper, the consolidation involves collecting and organizing the papers. If the defects are recorded electronically, search features can easily locate duplicate defects.

STEP 2: EVALUATION

Task 1: Analyze the Metrics

Metrics are used so that we can help make decisions more effectively and support the maintenance development process. The objective of this task is to apply the principles of metrics to control the testing process.

In a previous task, the metrics and metric points were defined for each test cycle to be measured. During the present task, the metrics that were measured are analyzed. This involves quantifying the metrics and putting them into a graphical format.

The following is the key information a test manager needs to know at the end of a test cycle:

- *Test Case Execution Status*—How many test cases have been executed, how many not executed, and how many discovered defects? This provides an indication of the tester productivity. If the test cases are not being executed in a timely manner, this raises a flag that more testers may need to be assigned to the project.
- *Defect Gap Analysis*—What is the gap between the number of defects that have been uncovered and the number that have been corrected? This provides an indication of maintenance development's ability to

correct defects in a timely manner. If there is a relatively large gap, this raises the flag that perhaps more developers need to be assigned to the project.

- *Defect Severity Status*—The distribution of the defect severity, e.g., critical, major, and minor. This provides an indication of the quality of the system. If there are a large percent of defects in the critical category, there probably exists a considerable number of design and architecture issues, which raises a flag.

- *Test Burnout Tracking*—Shows the cumulative and periodic number of defects being discovered. The cumulative, i.e., running total of defects, and defects by time period help predict when fewer and fewer defects are being discovered. This is indicated when the cumulative curve "bend" and the defects by time period approach zero. If the cumulative curve shows no indication of bending, it is a flag that discovery of defects is still very robust and that many more remain to be discovered in other test cycles.

Graphical examples of the above metrics can be seen in the "Publish the Metric Graphics" task of Part 30.

Task 2: Refine the Test Schedule

In a previous task a test schedule was produced that includes the maintenance testing steps (and perhaps tasks), target begin dates and target end dates, and responsibilities. During the course of maintenance development the testing schedule need to be continually monitored. The objective of this task is to update the test schedule to reflect the latest status. It is the responsibility of the test manager to

- Compare the actual progress to the planned progress
- Evaluate the results to determine the testing status
- Take appropriate action based upon the evaluation

If the maintenance testing progress is behind schedule, the test manager needs to determine the factors causing the slip. A typical cause is an underestimation of the test effort. Another factor could be that an inordinate number of defects are being discovered, causing a lot of the testing effort to be devoted to retesting old, corrected defects. In either case, more testers may be needed and/or overtime may be required to compensate for the slippage.

Task 3: Identify Requirement Changes

In a previous task the maintenance functional requirements were initially analyzed by the testing function, which consisted of the hierarchical functional decomposition, the functional window structure, the window standards, and the minimum system requirements of the system.

Between test cycles, new requirements may be introduced into the maintenance development process. It can consists of

- New GUI interfaces
- New functions
- Modified functions
- Eliminated functions
- New system requirements, e.g., hardware
- Additional system requirements
- Additional acceptance requirements

Each new maintenance requirement need to be identified, recorded, and analyzed.

Part 30
Prepare for the Next Test Cycle (Act)

Deming's continuous improvement process using the PDCA model is applied to the software testing process. We are now in the Act part of the model. Deming's continuous improvement process using the PDCA model (Exhibit 1) is applied to the software testing process.

Exhibit 2 outlines the steps and tasks associated with the Act part of maintenance testing. Each step and task is described, along with valuable tips and techniques.

STEP 1: REFINE THE TESTS

Task 1: Update the Function/GUI Tests

The objective of this task is to update the maintenance test design to reflect the new functional requirements. The GUI Function/Test Matrix which cross references the tests to the functions, needs to be updated. The new functions are added in the vertical list and the respective test cases are added to the horizontal list. The test case name is recorded on the matrix along with the number.

Next, any new GUI/Function test cases in the matrix need to be documented or scripted. The conceptual test cases are then transformed into reusable test scripts with test data created. Also, any new GUI requirements are added to the GUI tests.

Task 2: Update the System Fragment Tests

In a prior task the maintenance system fragment tests were defined. System fragment tests are sample subsets of full system tests that can be performed during each test loop. The objective of doing a fragment test is to provide early warning of pending problems that would arise in the full system test.

Candidate fragment system tests include function, performance, security, usability, documentation, and procedure. Some of these fragment tests should have formal tests performed during each test cycle, while others

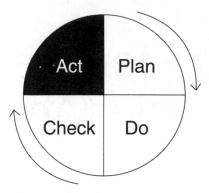

Exhibit 1. Maintenance Testing and Continuous Improvement

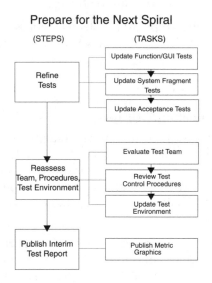

Exhibit 2. Prepare for the Next Test Cycle

should be part of the overall testing strategy. The objective of the present task is to update the system fragment tests defined earlier based upon new requirements. New baseline measurements are defined.

Task 3: Update the Acceptance Tests

In a prior task the initial list of maintenance acceptance tests was defined. Acceptance testing is an optional user-run test that demonstrates the ability of the application to meet the user's requirements. The motivation for this test is to demonstrate rather than be destructive, e.g., showing that the system works. If performed, acceptance tests typically are a subset of the system tests. However, the users sometimes define "special tests" such as intensive stress or volume tests to stretch the limits of the system even beyond what was tested during the system test.

The objective of the present task is to update the acceptance tests defined earlier based upon new requirements.

STEP 2: REASSESS THE TEAM, PROCEDURES, AND TEST ENVIRONMENT

Task 1: Evaluate the Test Team

Between each maintenance test cycle, the performance of the test team needs to be evaluated in terms of its quality and productivity. The test team leader directs one or more testers and assures that the right skill level is brought to the project. He or she makes sure that the test cases are being executed according to the plan, the defects are being reported and retested, the test automation is successful.

The basis for allocating dedicated testing resources is the scope of the functionality and the maintenance development time frame. If the testing is not being completed satisfactorily, the team leader needs to counsel one or more team members and/or request additional testers.

Task 2: Review the Test Control Procedures

In a prior task the maintenance test control procedures were set up before the first test cycle. The objective of this task is to review those procedures and make appropriate modifications. The predefined procedures include the following:

- Defect recording/tracking procedures
- Change request procedures
- Version control procedures
- Configuration build procedures
- Project issues resolution procedures
- Reporting procedures

The purpose of *defect recording/tracking procedures* is to record and correct defects and record metric information about the application under maintenance improvement. As the project progresses, these procedures may need tuning. Examples include new status codes or new fields in the defect tracking form, an expanded defect distribution list, and additional verification checks.

The purpose of *change request procedures* is to allow new change requests to be communicated to the maintenance development and testing team. As the project progresses, these procedures may need tuning. Examples include a new change control review board process, a new sponsor who has ideas of how the change request process should be implemented, a new change request database, and a new software configuration management tool.

The purpose of *version control procedures* is to uniquely identify each software component via a labeling scheme and allow for successive revisions. As the project progresses, these procedures may need tuning. Examples include a new software configuration management tool with a new versioning scheme or new labeling standards.

The purpose of *configuration build procedures* is to provide an effective means to assemble a software system from the software source components into executable components. As the project progresses, these procedures may need tuning. Examples include the addition of a new 4GL language, a new software configuration management tool, or a new delta build approach.

The purpose of *project issues resolution procedures* is to record and process testing issues that arise during the testing process. As the project progresses, these procedures may need tuning. Examples include a new project manager who requests a Lotus Notes approach, formation of a new issue review committee, an issue priority categorization scheme is updated, and a new issue submission process is implemented.

The purpose of *reporting procedures* is to facilitate the communication process and reporting. As the project progresses, these procedures may need tuning. Examples include a new project manager who requires weekly testing status reports, a new interim test report structure, or an expanded reporting distribution.

Task 3: Update the Test Environment

In a prior task the maintenance test environment was defined. A test environment provides a physical framework for testing necessary for the testing activity. During this task, the test environment needs are reviewed and updated.

The main components of the test environment include the physical test facility, technologies, and tools. The test facility component includes the physical setup. The technologies component includes all of the hardware platforms, physical network and all its components, operating system software, and other software such as utility software. The tools component includes any specialized testing software such as automated test tools, testing libraries, and support software. Example of changes to the test environment include

- Expanded test lab
- New maintenance testing tools required
- Addition maintenance test hardware required
- Addition network facilities
- Additional test database space required
- New Lotus Notes logons
- Additional software to support maintenance testing

STEP 3: PUBLISH INTERIM TEST REPORT

Task 1: Publish the Metric Graphics

Each maintenance test cycle should produce an interim report to describe the status of testing. These reports are geared to the testing team, the test manager, and the maintenance development manager, and will help them make adjustments for the next test cycle. The following minimal graphical reports are recommended between each test iteration.

Test Case Execution Status. The objectives of Exhibit 3 are to show the status of maintenance testing and predict when the testing and maintenance development group will be ready for production. Test cases run with errors have not yet been corrected.

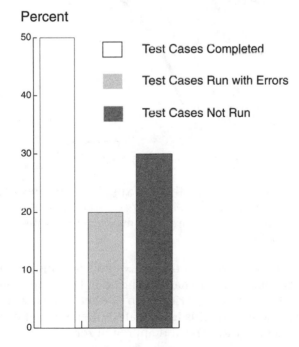

Exhibit 3. Test Execution Status

If there is a relatively large number of test cases that have not been run, the testing group needs to increase its productivity and/or resources. If there is a large number of test cases run with errors and not corrected, the maintenance development team also needs to be more productive.

Defect Gap Analysis. The objective of Exhibit 4 is to show the gap between the number of defects that have been uncovered and the number that have been corrected. If there is a large gap, this indicates that maintenance development needs to increase effort and resources to correct uncovered defects faster.

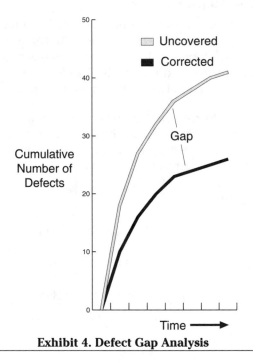

Exhibit 4. Defect Gap Analysis

Defect Severity Status. The objective of Exhibit 5 is to show the distribution of the three severity categories. A large percentage of defects in the critical category indicates that a problem may exist with the design or architecture of the application..

Test Burnout Tracking. The objective of Exhibit 6 is to indicate the rate of uncovering defects during maintenance. The cumulative, i.e., running total of defects, and defects by time period help predict when fewer and fewer defects are being discovered. This is indicated when the cumulative curve "bend" and the defects by time period approach zero

Test Exit Tracking. One of the most difficult and politically charged problems is deciding when to stop maintenance testing, since it is impos-

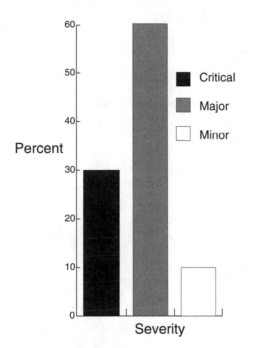

Exhibit 5. Defect Severity Status

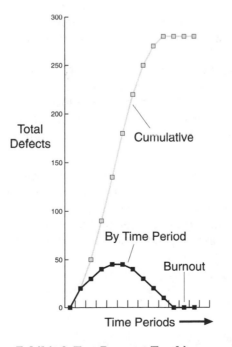

Exhibit 6. Test Burnout Tracking

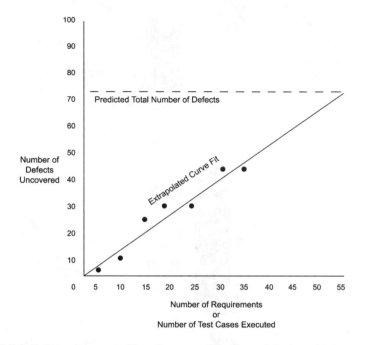

Exhibit 7. Requirements/Test Cases vs. Number of Defects Uncovered

sible to know when all the defects have been detected. This is true even though a test exit strategy was developed in the maintenance test plan. A technique that may be helpful deals with a successful requirement or test case coverage. Exhibit 7 shows a graph that tracks the number of requirements or test cases executed versus the number of defects uncovered to date. By measuring the percentage of requirements tested or test cases executed versus the number of uncovered defects, one can extrapolate the number of remaining defects given the remaining number of requirements or test cases.

The straight line is curve-fitted to the real number of requirements or test cases. The line is stretched to the vertical axis representing the total number of requirements or test cases. At this point, a horizontal line is drawn to the left-hand side number of defects uncovered. The crossover point represents a "gross" predication of the number of total defects.

Part 31
Maintenance System Testing

See Part 17, Conduct the System Test, for more details.

Conduct System Testing

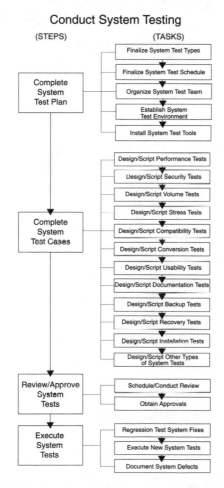

Exhibit 1. Conduct Maintenance System Testing

Part 32
Maintenance Acceptance Testing

See Part 18, Conduct Acceptance Testing, for more details.

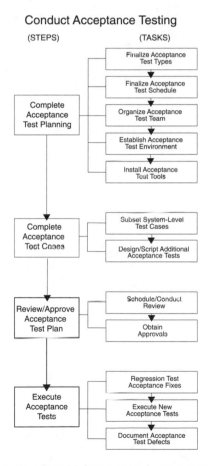

Exhibit 1. Conduct Maintenance Acceptance Testing

Part 33
Maintenance Summary Test Report

See Part 19, Summarize/Report Spiral Test Results, for more details.

Summarize/Report Maintenance Test Results

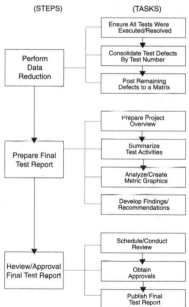

Exhibit 1. Summarize/Report Maintenance Test Results

Part 34
System Installation

The previous sections describe how to plan for and test maintenance enhancements and correct defects. This section describes how to verify the ability to successfully install the system. The time needed for actual installation is much less than that needed for monitoring the system to make sure it operates correctly and to take appropriate actions to resolve problems.

If the enhancement design changes and software have been tested properly, the bulk of the work has already been completed. However, circumstances can arise that were not anticipated during the testing.

Exhibit 1 illustrates the steps that need to be performed for a successful installation, from recovery planning to documenting any discovered system problems.

STEP 1: DEVELOP A RECOVERY PLAN

In the event the installed changes to the system do not function properly to the point that it has lost its integrity, a recovery process needs to be predefined and in place to be able to restore the old versions of the system. The process should enable the system to be backed up to its integrity level. The recovery plan needs to be tested and verified before attempting to install the new change(s).

STEP 2: PLACE MAINTENANCE CHANGES INTO PRODUCTION

Certain activities must take place to introduce the new changes and system into a production mode. One of the first is to prepare an installation checklist that will ensure that all parties are aware of the changes and new procedures. The list should describe the new changes and the operational impact of the changes from a functional and procedural point of view. The checklist should be reviewed by operations and should be signed off by the approval authorities. The users should sign off that the user community has had the proper training on the changes and is ready.

Version control is critical when the whole system is partially replaced. Each software component in the system production should be labeled when it is to be placed into production and when the old version is to be replaced. A history log of the changes to each software component must be made to be able to trace back.

System Installation

(Steps)

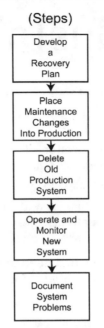

Exhibit 1. System Installation

The approved change(s) are entered into production and the respective parties are formally notified.

STEP 3: DELETE OLD PRODUCTION SYSTEM

Versions of the old production system must not be deleted until the new changes have been verified operationally. Procedures and standards need to be in place defining when the old system versions will be deleted. This requires authorization signatures.

STEP 4: OPERATE AND MONITOR NEW SYSTEM

After the new system changes are installed, the new system is put into an operational mode. Typically, if there are problems with the changes, these will surface immediately after the installation. It is, therefore, imperative that the new system is monitored closely. Interested parties include software maintenance group, system control group, users, and operations.

A change checklist describing the new changes should be used to indicate areas to monitor from a functional and operational procedural level.

STEP 5: DOCUMENT SYSTEM PROBLEMS

Problems encountered with the new change(s) must be formally document-ed and communicated. This should also include the severity, priority, risk analysis, and potential impact on the system. This information will enable the reporter to associate the problem with the respective change(s), which will help maintenance programmers to analyze and correct the problem.

Some installation metric points that were defined in a previous task are shown in Exhibit 2. The installation metric and derivation are shown. The gathering and analysis of these metrics should improve the installation process.

Exhibit 2. System Installation Metrics

Metric	Metric Point	Derivation
Installation effectiveness:	Number of installation conditions monitored	Count
Installation effectiveness:	Number of new software versions installed	Count
Installation effectiveness:	Number of old software versions deleted	Count
Test effectiveness:	Number of problems discovered during installation	Count
Installation effectiveness:	Number of software changes installed	Count
Installation effectiveness:	Number of software changes installed by application	Histogram
Installation effectiveness:	Number of software changes not installed on time	Count

Section VI
Modern Maintenance Tools

Software testing functions within maintenance departments must cope with the demands for software to provide more complex functions and features. Maintenance tools cover a wide range of activities and enable departments to build and enhance applications more effectively.

This section provides an overview of some popular maintenance test tools and demonstrates how they can improve the quality and productivity of a maintenance effort.

The objectives of this section are to

- Describe when a maintenance tool is useful.
- Provide a testing maintenance tool selection checklist.
- Discuss types of maintenance tools.
- Provide descriptions of modern and popular testing maintenance tools.

Part 35
Introduction to Maintenance Tools

Many testing tools are available today. Some of these tools are used for new development, and many are also especially suited to the maintenance area. Software testing is facilitated by the effective use of maintenance tools. In testing maintenance changes to software, the tester identifies the types of maintenance tools used by the maintenance team and determines whether they will be helpful in testing.

Software maintenance tools are computer programs that can be used in development, analysis, testing, maintenance, and management of other computer programs and their documentation. This section discusses some maintenance tools that can be useful in maintaining software systems.

Generally, there are two maintenance tool categories: technical and management. *Management maintenance tools* assist the maintenance manager in controlling and tracking all of the maintenance tasks. Some of the software maintenance tools in this category are discussed in the following sections.

Technical maintenance tools help analyze, change the source code and documentation, and test the system. A regression testing tool is an example of an automated technical tool to test the system repeatedly. It may be useful under the following circumstances:

- Tests need to be run every build of an application, e.g., time consuming, unreliability, and inconsistency using human resources.
- Tests are required using multiple data values for the same actions.
- Tests require detailed information from system internals such as SQL, GUI attributes that require an automated approach.

MAINTENANCE TESTING MAINTENANCE TOOL SELECTION CHECKLIST

Finding the appropriate maintenance tool can be difficult, and several questions need to be answered before selecting a maintenance tool. Exhibit 1 lists questions to help the maintenance test team evaluate and select a maintenance tool.

Exhibit 1. Testing Tool Selection Checklist

Item	Yes	No	N/A	Comments
1. How easy is the tool for your maintenance testers to use?				
2. Is it something that can be picked up quickly, or is a lot of training required?				
3. Do any of the team members already have experience using the maintenance tool?				
4. If training is necessary, are classes, books, or other forms of instruction available?				
5. Will the maintenance tool work effectively on the computer system currently in place?				
6. Or are more memory, faster processors, etc., going to be needed?				
7. Is the maintenance tool itself easy to use?				
8. Does it have a user-friendly interface?				
9. Is it prone to user error?				
10. Is the tool physically capable of testing your application? Many maintenance tools can only test in a non-GUI environment, while others in GUI environments.				
11. Can the maintenance tool handle full project testing? That is, is it able to run hundreds if not thousands of test cases for extended periods of time?				
12. Can the tool run for long periods of time without crashing, or is the tool itself full of bugs?				

Exhibit 1. (Continued) Testing Tool Selection Checklist

Item	Yes	No	N/A	Comments
13. Talk to customers who currently use or have previously used the maintenance tool. Did it meet their needs?				
14. How similar were their testing needs to yours and how well did the maintenance tool perform?				
15. Try to select a maintenance tool that is advanced enough so the costs of updating tests don't overwhelm any benefits.				
16. If a demo version is available, try it out before you make any decisions.				
17. Does the price of the maintenance tool fit in the QA Department or company budget?				
18. Does the maintenance tool meet the requirements of the company maintenance and testing methodology?				
19. If required, does the tool cover black-box and white-box features?				
20. Does the tool handle problem tracking effectively?				
21. Does the tool automatically correlate a defect to a test case for regression testing?				
22. Does the test library management system handle change control, version control, and configuration?				
23. Does the tool capture metric information?				
24. Does the tool provide management reporting and historical trends?				

TYPES OF MAINTENANCE TOOLS

This section is a taxonomy of testing tool types followed by a review of specific tool vendor products. (Also see Section IV — Modern Testing Tools, for other test tools, vendor names, and contact information.)

Code Complexity Tools

Metrics characterize software with numerical measures of complexity, which allows software engineers to identify software components that would be difficult to test or maintain.

Software complexity is one of the most pertinent metrics of computer programs, and its aim is to objectively associate a number with a program, based upon the presence or absence of certain characteristics of the software such as the number of errors left in the software; effort to design, test, or maintain a software product; development time; maintenance cost; etc. The importance of software complexity lies in the fact that knowing the complexity of a specific software product or its module enables one to

- Predict the cost of maintenance
- Assess the development time, effort, and cost
- Identify critical modules or parts of the software
- Compare programs, modules, programmers based upon according to software complexity

(See McCabe's McCabe QA.)

Regression Testing Tools

Each code change, enhancement, bug fix, and platform port necessitates retesting the entire application to ensure that the change has not hindered the quality. Manual testing can no longer keep pace in this rapidly developing environment. A regression maintenance testing tool facilitates the automation of the testing process, from test development to execution. Reusable test scripts are created that test and automatically verify the system's functionality. Prior to a release, one can execute these tests in an unattended mode, which fosters the detection of defects and ensures quality deliverables.

(See SunTest's JavaStar 1.2, Test Station, WinRunner 5, Xrunner, Rational Robot, and Rational TestFactory.)

Load and Performance Maintenance Tools

The purpose of maintenance load testing tools is to simulate a production environment to determine that normal or above-normal volumes of transactions can be completed successfully in an expected time frame. These tools test the availability and capacity of system resources, such as CPU, disk, memory, channel, and communication lines.

Exhibit 2. Vendor vs. Maintenance Tool Type (alphabetic order)

Vendor Name	Code Complexity	Regression	Load/ Performance	Problem Management	CM/Process Management	Web Site	Code Coverage	Runtime Error Analysis
ClearCase					x			
ClearCase MultiSite					x			
ClearDDTS				x				
ClearQuest				x				
JavaLoad			x					
JavaStar 1.2		x						
LoadRunner			x					
McCabe QA	x						x	
Other Maintenance Tools[a]						x		
Performance Studio			x					
PreVue			x					
Rational Robot		x						
Rational Visual Quantify			x					

Exhibit 2. (Continued) Vendor vs. Maintenance Tool Type (alphabetic order)

Vendor Name	Code Complexity	Regression	Load/ Performance	Problem Management	CM/Process Management	Web Site	Code Coverage	Runtime Error Analysis
Rational Purify 6.0								x
Rational TestFactory		x					x	x
Rational Visual PureCoverage 6.0							x	
SQA SiteCheck						x		
Test Station		x						
TestStudio								
WinRunner 5		x						
Xrunner		x						

[a]See Exhibits 3 through 8.

(See JavaLoad, LoadRunner, PreVue, Performance Studio, and Rational Visual Quantity.)

Problem Management Tools

Problem management tools fulfill two major functions: call tracking and problem tracking. *Call tracking* targets problems reported by customers often over telephone lines, receives inputs from a variety of geographically disperse locations, assigns a responsible person to the problem, and provides status monitoring and reporting.

Problem tracking handles development process management, change management authorization, task management (who, what, when, due date, status); provides statistics, metrics gathering, and reporting; manages historical records and facilitation of understanding; and integrates configuration management and testing tools.

Maintenance organizations need call tracking or problem tracking, or both. Many organizations choose to integrate their problem management and configuration management tools to gain better control of their development activities and to improve quality. Problem management tools may be purchased in any of at least three distinct packaging methods:

- Stand-alone, no integration with other tools
- Purchased separately, but integrated with one or more companion software engineering tools such as configuration management and test tools—may be from the same or from different vendors
- Bundled with other software engineering tools, usually a configuration management tool from the same vendor

(See ClearQuest and ClearDDTS.)

Configuration/Process Management Tools

Some maintenance tools provide configuration management, not development process management, others provide both but to varying degrees.

Software configuration management tools are concerned with labeling, tracking, and controlling changes in the software elements of a system. They control the evolution of a software system by managing versions of its software components and their relationships.

They identify all the interrelated components of software and control their evolution throughout the various life cycle phases. Software configuration management tools ensure that design and code are defined and cannot be changed without a review of the effect of the change itself and its documentation.

A process management tool controls all the software development phases and activities from requirements to maintenance. These tools are used to assure a repeatable, optimized development process. An example of

413

how they might be utilized in the maintenance environment is to verify that a problem report existed and had been approved for fixing and that the associated design, documentation, and review activities have been completed before allowing the code to be "checked in" again.

It is important to be certain to determine what form of management is most important for your project, then be certain the tools you consider provide that function.

(See ClearCase and ClearCase MultiSite.)

Web Site Test Tools

Web sites are essentially client/server applications—with web servers and "browser" clients. Web site management tools are designed to help the Webmaster or business manager manage every aspect of a rapidly changing site. It helps detect and repair defects in the structural integrity of their sites, e.g., broken links, orphaned pages, potential performance problems on Web sites, etc.

(See SQA SiteCheck and Exhibits 3 through 8.)

Code Coverage Tools

The purpose of coverage analysis tools is to monitor the system while a dynamic testing tool is executing. They are a form of white-box testing in which there is knowledge about the internal structure of the program of the system. Information is provided on how thorough the test was. Graphic analysis displays how much the system was covered during the test, such as the percentage of code executed and in which locations. This will provide the tester with information on weaknesses in the test design, which can be solved with additional test cases. Unit and integration coverage is provided with these tools. Unit coverage entails the coverage of the code and paths within a single program unit. Integration coverage comprises the interfaces between program units to determine the linkage between them.

(See McCabe QA, Rational TestFactory, and Rational Visual PureCoverage.)

Runtime Error Analysis Tools

A runtime error analysis tool automatically finds defects in an application and optionally builds a set of test scripts that optimize code coverage. It is a dynamic testing tool that exercises the application, exploring every option and selection. It then automatically generates a set of test scripts that cover both your application's user interface and source code to the greatest extent possible in the smallest number of steps. It also indicates which source code paths have been exercised and identifies untested lines and functions. It automatically detects program defects.

(See Rational Purify and Rational TestFactory.)

414

Exhibit 3. Java Testing Tools

Tool Name	Tool Vendor	Description
AppletLoad	RadView Software	Part of Radview's WebLoad tool set; for performance testing of Applets and Java-Implemented protocols.
AssertMate	RST	RST's code assertion toolkit for Java programmers and class level testers.
Assure for Java[a]	KAI	Java debugging pool—monitors memory, references, object creation, and lock acquisitions. Finds thread deadlocks, stalls, data race conditions, synchronization errors. Results displayed in browser with pointers to source code. For Win95/NT, Solaris.
DeepCover for Java	RST	Code coverage tool for Java from RST. For Solaris and Win95/NT.
DevPartner for Java	CompuWare Corp.	NuMega/Compuware's debugging/productivity tool to detect and diagnose Java bugs and performance problems, thread and event analysis, coverage analysis.
Documentary for Java	Power Software	Automated source code documentation tool; produces HTML documentation to all classes, methods, etc., in project as well as other reference information; for Windows, Solaris, HPUX.
Jprobe Profiler	KL Group	Java optimization and monitoring tool, allows drilling down to hotspots using nine performance metrics.
jtest!	ParaSoft	ParaSoft's automated white box Java test tool.
Krakatau Metrics for Java	Power Software	Software metrics tool includes more than 70 OO, procedural, complexity, and size metrics related to reusability, maintainability, testability, and clarity. Has online advisor for quality improvement; text, graphical, and HTML reporting capabilities. For Windows, Solaris, HPUX.

Exhibit 3. (Continued) Java Testing Tools

Tool Name	Tool Vendor	Description
Metamata Java Code Analysis Tools	Metamata	Suite of tools for analysis of Java source code quality, complexity and quality metrics, debugging, and more.
Optimizelt	Intuitive Systems	Java language profiling tool, analyzes use of memory and CPU resources to find bottlenecks and to solve Java performance problems.
RSM	Squared	Code metrics tool for C/C++/Java—style compliance, LOC, complexity, class metrics, hyperlinks to source, HTML reports. Runs on Win3.1/95/NT, Unix.
SilkBeans	Segue	Segue's Java test tool; part of their Silk Web Test tool suite.
TCAT for Java	TestWorks	Code coverage analyzer and code analysis for Java applets; written in Java. For Unix.
TotalMetric	RST	RST's Code metrics and OO metrics tool for Java.
Visual Test	McCabe & Associates	McCabe Visual Testing ToolSet and McCabe Quality ToolSet, with Java coverage and metrics capabilities.
VTune	Intel	Intel's performance tuning tool for applications running on Intel processors; includes Java support.

Cross-Reference Maintenance Tools

One of the most useful aids to maintenance is the cross-reference list that accompanies the compiler source listing. It usually provides a concise, ordered analysis of the data variables, including the location and number of times the variables are used, as well as other pertinent information about the program.

In large systems, it is often difficult to determine which modules are called or used by other programs and where in the system a specific module or parameter is used. What is often needed is the capacity to produce and develop a cross-reference listing on an inter-program basis rather than on an intra-program basis. This information can be obtained from some of the available cross-reference generators. Such information is useful to the maintenance staff attempting to backtrack to determine where an error occurred.

Exhibit 4. Web Link Checking Tools

Tool Name	Tool Vendor	Description
Alert Linkrunner	Viablesoft ware	Link check tool; evaluation version available. For Win95/98/NT.
CyberSpyder Link Test	Aman Software	Shareware link checker by Aman Software; capabilities include specified URL exclusions, ID/Password entries, test resumption at interruption point, page size analysis, 'what's new' reporting. For Win3.1/95/NT.
I-Control Web Weaver	Future ArtForms	Link checker; evaluation version available; for Win95/NT.
InfoLink	BiggByte Software	Link checker program from BiggByte Software; can be automatically scheduled; includes FTP link checking; multiple page list and site list capabilities; customizable reports; changed-link checking; results can be exported to database. Freeware and evaluation versions available.
Linkalarm	LinkAlarm	Low cost on-the-Web link checker; free trial period available. Automatically scheduled reporting by e-mail.
Linkbot	Tetranset Software	Tetranet's tool for checking links, missing page titles, slow pages, stale content, site mapping; from local drive or remote server. Evaluation copy available; for Win95/NT.
Link Scan	Electronic Software Publishing Corp.	Electronic Software Publishing Co.'s link checker/site mapping tool; capabilities include automated retesting of problem links, randomized order checking; can check for bad links due to specified problems such as server-not-found, unauthorized-access, doc-not-found, relocations, timeouts. Includes capabilities for central management of large multiple intranet/Internet sites. Evaluation copy available. For UNIX and NT servers. Requires Perl 5.
RiadaLinx!	Riada International	Link checker; evaluation copy available; for Win95/NT.

Exhibit 4. (Continued) Web Link Checking Tools

Tool Name	Tool Vendor	Description
Surf!	Segue	Link-testing tool used in Seque's Live Quality-Web Site Web test tool suite.
Theseus	Matter Form Media	Link checker for Mac; evaluation version available.

Exhibit 5. HTML Validation Tools

Tool Name	Tool Vendor	Description
CSE 3310 HTML Validator	Al Internet Solutions	Shareware HTML validator for Win95/NT. (This tool is also integrated into the 'HomeSite' Web development/authoring tool.)
Spyglass HTML Validator	SpyGlass	Free standalone local-drive HTML validator. Color-coded display, errors in list can link directly to error location in page; editable corrections within display; selectable validation levels; for Win95.

Comparator Maintenance Tools

Comparators are software maintenance tools that accept two or more sets of input and generate a report that lists the discrepancies between the input data sets. This maintenance tool can be used for finding changes in such areas as the source code, input data, and program output and is extremely useful in ascertaining whether a change made to the system caused it to fail or work differently. A comparator can also be used to ensure that one set of test results is identical to a previous set or to identify where the results have changed.

Most comparators are developed for a specific system. They may be general in nature or work on specific parts of the system and perform specific functions. They are relatively simple to build and are very valuable maintenance tools.

A comparator is a program used to compare two versions of source data to determine whether the two versions are identical or to specifically identify where any differences in the versions occur. Comparators are most effective during software testing and maintenance when periodic modifications to the software are anticipated.

Exhibit 6. Web Regression Tools

Tool Name	Tool Vendor	Description
Astra Quick Test	Mercury Interactive	Mercury's product for functional testing of Wed-based e-business applications; can emulate various browser types and versions and HTTP protocols. For Win95/NT.
AutoTester Web	AutoTester, Inc.	AutoTester Corp.'s link check and site test tool; includes scripting capabilities, automated documentation, reporting functionality, and the ability to test Java applets and ActiveX. Works with MSIE or Netscape browsers. For Win95/NT/AIX/ Solaris/Tandem/NextStep.
Compuware's QARun	Compuware Corp.	QARun for functional/regression testing of Web, character-based, and GUI systems; for Win95/NT.
e-Tester	RSW Software	Web functional/regression test tool from RSW. Includes record/playback, scripting language; can test image maps, frames, forms, links, ActiveX, Applets, VBScript, JavaScript. Includes SiteSpider site element detection and mapping tool, and a 'Data Banks' feature for data-driven automated testing. Supports external custom test logic via External Callout Facility. Special test extensions for Net Dynamics, Web Objects, Cold Fusion, Microsoft, and Silverstream. Evaluation version available. For Win95/98/NT.
FormAgent	Ventura Communications	VCI's FormAgent for automated form-filling; can be configured for multiple users. Can be adapted for partial automation of forms-based Web testing. Evaluation copy available; for Win95/NT, NS3.0+, MSIE3.x.
SilkTest	Segue	Seque's Web testing tool for functional and regression testing; includes capabilities for testing Java applets, HTML, ActiveX, images; works with MSIE, Netscape, includes capture/playback capabilities.
WebART	WebART	WebART, from OCLC, Inc., tool for functional, regression, and performance testing. Includes capture/playback/ and scripting language; can simulate 100–200 users in load testing. Evaluation copy available. For Win3.1/95/NT.

Exhibit 7. Web Security Tools

Tool Name	Tool Vendor	Description
HostCheck	DMW	Suite of security test and management tools from DMW Worldwide. Checks for presence of sniffers and insecure network configuration, secure file removal by repetitive overwriting of location, checks for preexisting security problems against vulnerability database, file/directory permissions management and monitoring, password security testing, user management and account security checking, security reporting and test scheduling. For UNIX platforms.
WebTrends Security Analyzer	Web Trends Corp.	Web site tool to detect and fix security problems. Includes periodically updated Expert knowledge base. For Win95/98/NT.
Compuware's QARun	Compuware Corp.	QARun for functional/regression testing of Web, character-based, and GUI systems; for Win95/NT.
Netsonar	Cisco Systems	Cisco's product for detecting and reporting on Internet server and network vulnerabilities; risk management; network mapping. Require Solaris and Netscape browser.
Inspectorscan	Shavlik Technologies	Shavlik Technologies' security analysis and reporting tool; for NT.
Netective Site	Netect Ltd.	Netect's product for analyzing internal and external security vulnerabilities. For Solaris.
CyberCop SCANNER	Network Associates	NT security auditing tool from Network Associates for intranets, Web servers, firewalls, and screening routers.
COAST Security Archive	Coast Security Archive	Purdue University's computer security site; includes extensive collection of links organized by subject to security tools, info resources, etc. Tools list of more than 100 security tools includes many test tools such as CRACK, COPS, IPSend, Tiger, Secure Sun, etc.; all tools listed are available for download from the COAST site.
NukeNabber	DSI	For monitoring TCP and UDP ports for intrusions; includes tracer utilities. Freeware from DSI; for Win95/98/NT.

420

Exhibit 7. (Continued) Web Security Tools

Tool Name	Tool Vendor	Description
NetRecon	Axent	Axent Technology's tools for testing vulnerability of network systems and resources from inside or outside the firewall; exploits IP and non-IP-based protocols; selective targeting capabilities; creates HTML reports; 'Intruder Alert' capability for 7x24 monitoring. Probes any platform type. Runs on NT4.0.
L0phtCrack	L0pht	Password auditing/security check tool from L0pht. Site also has Internet security advisory collections. Shareware. For Win95/NT.
Internet Scanner Toolset	ISS	Internet Security Systems' test tool for network vulnerability analysis and decision support. Can perform scheduled and selective security probes of network services, operating systems, configurations, applications, CGI, and routers for intranets, firewalls, Web servers. For NT/95, AIX, HP-UX, Solaris, SunOS, Linux.

Comparator (Windows File Revision Feature). With Windows File Revision feature one can compare two version of a document. The two documents being compared must have different file names or the same filename in different folders. To use this feature under Windows 95:

1. Open the edited version of the document.
2. On the Tools menu, click Revisions.
3. Click Compare Versions.
4. Click the name of the original document, or type its name in the File Name box.
5. Accept or reject the revisions.

Diagnostic Routines

Diagnostic Routines assists the maintenance staff by reducing the amount of time and effort required for problem resolution. Some common routines are:

- Trace—Generates an audit trail of actual operations during execution.
- Breakpoint—Interrupts program execution to initiate debugging activities.
- Save/restart—Salvages program execution status at any point to permit evaluation and reinitiation.
- Dump—Gives listings (usually unformatted or partially formatted) of all or selected portions of the program in main storage at a specific point in time.

Exhibit 8. Web Management Tools

Tool Name	Tool Vendor	Description
Adobe SiteMill	Adobe Systems Inc.	Adobe's product for Web site management, link checking/updating, page authoring and editing; available as add-on for PageMill; for Macintosh.
Astra SiteManager	Mercury Interactive	Mercury's Web site management tool; scans Web site and highlights functional areas with color-coded links and URLs to provide a visual map of site. Site map includes HTML, cgi scripts, applets, etc. Shows broken links, access problems, compares maps as site changes, identifies usage patterns and validates dynamically generated pages. Change management/tracking. Evaluation copy available. For Win95/NT.
BazaarAnalyzer Pro	BazaarSoft, Inc.	Aquas Software's Web management and analysis tool; runs on Web server, interface via any Java-enabled browser. Manage multiple sites, users, security; customizable Web report, realtime alerting for broken links, etc.; visitor analysis. For NT, Solaris, HP, Linux, SGI/IRIX, BSD/BSDI.
Blueprint	Brooklyn North Software Works, Inc.	Web site analysis and management tool, includes link checker, site mapper, reporting statistics, integrated ftp and uploading. For Win95/NT.
Chisel	Digital Technology, Inc.	Multifunction tool for behavior and performance testing of live network applications. Load and stress testing; verifies firewall effectiveness; supports HTTP, FTP, ping, SNMP, telnet, TCP, UDP, ODBC database applications. Can create and save user-defined test scenarios. Requires NT and MSIE.

Exhibit 8. (Continued) Web Management Tools

Tool Name	Tool Vendor	Description
COAST WebMaster	Coast Software	Coast Software, Inc. WebMaster site management tool; for Web site file management, link checking, site version comparisons, page download timing and estimating, server log file reporting. Includes HTML editor and file manager, page display verification, global search and replace. Evaluation copy available. For Win95/WinNT.
Cold fusion	Allaire Corp.	Allaire's Web development environment includes integrated test Web server for immediate site testing, automatic database query tester, version control. Evaluation version available. For Win95/NT/Solaris.
DynaBase	Inso Corp.	Inso's Web site publishing and development management product for multi-user control, version control, link verification, and site deployment. Capabilities include remote access, multiple editions, deployment. Capabilities include remote access, multiple editions, dynamic publishing.
e-Monitor	RSW Software	Web tool from RSW for 7x24 Web site monitoring. Can utilize test scripts created with their e-Tester tool; allows wide range of corrective action and notification responses. Includes a wizard script generator that generates scripts in standard Visual Basic. Evaluation version available. For Win95/98/NT.
Equalizer	Coyote Point Systems	Load balancing server appliance and site management tool from Coyote Point Systems. Web-based interface for load balancing administration, server failure detection, real-time server monitoring of server response time, number of pending requests, etc.
HotMetalPro	SoftQuad	SoftQuad's Web development tool for Web site authoring/development/management, includes capabilities link management, site mapping. For Win95/98/NT.

Exhibit 8. (Continued) Web Management Tools

Tool Name	Tool Vendor	Description
HP Firehunter	Hewlett Packard	HP's tool for monitoring, diagnosis, and management of Internet services; including performance, fault detection, reporting. Supports a variety of platforms.
HTML Grinder	Matterform Media	Matterform Media's Web site management/ authoring software with multi-file find and replace, file name management, TOC-builder, more. Evaluation version available. For Mac.
HTML PowerTools	Talicom	HTML validator, global search-and-replace. Data stamper, spell checker, Meta manager, image tag checker, HTML-to-text converter, customizable reports. Link checker. Validates against various HTML versions, NS and MSIE extensions; has updatable rulebase. From Talicom. Free 30-day evaluation copy. For Win3.1/95/NT.
Interwoven Team Site	Interwoven, Inc.	Web development, version control, access control, and publishing control tool; works with many servers, OS's, and platforms.
Intranet Solutions	International Network Services	VitalSign Software's suite of products for dynamically monitoring faults, response times, congestion, downtime, bottlenecks, timeouts, performance changes for intranet systems. For NT.
Microsoft FrontPage	Microsoft Corp.	Microsoft's 'Front Page' Web site authoring and site management tool; includes site management capabilities, link checking, etc. Evaluation copy available.
Microsoft SiteServer	Microsoft Corp.	Web site development, maintenance, management tool includes site mapping, link checker, publishing control, site analysis; formerly MS Backoffice Live: WebMapper and also formerly NetCarta WebMapper until bought out by Microsoft. For MS Internet Server on NT.

Exhibit 8. (Continued) Web Management Tools

Tool Name	Tool Vendor	Description
MS Visual Source Safe	Microsoft Corp.	Microsoft's version 5.0 of their software version control tool; includes site change management, Web link checker, site mapping; can integrate with MS FrontPage. For Win3.1/95/NT/DOS/UNIX/Mac.
NETClarity	LANQuest	Suite of browser-based Intranet performance management and diagnostic tools from LANQuest. Find network bottlenecks; capacity planning and analysis.
NetDialect	Uniscape	Multilingual Web site management solution; uses a scalable Oracle database that reuses translation memory across multiple sites/projects simultaneously. Extracts information kernels from their native HTML files, then checks extracted information against an accumulating repository of translated sentences, key words, or glossaries. Translated strings are automatically populated in the translation editor. Human or machine translation completes the translation process. After review for quality, the native file is automatically reassembled with the translated/updated information.
OpenDeploy	Interwoven	Interwoven's configurable control system for deploying from development to production environments. Includes automated deployment, security, and encryption capabilities. Rollback capabilities if used in conjunction with their TeamSite product.
PowerMapper	Electum Multimedia	For customizable automated site mapping, HTML validation, link checking. Evaluation copy available; for Win95/NT and MSIE 3.0 or later.
ServerCheck	Netmechanic	Netmechanic's on-the-Web tool checks a Web server's performance periodically for 8 hours; the resulting report sent by e-mail includes comparisons to other servers. Site also includes a link-checker, HTML validator, spell checker.

Exhibit 8. (Continued) Web Management Tools

Tool Name	Tool Vendor	Description
Site Scope	Freshwater Software	Freshwater Software's product for site monitoring and maintenance. Runs on servers and monitors server performance, links, connections, logs, etc., and provides notifications of problems. Includes published API for creating custom monitors. Monitors mimic users end-to-end actions. For NT or Unix.
Site/C	Locutus Codeware	'Set-and-forget' utility for periodic server monitoring for Web server connection problems, link problems; e-mail notifications, logging capabilities. Evaluation version available; for Win95/NT.
SiteBoss	Opposite Software	Opposite Software's tool for Web site management, meta tag management, spell checking, diagnosis, repair, and optimization; global search and replace, HTML-to-text converter, link checker, HTML validator; integrated HTML editor and browser. Updatable rulebase. Evaluation copy available for Win95/NT.
SITEMAN	Greyscale Systems	Web site management and editing tool collection from Greyscale Systems. Link checking. Global search and replace. Checks for orphan files. Call HTML editor from within program. Has freeware and shareware versions. Evaluation copy available. For Win31./95/NT.
SiteSweeper	Site Technologies, Inc.	Web site analysis tool checks for broken links, slow pages, missing meta tags, missing alt tags, etc. Creates browser-viewable reports, analyzes local or remote sites, includes image cataloging with thumbnails. Evaluation copy available. Free on-the-Web demo also available. Runs on Win/95/NT.

Exhibit 8. (Continued) Web Management Tools

Tool Name	Tool Vendor	Description
SM-Web	Service Metrics	Web site performance measurement service, measures from the end-user's perspective. Monitors various statistics such as Response Time, Throughput, End-to-End Time Comparison among 10 Select Cities.
SQA Sitecheck	Rational Software Corp.	Rational's Web site management tool includes link checker, finds slow pages, simulates both Netscape and MSIE browsers. SSL support. For Win95/NT. 30 day evaluation copy available.
StoryServer Web System	Vignette Corp.	For Web site collaborative content, publishing, management, and maintenance. Supports servers on Solaris, NT 4.0. Can optimize pages based on incoming browser, supports various attributes including: CSS, Cookies, DynaHTML, Frames, Java, JavaScript, Lynx, Macintosh, MSIE versions, Netscape versions, Tables, WebTV. Supports Oracle, Sybase, Informix, UC2, SQL Server, via native APIs. Supports NS Enterprise Server, Apache, OpenMarket, MS IIS; supports NSAPI to Netscape, ISAPI to Microsoft IIS and Fast CGI to Apache and OMI. Requires Java Runtime Environment.
TeamSite	Interwoven	Interwoven's collaborative Web site production control, administration, and management product for enterprise-wide Internet and intranet projects. Includes version control, browser interface, comparison capability, file edit merging, variable lock controls. Client side requires NS 3.01+ or MSIE 3.01+; server side compatible with many available Web servers.

Exhibit 8. (Continued) Web Management Tools

Tool Name	Tool Vendor	Description
TestWorks/Web	Software Research	Collection of Web test tools for capture/playback, load testing, Java testing from Software Research, Inc. Includes their CAPBAK/Web for Web test tool, XVirtual load generation tool, and TCAT for Java test coverage tool. For Win95/NT and UNIX platforms.
Unicenter TNG w/Web Management Option	Computer Associates, Inc.	Site management application from Computer Associates includes access and security control, monitoring, logging, metrics, server management, network management. For MS and Netscape Web servers.
WebSite Director	CyberTeam	Web-content workflow management system with browser-based interface includes configurable workflow management, e-mail submission of Web content, and e-mail notifications; allows defining and applying existing workflow and approval rules to Web content management process. For NT, UNIX systems.
WebSite Manager	Pro Solutions	Web site management tool from Pro Solutions Software; link checker, change management. Evaluation version available. For Win95/NT.
WebTrends Enterprise Suite	Web Trends Corp.	Web site management tool including log analysis, link analysis and quality control, content management and site visualization, alerting, monitoring and recovery, proxy server traffic analysis and reporting
WireTap	Platinum	Continuously monitors and manages network, intranet, and Internet performance; provides real-time Web traffic analysis, and monitors Web and SQL transaction response times. From Platinum Technologies. Supports AIX, HP-UX, Solaris, NT.

Compilers often provide diagnostic capabilities that can assist programmers in analyzing the execution flow and capturing a myriad of data at predetermined points in the process. In the hands of a skilled maintenance programmer, these diagnostics can help identify the sections of code that cause the error as well as identify what is taking place there.

Although these aids are extremely useful, they are after-the-fact maintenance tools used to help determine what has gone wrong with an operational system. Far more useful are diagnostic capabilities designed and implemented within the source code as it is developed. This type of diagnostic is normally disabled but can be turned on through the use of one or more control parameters.

Application Utility Libraries

Most operating systems provide support and utility libraries that contain standard functional routines (e.g., square roots, sine, cosine, absolute values). In addition, high-order language compilers have many built-in functions that can be used by the programmer to perform standard functions. Just as these libraries provide standardized routines to perform processes that are common to many applications, large systems should have a procedure library that contains routines common to various segments of the application system. These functions and utility routines should be available to everyone working on the system, from the developer to the maintenance staff. Application support utility libraries assist by

- Saving time (the programmer need not reinvent the wheel).
- Simplifying the changing of common code by changing all programs that use a module. This usually requires relinking or recompiling each affected program, but it eliminates the need to change lines of code in each program.
- Providing wider availability of utility procedures developed by one person or group to all persons working on the system.
- Facilitating maintenance of the system by keeping the code in a central library or set of libraries.

In addition to the stored library routines, all the source code for the application system should be stored in a centralized, online library. Access to this library should be controlled by a librarian who maintains the integrity of the library and the code.

Online Documentation Libraries

System documentation usually consists of one or more hard-copy folders or files stored at a central location. The need for the maintenance staff to have access to these documentation folders and the need to keep the documentation up to date and secure are sometimes at cross-purposes. It is therefore recommended that as much documentation as is practical also be kept online in documentation libraries that the maintenance staff can access at any time. A librarian should control updating of this library.

Online/Interactive Change and Debugging Facilities

Interactive debugging provides significant advantages over the batch method because of the convenience and speed of modification. With interactive processing, the maintenance programmer can analyze the problem area, make changes to a test version of the system, and test and debug the system immediately. The alternative—submitting a batch job to perform the testing—requires much more time to complete. Although this may be necessary in some cases because of system size or resource requirements, most maintenance activities (even perfective maintenance) are highly critical problems that must be addressed and solved as quickly as possible. Interactive processing provides a continuity that enables greater concentration on the problem and quicker response to the tests. Although estimates of the increase in productivity vary widely, there is clearly a substantial improvement when the maintenance programmer has online interactive processing capabilities.

VENDOR TOOL DESCRIPTIONS

The following is an overview of some of the major software maintenance tool vendors. No one tool is favored over another. Exhibit 2 cross-references the tool vendors with the tool types.

McCabe's McCabe QA

Product Description. This tool provides a comprehensive solution to the following issues: (1) What is the quality of the system? (2) Has it been constructed in an efficient and effective manner to minimize testing and maintenance costs? (3) How can we accurately measure risk and improve quality while still meeting critical deadlines? (4) Have new versions of the software increased or degraded the quality?

With its interactive, visual environment, one can quickly and objectively gauge the quality of the code. The tool combines cutting-edge graphical technology and industry standards of measurement to help focus resources where they will have the greatest impact on your projects.

Product Features.

- Module-by-module metric calculations that help identify where a program is more likely to contain errors.
- Graphical displays represent the structure of code and the metrics rankings to provide easy and valuable assessment of even large systems.
- A database of software characteristics including metrics and flowgraphs, used as a valuable resource for future software changes and upgrades.
- Metrics

— McCabe Cyclomatic Complexity
— McCabe Essential Complexity
— Module Design Complexity
— Integration Complexity
— Lines of Code
— Halstead

Platforms Supported.

Sun	Solaris 2.5.1 (Motif Only)	Ada, C
PC	Windows NT 4.0, Windows 95	C++, COBOL, FORTRAN
IBM	AIX 4.2	Java, Visual Basic
HP	HP-UX 10.2	
SGI	IRIX 5.3	

SunTest's JavaStar 1.2

Product Description. JavaStar is a tool for testing Java applications and applets through their graphical user interfaces (GUI). This tool helps you test your application by allowing you to record and automatically play back a series of user actions (e.g., typing, mouse clicks) on your application. At any time during playback, you can compare the state of your application with previous results; this allows you to automatically compare the behavior of your Java application on a number of platforms, and from one release version to the next.

JavaStar also supports powerful scripting and comparison capabilities for very thorough testing.

JavaStar is a very cost-effective way to test Java programs. You don't have to learn a new or difficult special-purpose proprietary testing language simply to make or modify your test scripts. Your code is Java, so use Java.

Product Features.

- *Runs on JDK 1.x or JDK2 compatible platforms and environments: it's truly cross-platform.* JavaStar leverages the benefits of Java technology for GUI regression testing. It is the first testing tool to test at the language level and the only GUI tool that runs anywhere that Java applications and applets run. Java's "write once, run anywhere" advantage simplifies the test creation process with only one set of tests to create and maintain, providing immediate return on investment.
- *Developers and QA engineers can speak the same language.* JavaStar's scripting language is Java. Since JavaStar's tests are written in the Java programming language, there are no machine-dependent scripting languages to learn, so QA engineers and developers are finally able to

work with a common language. Defects discovered during testing can be reproduced right on the developer's machine, increasing their confidence and understanding of test results.

- *Improved test thoroughness and accuracy: use Java to test Java.* Using the exact same test code to test an application on every platform increases test consistency and accuracy.

- *Lowered total cost of ownership.* Because JavaStar is written in Java and its scripting language is Java, only one tool needs to be learned and the same test will run on all platforms. This makes it is easier to learn and use than multiple-platform-specific tools, less expensive to support, and less expensive for total cost of ownership. This frees up test resources, reduces development cycle time, and improves overall software quality.

- *Internationalization: use the same test for internationalized versions.* Because JavaStar is running in the same process as a Java application, a test executes as intended regardless of the language the application's GUI displays, even if objects in the GUI have been moved around on the screen. This has substantial bottom line impact on developers who develop internationalized versions of applications.

- *JavaStar's modular approach provides a quick way to build robust tests.* Small, focused test scripts are quickly linked together into robust test suites using the point-and-click interface of the JavaStar Visual Test Composer. New tests can be created with these reusable task-specific test components to reduce the time and cost of developing applications.

- *Automatically creates a virtual tester.* JavaStar creates a virtual tester that behaves as a human tester would. JavaStar drives the application to a certain point, compares the data on screen and the state of components with previously captured expected results. JavaStar's automation makes testing faster, easier, and more cost-effective.

- *Advanced GUI and API test capabilities show JavaStar's power and flexibility.* JavaStar has fully editable Java scripting, GUI mapping, and visual-test composition. Through JavaStar, testers can access what appears in the GUI as well as control and verify non-GUI (API) events. Access to both GUI and API levels of the application increases a QA engineer's ability to produce rigorous, accurate tests.

- *Monitor real-time results or detailed reports.* JavaStar displays a test's execution graphically, flashing each node as it executes. QA engineers can track a test's real-time execution, review the detailed results in JavaStar's Results Viewer when convenient, or extract a report to HTML.

- *Easy updates to multiple tests with declaration files.* JavaStar makes it possible to update a whole collection of tests by simply editing one file they all reference. This reduces test maintenance when an application changes during the development lifecycle and produces significant time savings.

- *Increases test versatility by removing hard data.* JavaStar's tests are easily parameterizable, which makes it easy to change values in a test by replacing hard-coded data with references to data stored in external files. Tests that are independent of specific data have wider usability so fewer modules can be combined to make more varied tests.

System Requirements.

- 5 MB RAM
- 4 MB disk space
- Any additional requirements of the object under test

Platforms Supported. Developed completely in the Java language, and designed to run on all Java-compatible platforms. Requires a JDK 1.1.x or JDK 2 compliant Java Virtual Machine.

Rational Robot

Product Description. Rational Robot allows one to create, modify, and run automated tests on Web, ERP, and client/server applications. It is the only test automation solution that offers reusability and portability of test recordings across Windows platforms to provide one recording that plays back on all Windows platforms.

Rational Robot includes comprehensive Object Testing of object properties and data for C++ and other integrated development environments (IDEs).

Product Features.

- Part of a seamlessly integrated product suite for testing Windows NT, Windows 98, and Windows 95 client/server and Internet applications to deliver one of the industry's leading solution for testing cross-Windows client/server and Internet applications.
- Uses Object Testing to completely test 32-bit Windows objects and components, including ActiveX Controls, OLE Controls (OCXs), Visual Basic Controls (VBXs), Visual Basic objects, PowerBuilder objects, Oracle Developer/2000 objects, Win32 controls, and more.
- Delivers Rational's Object-Oriented Recording technology to provide the fastest, most intuitive test creation with the shortest learning curve.
- Includes SQABasic an integrated, Visual Basic syntax-compatible scripting environment to deliver the full power of an integrated programming environment for script development.
- Includes seamlessly integrated Web site testing power with Rational SiteCheck, to deliver comprehensive Web site analysis, performance measurement, and repair technology.

System Requirements.

Memory: 16 MB; 24 MB recommended

Disk Space: 40 MB

Computer: PC with 486 processor; Pentium-class processor recommended

Platforms Supported. Windows 98, Windows 95, or Windows NT

Rational TestFactory

Product Description. Rational TestFactory automatically detects runtime errors without user assistance and generates optimal scripts for regression testing. It is a unique automated software quality tool that does for quality engineers what the word processor did for writers. Rational TestFactory finds reliability defects in Visual Basic applications automatically, without recording or scripting.

This tool delivers on the promise of automated testing by exhaustively and automatically exercising the application to test every path through it for reliability defects. Whereas functionality testing requires user intervention, organizations can now perform reliability testing with Rational TestFactory automatically, without user intervention.

Rational TestFactory automates the tedious and error-prone aspects of reliability testing. Rational TestAccelerator helps you perform this reliability testing even faster by harnessing multiple computers to perform testing in parallel. Rational TestFactory lets you divide automated test development into a series of steps. Rational TestAccelerator lets you develop and run these steps on multiple computers. Rational TestAccelerator performs test generation and test execution in parallel, so you finish reliability testing faster.

Product Features.

- Finds defects in your applications automatically, without recording or scripting.
- Exhaustively and automatically exercises your application to test every path through it for defects.
- Creates optimized test scripts that can be used with Rational Robot for regression testing.
- Tests more of your application.

System Requirements.

- Rational TestFactory:

— 64 MB, 166 MHz
— 300 MB disk space for Rational TestStudio
- Rational TestAccelerator:
— 64 MB, 133 MHz
— 92 MB disk space

Platforms Supported.

- Rational TestFactory:
— Windows NT, Windows'95, or Windows'98 Visual Basic 4, 5, or 6
- Rational TestAccelerator:
— Windows NT, Windows'95, or Windows'98

AutoTester's Test Station Tool

Product Description. AutoTester Test Station is the automated testing solution designed specifically to help one increase the quality of character-based PC and host applications. AutoTester provides immediate productivity through capture/replay style test creation, yet stores the tests as well-documented, easily maintainable, object-aware tests. Both the skilled developer and expert application user benefit from AutoTester. The product includes an easy to use menu-driven interface as well as a powerful command set for advanced scripting needs.

Test Station and Test Library Manager work in tandem to give one the premier automated testing solution for character-based PC, midrange and mainframe applications. Test Station is an integrated environment that allows virtually anyone to develop, document, and execute a comprehensive automated test library. Test Library Manager is a central repository for the test library components that provides change and version control and global maintenance for tests across an entire application development life cycle.

Product Features.

- *Flexible test capture*—Lets one build consistent, documented tests that can be used over the life of the application from tester to tester and release to release. With Test Station, tests can be captured at any point in the software development process.
- *Unattended test execution*—Tests are intelligent scripts that provide dynamic verification of application responses against expected results, duplicating expectations and decision points. When unexpected application responses occur during test execution, the tests identify those responses and react accordingly. Recovery options log the details of application failures and then continue the testing process if possible. In addition, Test Station's playback synchronization provides proper test playback regardless of system performance.

- *Reusability and maintainability*—Helps one develop an automated test library that can be easily modified to account for new or different application behavior over time. For ease of maintenance, tests can be edited while in the application and then executed immediately, or they can be edited off-line with Test Station or any text editor.
- *Documentation and reporting*—Each step of every test is automatically documented in English for ease of understanding. Tests are identified with detailed descriptions, test case numbers, and test requirement identifiers for cross-reference purposes. After test execution, detailed results are available on-line or in report format for immediate review and analysis.
- *Scripting*—Includes the AutoTester Scripting Language. Designed to supplement the capabilities of Test Station, this language is a powerful command set that can accommodate unique testing needs and provide general task automation functionality.

System Requirements.

- Test Station:
  - IBM PC 386 or 100% compatible machines
  - MS-DOS or PC-DOS 5.0 or higher
  - 326K conventional memory or 30K with LIM 4.0 compliant expanded memory manager or DPMI 0.9 compliant extended memory manager
  - 10 MB minimum storage requirements
  - Supports most network terminal emulation and communications protocols, including IBM 3270, IBM 5250 (AS400), Hewlett-Packard 2392, Tandem 6530 and Unisys
- Windows 3.X:
  - IBM PC-386 or greater and 100% compatibles
  - 4 MB minimum memory plus Windows system requirements
  - 10 MB minimum disk storage
  - Supports Wall Data Rumba (Office 2.1A) and Attachmate Extra! V4.3A terminal emulation
- Windows'95 and Windows NT-16-BIT:
  - IBM PC-486 or greater and 100% compatibles
  - 4 MB minimum memory plus Windows'95 or Windows NT system requirements
  - 8 MB minimum disk storage per installed copy
- OS/2:
  - IBM PC-486 or greater and 100% compatibles
  - 4 MB minimum memory plus OS/2 system requirements
  - 10 MB minimum disk storage
  - Supports IBM OS/2 Communications Manager terminal emulation

Platforms Supported.

- Windows 3.1x
- Windows'95
- Windows NT – V4.x local testing 16-BIT applications only; no emulation supported

Mercury's WinRunner Tool 5

Product Description. WinRunner provides an easy way to test client/server GUI applications. It simplifies test automation, providing a powerful, productive, and cost-effective test solution. And with WinRunner's RapidTest scripting, new testers can overcome the initial barriers to test automation by giving the test script development process instant momentum. Application testers and developers can now get high quality software without compromising on-time deployment for Windows, Windows'95, and Windows NT.

WinRunner 4.0 features a powerful new approach to testing, RapidTest. RapidTest automatically creates a full suite of GUI tests from the application. RapidTest gets users started fast; instead of requiring users to create their first set of tests manually; they can use a Wizard to create test scripts directly from the application.

Today, test automation has successfully replaced manual test execution with automated test execution. But when it comes to building the automated tests, most conventional testing tools still rely exclusively on one-line-at-a-time scripting techniques like programming and object-oriented recording. These conventional tools merely transfer the burden from manual testing to manual test development.

Product Features.

Visually Integrated Scripting features:

- Visual Testing for powerful, flexible test creation productivity.
- Interpreted Development Workspace with test script interpreter and Multiple Document Interface for simple management of script development.
- Powerful Script Language to test everything that needs to be tested.
- Exception Handing with built-in routines for automatic recovery.
- Powerful Script Debugger to quickly "test" and fix scripts when problems occur.
- Flexible Verification to know exactly whether the application is working.
- New Visual Reporting that integrates high-level summary reports with detailed records for every test verification result, in a new, interactive reporting tool.

Script Mapping features:

- Handles application changes automatically, using Script Mapping for adaptable and reusable tests.
- Learns the application hierarchy, organizing objects by window. It also handles independent GUI maps for separate applications simultaneously, and can invoke them automatically during testing.
- GUI map provides a single point of control for multiple tests by updating one attribute of an object in the map—its effect updates all scripts automatically.
- Includes an interactive editing tool for viewing or modifying the map file. Users can choose which attributes to track for which objects, and what to name the objects in the test script, affording complete flexibility for defining how WinRunner looks for and identifies application objects.

Custom Control features:

- Integrated object support for major development tools and industry standard controls.
- Open API for custom controls to enable users to define their own testing support for objects.
- Analog recording and text recognition as an alternative for verification.

Powerful Client/Server GUI Test Automation:

- Provides a new, fully documented Open Testing API enabling users to create full automated testing support for custom objects—capture, replay, and verification.
- Supports point-to-point mouse movements, bitmap comparisons or bitmapped test based on fixed window coordinates.
- Can automate tests that depend on movement between fixed window coordinates, such as in graphical or drawing programs and programs that do not have GUI objects.
- Text recognition makes it possible to read text displayed by these objects as alphanumeric data and provides the ability to perform key test operations when hooks are not available to retrieve text data from displayed objects.

System Requirements.

- Minimum 16 MB RAM
- Minimum 16 MB disk space

Platforms Supported.

- Windows'95
- Windows NT

Mercury's XRunner (Unix) Tool 4

Product Description. XRunner offers a toolset for GUI test automation to run quickly and smoothly. Its fully integrated Visual Testing environment makes test development easier by incorporating simplified test script management, point-and-click selection, interactive debugging and more. To help one get started, XRunner's Script Wizard learns the application by navigating its way through all available UI paths to create a complex test script suite. With XRunner, one is guaranteed that GUI application testing is fast, reliable, and complete across all UNIX platforms.

XRunner extends a powerful set of automated testing utilities to ensure GUI reducing the time and expertise needed for creating, running, and maintaining automated tests. XRunner runs on all UNIX platforms and may be ported for testing across multiple environments such as Microsoft's Windows 3.x, Window'95 and Windows NT. One can develop a test once on one platform, and replay it on another for added versatility.

Product Features.

Automated GUI Regression Testing features:

- XRunner runs on all UNIX platforms and may be ported for testing across multiple environments.
- RapidTestTM Script Wizard, which automatically learns the entire application and generates tests for unattended regression testing.
- Visual Testing environment for combining object-oriented recording.
- Point-and-click test generation and test script logic into a single environment.
- Flexible verification and replay options.
- Sophisticated reporting tools.
- Portability across multiple platforms and more.

Automatic Test Generation features:

- A GUI Regression Test, which captures a baseline checkpoint of GUI attributes for every window that opens.
- A Bitmap Regression Test, which compares bitmaps between versions by creating a screen capture for every window that opens.
- A User Interface (UI) Test, which checks adherence to X Window UI conventions for every window that opens.
- A Template Test, which creates a test framework for future use.

Fully Integrated Scripting Environment features:

- Provides flexibility to create test scripts as one uses the application and offers point-and-click, recording, and programming.

- Records actions performed on a widget, such as selecting an item from a list or pressing a specific button, XRunner records a context-sensitive test script. XRunner is smart enough to select the item or press the button even when the UI changes.
- XRunner also supports analog test scripts when the tests are dependent upon movements between fixed window coordinates and do not have individual GUI objects. An analog test script will replay exact mouse movements or clicks and keystrokes—such as clicking the left mouse button.
- One can also use the programming method when enhancing tests created by recording, adding loops for flow control, setting and using variables, using conditional branching, filtering and report messaging. XRunner's Test Script Language (TSL) is based on the C programming language with added testing functions. By implementing the programming test method, users can tailor their tests to meet specific functions.
- XRunner's test script interpreter gives one test development power, since it supports simultaneous point-and-click test development, recording of user operations, and enhanced test script programming.
- To create the best possible script based on the testing requirements, XRunner fully supports mixing test script methods rather than requiring one to use them separately. It also provides a interactive debugger that enables one to "test the tests" for optimal performance.

Flexible Verification features:

- Using a point-and-click verification method of selecting the objects on the screen, one chooses the type of checkpoint to insert in the test script.
- Text recognition is a verification option exclusive to XRunner.
- XRunner is the only tool with a complete Optical Character Recognition (OCR) engine to recognize text such as checking console windows for error messages.
- XRunner can also verify images, objects, files, and tables. For example, XRunner supports tables in Oracle Developer/2000 applications.
- Likewise, XRunner provides open systems extensions that will allow one to launch shell scripts, system utilities, and tools.
- XRunner can also verify Motif programs using WidgetLint, a set of verification functions used to test Motif applications. XRunner detects widget color and attachment problems, as well as any unmanaged widgets to help one effectively debug Motif applications. Its open API allows one to implement WidgetLint verification functions.

Enhanced Replay Modes:

- XRunner provides several test script replay modes. Built-in automatic and custom synchronization allows one to run tests unattended—overnight or during the weekend—to maximize the application development time.

- In addition, XRunner can run in background mode, freeing up the workstation during the day. One can continue writing code while XRunner executes test scripts.
- Provides exception handling to keep test execution on track. Exception handling offers automatic built-in recovery, including

  — Overcoming unexpected conditions and resuming test execution without halting the test,
  — Invoking a series of procedures to dismiss unexpected objects,
  — Rewinding test script execution to a previous step,
  — Navigating elsewhere in the application,
  — Recording errors in the test log along with steps taken to resume testing,
  — Exiting the test when encountering certain surprise conditions.

- XRunner also enables one to define error recovery routines to ensure reliable replay and keep tests from coming to an abrupt halt.

Interactive Reporting Tool features:

- XRunner's interactive reporting tool combines a high-level view with detailed statistics about what bugs were found by the test and where.
- Includes the ability to drill down errors into greater detail, pinpointing the exact line in a test script. Both graphical and textual reports chart the testing results for further analysis.
- Interactive reporting identifies bugs that were found by the test both in summary and in detail. A color-coded tree shows all executed tests along with their results.

Script Mapping features:

- XRunner handles application changes automatically using Script Mapping for Adaptable, Reusable Tests (SMARTest), which automatically maintains object specific data independent of individual scripts.
- XRunner's SMARTest monitors GUI application changes automatically so that the tests will run correctly.
- Automatically creates a SMARTest GUI map for the tested application. When SMARTest learns the application hierarchy, it captures key application attributes and organizes objects hierarchically, window by window. SMARTest guarantees test scripts will work correctly when the application changes without requiring rework.

Portability features:

- XRunner's TSL is designed to port tests across all UNIX and Microsoft Windows (Windows 3.x, Windows NT, Windows'95) platforms.

- It provides the only scalable load testing solution for managing the risks of client/server systems.

System Requirements.

- 16 MB minimum RAM
- Approximately 100 MB disk space

Platforms Supported.

- UNIX

SunTest's JavaLoad

Product Description. Implementations of applications and applets written for the Java platform have emerged as the leading technology to implement client/server and Internet-based applications. It is crucial to understand how these applications behave and react under a variety of load conditions before they are deployed. JavaLoad software allows developers to target load testing at every point in an application's architecture and the development process. From running GUI clients directly to targeting server-side interfaces using protocols like HTTP, CORBA/IIOP, RMI, JDBC, or proprietary networked protocols, JavaLoad software helps you ensure that your Java-technology-based distributed application is solid—end to end.

System developers depend on load testing to isolate potential bottlenecks or problems before deploying their business-critical Java-technology-based applications and applets. Because JavaLoad software is written in the Java programming language, it can load test your application at every tier of the system, employing any number of client machines. JavaLoad software can test clients and servers in a heterogeneous environment—the norm in real-world enterprises. From a single point of contact, JavaLoad software stresses your entire system to isolate and identify potential client and server bottlenecks.

Product Features.

- *Cross-platform*—Since JavaLoad software is the only load testing tool written in the Java programming language, only the JavaLoad product is cross-platform. It will run anywhere your Java-technology-based application or applet can. Developers and QA engineers can use one tool to test distributed Java-technology-based applications on all platforms compatible with Java technology.
- *JavaLoad console provides a single-stop testing point of contact, anywhere you are*—JavaLoad software's powerful GUI console provides a central point of contact, control, and analysis. Even better, you can access the Commander network, and control enterprise-wide load test-

ing from any machine, anywhere in the network, so your single point of contact can move with you.

- *End-to-end load testing*—With JavaLoad software you can design load tests to meet specific requirements. JavaLoad software can load test an enterprise application from a pure client perspective or isolate each server-side interface and protocol. Testing with JavaLoad software helps ensure your enterprise application can handle the load it needs to handle, without creating problems elsewhere.
- *Development life cycle load testing*—JavaLoad software can be used throughout the product development life cycle. JavaLoad software is compelling among load testing tools, because it can validate architectures, benchmark hardware, and stress the integrated system.
- *Tightly integrated with JavaStar tool*—Coupled with Sun's JavaStar product, a Java GUI capture/relay tool, JavaLoad software can concurrently invoke numerous JavaStar scripts that faithfully replay user events using the actual Java-technology-based GUI clients of an enterprise application. Using JavaStar timers, any event can be timed and recorded, reporting the true response time a user will experience under loaded conditions.
- *Get load test results at your convenience*—Using the JavaLoad console, from any machine accessible to the JavaLoad test, the JavaLoad product conveniently generates reports of all test data, including the number of simulated users engaged, the average response time per user, an analysis of the session, and a comparison of different test sessions. The data are critical not only to finding but also to fixing the problems that decrease productivity and compromise enterprise information assets. Because JavaLoad software leverages the Java technology's animation capabilities, you can run enterprise-wide load testing, and see graphical reporting on bottleneck and performance problems all over the enterprise, in real time. This lets developers find problems, understand causes more clearly, and fix them more rapidly.
- *Telemetry channels monitor each tier of the system*—Whether it is client response time, number of simulated users, or database server data access time, any telemetry data that can be expressed as a name-value pair can be accessed, monitored, and reported—in real time or as a post-load test report or chart.
- *Synchronized test information*—JavaLoad software stores all test information in the JavaLoad Central Repository including the programs and data files that comprise the load tests, and all result data generated from the load sessions. JavaLoad software automatically synchronizes this data across the test network without relying on any file system protocol such as NFS or FTP. JavaLoad software ensures that all load tests on each host are running the same version. After running test sessions, JavaLoad software collects all test results and records

them in a central repository, making automatically generated Web-based load test reports available any time.

- *Simulates user activity*—With JavaLoad software, load testing is performed by the virtual user. A virtual user can be designed to perform a list of tasks. The tasks performed by a virtual user can be the invocation of any Java or non-Java technology-based program. This allows the JavaLoad product to be customized to simulate any user, using existing tests or creating new ones. Once a virtual user is defined, it can be replicated and deployed throughout the enterprise network to simulate real usage loads, no matter where in the enterprise they occur—in the test lab or the call center floor.
- *Completely reusable components*—Once designed, any components you need are always available to you to construct future tests, saving both time and money.
- *Web application load testing*—JavaLoad software comes packaged with a Web plug-in that can capture and replay HTTP events using any Web browser. The plug-in is designed to capture all HTTP events and create a Java program that will faithfully replay and time the recorded events, and ensure that all recorded Web server response codes are received. When invoked by the JavaLoad product, the plug-in playback program can be replicated and distributed over your entire test network to simulate a few dozen to thousands of users accessing your Web-based application concurrently.

Today, applications in many sectors, including e-commerce, the Web, telephony, order-entry, ERP, call center, and manufacturing, need load testing. Because Java technology links together heterogeneous environments, load testing these applications becomes more important than ever.

System Requirements.

- 3 MB RAM per Java virtual machine
- 3 MB RAM per GUI client user
- 60 KB per network user
- Any additional requirements of the system under test

Platforms Supported. Certified Java-compliant platform that conforms to JDK software, version 1.1.5, 1.1.6, 1.1.7, 1.1.7A.

Mercury's LoadRunner Tool

Product Description. LoadRunner is the integrated client, server, and Web load testing tool. It provides a scalable load testing solution for managing the risks of client/server systems. Using a minimum of hardware resources, LoadRunner provides consistent, repeatable, and measurable load to exercise a system. It exercises the client, server, and Web system just like real users. It contains a single point of control for client, server, and Web load testing and supports hundreds or even thousands of virtual users.

By automating both client and server load testing from a single point of control, LoadRunner helps developers get an accurate view of system behavior and performance throughout the application development life cycle.

Product Features.

Client Load Testing features:

- Exercises the system just like real users, driving real applications through the virtual clients simultaneously from a single point of control.
- Includes an integrated set of new load testing components: Virtual User Generator, ScenarioWizard, Visual Controller and Load Analyzer.
- Synchronizes all virtual users to create peak loads, pinpoint bottlenecks, and isolate problems.
- Records test scripts automatically at GUI, SQL, Web, and terminal levels.
- Aids in isolating problems at client, server, and network level.

Server Load Testing features:

- Supports both two-tier and three-tier client/server architectures.
- Generates an abstract data file of virtual users for non-programmers.
- Generates a simple C code file of virtual users for programmers.
- Verifies data retrieved from the server.
- Supports multiple client/server protocols.

Data Analysis features:

- Presents clear, attractive graphs and reports for analyzing load testing data.
- Compares data across platform configurations and virtual users to help isolate and pinpoint problems.
- Displays both code and GUI.
- Measures performance "end-to-end" from client through application server and to the database.
- Handles GUI changes automatically by maintaining scripts at object level.

Web Load Testing features:

- Supports HTTP, HTML, and Java applets.
- Defines transactions automatically for individual and groups of HTTP messages.
- Supports GET, POST, CGI messages.

- Creates test scripts by recording the actions of a user or user groups surfing a Web site.
- Determines maximum number of concurrent users a Web site can handle.

RTE Load Testing features:

- Records user interactions with character-based applications to create test scripts.
- Inserts synchronization points automatically on unique text or cursor positions on the screen.
- Generates a log file for debugging scripts and scenarios.
- Replays RTE virtual user sessions just like a movie recording.
- Verifies values as defined by row, column or screen while server is under peak conditions data from the server visually with an on-line server monitor.
- Exports data to standard formats (Microsoft Word, Microsoft Excel, Lotus 1-2-3, e-mail and more).

System Requirements.

- Controller
  — 32 MB RAM
  — 70 MB disk space
- Virtual Users
  — Minimum 2 MB per virtual user
  — 256 MB/100 virtual users
  — Disk space: 10 MB each

Platforms Supported.

- Windows 3.x
- Windows NT
- Windows'95
- Sun OS, Solaris, HP-UX, IBM AIX, NCR

Client/Server Protocols Supported.

- SQL: Oracle OCI, Oracle UPI, Sybase dbLib, Sybase CtLib, Informix I-net
- ODBC
- TP Monitors: Tuxedo
- Messaging: WinSocket
- Web: HTTP, Java
- Character-based: TTY, IBM 5250, IBM 3270
- Applications: SAP R/3, Oracle Financials, PeopleSoft, Baan

Rational's preVue Tool

Product Description. With preVue, Rational offers enterprisewide testing solutions. Products and services are provided that reduce risk, lower costs, and increase user satisfaction when deploying applications for client/server, X Window, ASCII, and Web environments.

The newest release of the preVue product line, release 5.0, offers extended graphical analysis capabilities, expanded client/server support for load testing, and the new preVue-Web extension. preVue-Web allows performance testing of the WW server with thousands of Web users.

preVue-C/S applies heavy user loads to database servers and application servers to give accurate performance and salability data. Understanding system limitations and pinpointing potential breakpoints before they are seen by end users is only possible when a real-life user load is applied to a server.

preVue-Web records HTTP traffic, downloaded Java applets, user think-time, number of bytes received, connects and disconnects generated by any browser, running on any platform. By not requiring any recording software to be installed on the client browser or server machines, the traffic recorded can be used to generate heavy user loads against a Web server even as the environment changes. preVue-Web can record Internet and intranet application traffic from any Windows, Windows'95, Windows NT, MacOS, OS/2 or UNIX system. preVue-Web software is supported on all major UNIX platforms and Windows NT.

preVue-X automates both GUI regression testing and load testing for X Window applications and does not require special hooks into the application or X libraries. The tool operates at the X protocol level, between the X server and the X client applications. It operates independently from the graphical user interface (Open Look, Motif, CDE, etc.), toolkits, and network.

preVue-ASCII (Version 5.0 is a remote terminal emulator (RTE) that replicates users running applications on a system under test (SUT). preVue-ASCII automates multi-user testing of the applications by replacing both users and physical devices with software scripts that deliver an accurate workload of user activity. It cost-effectively measures the quality and performance of the applications under large user loads.

Product Features.

preVue-C/S features:

- Emulates 2-tier and 3-tier network traffic.
- SQL, HTTP, and Tuxedo traffic is captured and automatically turned into client emulation scripts.

- Supports testing of Oracle, Sybase, Informix, and SQL Server databases.
- Presentation-quality data analysis tools.
- Real-time test monitoring.
- Measures server response time under varying user loads.
- Integrated reporting with performance monitoring tools.
- Easily varies the user workload during playback.
- Tests are independent of client operating system and hardware environment.

preVue-Web features:

- Measures Web server response times under large user loads.
- Automatically captures and plays back HTTP traffic and downloading of Java applets.
- Accurately emulates and timestamps concurrent responses to multiple HTTP requests.
- Provides emulation of users of any Web browser, running on any client platform.
- Supported on all major UNIX platforms and Windows NT.
- Integrates with preVue-C/S to test both database and Web servers.

preVue-X features:

- A single tool for both GUI and performance testing.
- Nonintrusive approach lets one "test what you ship."
- Tests all versions of UNIX, X server, GUI toolkits, etc.
- Automatically generates test scripts reproducing user inputs and system responses.

preVue-ASCII features:

- Cost-effectively and accurately emulates large user loads.
- Tests any screen-based application in any operating system environment.
- Measures the user's perception of performance-response times at the user's terminal.
- Automatically generates test scripts reproducing user inputs and system responses.
- Provides the realism of actual users, yet tests are reproducible.
- Support on all major UNIX platforms.
- Uncovers quality and performance problems with new software releases before the users see them.
- Determines how the applications perform with new system hardware or software upgrades.
- Verifies the quality of applications following Year 2000 code changes.
- Tests the capacity of the current system as the number of users increases.

System Requirements.
N/A

Platforms Supported.

- UNIX
- Windows NT

Rational's PerformanceStudio

Product Description. PerformanceStudio integrates functional and load testing with test-system performance and delivers information needed to make critical deployment and resource planning decisions. It includes Rational's award-winning Robot product for script recording and built-in test-asset management, as well as innovations such as data-smart recording, client-smart pacing, load-smart scheduling, and server-smart playback aimed at improving ease-of-use, accuracy, and scalability.

Product Features.

- **DataSmart Recording** automates the use of multiple transactions from a single test script.
- **LoadSmart Scheduling** automates the creation of workloads for 10 or 10,000+ users. Recently, performance-testing technology scored a significant new benchmark by simultaneously supporting 30,000 virtual users during a test run.
- **ClientSmart Pacing** automates the insertion of production level timing characteristics.
- **ServerSmart Playback** ensures the integrity of the results you are producing.

These innovations of PerformanceStudio are equally suited to address the needs of legacy systems such as two and n-tier client server architectures, ERP, as well as the ever changing e-commerce environments.

System Requirements.

NT Master Station:

- 99 MHz Pentium or higher (166 MHz for test runs greater than 50 virtual users)
- 80 MB free disk space

NT Agent:

- Pentium, 99 MHz Pentium or higher (166 MHz recommended)
- 40 MB free disk space

Platforms Supported.

- Unix Agent
- Sun Solaris, HP, UX, IBM, AIX, additional port on request

Rational's Visual Quantify Tool

Product Description. Quantify is a powerful, easy-to-use performance analysis tool that gives developers an easy way to identify application performance bottlenecks. Using Rational's patented Object Code Insertion (OCI) technology, Quantify actually counts the individual machine instruction cycles it takes to execute an application and records the exact amount of time the application spends in any given block of code. With Quantify, developers get the accurate and repeatable performance data they need to quickly and easily improve application performance.

Product Features.

- Pinpoints performance bottlenecks in all parts of an application, including user functions, system calls, shared and third-party libraries.
- Detects performance problems everywhere in Unix applications:
  — C and C++ source code
  — Third party libraries
  — Shared or system libraries
- Detects performance problems everywhere in Windows applications:
  — C and C++, Visual Basic, and Java source code
  — ActiveX, DirectX, OLE and COM components
  — Dynamic Link Libraries (DLLs)
  — Third-party DLLs
  — Windows operating system code
- Presents accurate, repeatable performance data in an easy to read graphical displays.
- Offers multiple, complementary views of performance data.
- Collects per-thread performance data.
- Automatically compares runs for fast verification of performance improvements.

Platforms Supported.

- UNIX:
  — Sun SPARC workstations running SunOS 4.x, Solaris 2.3–2.6
  — HP9000 Series 700/800 workstations running HP-UX 9.0.x through 10.30
- Windows NT:
  — Intel architecture only
  — Windows NT 3.51 or above

— Visual C++ 2.2 or above
— Visual Basic 5.0 or above
— Java applications run through the Microsoft Virtual Machine for Java

Rational's ClearDDTS

Product Description. ClearDDTS is a change request management product specifically designed to track and manage product defects and enhancement requests uncovered during product development and quality assurance testing. It can be tightly integrated with software configuration management products, such as ClearCase, to help users effectively manage change throughout the software development life cycle.

Product Features.

- Organizes change requests for easy retrieval.
- Provides an easy-to-use querying facility.
- Offers a Web interface to support multiple platforms and remote projects.
- Integrates with electronic mail for remote submission and notification.
- Features an SQL interface to the Oracle RDBMS and includes a SQL-capable database as part of the product.
- Includes management reports—more than 40 types.
- Integrates with ClearCase, ClearGuide, ClearSupport, and other popular software development and call tracking tools.

System Requirements.

Server:

- Approximately 55 MB of disk space
- At least 32 MB of RAM

Platforms Supported.

- Sun Solaris 2.5, 2.5.1, 2.6
- HP-UX 10.20, 11.00
- DEC OSF1 4.0d
- IBM AIX 4.2x
- SGI IRIX 6.2, 6.4
- Apache 1.2, 1.3.4
- Netscape Enterprise 3.0, 3.01, 3.6
- Microsoft Internet Explorer 4.0 or higher
- Netscape Navigator 3.0 or higher
- Oracle 7.1.6 or higher

Rational's ClearQuest

Product Description. Rational ClearQuest is a scalable and configurable defect tracking/change request management product for tracking and reporting on defects and other types of change requests throughout the development life cycle. ClearQuest shortens development cycles by unifying all team members—project managers, QA managers, testers, developers—in managing software development change.

Product Features.

- Complete out-of-the-box solution includes automatic e-mail submission and notification, Web interface, Crystal Reports, and Sybase SQL Anywhere.
- Integrates with software configuration management solutions including Rational ClearCase and Microsoft Visual SourceSafe.
- Integrates with testing solutions including Rational Suite TestStudio, TeamTest, Purify, and more.
- Supports Oracle, SQL Server, SQL Anywhere, and Access databases.
- Enables easy customization of request process lifecycle, database fields, user interface layout, and more.

System Requirements.

ClearQuest Client

- Windows NT 4.0 with Service Pack 4, or Windows 95/98
- Approximately 80 MB of disk space
- At least 32 MB of RAM (recommended: 64 MB of RAM)

ClearQuest Web Server

- Windows NT Server 4.0 with Service Pack 4
- Microsoft Internet Information Server (IIS) 4.0
- 50 MB of hard disk space
- 128 MB of RAM

Platforms Supported.

- Windows'95/'98/NT
- Microsoft IIS
- Microsoft Internet Explorer
- Netscape Navigator
- Sybase SQL/Anywhere 5.5.04
- Oracle 7.3.4 or higher
- SQL Server 6.5 with Service Pack 5 or SQL Server 7.0

Rational's ClearCase

Product Description. ClearCase provides a comprehensive configuration management solution, including version control, workspace management, build management, and process control. ClearCase offers a uniquely transparent, nonintrusive approach, and supports multiple platforms and IDEs, making it easy to deploy and maintain, without forcing you to change your existing environment, your tools, or the way you work.

Product Features.

- Goes far beyond version control by also offering powerful workspace management, build management, and process control capabilities.
- Enables parallel development—even across geographically distributed sites.
- Integrates with Microsoft Developer Studio, PowerBuilder, Oracle Developer/2000, and many of Rational's software development solutions.
- Provides disconnected usage model, so that users can work at home with ease and then reliably merge work back into the mainline of development.
- Offers advanced build auditing, enabling teams to guarantee what went into any build.
- Performs automatic, graphical merges of files and directories highlighting code conflicts and safely resolving inconsistencies.
- Versions everything that evolves in development—including source code, binaries, executables, documentation, test suites, libraries, and directories.
- Tightly integrated with change request management products to track which defects were fixed in each release.

System Requirements. Client Only: Windows 95, 98

Platforms Supported. Client and server: Windows NT, Solaris, HP, AIX, SGI, Digital Unix, Sun OS, Siemens Sinix, UnixWare

Rational's ClearCase MultiSite

Product Description. ClearCase MultiSite is a ClearCase product option that enables parallel development across geographically distributed project teams. Available on Windows NT and UNIX, ClearCase MultiSite extends ClearCase's reach to team members down the street or across the world, delivering automated, error-free replication of project databases and transparent access to all software elements.

Product Features.

- Features the safest and most reliable means to exchange multi-site ClearCase repository-based information.
- Automatically resends information in the event of network failure and recovers repositories in the event of system failure.
- Scales easily to support projects regardless of size of team, location of members, or platform usage.
- Offers the most efficient means to update team members by only transmitting incremental changes that appear in ClearCase's project repositories. A network resource and time saver.
- Facilitates distributed development across networked and non-networked sites by offering update mechanisms that support both network and tape transfers.

System Requirements. Client only: Windows 95, 98

Platforms Supported. Client and server: Windows NT, Solaris, HP, AIX, SGI, Digital Unix, Sun OS, Siemens Sinix, UnixWare

Rational's SQA SiteCheck Tool

Product Description. SQA SiteCheck is a powerful, yet easy to use, Website management tool for the Intranet or World Wide Web site. It is designed to help the Webmaster or business manager keep up with every aspect of the rapidly changing site. The primary purpose of SQA SiteCheck is to detect broken links, orphaned pages, and potential performance problems on Web sites. SQA SiteCheck helps Webmasters and Web site administrators detect and repair defects in the structural integrity of their sites.

SQA SiteCheck includes many features that allow it to test Web sites that use the most current technology to present active content such as HTML forms and Java applets. It is also capable of testing secure sites making use of SSL, proxy servers, and multiple security realms to protect the data sent to and from the site. SQA SiteCheck's advanced level of integration with McAfee VirusScan enables one to detect infected documents on a site before visitors do.

Product Features.

- A fully integrated internal browser and HTML editor.
- Full support of the Secure Sockets Layer (SSL).
- Filters for Web-based forms, frames, Java, JavaScript, ActiveX, and VBScript.
- Automatic tracking of moved or orphan pages and broken links.
- Fixes links without needing a separate editor.
- Includes automatic virus scanning.

- Pinpoints all slow pages and predicts performance time for all communication paths.
- Can impersonate both Microsoft Internet Explorer and Netscape Navigator to see the different server responses to the different browsers.
- Integration with SQA Suite: SQA Robot as the Web Site Test Case.

System Requirements.

- 16 MB, 32 MB recommended for NT
- 10 MB
- PC with 486 processor, Pentium-class processor recommended

Platforms Supported.

- Microsoft Windows 95 or Windows NT 4.0 or later
- ActiveScan View requires Microsoft Internet Explorer v3.0 or later

Rational Visual PureCoverage 6.0

Product Description. Comprehensive testing of applications and fast identification of problem areas throughout the development process is essential to producing high-quality software. However, without tools that help you identify which parts of the application have and have not exercised in a test run, you'll waste valuable time trying to guess where the problem areas are and what you have to do to fix them.

Visual PureCoverage helps you quickly identify untested code, so you can be sure you've checked your entire application for potential problems, not just part of it. An essential tool for Visual Basic, Visual C++, or Java applications, Visual PureCoverage will speed testing efforts, save precious development time, and enable you to deliver higher quality software faster and within budget.

Product Features.

- Automatically pinpoints untested code.
- No source code or special builds required.
- PowerCov controls the level of data collected.
- Identifies untested code everywhere, including:
  — ActiveX, DirectX, OLE, and COM components
  — Dynamically linked libraries (DLLs)
  — Source code
  — Third party controls and DLLs
  — System DLLs
- Integrated with Microsoft Visual Studio 6.0
- Supports Visual Basic, Visual C++, and Java applications
- Integrated with Visual Test, and ClearQuest

Version 6.0 enhancements include:

- Microsoft Visual Studio 6.0 integration.
- Support for Microsoft Visual C++ 6.0 and Microsoft Visual Basic 6.0.
- Now supports merging different executables for determining the coverage of DLL's that are used by multiple programs.
- Enhanced Visual Basic functionality.
- Integrated with Rational Visual Test and ClearQuest.

System Requirements.

- PC-compatible system, Intel 486 or Pentium processor
- Microsoft Windows NT 4.0 with Service Pack 3 or greater
- 32 MB RAM required, 64 Mb RAM recommended
- Approximately 20 MB free disk space
- 150 MB minimum swap space recommended

Platforms Supported.

- Intel architecture
- Windows NT 4.0 or above (including Japanese Windows NT 4.0)
- Visual Basic 5.0, 6.0
- Visual C++ 4.2-6.0
- Microsoft Visual Studio 5.0, 6.0
- Microsoft VJ++ 1.11 VM build 2553 or higher
- Windows CE applications run in emulation mode on Windows NT; emulation software available with Windows CE SDK

Rational Purify 6.0

Product Description. Run-time or memory-access errors are some of the most difficult problems for Windows NT programmers to solve. These problems are even greater when developing software with components—whether purchased from third parties, downloaded off the Internet, or reused from a previous project. Errors in these components can be disastrous and may take weeks to find and fix. Only Purify will pinpoint error in components as well as any application code you've written. Purify helps you get to the root of your run-time problem so you can quickly fix the error, rather than spend a lot of time trying to debug it.

With Purify, no special build is required. Just select an executable and Purify will automatically begin checking for run-time errors and memory leaks. Integration with Microsoft Visual Studio allows Purify to interact with the IDE and debugger, and gives developers immediate run-time error checking without making any changes to any tools in use.

Product Features.

- Automatically pinpoints hard-to-find run-time errors.
- Checks for run-time errors in all your code, including components.
- Quickly analyzes your executables—no rebuild is required.
- Checks for errors in Windows API calls and OLE methods.
- Lets you control the level of error checking per code module.
- Companion tool for Rational Visual Quantify and Visual PureCoverage, and integrated with Rational Visual Test and ClearQuest.
- Integrated with Microsoft Visual Studio 6.0.

Version 6.0 enhancements include:

- Microsoft Visual Studio 6.0 Integration
- Support for Visual C++ 6.0
- Significant improvements in instrumented program performance, making Purify even faster!
- Integrated with Rational Visual Test and ClearQuest.

System Requirements.

- PC-compatible system, Intel 486 or Pentium processor
- Microsoft Windows NT 4.0 with Service Pack 2 or greater
- 32 MB RAM required, 64 MB RAM recommended
- Approximately 20 MB free disk space
- 150 MB minimum swap space recommended

Platforms Supported.

- Intel architecture
- Windows NT 4.0 or above (including Japanese Windows NT 4.0)
- Visual C++ 4.2–6.0
- Visual Studio 5.0, 6.0
- Windows CE applications run in emulation mode on Windows NT; emulation software available with Windows CE SDK

Other Maintenance Tools

See Exhibits 3, 4, 5, 6, 7, and 8.

Appendix A
Spiral Testing Methodology

The following is a graphical representation of the spiral testing methodology and consists of an overview relating the methodology to Deming's Plan–Do–Check–Act (PDCA) quality wheel, parts, steps, and tasks.

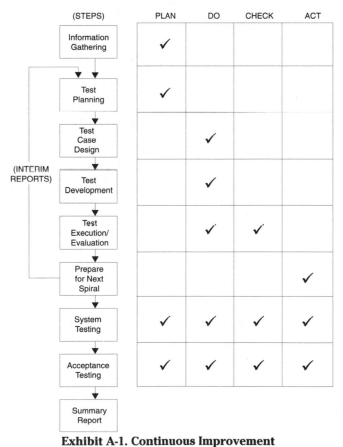

Exhibit A-1. Continuous Improvement

Information Gathering

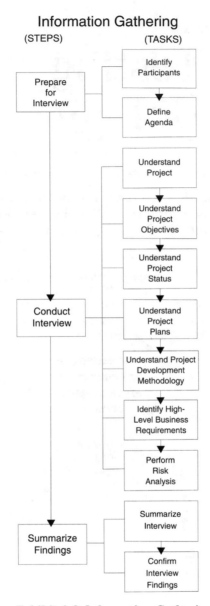

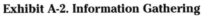

Exhibit A-2. Information Gathering

Test Planning

(STEPS)   (TASKS)

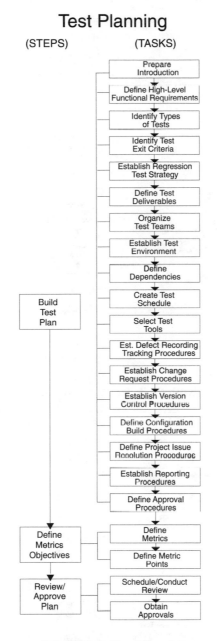

Exhibit A-3. Test Planning

Test Case Design

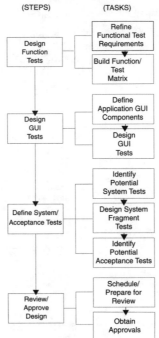

Exhibit A-4. Test Case Design

Test Development

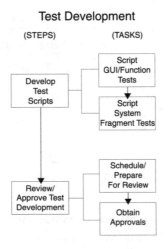

Exhibit A-5. Test Development

Test Execution/Evaluation

(STEPS) (TASKS)

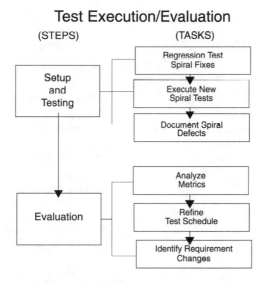

Setup and Testing
- Regression Test Spiral Fixes
- Execute New Spiral Tests
- Document Spiral Defects

Evaluation
- Analyze Metrics
- Refine Test Schedule
- Identify Requirement Changes

Exhibit A-6. Test Execution/Evaluation

Prepare for the Next Spiral

(STEPS) (TASKS)

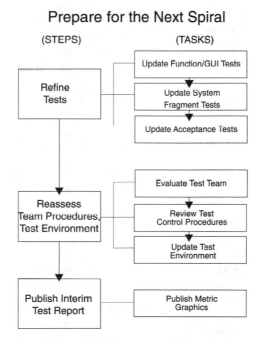

Refine Tests
- Update Function/GUI Tests
- Update System Fragment Tests
- Update Acceptance Tests

Reassess Team Procedures, Test Environment
- Evaluate Test Team
- Review Test Control Procedures
- Update Test Environment

Publish Interim Test Report
- Publish Metric Graphics

Exhibit A-7. Prepare for the Next Spiral

Conduct System Testing

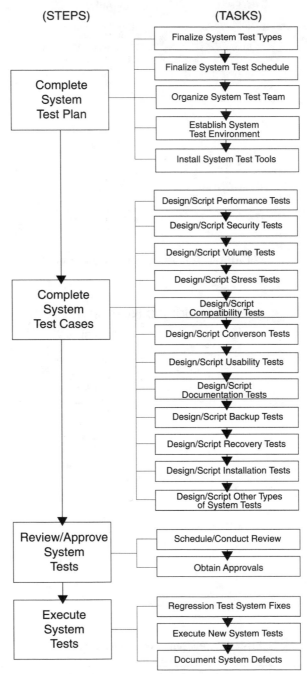

Conduct Acceptance Testing

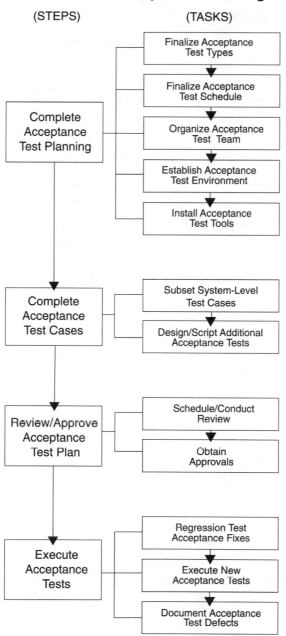

(STEPS)

(TASKS)

Complete Acceptance Test Planning
- Finalize Acceptance Test Types
- Finalize Acceptance Test Schedule
- Organize Acceptance Test Team
- Establish Acceptance Test Environment
- Install Acceptance Test Tools

Complete Acceptance Test Cases
- Subset System-Level Test Cases
- Design/Script Additional Acceptance Tests

Review/Approve Acceptance Test Plan
- Schedule/Conduct Review
- Obtain Approvals

Execute Acceptance Tests
- Regression Test Acceptance Fixes
- Execute New Acceptance Tests
- Document Acceptance Test Defects

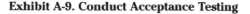

Exhibit A-9. Conduct Acceptance Testing

Summarize/Report Spiral Test Results

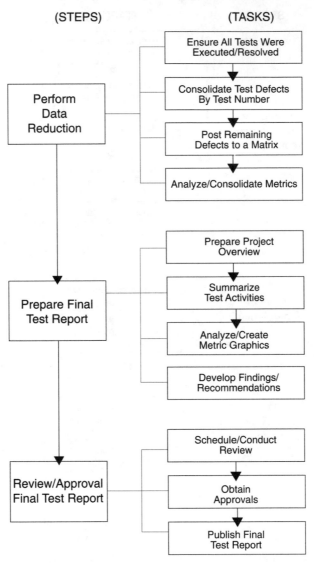

(STEPS)   (TASKS)

Exhibit A-10. Summarize/Report Spiral Test Results

Appendix B
Software Quality Assurance Plan

This appendix provides a sample software quality assurance plan for an application project. The details of the project are obscured to emphasize the plan's general philosophy and techniques.

1. **Purpose**
2. **Reference Document**
   - 2.1 The MIS Standard
   - 2.2 MIS Software Guidelines
   - 2.3 The Software Requirements Specification
   - 2.4 The Generic Project Plan
   - 2.5 The Generic Software Test Plan
   - 2.6 The Software Configuration Management Plan
3. **Management**
   - 3.1 The Organizational Structure
   - 3.2 Tasks and Responsibilities
     - 3.2.1 Project Leader (Lead Software Engineer)
     - 3.2.2 Software Development Groups
     - 3.2.3 The Testing Subcommittee
4. **Documentation**
   - 4.1 The Software Requirements Specification
   - 4.2 System User Guide
   - 4.3 The Installation Guide
   - 4.4 Test Results Summary
   - 4.5 Software Unit Documentation
     - 4.5.1 The Preliminary Design Document
     - 4.5.2 Detailed Design Document
     - 4.5.3 Other Documents
   - 4.6 Translator Software Units
5. **Standards, Practices, and Conventions**
6. **Reviews and Inspections**
7. **Software Configuration Management**
8. **Problem Reporting and Corrective Action**
9. **Tools, Techniques, and Methodologies**

APPENDIX B

10. Code Control
11. Media Control
12. Supplier Control
13. Records Collection, Maintenance, and Retention
14. Testing Methodology

Appendix C
Requirements Specification

The requirements specification is a specification for a software product, program, or application that performs functions in a specific environment organized by feature (source: IEEE Recommended Practice for Software Requirements Specifications).

3.2 System Features
   3.2.1   System Feature 1
         3.2.1.1   Introduction/Purpose of Feature
         3.2.1.2   Stimulus/Response Sequence
         3.2.1.3   Associated Functional Requirements
         3.2.1.4   Introduction/Purpose of Feature
         3.2.1.5   Stimulus/Response Sequence
         3.2.1.6   Associated Functional Requirements
                 3.2.1.3.1   Functional Requirements 1
                    .
                    .
                    .
                 3.2.1.3.n   Functional Requirements n
   3.2.2   System Feature 2
     .
     .
     .
   3.2.m   System Feature m
     .
     .
     .

3.3 Performance Requirements
3.4 Design Constraints
3.5 Software System Attributes
3.6 Other Requirements

4. Supporting Information
   4.1 Table of Contents and Index
   4.2 Appendices

Appendix D
Change Request Form

The sample change request form below serves as the document vehicle to record and disseminate the actions of change control.

Exhibit D-1. Change Request Form

Change Request Form
Report Number: _____ Change Request No: _____
System Affected:
Subsystem Affected:
Documentation Affected:
Problem Statement:
Action Required:

Appendix E
Test Templates

E1: UNIT TEST PLAN

The unit test plan is based on the program or design specification and is required for a formal test environment. The following is a sample unit test plan table of contents.

1. **Introduction Section**
   a.   Test Strategy and Approach
   b.   Test Scope
   c.   Test Assumptions
2. **Walkthrough (Static testing)**
   a.   Defects Discovered and Corrected
   b.   Improvement Ideas
   c.   Structured Programming Compliance
   d.   Language Standards
   e.   Development Documentation Standards
3. **Test Cases (Dynamic testing)**
   a.   Input Test Data
   b.   Initial Conditions
   c.   Expected Results
   e.   Test Log Status
4. **Environment Requirements**
   a.   Test Strategy and Approach
   b.   Platform
   c.   Libraries
   d.   Tools
   e.   Test Procedures
   f.   Status Reporting

E2: SYSTEM/ACCEPTANCE TEST PLAN

The system or acceptance test plan is based on the requirement specifications and is required for a formal test environment. System testing evaluates the functionality and performance of the whole application and consists of a variety of tests including: performance, usability, stress, documentation, security, volume, recovery, etc. Acceptance testing is a user-run test which demonstrates the application's ability to meet the original business objectives and system requirements and usually consists of a subset of system tests.

The following is a sample test plan table of contents.

1. **Introduction**
    a. System Description (i.e., brief description of system)
    b. Objective (i.e., objectives of the test plan)
    c. Assumptions (e.g., computers available all working hours, etc.)
    d. Risks (i.e., risks if unit testing is not completed)
    e. Contingencies (e.g., backups procedures, etc.)
    f. Constraints (e.g., limited resources)
    g. Approval Signatures (e.g., authority to sign-off document)
2. **Test Approach and Strategy**
    a. Scope of Testing (i.e., tests to be performed)
    b. Test Approach (e.g., test tools, black-box)
    c. Types of Tests (e.g., unit, system, static, dynamic, manual)
    d. Logistics (e.g., location, site needs, etc.)
    e. Regression Policy (e.g., between each build)
    f. Test Facility (i.e., general description of where test will occur)
    g. Test Procedures (e.g., defect fix acceptance, defect priorities, etc.)
    h. Test Organization (e.g., description of QA/test team)
    i. Test Libraries (i.e., location and description)
    j. Test Tools (e.g., capture/playback regression testing tools)
    k. Version Control (i.e., procedures to control different versions)
    l. Configuration Building (i.e., how to build the system)
    m. Change Control (i.e., procedures to manage change requests)
3. **Test Execution Setup**
    a. System Test Process (e.g., entrance criteria, readiness, etc.)
    b. Facility (e.g., details of test environment, lab)
    c. Resources (e.g., staffing, training, timeline)
    d. Tool Plan (e.g., specific tools, packages, special software)
    e. Test Organization (e.g., details of who, roles, responsibilities)
4. **Test Specifications**
    a. Functional Decomposition (e.g., what functions to test from functional specification)
    b. Functions Not to Be Tested (e.g., out of scope)
    c. Unit Test Cases (i.e., specific unit test cases)
    d. Integration Test Cases (i.e., specific integration test cases)
    e. System Test Cases (i.e., specific system test cases)
    f. Acceptance Test Cases (i.e., specific acceptance test cases)
5. **Test Procedures**
    a. Test Case, Script, Data Development (e.g., procedures to develop and maintain)
    b. Test Execution (i.e., procedures to execute the tests)

    c.   Correction (i.e., procedures to correct discovered defects)

    d.   Version Control (i.e., procedures to control software component versions)

    e.   Maintaining Test Libraries

    f.   Automated Test Tool Usage (i.e., tool standards)

    g.   Project Management (i.e., issue and defect management)

    h.   Monitoring and Status Reporting (i.e., interim vs. summary reports)

6. Test Tools

    a.   Tools to Use (i.e., specific tools and features)

    b.   Installation and Setup (i.e., instructions)

    c.   Support and Help (e.g., vendor help line)

7. Personnel Resources

    a.   Required Skills (i.e., manual/automated testing skills)

    b.   Roles and Responsibilities (i.e., who does what when)

    c.   Numbers and Time Required (e.g., resource balancing)

    d.   Training Needs (e.g., send staff to tool training)

8. Test Schedule

    a.   Development of Test Plan (e.g., start and end dates)

    b.   Design of Test Cases (e.g., start and end dates by test type)

    c.   Development of Test Cases (e.g., start and end dates by test type)

    d.   Execution of Test Cases (e.g., start and end date by test type)

    e.   Reporting of Problems (e.g., start and end dates)

    f.   Developing Test Summary Report (e.g., start and end dates)

    g.   Documenting Test Summary Report (e.g., start and end dates)

E3: REQUIREMENTS TRACEABILITY MATRIX

A requirements traceability matrix (Exhibit E-1) is a document that traces user requirements from analysis through implementation. It can be used as a completeness check to verify that all requirements are present or that there are no unnecessary/extra features, and as a maintenance guide for new personnel. At each step in the development cycle, the requirements, code, and associated test cases are recorded to ensure that the user requirement is addressed in the final system. Both the user and developer have the ability to easily cross-reference the requirements to the design specifications, programming, and test cases.

E4: TEST PLAN (CLIENT/SERVER AND INTERNET SPIRAL TESTING)

The client/server test plan is based on the information gathered during the initial interview(s) with development and any other information that becomes available during the course of the project. Since requirement specifications are probably not available in the spiral development environment, this test plan is a "living document." Through every spiral, new information is added, and old information is updated as circumstanc-

Exhibit E-1. Requirements Traceability Matrix

User Requirement Reference	System Requirements Reference	Design Specification	Coding Component Reference	Unit Test Case Reference	Integration Test Case Reference	System Test Case Reference	Acceptance Test Case Reference
1.1 Customer must be valid	1.1.2 Online customer screen	Customer screen specification	CUS105, CUS217	CUS105.1.1, CUS2171.1	Int1.25, Int1.26	Sys4.75, Sys4.76	Acc2.25, Acc2.26
•	•	•	•	•	•	•	•
•	•	•	•	•	•	•	•
•	•	•	•	•	•	•	•

es change. The major testing activities are the function, GUI, system, acceptance, and regression testing. These tests, however, are not necessarily performed in a specific order and may be concurrent.

The cover page of the test plan includes the title of the testing project, author, current revision number, and date last changed. The next page includes an optional section for signoffs by the executive sponsor, development manager, testing manager, quality assurance manager, and others as appropriate.

The following is a sample test plan table of contents.

1. Introduction
    1.1 Purpose
    1.2 Executive Summary
    1.3 Project Documentation
    1.4 Risks
2. Scope
    2.1 In Scope
    2.2 Test Requirements
        2.2.1 High-Level Functional Requirements
        2.2.2 User Business/Interface Rules
    2.3 GUI Testing
    2.4 Critical System/Acceptance Testing
        2.4.1   Performance Testing
        2.4.2   Security Testing
        2.4.3   Volume Testing
        2.4.4   Stress Testing
        2.4.5   Compatibility Testing
        2.4.6   Conversion Testing
        2.4.7   Usability Testing
        2.4.8   Documentation Testing
        2.4.9   Backup Testing
        2.4.10 Recovery Testing
        2.4.11 Installation Testing
    2.5 Regression Testing
    2.6 Out of Scope
3. Test Approach
    3.1 General Test Structure
    3.2 Data
    3.3 Interfaces
    3.4 Environmental/System Requirements
    3.5 Dependencies
    3.6 Regression Test Strategy
    3.7 Defect Tracking and Resolution
    3.8 Issue Resolution

E5: FUNCTION/TEST MATRIX

The function/test matrix (Exhibit E-2) cross references the tests to the functions. This matrix provides proof of the completeness of the test strategies and illustrates in graphic format which tests exercise which functions.

E6: GUI COMPONENT TEST MATRIX
(CLIENT/SERVER AND INTERNET SPIRAL TESTING)

With a GUI component test matrix (Exhibit E-3), each GUI component is defined and documented by name and GUI type. During GUI testing, each component is tested against a predefined set of GUI tests.

E7: GUI-BASED FUNCTIONAL TEST MATRIX
(CLIENT/SERVER AND INTERNET SPIRAL TESTING)

Exhibit E-4 is a GUI-based Function Test Matrix template that can be used to document GUI-based test cases. It includes functions and associated GUI objects or foundation components (windows, menus, forms, icons, and controls). Each test includes a requirements number, test objective, test procedure (step or script), expected results, whether the test passed or failed, the tester, and the date of the test. It thus also serves as a test case log.

E8: TEST CASE

A test case (Exhibit E-5) defines the step-by-step process whereby a test is executed. It includes the objectives and conditions of the test, the steps needed to set up the test, the data inputs, and the expected and actual results. Other information, such as the software, environment, version, test ID, screen, and test type, are also provided.

Exhibit E-2. Function/Test Matrix

	Test Case				
	1	**2**	**3**	**4**	**5**
Business Function					

Exhibit E-3. GUI Component Test Matrix

Name	Window	GUI Type				P/F	Date	Tester
		Menu	Form	ICON	Control			
Main-Window	√							
Customer-Order Window	√							
Edit-Order Window	√							
Menu Bar		√						
Tool Bar					√			
.								
.								
.								

Exhibit E-4. GUI-Based Function Test Matrix

Function (enter the name)

Case No.	REQ No.	Test Objective	Case Steps	Expected Results	(P/F)	Tester	Date
			1. 2. 3.				
GUI object (menu, icon, List Box etc.)							
			1. 2. 3.				
GUI object (menu, icon, List Box etc.)							
			1. 2. 3.				
GUI object (menu, icon, List Box etc.)							
			1. 2. 3.				
GUI object (menu, icon, List Box etc.)							
			1. 2. 3.				

Exhibit E-5. Test Case

Date: _____   Tested by: _____

System:_____   Environment: _____

Objective:_____   Test ID _____ Req ID _____

Function:_____   Screen: _____

Version:_____   Test Type: _____

(Unit, Integ., System, Accept.)

Condition to Test:

_____

_____

_____

_____

Data/Steps to Perform:

_____

_____

_____

_____

Expected Results:

_____

_____

_____

Actual Results: Passed ☐   Failed ☐

_____

_____

_____

_____

E9: TEST CASE LOG

The test case log (Exhibit E-6) documents the test cases for a test type to be executed during testing. It also records the results of the tests, which provides the detailed evidence for the test log summary report and enables one to reconstruct the test, if necessary.

Exhibit E-6. Test Case Log

Test Name:	Enter Name of Test
Test Case Author:	Enter Test Case Author Name
Tester Name:	Enter Tester Name
Project ID/Name:	Enter Name of Project
Test Cycle ID:	Enter Test Cycle ID
Date Tested:	Enter Date Test Case Was Completed

Test Case ID	Test Objective ID	Category	Condition	Expected Results	Actual Results	Requirement ID
Enter ID	Enter ID from Test Plan	Enter the Test Category (edit, numeric, presentation, etc.)	Enter Specific Test Condition	Describe the Specific Results Expected Upon Executing the Condition	Record "Pass" or "Fail"	Enter the ID that Traces Back to the Specific Requirement

E10: TEST LOG SUMMARY REPORT

A test log summary report (Exhibit E-7) documents the test cases from the tester's test logs, eight in progress or completed, for the status reporting and metric collection.

Exhibit E-7. Test Log Summary Report

Completed By:	Enter the Tester Name of the Report	Report Date:	Enter Date of the Report
Project ID/Name	Enter Project Identifier/Name	Testing Name/Event:	Enter the Name of the Type of Test (Unit, Integration, System, Acceptance)
Total Number of Test Cases	Enter Total Number of Test Cases	Testing Sub-Type:	Enter Name of Testing Subtype (Interface, Volume, Stress, User, Parallel Testing)

Week/ Month	Current Period	Project to Date	% Started	Current Period	% Open	Current Period	Project to Date	% Completed
Enter Test Period	Enter Number of Test Cases Started for the Period	Enter Total Test Cases Started to Date	Total Number Test Cases Started/ Total Number of Test Cases	Enter Number of Test Cases Started for this Period	Total Number Started/ Total Number of Test Cases	Enter Number of Test Cases Started for this Period	Enter Total Test Cases Started to Date	Total Number Test Cases Started/ Total Number of Test Cases
Total:								

E11: SYSTEM SUMMARY REPORT

A system summary report should be prepared for every major testing event. Sometimes it summarizes all the tests. The following is an outline of the information that should be provided.

1. **General Information**
    1.1 **Test Objectives.** The objectives of the test, including the general functions of the software tested and the test analysis performed, should be summarized. Objectives include functionality, performance, etc.
    1.2 **Environment.** The software sponsor, development manager, the user organization, and the computer center at which the software is to be installed should be identified. The manner in which the

test environment may be different from the operation environment should be noted, and the effects of this difference assessed.

1.3   References. Applicable references should be listed, including:

    a. Project authorization
    b. Previously published documents on the project
    c. Documentation concerning related projects
    d. Standards and other reference documents

2. Test Results and Findings

The results and findings of each test should be presented separately.

2.1   Test (Identify)

    2.1.1   Validation Tests. Data input and output results of this test, including the output of internally generated data, should be compared with the data input and output requirements. Findings should be included.

    2.1.2   Verification Tests. Variances with expected results should be listed.

2.2   Test (Identify). The results and findings of the second and succeeding tests should be presented in a manner similar to the previous paragraphs.

3. Software Function and Findings

3.1   Function (Identify)

    3.1.1   Performance. The function should be briefly described. The software capabilities that were designed to satisfy this function should be described. The findings on the demonstrated capabilities from one or more tests should be included.

    3.1.2   Limits. The range of data values tested should be identified. The deficiencies, limitations, and constraints detected in the software during the testing with respect to this function should be noted.

3.2   Function (Identify). The findings on the second and succeeding functions should be presented in a manner similar to paragraph 3.1.

4. Analysis Summary

4.1   Capabilities. The capabilities of the software as demonstrated by the tests should be described. When tests were to demonstrate fulfillment of one or more specific performance requirements, findings showing the comparison of the results with these requirements should be prepared. The effects of any differences in the test environment compared with the operational environment should be assessed.

4.2   Deficiencies. Software deficiencies as demonstrated by the tests should be listed, and their impact on the performance of the software should be assessed. The cumulative or overall impact on performance of all detected deficiencies should be summarized.

4.3 Graphical Analysis. Graphs can be used to demonstrate the history of the development project including defect trend analysis, root cause analysis, etc. (Project wrap-up graphs are recommended as illustrations.)

4.4 Risks. The business risks faced if the software is placed in production should be listed.

4.5 Recommendations and Estimates. For each deficiency, estimates of time and effort required for its correction should be provided along with recommendations on:

a. Urgency of each correction

b. Parties responsible for corrections

c. How the corrections should be made

4.6 Opinion. The readiness of the software for production should be assessed.

E12: DEFECT REPORT

A defect report (Exhibit E-8) documents an anomaly discovered during testing. It includes all the information needed to reproduce the problem, including the author, release/build number, open/close dates, problem area, problem description, test environment, defect type, how it was detected, who detected it, priority, severity, status, etc.

E13: TEST SCHEDULE

A test schedule (Exhibit E-9) includes the testing steps (and perhaps tasks), the target begin and end dates, and responsibilities. It should also describe how the test will be reviewed, tracked, and approved.

E14: RETEST MATRIX

A retest matrix is a tool that relates test cases to functions (or program units) as shown in Exhibit E-10. A check entry in the matrix indicates that the test case is to be retested when the function (or program unit) has been modified due to an enhancement(s) or correction(s). No entry means that the test does not need to be retested. The retest matrix can be built before the first testing spiral but needs to be maintained during subsequent spirals. As functions (or program units) are modified during a development spiral, existing or new test cases need to be created and checked in the retest matrix in preparation for the next test spiral. Over time with subsequent spirals, some functions (or program units) may be stable with no recent modifications. Consideration to selectively remove their check entries should be undertaken between testing spirals.

Exhibit E-8. Software Problem Report

Software Problem Report

Defect ID: *(Required)*
Computer generated

Author: *(Required)*
Computer generated

Release/Build#: *(Required)*
Build where issue was discovered

Open Date: *(Required)*
Computer generated

Close Date: *(Required)*
Computer generated when QA closes

Problem Area: *(Required)*
E.g., add order, etc.

Defect or Enhancement: *(Required)*
Defect (default)
Enhancement

Problem Title: *(Required)*
Brief, one-line description

Problem Description:
A precise problem description with screen captures, if possible

Current Environment: *(Required)*
E.g. Win95T/Oracle 4.0 NT

Other Environment(s):
E.g., WinNT/Oracle 4.0 NT

Defect Type: *(Required)*
Architectural
Connectivity
Consistency
Database Integrity
Documentation
Functionality (default)
GUI
Installation
Memory
Performance
Security and Controls
Standards and Conventions
Stress
Usability

Exhibit E-8. (Continued) Software Problem Report

Who Detected: *(Required)*
External Customer
Internal Customer
Development
Quality Assurance (default)

How Detected: *(Required)*
Review
Walkthrough
JAD
Testing (default)

Assigned To: *(Required)*
Individual assigned to investigate problem

Priority: *(Required)*
Critical
High (default)
Medium
Low

Severity: *(Required)*
Critical
High (default)
Medium
Low

Status: *(Required)*
Open (default)
Being Reviewed by Development
Returned by Development
Ready for Testing in the Next Build
Closed (QA)
Returned by (QA)
Deferred to the Next Release

Status Description:
(Required when Status = "Returned by Development," "Ready for Testing in the Next Build")

Fixed by:
(Required when Status = "Ready for Testing in the Next Build")

Planned Fix Build#:
(Required when Status = "Ready for Testing in the Next Build")

Exhibit E-9. Test Schedule

Test Step	Begin Date	End Date	Responsible
First Spiral			
Information gathering			
Prepare for Interview	x•xx•xx	x•xx•xx	
Conduct Interview	x•xx•xx	x•xx•xx	
Summarize Findings	x•xx•xx	x•xx•xx	
Test Planning			
Build Test Plan	x•xx•xx	x•xx•xx	
Define the Metric Objectives	x•xx•xx	x•xx•xx	
Review/Approve Plan	x•xx•xx	x•xx•xx	
Test Case Design			
Design Function Tests	x•xx•xx	x•xx•xx	
Design GUI Tests	x•xx•xx	x•xx•xx	
Define the System/Acceptance Tests	x•xx•xx	x•xx•xx	
Review/Approve Design	x•xx•xx	x•xx•xx	
Test Development			
Develop Test Scripts	x•xx•xx	x•xx•xx	
Review/Approve Test Development	x•xx•xx	x•xx•xx	
Test Execution/Evaluation			
Setup and Testing	x•xx•xx	x•xx•xx	
Evaluation	x•xx•xx	x•xx•xx	
Prepare for the Next Spiral			
Refine the tests	x•xx•xx	x•xx•xx	
Reassess Team, Procedures, and Test Environment	x•xx•xx	x•xx•xx	
Publish Interim Report	x•xx•xx	x•xx•xx	
•			
•			
•			
Last Spiral...			

Exhibit E-9. (Continued) Test Schedule

Test Step	Begin Date	End Date	Responsible
Test Execution/Evaluation			
Setup and Testing	xx•xx•xx	xx•xx•xx	
Evaluation	xx•xx•xx	xx•xx•xx	
•			
•			
•			
Conduct System Testing			
Complete System Test Plan	xx•xx•xx	xx•xx•xx	
Complete System Test Cases	xx•xx•xx	xx•xx•xx	
Review/Approve System Tests	xx•xx•xx	xx•xx•xx	
Execute the System Tests	xx•xx•xx	xx•xx•xx	
Conduct Acceptance Testing			
Complete Acceptance Test Plan	xx•xx•xx	xx•xx•xx	
Complete Acceptance Test Cases	xx•xx•xx	xx•xx•xx	
Review/Approve Acceptance Test Plan	xx•xx•xx	xx•xx•xx	
Execute the Acceptance Tests	xx•xx•xx	xx•xx•xx	
Summarize/Report Spiral Test Results			
Perform Data Reduction	xx•xx•xx	xx•xx•xx	
Prepare Final Test Report	xx•xx•xx	xx•xx•xx	
Review/Approve the Final Test Report	xx•xx•xx	xx•xx•xx	

E15: SPIRAL TESTING SUMMARY REPORT (CLIENT/SERVER AND INTERNET SPIRAL TESTING)

The objective of the final spiral test report is to describe the results of the testing, including not only what works and what does not, but the test team's evaluation regarding performance of the application when it is placed into production.

For some projects, informal reports are the practice, while in others very formal reports are required. The following is a compromise between

Exhibit E-10. Retest Matrix

	Test Case				
	1	**2**	**3**	**4**	**5**
Business Function					
Order Processing					
Create New Order					
Fulfill Order					
Edit Order					
Delete Order					
Customer Processing					
Create New Customer					
Edit Customer					
Delete Customer					
Financial Processing					
Receive Customer Payment					
Deposit Payment					
Pay Vendor					
Write a Check					
Display Register					
Inventory Processing					
Acquire Vendor Products					
Maintain Stock					
Handle Back Orders					
Audit Inventory					

Exhibit E-10. Retest Matrix

	Test Case				
	1	**2**	**3**	**4**	**5**
Adjust Product Price					
Reports					
Create Order Report					
Create Account Receivables Report					
Create Account Payables					
Create Inventory Report					

the two extremes to provide essential information not requiring an inordinate amount of preparation.

I. **Project Overview**
II. **Test Activities**
    A.   **Test Team**
    B.   **Test Environment**
    C.   **Types of Tests**
    D.   **Test Schedule**
    E.   **Test Tools**
III. **Metric Graphics**
IV. **Findings/Recommendations**

Appendix F
Checklists

A very powerful quality control testing tool is a checklist. It is powerful because it statistically differentiates between two extremes. It can be used for fact gathering during problem identification, cause analysis, or it can check progress during implementation of a solution.

Observed results or conditions are recorded by entering or not entering check marks opposite items on a list. Information gathered in this way is limited to simple yes/no answers. It also quantifies or counts the data entered for subsequent tallying and analysis.

F1: REQUIREMENTS PHASE DEFECT CHECKLIST

The requirements phase defect checklist (Exhibit F-1) is used to verify the functional needs and specifications for the system. A check in the Missing column means that the item was not included. A check in the Wrong column means the item was incorrectly used. A check in the Extra column means that the item has been discovered but not originally identified. The total column totals the number of missing and extra items.

F2: LOGICAL DESIGN PHASE DEFECT CHECKLIST

The logical design phase defect checklist (Exhibit F-2) is used to verify the logical design of the system. A check in the Missing column means that the item was not included. A check in the Wrong column means the item was incorrectly used. A check in the Extra column means that the item has been discovered but not originally identified. The total column totals the number of missing and extra items.

F3: PHYSICAL DESIGN PHASE DEFECT CHECKLIST

The physical design phase defect checklist (Exhibit F-3) is used to verify the physical design of the system. A check in the Missing column means that the item was not included. A check in the Wrong column means the item was incorrectly used. A check in the Extra column means that the item has been discovered but not originally identified. The total column totals the number of missing and extra items.

Exhibit F-1. Requirements Phase Checklist

Defect Category	Missing	Wrong	Extra	Total
1. Business rules (or information) are inadequate or partially missing.				
2. Performance criteria (or information) are inadequate or partially missing.				
3. Environment information is inadequate or partially missing.				
4. System mission information is inadequate or partially missing.				
5. Requirements are incompatible.				
6. Requirements are incomplete.				
7. Requirements are missing.				
8. Requirements are incorrect.				
9. The accuracy specified does not conform to the actual need.				
10. The data environment is inadequately described.				
11. The external interface definitions are erroneous.				
12. User training has not been considered adequately.				
13. Initialization of the system state has not been considered.				
14. The functions have not be adequately defined.				
15. The user needs are inadequately stated.				
16. Quality metrics have not been specified adequately, e.g., maintainability, transportability, etc.				

Exhibit F-2. Logical Design Phase Checklist

Defect Category	Missing	Wrong	Extra	Total
1. The data has not been adequately defined.				
2. Entity definition is incomplete.				
3. Entity cardinality is incorrect.				
4. Entity attribute is incomplete.				
5. Normalization is violated.				
6. Incorrect primary key				
7. Incorrect foreign key				
8. Incorrect compound key				
9. Incorrect entity subtype				
10. The process has not been adequately defined.				
11. Parent process is incomplete.				
12. Child process is incomplete.				
13. Process inputs/outputs are incorrect.				
14. Elementary processes are not defined correctly.				
15. Mutually exclusive process problem.				
16. Parallel links problem.				
17. Event-triggered processes not defined properly.				
18. Incorrect entity/process create association.				
19. Incorrect entity/process read association.				
20. Incorrect entity/process update association.				
21. Incorrect entity/process delete association.				

Exhibit F-3. Physical Design Phase Checklist

Defect Category	Missing	Wrong	Extra	Total
1. Logic or sequencing is erroneous.				
2. Processing is inaccurate.				
3. Routine does not input or output required parameters.				
4. Routine does not accept all data within the allowable range.				
5. Limit and validity checks are made on input data.				
6. Recovery procedures are not implemented or are inadequate.				
7. Required processing is missing or inadequate.				
8. Values are erroneous or ambiguous.				
9. Data storage is erroneous or inadequate.				
10. Variables are missing.				
11. Design requirements are inaccurately or incorrectly understood.				
12. Database is not compatible with the data environment.				
13. Modular decomposition reflects a high intermodular dependence.				
14. Major algorithms are not evaluated for accuracy or speed.				
15. Control structure is not expandable.				
16. Control structure ignores the processing priorities.				
17. Interface protocols are incorrect.				
18. Logic to implementing algorithms is incorrect.				
19. Data is not converted according to correct format.				
20. No consideration is given to the effects of round-off or truncation.				
21. Indices are not checked for validity.				
22. Infinite loops are permitted.				
23. Module specifications are incorrectly understood.				
24. Database rules are violated.				
25. Logic is incomplete for all cases.				
26. Special cases are neglected.				

Exhibit F-3. (Continued) Physical Design Phase Checklist

Defect Category	Missing	Wrong	Extra	Total
27. Error handling is deficient.				
28. Timing considerations are neglected.				
29. Requirement specifications are misallocated among the various software modules.				
30. Interface specifications are misunderstood or misimplemented.				
31. System is functionally correct but does not meet performance requirements.				
32. Software is not sufficiently complex to match the problem being solved.				
33. Arithmetic overflow and underflow are not properly addressed.				
34. Actions in response to given inputs are inappropriate or missing.				
35. Algorithmic approximations provide insufficient accuracy or erroneous results for certain values of the input.				
36. There are errors in the detailed logic developed to solve a particular problem.				
37. Singular or critical input values may yield unexpected results that are not appropriately accounted for in the code.				
38. An algorithm is inefficient or does not compute the result as rapidly as a more efficient algorithm.				
39. An algorithm does not cover all the necessary cases.				
40. An algorithm is incorrect or converges to the wrong solution.				
41. Logic errors exist.				
42. A design oversight occurs.				

F4: PROGRAM UNIT DESIGN PHASE DEFECT CHECKLIST

The program unit design phase defect checklist (Exhibit F-4) is used to verify the unit design of the system. A check in the Missing column means that the item was not included. A check in the Wrong column means the item was incorrectly used. A check in the Extra column means that the item has been discovered but not originally identified. The total column totals the number of missing and extra items.

APPENDIX F

Exhibit F-4. Program Unit Design Phase Checklist

Defect Category	Missing	Wrong	Extra	Total
1. Is the if-then-else construct used incorrectly?				
2. Is the dowhile construct used incorrectly?				
3. Is the dountil construct used incorrectly?				
4. Is the case construct used incorrectly?				
5. Are there infinite loops?				
6. Is it a proper program?				
7. Are there goto statements?				
8. Is the program readable?				
9. Is the program efficient?				
10. Does the case construct contain all the conditions?				
11. Is there dead code?				
12. Does the program have self-modifying code?				
13. Is the algorithm expression too simple?				
14. Is the algorithm expression too complicated?				
15. Is the nesting too deep?				
16. Is there negative Boolean logic?				
17. Are there compounded Boolean expressions?				
18. Is there jumping in and out of loops?				

F5: CODING PHASE DEFECT CHECKLIST

The coding phase defect checklist (Exhibit F-5) is used to verify the conversion of the design specifications into executable code. A check in the Missing column means that the item was not included. A check in the Wrong column means the item was incorrectly used. A check in the Extra column means that the item has been discovered but not originally identified. The total column totals the number of missing and extra items.

Exhibit F-5. Coding Phase Checklist

Defect Category	Missing	Wrong	Extra	Total
1. Decision logic or sequencing is erroneous or inadequate.				
2. Arithmetic computations are erroneous or inadequate.				
3. Branching is erroneous.				
4. Branching or other testing is performed incorrectly.				
5. There are undefined loop terminations.				
6. Programming language rules are violated.				
7. Programming standards are violated.				
8. The programmer misinterprets language constructs.				
9. Typographical errors exist.				
10. Main storage allocation errors exist.				
11. Iteration schemes are unsuccessful.				
12. I/O format errors exist.				
13. Parameters or subscripts are violated.				
14. Subprogram invocations are violated.				
15. Data errors exist.				
16. A subprogram is nonterminating.				
17. There are errors in preparing or processing input data.				
18. Tape handling errors exist.				
19. Disk handling errors exist.				
20. Output processing errors exist.				
21. Error message processing errors exist.				
22. Software interface errors exist.				
23. Database interface errors exist.				
24. User interface errors exist.				
25. Indexing and subscripting errors exist.				
26. Iterative procedural errors exist.				
27. Bit manipulation errors exist.				
28. Syntax errors exist.				

Exhibit F-5. (Continued) Coding Phase Checklist

Defect Category	Missing	Wrong	Extra	Total
29. Initialization errors exist.				
30. There is confusion in the use of parameters.				
31. There are errors in loop counters.				
32. Decision results are incorrectly handled.				
33. Variables are given multiple names or are not defined.				
34. Errors are made in writing out variable names.				
35. Variable type and dimensions are incorrectly declared.				
36. There is confusion about library program names.				
37. External symbols are incorrectly resolved.				
38. Compiler errors exist.				
39. Singularities and external points exist.				
40. Floating point underflow errors exist.				
41. Floating point overflow errors exist.				
42. Floating point and integer division by zero is allowed.				
43. A sequencing error exists.				
44. There is a failure to save and restore appropriate registers in real-time systems.				
45. The software interface to connected hardware systems is incorrect.				

F6: FIELD TESTING CHECKLIST

A field test (Exhibit F-6) is limited to a specific field or data element and is intended to validate that all of the processing related to that specific field is performed correctly.

F7: RECORD TESTING CHECKLIST

A record test (Exhibit F-7) validates that records can be created, entered, processed, stored, and output correctly.

Exhibit F-6. Field Testing Checklist

Item	Yes	No	N/A	Comments
1. Were all codes validated?				
2. Can fields be updated properly?				
3. Is the field large enough for collecting the totals?				
4. Is the field adequately described in the program?				
5. Can the field be initialized properly?				
6. Do all references to the field use the proper field name?				
7. If the field's contents are restricted, are those restrictions validated?				
8. Were rules established for identifying and processing invalid field data? (If not, this data must be developed for the error-handling transaction type. If so, test conditions must be prepared to validate the specification processing for invalid field data.)				
9. Is a wide range of typical valid processing values included in the test conditions?				
10. For numerical fields, have the upper and lower values been tested?				
11. For numerical fields, has a zero value been tested?				
12. For numerical fields, has a negative test condition been prepared?				
13. For alphabetical fields, has a blank condition been prepared?				
14. For an alphabetic or alphanumeric field, has a test condition longer than the field length been prepared to check truncation processing?				
15. Were all valid conditions tested on the basis of the data dictionary printout?				
16. Were systems specifications reviewed to determine whether all valid conditions are tested?				
17. Do owners of data elements know whether all valid conditions are tested?				
18. Have owners of data elements reported their results?				

Exhibit F-7. Record Testing Checklist

Item	Yes	No	N/A	Comments
1. Were conditions prepared for testing the processing of the first record?				
2. Were conditions determined for validating the processing of the last record?				
3. Were all multiple records per transaction processed correctly?				
4. Were all multiple records on a storage medium (i.e., permanent or temporary file) processed correctly?				
5. Were all variations in record size tested (e.g., a header with variable length trailers)?				
6. Can the Iob control language be checked for each record type?				
7. Can processing be done for two records with the same identifier (e.g., two payments for the same accounts receivable file)?				
8. Can the first record stored on a storage file be retrieved?				
9. Can the last record stored on a storage file be retrieved?				
10. Can all of the records entered be stored properly?				
11. Can all of the stored records be retrieved?				
12. Do interconnecting modules have the same identifier for each record type?				
13. Can the data entry function prepare the proper records from the data entry documentation?				
14. Is the user documentation useful to users?				
15. Do individual module record descriptions conform to the system record descriptions?				
16. Does the storage definition of records conform to the system definition of records?				
17. Are record descriptions common throughout the entire software system?				
18. Do current record formats coincide with the formats used on files created by other systems?				

F8: FILE TEST CHECKLIST

A file test (Exhibit F-8) verifies that all needed files are included in the system being tested, that they are properly documented in the operating infrastructure, and that the files connect properly with the software components that need data from those files.

Exhibit F-8. File Test Checklist

Item	Yes	No	N/A	Comments
1. Is a condition available for testing each file?				
2. Is a condition available for testing each file's interface with each module?				
3. Are test conditions available for validating each job control condition (or the equivalent in environments in which there is no JCL)?				
4. Is a condition available for validating that the correct version of each file will be used?				
5. Is a condition available for testing that records placed on a file will be returned intact?				
6. Are conditions available for validating that each file is properly closed after the last record is processed for that file?				
7. Are conditions available for validating that each record type can be processed from beginning to end of the system intact?				
8. Are conditions available for validating that all records entered are processed through the system?				
9. Are conditions available for validating that files that are mounted but not used are properly closed at the end of processing?				
10. Are test conditions available for creating a file for which no prior records exist?				
11. Is a condition available for validating the correct closing of a file when all records on the file have been deleted?				
12. Are conditions available for validating the correctness of all the job control statements?				

F9: ERROR TESTING CHECKLIST

An error test (Exhibit F-9) identifies errors in data elements, data element relationships, record and file relationships, as well as logical processing conditions.

Exhibit F-9. Error Testing Checklist

Item	Yes	No	N/A	Comments
1. Were functional errors identified by the brainstorming session with end users/customers?				
2. Were structural error conditions identified by the brainstorming session with project personnel?				
3. Were functional error conditions identified for the following cases:				
Rejection of invalid codes?				
Rejection of out-of-range values?				
Rejection of improper data relationships?				
Rejection of invalid dates?				
Rejection of unauthorized transactions of the following types:				
• Invalid value?				
• Invalid customer?				
• Invalid product?				
• Invalid transaction type?				
• Invalid price?				
Alphabetic data in numeric fields?				
Blanks in a numeric field?				
An all-blank condition in a numeric field?				
Negative values in a positive field?				
Positive values in a negative field?				
Negative balances in a financial account?				
Numeric in an alphabetic field?				
Blanks in an alphabetic field?				
Values longer than the field permits?				
Totals that exceed maximum size of total fields?				

Exhibit F-9. (Continued) Error Testing Checklist

Item	Yes	No	N/A	Comments
Proper accumulation of totals (at all levels for multiple-level totals)?				
Incomplete transactions (i.e., one or more fields missing)?				
Obsolete data in the field (i.e., a formerly valid code no longer valid)?				
A new value that will become acceptable but is not acceptable now (e.g., a new district code for which the district has not yet been established)?				
A postdated transaction?				
Change of a value that affects a relationship (e.g., if the unit digit is used to control year, switching from 9 in 89 to 0 in 90 can still be processed)?				
4. Does the data dictionary list of field specifications generate invalid specifications?				
5. Are tests performed for the following architectural error conditions:				
Page overflow?				
Report format conformance to design layout?				
Posting of data to correct portion of reports?				
Printed error messages representative of the actual error condition?				
All instructions executed?				
All paths executed?				
All internal tables?				
All loops?				
All PERFORM type routines?				
All compiler warning messages?				
The correct version of the program?				
Unchanged portions of the system revalidated after any part of the system is changed?				

F10: USE TEST CHECKLIST

A use test (Exhibit F-10) tests the end user's ability to use the system and involves an understanding of both system output and that output's ability to lead to a correct action.

Exhibit F-10. Use Test Checklist

Item	Yes	No	N/A	Comments
1. Are all end-user actions identified?				
2. Are they identified in enough detail so that contribution of information system output items can be related to those actions?				
3. Is all the information used in taking an action identified and related to the action?				
4. Is the output from the system under test related to specific actions?				
5. Does the end user correctly understand the output reports and screens?				
6. Does the end user understand the type of logic and computation performed to produce the output?				
7. Can the end user identify the contribution the output makes to the actions taken?				
8. Can the end user identify whether the actions taken are correct?				
9. If not, can another party determine the correctness of the actions taken?				
10. Is the relationship between system output and business actions defined?				
11. Does interpretation of the matrix indicate that the end user does not have adequate information to take an action?				
12. Does analysis of the matrix indicate that the end user is making an abnormal number of incorrect actions?				
13. If so, is the end user willing to let the system be modified to provide better information for taking actions?				

F11: SEARCH TEST CHECKLIST

A search test (Exhibit F-11) verifies locating records, fields, and other variables, and helps validate that the search logic is correct.

Exhibit F-11. Search Test Checklist

Item	Yes	No	N/A	Comments
1. Were all internal tables identified?				
2. Were all internal lists of error messages identified?				
3. Were all internal logic paths (when there are multiple choices) identified?				
4. Was the search logic identified? (In some cases, algorithms are used to identify the needed entity.)				
5. Were all authorization routines identified?				
6. Were all password routines identified?				
7. Was all business processing logic requiring a search identified (e.g., logic requiring the lookup of a customer record)?				
8. Were database search routines identified?				
9. Were subsystem searches identified (e.g., finding a tax rate in a sales tax subsystem)?				
10. Were complex search logics identified (e.g., those requiring two or more conditions or two or more records-searching for accounts more than both 90 days old and $100)?				
11. Were search routines for processing modules identified?				
12. Were test conditions graded for all of the preceding search conditions?				
13. Was the end user interviewed to determine the type of one-time searches that might be encountered in the future?				
14. If so, can these searches be done with reasonable effort (confirmed by the project group)?				
15. If no, was the end user informed of the cost of conducting the searches or reconstructing the system to meet those needs?				

F12: MATCH/MERGE CHECKLIST

A match/merge test (Exhibit F-12) ensures that all the combinations of merging and matching are adequately addressed. The test typically involves two or more files, and an input transaction and one or more files or an input transaction and an internal table.

Exhibit F-12. Match/Merge Checklist

Item	Yes	No	N/A	Comments
1. Were all files associated with the application identified? (In this transaction, files include specialized files, databases, and internal groupings of records used for matching and merging.)				
2. Were the following match/merge conditions addressed:				
Match/merge of records of two different identifiers (e.g., inserting a new employee on the payroll file)?				
A match/merge on which there are no records on the matched/merged file?				
A match/merge in which the matched/merged record is the lowest value on the file?				
A match/merge in which the matched/merged record is the highest value on the file?				
A match/merge in which the matched/merged record is the same value as an item on a file, e.g., adding a new employee when the employee's payroll number is the same as an existing payroll number on the file)?				
A match/merge for which there is no input file or transactions being matched/merged? (The objective is to see that the matched/merged file is adequately closed.)				
A match/merge in which the first item on the file is deleted?				
A match/merge in which the last item on the attached/merged file is deleted?				
A match/merge in which two incoming records have the same value?				
A match/merge in which two incoming records indicate a value on the matched/merged file is to be deleted?				
A match/merge condition when the last remaining record on the matched/merged file is deleted?				
A match/merge condition in which the incoming matched/merged file is out of sequence or has a single record out of sequence?				
Were these test conditions applied to the totality of match/merge conditions that can occur in the software being tested?				

F13: STRESS TEST CHECKLIST

A stress test (Exhibit F-13) validates the performance of software that is subjected to a large volume of transactions.

Exhibit F-13. Stress Test Checklist

Item	Yes	No	N/A	Comments
1. Were all desired performance capabilities identified?				
2. Were all system features contributing to the test identified?				
3. Were the following system performance capabilities identified:				
Data entry operator performance?				
Communications line performance?				
Turnaround performance?				
Availability and uptime performance?				
Response time performance?				
Error-handling performance?				
Report-generation performance?				
Internal computational performance?				
Performance in developing actions?				
4. Are the following system features (that can impair performance) identified:				
Internal computer processing speed?				
Communications line transmission speed?				
Efficiency of programming language?				
Efficiency of database management system?				
Number of input terminals and entry stations?				
Skill level of data entry staff?				
Backup for computer terminals?				
Backup for data entry staff?				
Expected downtime with central processing site?				
Expected frequency and duration of abnormal software terminations?				
Queuing capabilities?				
File-storage capabilities?				
5. Are the stress conditions realistic for validating software performance (as confirmed by project personnel)?				

F14: ATTRIBUTES TESTING CHECKLIST

An attribute test (Exhibit F-14) involves verifying the attributes which are quality and productivity characteristics of a system being tested. An example includes the ease of introducing changes into the software.

Exhibit F-14. Attributes Testing Checklist

Item	Yes	No	N/A	Comments
1. Have software attributes been identified?				
2. Have software attributes been ranked?				
3. Do end users or customers agree with the attribute ranking?				
4. Have test conditions been developed for the very important attributes?				
5. For correctness attributes, are the functions accurate and complete?				
6. For the file integrity attribute, is the integrity of each file or subschema validated?				
7. For the authorization attribute, are there authorization procedures for each transaction?				
8. For the audit trail attribute, do test conditions verify that each business transaction can be reconstructed?				
9. For the continuity-of-processing attribute, can the system be recovered within a reasonable time span and transactions captured or processed during the recovery period?				
10. For the service attribute, do turnaround and response times meet user needs?				
11. For the access control attribute, is the system limited to authorized users?				
12. Does the compliance attribute conform to MIS standards, the systems development methodology, and appropriate policies, procedures, and regulations?				
13. For the reliability attribute, is incorrect, incomplete, or obsolete data processed properly?				
14. For the ease-of-use attribute, can users use the system effectively, efficiently, and economically?				
15. For the maintainability attribute, can the system be changed or enhanced with reasonable effort and on a timely basis?				
16. For the portability attribute, can the software be moved efficiently to other platforms?				

Exhibit F-14. (Continued) Attributes Testing Checklist

Item	Yes	No	N/A	Comments
17. For the coupling attribute, can the software integrate properly with other systems?				
18. For the performance attribute, do end users consider the software's performance acceptable?				
19. For the ease-of-operation attribute, are operations personnel able to effectively, economically, and efficiently operate the software?				

F15: STATES TESTING CHECKLIST

A states test (Exhibit F-15) verifies special conditions relating to both the operating and functional environments that may occur.

Exhibit F-15. States Testing Checklist

Item	Yes	No	N/A	Comments
1. Has the state of empty master files been validated?				
2. Has the state of empty transaction files been validated?				
3. Has the state of missing master records been validated?				
4. Has the state of duplicate master records been validated?				
5. Has the state of empty tables been validated?				
6. Has the state of insufficient quantity been validated?				
7. Has the state of negative balances been validated?				
8. Has the state of duplicate input been validated?				
9. Has the state of entering the same transaction twice (particularly from a terminal) been validated?				
10. Has the state of concurrent updates (i.e., two terminals calling on the same master record at the same time) been validated?				
11. Has the state in which there are more requests for service or products than there are services and products to support them been validated?				

F16: PROCEDURES TESTING CHECKLIST

A procedures test (Exhibit F-16) verifies the software to verify the operating, terminal, and communications procedures.

Exhibit F-16. Procedures Testing Checklist

Item	Yes	No	N/A	Comments
1. Have start-up procedures been validated?				
2. Have query procedures been validated?				
3. Have file mounting procedures been validated?				
4. Have updating procedures been validated?				
5. Have backup procedures been validated?				
6. Have off-site storage procedures been validated?				
7. Have recovery procedures been validated?				
8. Have terminal operating procedures been validated?				
9. Have procedures needed to operate the terminal when the main computer is down been validated?				
10. Have procedures needed to capture data when the terminals are down been validated?				

F17: CONTROL TESTING CHECKLIST

A control test (Exhibit F-17) validates the ability of internal controls to support accurate, complete, timely, and authorized processing. These controls are usually validated by auditors assessing the adequacy of control, which is typically dictated by law.

Exhibit F-17. Control Testing Checklist

Item	Yes	No	N/A	Comments
1. Have the business transactions processed by the software been identified?				
2. Has a transaction flow analysis been prepared for each transaction?				
3. Have controls for the transaction flow been documented?				
4. Do data input controls address:				
Accuracy of data input?				
Completeness of data input?				
Timeliness of data input?				
Conversion of data input into a machine-readable format?				
The keying of input?				
Data input processing schedules?				
Assignment of data input duties (e.g., originating, entering, and processing data and distributing output)?				
End users' input (with the help of the control group)?				
Input of all source documents?				
Batching techniques?				
Record counts?				
Predetermined control totals?				
Control logs?				
Key verification?				
Preprogrammed keying formats?				
Editing for input?				
Input data elements?				
Data validation editing techniques?				
Monitoring for overrides and bypasses?				
Restriction of overrides and bypasses to supervisory personnel?				
Automatic recording and submission of overrides and bypasses to supervisors for analysis?				

Exhibit F-17. (Continued) Control Testing Checklist

Item	Yes	No	N/A	Comments
Automatic development of control counts during data entry?				
Recording of transaction errors?				
Monitoring of rejected transactions for correcting and reentering them on a timely basis?				
Written procedures for data input processes?				
Appropriate error messages for all data error conditions?				
Security for data entry terminals?				
Passwords for entering business transactions through terminals?				
Shutting down of terminals after predefined periods of inactivity?				
Reports of unauthorized terminal use?				
Built-in identification codes for terminals?				
Logs of transactions entered through terminals? Interactive displays that tell terminal operators which data is entered?				
5. Do data entry controls include the following controls:				
Accuracy of new data?				
Completeness of new data?				
Timely recording of new data?				
Procedures and methods for creating new data?				
Security for blank source documents?				
Checking of cross-referenced fields?				
Pre-numbered documents?				
Transaction authorization?				
Systems overrides?				
Manual adjustments?				
Batching of source documents?				
Control totals for source documents?				
A correction procedure for errors made on source documents?				

Exhibit F-17. (Continued) Control Testing Checklist

Item	Yes	No	N/A	Comments
A retention repository for source documents?				
Transmission of source documents for data entry?				
Confirmation by the data entry function to the source document function that the documents are entered? (For online systems, data origination and data entry are performed concurrently.)				
Prompt messages for data entry operators?				
6. Do processing controls address:				
Input throughout processing?				
Instructions for operations personnel on how to control processing?				
Abnormal termination or conditions?				
Operation logs for review by supervisors?				
Procedures for reconciling record counts and control totals?				
Reconciliation of processing control totals and manually developed control totals?				
Procedures ensuring that the right versions of programs are run?				
Procedures ensuring that the right versions of files are used?				
Maintenance of run-to-run totals?				
Reconciliation of processing from last to current run (or between different time periods)?				
Validation of new data?				
Manual validation of override and bypass procedures after processing?				
Maintenance of transaction history files?				
Procedures for controlling errors?				
Correct and timely reentry of rejected transactions?				
Recording of correct accounting classifications?				
Concurrent update protection procedures?				
Error messages printed out for each error condition?				

Exhibit F-17. (Continued) Control Testing Checklist

Item	Yes	No	N/A	Comments
Identical procedures for processing corrected and original transactions?				
7. Do data output controls address:				
Accountable documents (e.g., bank checks)?				
Accountable documents damaged in output preparation?				
Completeness of output?				
Review of output documents for acceptability and completeness?				
Reconciliation of output documents for record counts and control totals?				
Identification of output products?				
Delivery of output products to the right locations?				
Delivery of output products on a timely basis?				
Appropriate security for output products?				
The end user's assigned responsibility for the accuracy of all output?				
Logs for output production and delivery?				
Clear output error messages?				
A history of output errors?				
Users informed of output product errors?				
Users informed of abnormal terminations?				
A phone number users can call for help in understanding output?				
A phone number users can call for information about the output production schedule?				
The number of copies of output?				
Procedures that determine who gets online output?				
Control totals for online output?				
Written procedures for online output?				
Procedures for user responses made on the basis of output information?				
8. Has the level of risk for each control area been identified?				

Exhibit F-17. (Continued) Control Testing Checklist

Item	Yes	No	N/A	Comments
9. Has this level of risk been confirmed by the audit function?				
10. Have end users or customers been notified of the level of control risk?				

F18: CONTROL FLOW TESTING CHECKLIST

A control flow test (Exhibit F-18) validates the control flow of transactions through the system under test. It determines whether records can be lost or misprocessed during processing.

Exhibit F-18. Control Flow Testing Checklist

Item	Yes	No	N/A	Comments
1. Have all branches been tested in both directions?				
2. Have all statements been executed?				
3. Have all loops been tested?				
4. Have all iterations of each loop been tested?				
5. Have all execution paths been tested?				
6. Have all subroutines and libraries been called in and executed during testing?				

F19: TESTING TOOL SELECTION CHECKLIST

Finding the tool that is appropriate for a project can be difficult. Several questions need to be answered before selecting a tool. The testing tool selection checklist (Exhibit F-19) lists the questions to help the QA team evaluate and select an automated testing tool.

Exhibit F-19. Testing Tool Selection Checklist

Item	Yes	No	N/A	Comments
1. How easy is the tool for your testers to use? Is it something that can be picked up quickly, or is training going to be required?				
2. Do any of the team members already have experience using the tool?				
3. If training is necessary, are classes, books, or other forms of instruction available?				
4. Will the tool work effectively on the computer system currently in place?				
5. Or is more memory, faster processors, etc., going to be needed?				
6. Is the tool itself easy to use?				
7. Does it have a user-friendly interface?				
8. Is it prone to user error?				
9. Is the tool physically capable of testing your application? Many testing tools can only test in a GUI environment, while others test in nonGUI environments.				
10. Can the tool handle full project testing? That is, is it able to run hundreds if not thousands of test cases for extended periods of time?				
11. Can it run for long periods of time without crashing, or is the tool itself full of bugs?				
12. Talk to customers who currently or previously have used the tool. Did it meet their needs?				
13. How similar were their testing needs to yours and how well did the tool perform?				
14. Try to select a tool that is advanced enough so the costs of updating tests don't overwhelm any benefits of testing.				
15. If a demo version is available, try it out before you make any decisions.				
16. Does the price of the tool fit in the QA department or company budget?				
17. Does the tool meet the requirements of the company testing methodology?				

Appendix G
Integrating Testing into Development Methodology

The following describes testing as a process rather than a life cycle phase. A quality assurance department treating testing as a life cycle phase must integrate the concepts in this manual into its current systems development methodology. If the development methodology provides for testing throughout the design and maintenance methodology but is not well defined, the testing approach must be expanded and modified to correspond to the process described in this manual.

Testing must be integrated into the systems development methodology. Considered as a separate function, it may not receive the appropriate resources and commitment. Testing as an integrated function, however, prevents development from proceeding without testing.

Integration of testing into a systems development methodology is a two-part process. First, the testing steps and tasks are integrated into the systems development methodology through addition or modification of tasks for developmental personnel to perform during the creation of an application system. Second, defects must be recorded and captured. This process is the equivalent of problem reporting in operational application systems. The test manager must be able to capture information about the problems or defects that occur; without this information, it is difficult to improve testing.

Usually, the person responsible for the systems development methodology integrates testing into it. In many organizations, this is the quality assurance function. If no one is directly responsible for the systems development methodology, the test manager should assume responsibility for testing integration. If testing, which can take half of the total development effort, is not already an integral part of the current systems development methodology, the integration process will be especially time consuming.

STEP 1: ORGANIZE THE TEST TEAM

Integrating a new test methodology is difficult and complex. Some organizations habitually acquire new design methodologies without fully implementing them, a problem that can be obviated with proper planning and management direction.

To make a test design methodology work, a team of key people from the testing function must be appointed to manage it. The group should be representative of the overall testing staff and respected by their peers. The test management team should consist of three to seven individuals. With fewer than three members, the interaction and energy necessary to successfully introduce the testing methodology may not occur. With more than seven members, management of the team becomes unwieldy.

Whether a supervisor is appointed chairperson of the test management team or a natural leader assumes the role, this individual ensures that the team performs its mission.

The MIS director should ensure that the test management team:

- Understands testing concepts and the standard for software testing discussed in this manual.
- Customizes and integrates the standard for software testing into the organization's systems design and maintenance methodology.
- Encourages adherence to and support of the integrated test methodology and agrees to perform testing in the manner prescribed by the methodology.

Management should not attempt to tell the test management team which aspects of the software testing standard should be adopted, how that testing methodology should be integrated into the existing design methodology, or the amount of time and effort needed to perform the task. Management should set the tone by stating that this manual will be the basis for testing in the organization but that the test management team is free to make necessary modifications.

STEP 2: IDENTIFY TEST STEPS AND TASKS TO INTEGRATE

Section III defines the steps and tasks involved in the client/server and internet testing methodology. These should be evaluated to determine which are applicable to the organization and design methodology. Some of the tasks may already be performed through design methodology, the test management team may consider them unnecessary, or the team may decide to combine tasks.

The test team must consider three areas when performing this step. First, the test team must agree on the general objectives of testing. Second, it must understand how the design methodology works. Third, it must understand the test methodology presented in this manual.

STEP 3: CUSTOMIZE TEST STEPS AND TASKS

The material covered in this text may not be consistent with the methodology in place and will need customizing for each organization. The test team can either perform this task itself or assign it to others (e.g., to the group in charge of design methodology).

Customization usually includes:

- Standardizing vocabulary — Vocabulary should be consistent throughout the design methodology. If staff members understand and use the same vocabulary, they can easily move from job to job within the organization. Vocabulary customization may mean changing vocabulary in the testing standard or integrating the testing vocabulary into the systems development methodology.
- Changing the structure of presentation — The way the testing steps and tasks have been described may differ from the way other parts of the design methodology are presented. For example, this manual has separate sections for forms and text descriptions of the software testing tools. If the systems development methodology integrates them into single units, they may need to be rearranged or reordered to make them consistent with the development manual.

Customization can work two ways. First, the process can be customized for individual application systems. During test planning, the test team would determine which tasks, worksheets, and checklists are applicable to the system being developed and then create a smaller version of the process for test purposes. Second, the processes described in this manual can be customized for a particular development function. The test standards and procedures can be customized to meet specific application and test needs.

STEP 4: SELECT INTEGRATION POINTS

This step involves selecting points in development methodology to integrate test steps and tasks. It requires a thorough understanding of the systems development methodology and the software tasks. The two key criteria for determining where to integrate these tasks are:

- What data is needed — The test task can be inserted into the design methodology only after the point at which the needed information has been produced.
- Where the test products are needed — The testing tasks must be completed before the products produced by that task are needed in the systems development methodology.

If these two rules are followed, both the earliest and latest points at which the tasks can be performed can be determined. The tasks should be inserted in the systems development methodology within this time frame.

STEP 5: MODIFY THE DEVELOPMENT METHODOLOGY

This step generally involves inserting the material into the systems development methodology documentation and must be performed by someone familiar with the design process. All the information needed to modify the systems development methodology is available at this point.

STEP 6: INCORPORATE DEFECT RECORDING

An integral part of the tester's workbench is the quality control function, which can identify problems and defects uncovered through testing as well as problems in the testing process itself. Appropriate recording and analysis of these defects is essential to improving the testing process.

The next part of this section presents a procedure for defect recording and analysis when the testing process is integrated into the systems development methodology. This procedure requires categorizing defects and ensuring that they are appropriately recorded throughout the systems development methodology.

The most difficult part of defect recording is convincing development staff members that this information will not be used against them. This information is gathered strictly for the improvement of the test process and should never be used for performance appraisals or any other individual evaluations.

STEP 7: TRAIN IN USE OF THE TEST METHODOLOGY

This step involves training analysts, users, and programmers in use of the test methodology. Once testing is integrated into the systems development methodology, people must be trained and motivated to use the test methodology, a more difficult job.

Test management team members play a large role in convincing their peers to accept and use the new methodology — first, by their example, and second, by actively encouraging co-workers to adopt the methodology. An important part of this step is creating and conducting testing seminars, which should cover the following:

- Testing concepts and methods — This part of the training recaps the material in Appendix F.
- Test standards — Individuals responsible for testing must know the standards they are measured against. The standards should be taught first, so team members know why they are performing certain tasks

(e.g., test procedures), and the procedures second. If they feel that the procedures are just one way of testing, they may decide there are better ways. On the other hand, if they know the objective for performing the test procedures (e.g., meeting test standards), they are more likely to take an interest in learning and following the test procedures.

- Test methodology — The methodology incorporated into the systems development methodology should be taught step by step and task by task. An analyst, user, or programmer should initially perform tasks under the direction of an instructor. This helps ensure that these professionals fully understand how the task should be performed and what results should be expected.

Until the individuals responsible for testing have been trained and have demonstrated proficiency in testing processes, management should allow for some testing errors. In addition, until individuals have demonstrated mastery of the test procedures, they should be closely supervised during the execution of those procedures.

Appendix H
Software Testing Techniques

H1: BASIS PATH TESTING

Basis path testing is a white-box technique that identifies test cases based on the flows or logical paths that can be taken through a program. A basis path is a unique path through the program where no iterations are allowed. Basis paths are atomic level paths, and all possible paths through the system are linear combinations of them. Basis path testing also produces a cyclomatic metric, which measures the complexity of a source code module by examining the control structures.

Consider the following small program, which reads records from a file and tallies the numerical ranges of a field on each record to illustrate the technique.

PROGRAM: FIELD-COUNT.

```
Node  Statement
1.    Dowhile not EOF
          read record
2.            if FIELD_COUNTER > 7 then
3.                increment COUNTER_7 by 1
          else
4.                if FIELD_COUNTER > 3 then
5.                    increment COUNTER_3 by 1
              else
6.                    increment COUNTER_1 by 1
7.                endif
8.            endif
9.        End_While
10.   End
```

In theory, if the loop were to be iterated 100 times, 1.5×10 test cases would be required to perform exhaustive testing, which is not achievable.

On the other hand, with basis testing there are four basis test cases required to test the program, as shown below.

$1{\to}10$

$1{\to}2{\to}3{\to}8{\to}9{\to}1{\to}10$

$1{\to}2{\to}4{\to}5{\to}7{\to}8{\to}9{\to}1{\to}10$

$1{\to}2{\to}4{\to}6{\to}7{\to}8{\to}9{\to}1{\to}10$

Mathematically, all possible paths in the program can be generated by linear combinations of the four basis paths. Experience shows that most of the potential defects will be discovered by executing the four basis path test cases, which demonstrates the power of the technique. The number of basis paths is also the cyclomatic complexity metric. It is recommended that the cyclomatic for a program module should not exceed 10. As the calculations are very labor intensive, there are testing tools to automate the process. See Section IV, Modern Testing Tools, for more details.

Basis path testing can also be applied to integration testing when program modules are integrated together. The use of the technique quantifies the integration effort involved as well as the design-level complexity.

H2: BLACK-BOX TESTING

Black-box or functional testing is one in which test conditions are developed based on the program or system's functionality, i.e., the tester requires information about the input data and observed output, but does not know how the program or system works. Just as one does not have to know how a car works internally to drive it, it is not necessary to know the internal structure of a program to execute it. The technique focuses on testing the program's functionality against the specification. With black-box testing, the tester views the program as a black-box and is completely unconcerned with the internal structure of the program or system. Some examples in this category include: decision tables, equivalence partitioning, range testing, boundary value testing, database integrity testing, cause-effect graphing, orthogonal array testing, array and table testing, exception testing, limit testing, and random testing.

A major advantage of black-box testing is that the tests are geared to what the program or system is supposed to do, and it is natural and understood by everyone. This should be verified with techniques such as structured walkthroughs, inspections, and JADs. A limitation is that exhaustive input testing is not achievable, because this requires that every possible input condition or combination be tested. Additionally, since there is no knowledge of the internal structure or logic, there could be errors or deliberate mischief on the part of a programmer, which may not be detectable with black-box testing. For example, suppose a disgruntled payroll programmer wanted to insert some job security into a payroll application he or she is developing. By inserting the following extra code into the application, if the employee were to be terminated, i.e., if his or her employee ID no longer exists in the system, justice would sooner or later prevail.

Extra Program Logic

> if my employee ID exists
>
>> deposit regular pay check into my bank account
>
> else
>
>> deposit an enormous amount of money into my bank account
>>
>> erase any possible financial audit trails
>>
>> erase this code

H3: BOTTOM-UP TESTING

The bottom-up testing technique is an incremental testing approach where the lowest-level modules or system components are integrated and tested first. Testing then proceeds hierarchically to the top level. A driver, or temporary test program that invokes the test module or system component, is often required. Bottom-up testing starts with the lowest-level modules or system components with the drivers to invoke them. After these components have been tested, the next logical level in the program or system component hierarchy is added and tested driving upward.

Bottom-up testing is common for large, complex systems, and it takes a relatively long time to make the system visible. The menus and external user interfaces are tested last, so users cannot have an early review of these interfaces and functions. A potential drawback is that it requires a lot of effort to create drivers, which can add additional errors.

H4: BOUNDARY VALUE TESTING

The boundary value testing technique is a black-box technique that focuses on the boundaries of the input and output equivalence classes (see Equivalence Class Partitioning Testing). Errors tend to congregate at the boundaries. Focusing testing in these areas increases the probability of detecting errors.

Boundary value testing is a variation of the equivalence class partitioning technique, which focuses on the bounds of each equivalence class, e.g., on, above, and below each class. Rather than select an arbitrary test point within an equivalence class, boundary value analysis selects one or more test cases to challenge each edge. Focus is on the input space (input equivalence classes) and output space (output equivalence classes). It is more difficult to define output equivalence classes and, therefore, boundary value tests.

Boundary value testing can require a large number of test cases to be created because of the large number of input and output variations. It is recommended that at least nine test cases be created for each input variable. The inputs need to be thoroughly understood, and the behavior must be consistent for the equivalence class. One limitation is that it may be very difficult to define the range of the equivalence class if it involves complex calculations. It is, therefore, imperative that the requirements be as detailed as possible. The following are some examples of how to apply the technique.

Numeric Input Data

Field Ranges. Ex. "Input can range from *integers* 0 to 100," test cases include –1, 0, 100, 101

Ex. "Input can range from *real numbers* 0 to 100.0," test cases include –.00001, 0.0, 100.0, 100.00001

Numeric Output Data

Output Range of Values. Ex. "Numerical range outputs of actuarial tables can be from \$0.0 to \$100,000.00," e.g., attempt to create conditions which produces negative amount, \$0.0, \$100,000.00, \$100,000.01

Non-numeric Input Data

Tables or Arrays. Ex. Focus on the first and last rows, e.g., read, update, write, delete

Ex. Try to access a non-existent table or array

Number of Items. Ex. "Number of products associated with a model is up to 10," e.g., enter 0, 10, 11 items

Non-numeric Output Data

Tables or Arrays. Ex. Focus on the first and last rows, e.g., update, delete, insert operations

Number of Outputs. Ex. "Up to 10 stocks can be displayed," e.g., attempt to display 0, 10, and 11 stocks

GUI

1. Vertically and horizontally scroll to the end of scroll bars

2. Upper and lower limits of color selection
3. Upper and lower limits of sound selection
4. Boundary gizmos, e.g., bounds available sets of available input values
5. Spinners, e.g., small edit field with two half-height buttons
6. Flip-flop menu items
7. List box bounds

H5: BRANCH COVERAGE TESTING

Branch coverage or decision coverage is a white-box testing technique in which test cases are written to ensure that every decision has a true and false outcome at least once, e.g., each branch is traversed at least once. Branch coverage generally satisfies statement coverage (see Statement Coverage testing technique), since every statement is on the same subpath from either branch statement.

Consider the following small program which reads records from a file and tallies the numerical ranges of a field on each record to illustrate the technique.

PROGRAM: FIELD-COUNT

```
Dowhile not EOF
    read record
    if FIELD_COUNTER > 7 then
        increment COUNTER_7 by 1
    else
        if FIELD_COUNTER > 3 then
            increment COUNTER_3 by 1
        else
            increment COUNTER_1 by 1
        endif
    endif
End_While
End
```

The test cases to satisfy branch coverage are as follows:

Test Case	Value (FIELD_COUNTER)
1	>7, ex. 8
2	<= 7, ex. 7
3	>3, ex. 4
4	<= 3, ex. 3

For this particular example, Test Case 2 is redundant and can be eliminated.

H6: BRANCH/CONDITION COVERAGE TESTING

Branch/condition coverage is a white-box testing technique in which test cases are written to ensure that each decision and the conditions within a decision takes on all possible values at least once. It is a stronger logic-coverage technique than decision or condition coverage because it covers all the conditions that may not be tested with decision coverage alone. It also satisfies statement coverage.

One method of creating testing cases using this technique is to build a truth table and write down all conditions and their complements. Then, if they exist, duplicate test cases are eliminated. Consider the following small program, which reads records from a file and tallies the numerical ranges of a field on each record to illustrate the technique.

PROGRAM: FIELD-COUNT

```
Dowhile not EOF
    read record
    if FIELD_COUNTER > 7 then
        increment COUNTER_7 by 1
    else
        if FIELD_COUNTER > 3 then
            increment COUNTER_3 by 1
        else
            increment COUNTER_1 by 1
        endif
    endif
End_While
End
```

The test cases to satisfy branch/condition coverage are as follows:

Test Case	Value (FIELD_COUNTER)
1	>7, ex. 8
2	<= 7, ex. 7
3	>3, ex. 4
4	<= 3, ex. 3

For this particular example there is only one condition for each decision. If there were more, each condition and its complement would be tested. Again, Test Case 2 is redundant and can be eliminated.

H7: CAUSE-EFFECT GRAPHING

Cause-effect diagrams (also known as Ishikawa or Fishbone diagrams) are useful tools to analyze the causes of an unsatisfactory condition. They have several advantages. One is that they provide a visual display of the relationship of one cause to another. This has proven to be an effective way to stimulate ideas during the initial search. Another benefit is that it provides a way to keep searching for root causes by asking why?, what?, where?, who?, and how? Another is that it is a graphical representation in which the cause-relationships are easily discernible.

One application of cause-effect graphs was undertaken to understand the inspection process. It discovered that (1) excessive size of materials to be inspected leads to a preparation rate that is too high, (2) a preparation rate that is too high contributes to an excessive rate of inspection, and (3) an excessive rate of inspection causes fewer defects to be found. This analysis using cause-effect graphics provided insights to optimize the inspection process by limiting the size of materials to be inspected and the preparation rate.

Proper preparation for construction of cause-effect diagrams is essential. Visibility is a key requirement. It is advisable to leave a good deal of space between the causes as they are listed, so there can be room for additional notations as the work continues.

Several stages of construction should be expected before a "finished" product is developed. This often consists of enlarging a smaller section of the cause-effect diagram by taking one significant cause and making it the "effect" to be analyzed on another cause-effect diagram.

Cause-effect graphics can also be applied to test case design, particularly function testing. They are used to systematically select a set of test cases that have high probability of detecting program errors. This technique explores the input and combinations of input conditions of a program to develop test cases but does not examine the internal behavior of the program. For each test case derived, the technique also identifies the expected output. The input and output are determined through the analysis of the requirement specifications (see Section IV, Modern Testing Tools which automates the process).

The following is a brief overview of the methodology to convert requirements to test cases using cause-effect diagrams. It is followed by an example of how to apply the methodology.

Cause-Effect Methodology

1. Identify all the requirements.
2. Analyze the requirements and identify all the causes and effects.
3. Assign each cause and effect a unique number.
4. Analyze the requirements and translate it into a Boolean graph linking the causes and effects.

5. Convert the graph into a decision table.
6. Convert the columns in the decision table into test cases.

Example. A database management system requires that each file in the database have its name listed in a master index identifying the location of each file. The index is divided into 10 sections. A small system is being developed that allows the user to interactively enter a command to display any section of the index at the terminal. Cause-effect graphing is used to develop a set of test cases for the system. The specification for this system is explained in the following paragraphs.

Specification

To display one of the 10 possible index sections, a command must be entered consisting of a letter and a digit. The first character entered must be a D (for display) or an L (for list), and it must be in column 1. The second character entered must be a digit (0 through 9) in column 2. If this command occurs, the index section identified by the digit is displayed on the terminal. If the first character is incorrect, error message "Invalid Command" is printed. If the second character is incorrect, error message "Invalid Index Number" is printed.

The causes and effects are identified as follows:

Causes

1. Character in column 1 is D.
2. Character in column 1 is L.
3. Character in column 2 is a digit.

Effects

50. Index section is displayed.
51. Error message "Invalid Command" is displayed.
52. Error message "Invalid Index Number" is displayed..

A Boolean graph (see Exhibit H-1) is constructed through analysis of the specification. This is accomplished by (1) representing each cause and effect by a node by its unique number, (2) listing all the cause nodes vertically on the left side of a sheet of paper and listing the effect nodes on the right side, (3) interconnecting the cause and effect nodes by analyzing the specification. Each cause and effect can be in one of two states: true or false. Using Boolean logic, set the possible states of the causes and determine under what conditions each effect is present, and (4) annotating the graph

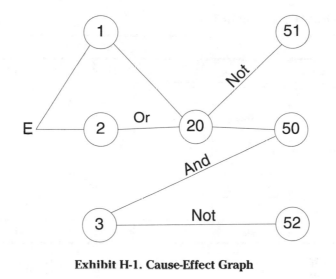

Exhibit H-1. Cause-Effect Graph

with constraints describing combinations of causes and effects that are impossible because of syntactic or environmental constraints.

Node 20 is an intermediate node representing the Boolean state of node 1 or node 2. The state of node 50 is true if the states of nodes 20 and 3 are both true. The state of node 20 is true if the state of node 1 or node 2 is true. The state of node 51 is true if the state of node 20 is not true. The state of node 52 is true if the state of node 3 is not true. Nodes 1 and 2 are also annotated with a constraint that states that causes 1 and 2 cannot be true simultaneously.

Exhibit H-2 shows Exhibit H-1 converted into a decision table. This is accomplished by (1) tracing back through the graph to find all combinations of causes that make the effect true for each effect, (2) representing each combination as a column in the decision table, and (3) determining the state of all other effects for each such combination. After completing this, each column in Exhibit H-2 represents a test case.

For each test case, the bottom of Exhibit H-2 indicates which effect is present (indicated by a 1). For each effect, all combinations of causes that result in the effect are represented by the entries in the columns of the table. Blanks in the table mean that the state of the cause is irrelevant.

Exhibit H-2. Decision Table

		Test Cases		
Causes	1	2	3	4
1	1	0	0	
2	0	1	0	
3	1	1		1
Effects				
50	1	1	0	0
51	0	0	1	0
52	0	0	0	1

Each column in the decision table is converted into the four test cases shown below.

Test Case Number	Input	Expected Results
1	D5	Index Section 5 is displayed
2	L4	Index Section 4 is displayed
3	B2	"Invalid Command"
4	DA	"Invalid Index Number"

Cause-effect graphing can produce a useful set of test cases and can point out incompleteness and ambiguities in the requirement specification. It can be applied to generate test cases in any type of computing application when the specification is clearly stated and combinations of input conditions can be identified. Although manual application of this technique is tedious, long, and moderately complex, there are automated testing tools that will automatically help convert the requirements to a graph, decision table, and test cases. See Section IV, Modern Test Tools, Bender & Associates, for more details.

H8: CONDITION COVERAGE

Condition coverage is a white-box testing technique in which test cases are written to ensure that each condition in a decision takes on all possible outcomes at least once. It is not necessary to consider the decision branches with condition coverage using this technique. Condition coverage guarantees that every condition within a decision is covered. However, it does not necessarily traverse the true and false outcomes of each decision.

One method of creating testing cases using this technique is to build a truth table and write down all conditions and their complements. If they exist, duplicate test cases are eliminated.

Consider the following small program, which reads records from a file and tallies the numerical ranges of a field on each record to illustrate the technique.

PROGRAM: FIELD-COUNT

```
Dowhile not EOF
    read record
    if FIELD_COUNTER > 7 then
        increment COUNTER_7 by 1
    else
        if FIELD_COUNTER > 3 then
            increment COUNTER_3 by 1
        else
            increment COUNTER_1 by 1
        endif
    endif
End_While
End
```

The initial test cases to satisfy condition coverage are as follows:

Test Case	Values (FIELD_COUNTER)
1	>7, e.g., 8
2	<= 7, e.g., 7
3	>3, e.g., 6
4	<= 3, e.g., 3

Notice that test cases 2 and 3 are redundant and one of them can be eliminated, resulting in three test cases.

H9: CRUD TESTING

A CRUD matrix, or process/data matrix, is optionally developed during the analysis phase of application development which links data and process models. It helps ensure that the data and processes are discovered and assessed. It identifies and resolves matrix omissions and conflicts and helps refine the data and process models, as necessary. It maps processes against entities, showing which processes create, read, update, or delete the instances in an entity.

APPENDIX H

The CRUD matrix in Exhibit H-3 is developed at the analysis level of development before the physical system or GUI (physical screens, menus etc.) have been designed and developed. As the GUI evolves, a CRUD test matrix can be built, as shown in Exhibit H-3. It is a testing technique that verifies the life cycle of all business objects. In Exhibit H-3, each CRUD cell object is tested. When an object does not have full life cycle operations a "–" can be placed in a cell.

Exhibit H-3. CRUD Testing

Object	C (pass/fail)	R (pass/fail)	U (pass/fail)	D (pass/fail)	Delete Confirm (yes/no)	Tester	Date (m/d/y)
Customer	x	x	x	x			
Order	-	x	x	-			
Payment	-	x	x	-			
Vendor	x	x	x	x			
Check	x	x	-	x			
Register	x	x	x	x			
Product	-	x	x	-			
Stock	x	x	x	x			
Back Order	-	x	x	-			
Inventory	x	-	x	-			
Report	x	x	-	-			
.							
.							
.							
.							

A variation of this is to also make unit performance measurements for each operation during system fragment testing.

H10: DATABASE TESTING

The following provides a description of how to test databases. It also includes an overview of relation database concepts, which will serve as a reference to the tester.

Integrity Testing

Database integrity testing verifies: the structure and format, compliance with integrity constraints, business rules and relationships, edit controls on updates which refresh databases, and database normalization, or denormalization per performance constraints. There are at least six types of integrity tests that need to be performed to verify the integrity of the database.

Entity Integrity. Entity integrity states that each row must always have a primary key value. For example, if team ID is the primary key of the team table, no team can lack a team ID. This can be tested and verified with database integrity reports or queries.

Primary Key Integrity. The value of each primary key must be unique and valid. For example, two teams cannot have the same team ID, and a team ID of "ABC" is invalid when numeric values are required. Another rule is that the primary key must not contain a null value (be empty). This can be tested and verified with database integrity reports or queries.

Column Key Integrity. The values in a column have column-specific rules. For example, the values in a column for the number of members on a team must always be a positive and numeric number and not exceed 7. This can be tested and verified with database integrity reports or queries. It can also be verified with the following testing techniques: range testing, boundary value testing, field integrity testing, and positive and negative testing.

Domain Integrity. A domain is an object that is a set of data and characteristics that describe those values. For example, "date" could be defined as a basic data type which has a field length, format, and validation rules. Columns can be defined based on domains; in this case a column might be defined as an order date. This can be tested and verified with database queries. It can also be verified with the following testing techniques: range testing, boundary value testing, field integrity testing, and positive and negative testing.

User-Defined Integrity. User-defined integrity checks are specialized validation rules that go beyond the standard row and column checks. User-defined rules for particular data items often must be written manually, using a procedural language.

Another option instead of writing procedures is the use of assertions, if available. Assertions are stand-alone validation checks that are not linked to a particular row or column, but that are automatically applied.

Referential Integrity. The primary key is a candidate key to uniquely identify a particular entity. With a table of teams, the primary key could be the team number. A foreign key is a key that refers to a primary key in another entity, as a cross reference. For example, part of the key to a member name (from a member entity) may be a team ID, which is the primary key to the team entity.

A table has business rules that govern the relationships among entities. For example, a member must be related to a team, and only one team. A team, on the other hand, may at any given time have no members, only one member, or many members. This is referred to as the cardinality of the entity relationship. Any member "floating around" in the system, without being associated with a team, is an invalid order. A record such as this is referred to as an orphan.

As an example, assume that a team can have one, none, or more members, but a member cannot exist without a team. The test cases shown in Exhibit H-4 should be created to verify referential integrity.

Exhibit H-4. Referential Integrity Test Cases

Test case	Expected Results
1. Insert a team	No association with the member entity for this record
2. Insert a member	There exists a foreign key relationship to the team entity
3. Attempt to delete a team which has a relationship (foreign key) in the member	Should not do automatically but provide a confirmation prompt
4. Update a member	Team foreign key relation exists to the team entity

Other database testing approaches include the following:

- **Control Testing**
  Control testing includes a variety of control issues, which need to be tested:
  - Security Testing — protects the database from unauthorized access
  - Backup Testing — verifies the ability to backup the system
  - Recovery Testing — verifies the restoration of a database to a state known to be correct after some failure has rendered it unreliable
  - Concurrency Testing — ensures that parallel processes such as queries and updates do not interfere with each other

- Deadlock Control — ensures that two concurrent processes do not form a "gridlock" and mutually exclude each other from adequate completion
- **Data Content Verification**
  Periodic audits and comparisons with known reference sources
- **Refresh Verification**
  Verify external systems which refresh the database, data conversions
- **Data Usage**
  This includes verifying database editing and updating. Many times, the developer does not create enough or may include too many characters for the columns of an entity. The tester should compare the number of characters on each GUI field to the respective entity field lengths to verify they are the same. Tip: one way to make sure the database column lengths are large enough is to copy a very large document using the Window copy edit feature and then paste it into each GUI field. Some of the testing techniques which can be employed to generate data include range testing, boundary value testing, field integrity testing, and positive and negative testing. Most databases have query facilities which enable the tester to verify that the data is updated and edited correctly in the database.
- **Stored Procedures**
  These procedures are stored and invoked when specific triggers from the application occur.

Data Modeling Essentials

The purpose of this section is to familiarize the reader with data modeling concepts and terminology in order to perform database and GUI field testing against a relational design (see below, Database Integrity Testing, Range Testing, Positive and Negative Testing, and Table and Array Testing). It will also serve as a useful reference to relational database design in the context of testing.

What Is a Model? A model is a simplified description of a real-world system that assists its user in making calculations and predictions. Only those aspects of the system that are of interest to the user are included in the model; all others are omitted.

Many different materials are used in creating models:

1. Metal
2. Wood
3. Clay

The most appropriate material is used for the model, even though it may differ from the material used for the system being modeled. The written specifications of a system may be used by themselves as a model of the real world.

A model may be considered as having two features:

- Shape or structure
- Content

The structure of the model reflects the invariant aspects of the system, while the content reflects the dynamic aspects. For example, the structure of a predictive meteorological model consists of formulae, while the content consists of data (temperature, humidity, wind speed, atmospheric pressure) gathered from many points over a period of time.

Why Do We Create Models? We must be able to measure real-world systems to be able to understand them, use them effectively, monitor their performance, and predict their future performance. Often, it is impossible to measure the actual system. It may be too expensive or too dangerous. Before an aircraft manufacturer sends a pilot up in a new plane, there must be some assurance that the plane will fly. An automobile manufacturer wants to know what a car will look like before tooling up an assembly line to make it.

We have a requirement to understand, measure, and control a real-world system — the user's business. The easiest way to make timely, cost-effective measurements and predictions about the business system is to create a model of the business. Data is the most appropriate material for our model — hence the name Data Model. The structure of our data model should represent the aspects of the user's business that change very little over time. The content of the model (the values stored in the model) represents the information that changes with time. The result is a data model whose structure is stable and, therefore, easily maintained.

Applications that we create will be responsible for adding, changing, and deleting the content of the model and for reporting on the content.

The use of this technique results in the following benefits:

1. The relatively stable nature of the data model will allow us to be more responsive to changing business needs. Business changes usually result in changes in how the content is maintained and reported. Changes to the structure of the model occur less frequently and are usually minor.
2. The technique we will use will create a data model that is independent of both current business processes (but not business policy) and current data processing technology.
3. An additional benefit of this technique is that it can be used in situations where current process-oriented techniques do not work. For

example, there are no clearly identifiable processes involved in a management information application. The users cannot specify exactly how data will be used. By creating a data model whose structure reflects the structure of the business, we can support any reasonable inquiry against the data.

4. Data analysis starts from the development of the data model.

Tables — A Definition. A table is a list of facts, numbers, etc., systematically arranged in columns.

Tables are used whenever we need to order information for storage or presentation. They are relatively easy to create and maintain and present information in a clear, unambiguous, simple format. Examples of tables that we may encounter are:

- Table of Contents
- Metric Conversion Table
- Table of Weights and Measures
- Tax Table

Exhibit H-5 illustrates the features of a table.

Exhibit H-5. Sample Table

Name	Address	Telephone Number
Bill Smith	3290 Oak Lane, Dallas, Texas	(972) 329-6723
Joe Jones	129 Cliff Avenue, Austin, Texas	(812) 456-2198
Sue Maddox	1421 Millington Drive, Boca Raton, Florida	(305) 402-5954
Jerry Jones	112 Cowboys Drive, Portland, Oregon	(265) 693-2319

Table Names. A table is identified by its name. Therefore, its name must be unique within the scope of the business.

Columns. A table is divided vertically into columns. All entries in a given column are of the same type and have the same format. A column contains a single piece of data about all rows in the table. Each column must have a name unique within the table. The combination of table name and column name is unique within the business. Examples might be CUSTOMER.NAME, CUSTOMER. NUMBER, EMPLOYEE.NAME, and EMPLOYEE. NUMBER.

Rows. A table is divided horizontally into rows. Each row must be uniquely identifiable. Each row has the same number of cells and contains a piece of data of a different type and format.

Order. The order of rows and columns in a table is arbitrary. That is, the order in which rows and columns are presented does not affect the meaning of the data. In fact, each user of a table may have unique requirements for ordering rows and columns. For this reason, there must be no special significance to the order.

Based on the above definition, tables are useful for documenting data requirements. They can be easily understood by both development and user personnel.

We will define a table to represent each object in our model. The table columns will provide descriptive information about the object, and the rows will provide examples of occurrences of the object.

Entities — A Definition.

> An entity is a uniquely identifiable person, place, thing, or event of interest to the user, about which the application is to maintain and report data.

When we create a data model, we must first decide which real-world objects are to be included. We will include only those objects that are of interest to the users. Furthermore, we will include only those objects required by computer applications.

We organize the objects (entities) to be included into groups called entity types. For example, a clothing store might identify customers, products sold, and suppliers of those products as objects to be included in a data model. This grouping, however, is not adequate for a useful model of the real world. Depending on the type of clothing sold by the store, the user may wish to group products by style, type, size, color, etc. The identification of objects is made difficult by the fuzzy definitions used in the real world. In our model, we must be specific; therefore, we will define as entity types only groups of objects in which each occurrence can be uniquely identified.

Each entity type is given a unique name. Examples are CUSTOMER, SUPPLIER, and EMPLOYEE.

Identification — Primary Key.

> Every entity must have a primary key.

To allow us to uniquely identify each occurrence of an entity type, we must define a key called the primary key. Its value may be assigned by the user or by the application. There may be more than one choice for the primary key. For the entity type EMPLOYEE we might choose SOCIAL INSURANCE NUMBER or invent an EMPLOYEE NUMBER. The major requirement is that each value be unique. It is also important that the primary key be one by which the user would naturally identify an occurrence of the entity. You should also choose a key that is not likely to change. It should be as short as possible. This is why serial numbers are popular keys; they are assigned once, they do not change, and they are unique. (Be careful. In the real world, duplicate serial numbers may be inadvertently assigned.)

Note: A key is not an access path. It is only a unique identifier.

Compound Primary Keys. A primary key may be composed of more than one column. For example, an automobile can be uniquely identified only by the combination MAKE + MODEL+VEHICLE IDENTIFICATION NUMBER. A key composed of more than one column is a *compound key*.

Null Values. In any descriptive information about an entity, it is possible to have a situation where a piece of data for a particular occurrence is not known. For example, when an employee description is added to a personnel application for the first time, the employee's department number or phone number might not be known. The correct value is not zero or blank; it is unknown. We refer to an unknown value as a *null* value. We might use blanks or zero or some special indicator to reflect this in a computer application. However, since null means unknown, you cannot compare null values (e.g., for equal). You also cannot use them in numeric computations, since the result would also be unknown. In our data model, we will indicate which columns may contain null values.

We bring this point up here because of the following rule:

A primary key may not be null.

It is important to remember this. A null value means we do not know what the correct value is, but primary key values must be known to uniquely identify each occurrence of the entity type to which they refer. In a compound key, it is possible for the key to contain null values in some, but NOT all columns.

Identifying Entities. Consider the following list.

Which is an entity type?
Which is an entity occurrence?
Which is neither?
What would be a suitable key?

1. Automobile
2. Ford
3. Superman
4. Nietzsche
5. Telephone
6. Telephone number
7. House

8. Postal code
9. Aquamarine
10. Seven
11. Marriage

One thing you will discover when trying to identify the entity types and occurrences in the above list is that the user context is important. Consider Automobile. If the user is an automobile dealer, then automobile could be an entity type. However, if the user is attempting to keep track of types of transportation, automobile could be an entity occurrence. Ford might be a make of automobile, a U.S. President, or a way to cross a river.

Telephone number is often treated as if it were an entity type. You might instead think of it as the key that identifies a telephone. It cannot identify a specific physical phone, however, because you can replace the phone with a new one without changing the telephone number. It doesn't identify a specific telephone line, because you can often take the phone number with you when you move to a new location. In fact, the telephone number really identifies a telephone company account.

Aquamarine might be an entity occurrence. What would be the entity type? If your user is a jeweler, the entity type might be Precious Stone; if a paint manufacturer, Color

Entity Classes. Entities may be grouped for convenience into various classes. Consider the following:

Major Entity: An entity that can exist without reference to other entities (e.g., CUSTOMER, ORDER). These entity types are typically identified early in the data analysis process. In most cases, the primary key of a major entity will consist of a single column.
Dependent Entity: An entity that depends upon and further defines another entity (e.g., ORDER LINE ITEM). These entity types will often be identified during the process of defining relationships or normalizing and refining the model. The primary key of a dependent entity is always a compound key. These topics will be covered later.
Minor Entity: An entity that is used primarily to define valid values within the model (e.g., EMPLOYEE TYPE, CREDIT CODE). These may be ignored in some cases (e.g., if the only valid values are Y and N). The primary key of a minor entity is almost always a single column.

Relationships — A Definition

Each entity in a data model; does not exist in solitary splendor. Entities are linked by relationships. A relationship is an association between two or more entities, of interest to the user, about which the application is to maintain and report data.

This is similar to the definition of an entity, and we will see that a relationship can be considered as a special type of entity.

Relationship Types. There are three types of relationships:

- One-to-One
- One-to-Many
- Many-to-Many

We will examine each type and see how we document them.

One-to-One. One-to-one relationships are the simplest and, unfortunately, the least common.

A one-to-one relationship links a single occurrence of an entity to zero or one occurrence of an entity. The related entity occurrences are usually of different types, but there is no rule prohibiting them from being of the same type. When the related entities are of the same type, the relationship is called a *recursive relationship.*

Let's consider a hypothetical example. An enlightened company, which shall remain nameless, has determined that employees work best when they are not forced to share desks or workstations. As a result, each desk is assigned to only one employee and each employee is assigned to one desk.

We document this happy relationship by placing the primary key of either entity into the description of the other entity as a foreign key.

Either Exhibit H-6 or Exhibit H-7 can be used to illustrate the relationship. Look first at Exhibit H-6 — the EMPLOYEE table.

Exhibit H-6. Employee Table

EMPLOYEE

EMPLOYEE NUMBER	DESK NUMBER
PK	FK
	ND
12345	004
23456	003
98751	001

The PK in the column headed EMPLOYEE NUMBER indicates that this is the primary key. The FK in the column headed DESK NUMBER indicates that this is a foreign key (i.e., it is a primary key in some other table). The ND in this column enforces the one-to-one relationship by indicating that

Exhibit H-7. Employee Table

DESK

DESK NUMBER	EMPLOYEE NUMBER
PK	FK
	ND, NL
003	23456
001	98751
002	-NULL-
004	12345

there can be no duplicate values (the same desk cannot be assigned to two different employees).

Exhibit H-7 illustrates the same relationship. The ND indicates that an employee may not be assigned to two different desks. Note, however, that there is an NL indication in the EMPLOYEE NUMBER column in this table. This indicates that a desk may be unassigned.

While the relationship may be documented either way, there are some guidelines:

1. Do NOT document the relationship both ways. Choose one.
2. Choose the way that reduces or eliminates the need to record nulls. Note that this typically means placing the foreign key in the entity with the fewest occurrences.

Based on the above guidelines, the relationship in our example is best represented, as in Exhibit H-6, by recording the desk number as a foreign key of the employee (although Exhibit H-7 is not wrong).

One-to-Many. One-to-many relationships are the most common, and the documentation technique is straightforward. A one-to-many relationship links one occurrence of an entity type to zero or more occurrences of an entity type.

As an example, let's look again at the company described above. When it comes to the assignment of telephones to employees, the company is not so enlightened. Each employee must share a single telephone number and line with other employees. Exhibit H-8 and Exhibit H-9 illustrate the relationship between telephone numbers and employees.

The documentation of this relationship appears to be the same as for a one-to-one relationship. However, there is only one way to represent a one-to-many relationship. We record the one in the many. In Exhibit H-8 and

Exhibit H-8. Employee Table

EMPLOYEE

EMPLOYEE NUMBER	TELEPHONE NUMBER
PK	FK
12345	1111
23456	1954
98751	2654

Exhibit H-9. Telephone Line Table

TELEPHONE LINE

TELEPHONE NUMBER
PK
1954
2222
1111
2654

Exhibit H-9, we record the telephone number as a foreign key of the EMPLOYEE. To record the relationship the other way would require an array of employee numbers of indeterminate size for each telephone number. There is another important difference. We did not place ND (no duplicates) in the foreign key column. This is because duplicates are allowed — the same telephone number can be assigned to more than one employee.

So the rule here is easy to remember. There is only one correct way:

Record the one in the many.

Many-to-Many. Many-to-many relationships are the most difficult to deal with. They also occur frequently enough to make data analysis interesting. A many-to-many relationship links many occurrences of an entity type to many occurrences of an entity type. For an example of this type of relationship, let us again examine the nameless company.

Management believes that the more people assigned to a given project, the sooner it will be completed. Also, because they become nervous at the

APPENDIX H

sight of idle employees, they give each employee several assignments to work on simultaneously.

We cannot document a many-to-many relationship directly, so we will create a new entity (see Exhibits H-10, 11, and 12) and link it to each of the entities involved, by a one-to-many relationship (we already know how to do that).

Exhibit H-10. Employee Table

EMPLOYEE

EMPLOYEE NUMBER
PK

Exhibit H-11. Project Table

PROJECT

PROJECT NUMBER
PK

Exhibit H-12. Employee/Project Table

EMPLOYEE/PROJECT

EMPLOYEE NUMBER	PROJECT NUMBER
PK	
FK	FK

The EMPLOYEE/PROJECT entity has been created to support the relationship between EMPLOYEE and PROJECT. It has a primary key consisting of the primary keys of the entity types it is relating. They are identified as foreign keys. This is an example of a compound key. Any entity may have a compound key which may be completely or partly made up of foreign keys from other entities. This commonly occurs with dependent entities. The EMPLOYEE/PROJECT entity we have created is dependent on EMPLOYEE and PROJECT; it wouldn't exist except for the relationship between them.

Note that the foreign keys that make up the primary key in this entity support one-to-many relationships between EMPLOYEE and EMPLOYEE/PROJECT and between PROJECT and EMPLOYEE/PROJECT. We must now demonstrate that this is equivalent to a many-to-many relationship between EMPLOYEE and PROJECT. An example will best illustrate the approach.

Given 2 employees and 2 projects, as in Exhibit H-13 and Exhibit H-14, we can show that both employees work on both projects by creating occurrences of the EMPLOYEE/PROJECT entity, as in Exhibit H-15.

Exhibit H-13. Employee Table

EMPLOYEE

EMPLOYEE NUMBER
11111
22222

Exhibit H-14. Project Table

PROJECT

PROJECT NUMBER
ABCD
WXYZ

Exhibit H-15. Employee/Project Table

EMPLOYEE/PROJECT

EMPLOYEE NUMBER	PROJECT NUMBER
11111	ABCD
11111	WXYZ
22222	ABCD
22222	WXYZ

We can see that EMPLOYEE 11111 is related to 2 EMPLOYEE/PROJECT occurrences (11111ABCD and 11111WXYZ). Each of these EMPLOYEE/PROJECT entities is in turn related to one PROJECT entity. The result is that each EMPLOYEE occurrence may be related to many PROJECT occurrences through the EMPLOYEE/PROJECT entity. By the same technique, each PROJECT occurrence may be related to many EMPLOYEE occurrences.

Multiple Relationships. There will sometimes be more than one type of relationship between occurrences of the same entity types. When you encounter this situation, identify and document each relationship independently of any others. For instance, in the last example, there might have been a requirement to record the project leader of each project independently of any other employees assigned to the project. This relationship might have been a one-to-many relationship with PROJECT LEADER EMPLOYEE NUMBER a foreign key in the PROJECT table.

Entities vs. Relationships. The distinction between entities and relationships is not always clear. Consider the following example.

A customer buys an automobile from a dealer. The sale is negotiated by a salesperson employed by the dealer. The customer may have purchased automobiles from this dealer before, but may have dealt with a different salesperson.

Is the purchase a relationship between customer and salesperson? Is it an entity that is related to customer, salesperson and automobile? How to treat such a real-world situation is often an arbitrary decision. There is no formal rule to guide you. Fortunately, the technique we use to document entities and relationships can reduce or eliminate the problem.

If we consider a purchase agreement to be an entity, we select a primary key, such as AGREEMENT NUMBER, and define relationships to other entities. There is a one-to-many relationship between SALESPERSON and PURCHASE AGREEMENT and, if we have satisfied customers, between CUSTOMER and PURCHASE AGREEMENT. We document these relationships in Exhibit H-16 by placing CUSTOMER NUMBER and EMPLOYEE NUMBER as foreign keys in PURCHASE AGREEMENT.

Exhibit H-16. Purchase Agreement Table

PURCHASE AGREEMENT

AGREEMENT NUMBER	CUSTOMER NUMBER	EMPLOYEE NUMBER
PK	FK	FK

If we do not consider the purchase agreement to be an entity, we must then document the relationship between CUSTOMER and SALESPERSON (see Exhibit H-17). Since, in the general case, there is a many-to-many relationship between customers and salespeople, we must create a new entity — CUSTOMER/SALESPERSON with a compound key of CUSTOMER NUMBER + EMPLOYEE NUMBER. We will probably have to add VEHICLE MAKE and IDENTIFICATION NUMBER to the primary key to ensure uniqueness.

Exhibit H-17. Customer/Salesperson Table

CUSTOMER/SALESPERSON

CUSTOMER NUMBER	EMPLOYEE NUMBER	VEHICLE MAKE	VIN
PK			
FK	FK		

To change this relationship to an entity, we need only rename it and change the primary key. The columns already in the table will probably still be required.

Attributes — A Definition

> An attribute is a characteristic quality of an entity or relationship, of interest to the user, about which the application is to maintain and report data.

Attributes are the data elements or fields that describe entities and relationships. An attribute is represented by a column in a table.

- Primary keys are attributes or sets of attributes that uniquely identify entities.
- Foreign keys are attributes that define relationships between entities.
- Non-key attributes provide additional information about entities (e.g., EMPLOYEE NAME) and relationships (e.g., QUANTITY ORDERED on an order line).

The information in this section applies to all types of attributes. All attributes base their values on domains.

Domain

> A domain is a set of possible values of an attribute.

To determine which values are valid for a given attribute, we need to know the rules for assigning values. The set of values that may be assigned to a given attribute is the domain of that attribute.

All attributes of the same type must come from the same domain. For example, the following attributes could describe different entities or relationship.

Department Number
Sales Branch Number
Service Branch Number

They are all based on the domain of possible department numbers. The domain is *not* a list of the assigned department numbers but a set of the possible department numbers from which values may be selected.

The definition of domains is somewhat arbitrary, and there may be a temptation to create general domains that allow too much freedom. Consider CUSTOMER NUMBER and DEPARTMENT NUMBER. If these attributes are both defined to be based on a domain of any numbers, we could end up with the following:

Customer	−12345
Department	12.34

By restricting the domain to positive integers, we can avoid negative numbers and decimal fractions. However, with a definition this general, we can still combine customers and departments. For example, someone might decide that, whenever an internal order is processed, the CUSTOMER NUMBER field on the order will be sent to the ordering DEPARTMENT NUMBER. To satisfy processing requirements, we would have to place department numbers in the CUSTOMER table, since all valid customers appear there. Now, whenever we reorganize the business, we must update the customer data.

The safest approach in our example is to define the domain of CUSTOMER NUMBERS and the domain of DEPARTMENT NUMBERS separately.

Note: Be careful when defining the domain of fields such as customer number, employee number, or part number. It is natural to think of such fields as numeric. It may even be true that, currently, all assigned values are numeric. Alphabetic characters, however, have a nasty habit of showing up in these identifiers sooner or later.

Domain Names. Each domain should have a name that is unique within the organization. The name and the rules for defining values within the domain should be documented. A single column primary key based on a domain will usually have the same name as the domain (e.g., customer number). If a key (primary or foreign) is compound, each column will usually have the same name as the domain. Where the same domain is referenced more than once by attributes of an entity (e.g., date born, date hired for an employee), the domain name should be part of the attribute column name.

Domains, and the attributes based on them, must be nondecomposable.

The statement above does not mean that attributes should not decay or fall apart from old age. As an example of a decomposable domain and attribute, consider the following:

Whenever an order is recorded, it is assigned an order number. The order number is created according to the following rules:

1. The customer number makes up the first (high order) part of the order number.
2. The order entry date, in the form YYMMDD is the next part of the order number.
3. The last two positions of the order number hold a sequence number to ensure uniqueness if a customer submits several orders in one day.

Because we use the term *order number,* there is a temptation to treat this as a single column. Resist the temptation. The primary key in this example is a compound key made up of customer number, order entry date, and a sequence number. Each attribute making up the compound key is based on a different domain. It is now possible to document the fact that there is an attribute in the order that is based on the domain of customer numbers. Any changes in the rules for that domain can be checked for their impact on the order entity.

Having said that all domains must be nondecomposable, we will now state two exceptions:

Date
Time

Date is usually in the form month/day/year. There is usually no need to record this as three separate attributes. Similarly, time may be left as hours/minutes.

Attributes vs. Relationships. Just as there is a somewhat arbitrary choice between entities and relationships, there is a similar choice between attributes and relationships. You could consider an attribute as a foreign key from a table of valid values for the attribute. If, for example, you were required to record color of eyes as an attribute of employee, you might set up an entity called COLOR with a primary key of COLOR NAME. You could then create EYE COLOR as a foreign key in EMPLOYEE. This would probably not provide much advantage over a simple attribute. You might even get into trouble. If you chose to add HAIR COLOR as a foreign key related to the same primary key, you could end up with an employee with blue hair and red eyes.

While the above example may seem trivial, real-world choices are often more subtle. You might choose a foreign key over a simple attribute if you wished to have a table for edit checking or if you needed a long description on reports. The description could be an attribute in the table in which the foreign key was a primary key.

Normalization. What Is Normalization? Normalization is the process of refining an initial set of entities into an optimum model. The purpose is to eliminate data redundancy and to ensure that the data structures are as flexible, understandable, and maintainable as possible.

Normalization is achieved by ensuring that an entity contains only those attributes that depend on the key of the entity. By *depend on* we mean that each value of the key determines only one value for each attribute of the entity. If the concept is unclear at this point, don't be discouraged; it will be explained later in this section. Said another way, normalization means ensuring that:

Each attribute depends on

<div align="center">The Key, The Whole Key, and Nothing But the Key</div>

Problems of Un-normalized Entities. Exhibit H-18 illustrates the problems that will occur in attempting to maintain an un-normalized entity. The example in Exhibit H-18 is un-normalized because the department name is dependent on the department number, not on the employee number, which is the key of the entity. Consider the effects of the design on the application.

Exhibit H-18. Employee Table

EMPLOYEE

EMPNO	NAME	SALARY	DEPT	DEPTNAME
PK				
00100	CODD, E.F.	65736	220	DEEP THOUGHT
00135	KENT, W.	58200	220	DEEP THOUGHT
00171	LEWIS, W.	49900	220	DEEP THOUGHT
00190	SMITH, S.	64000	220	DEEP THOUGHT
00215	DATE, C.J.	51500	114	PUBLISHING
00529	FLAVIN, M.	35700	354	ADVERTISING
00558	CLARK, G.	33600	354	ADVERTISING

1. Modification Anomaly
   Suppose a corporate reorganization makes it necessary to change the name of department 354 to Advertising and Promotion. A special purpose program will be required to modify this information *accurately and completely* everywhere that it appears in the database.
2. Insertion Anomaly
   A new employee is hired for department 220. The clerk maintaining the data may not have all the relevant information. Either he will

have to scan the data looking for existing names for dept. 220 or, probably, he will guess and assign our new employee to department 220, with DEPTNAME SHALLOW THOUGHT. What is the correct name of the department now?

3. Deletion Anomaly

   Employee number 00215 has retired. Her replacement starts next week. However, by deleting the entry for employee 00215, we have lost the information that tells us that the publishing department exists.

4. Redundancy

   It is possible to reduce the impact of these anomalies by designing programs that take their existence into account. Typically, this results in code that is more complex than it needs to be, and in additional code to resolve inconsistencies. These increase the cost of development and maintenance without eliminating the problems. In addition, the duplication of data will increase file or database sizes and will result in increased operating costs for the application.

All of the above problems are collectively known as the *update anomaly*.

Steps in Normalization. We will explain normalization by discussing a series of examples which illustrate the three basic steps to be followed in reducing un-normalized data to third normal form.

First Normal Form (1NF).

Each attribute depends on **THE KEY**

Each attribute can only have a single value for each value of a key. The first step in normalization is to remove attributes that can have multiple values for a given value of the key and form them into a new entity.

For example, consider the following entity (CUSTOMER) whose key attribute is CUSTNO (Customer Number) shown in Exhibit H-19.

In this case, the multivalued attribute consists of the three "attributes" ADDR_LINE_1, ADDR_LINE_2, ADDR_LINE_3. In fact, these are really three elements of an array. The first normal form of this entity is shown in Exhibit H-20 and Exhibit H-21.

We have created a new entity (CUSTOMER ADDRESS), with a compound key of customer number and line number (to identify each line of a customer's address). This new entity is *dependent* on the CUSTOMER entity and allows an address to have a variable number of lines (0 to 99).

Multivalued attributes can usually be identified because they are recorded as arrays (ADDR(1), ADDR(2)), including arrays of structures, where each element of the array is, in fact, a different value of the attribute. In some cases, as in the example above, the fact that an attribute

Exhibit H-19. Customer Table

CUSTOMER

CUSTNO	BRAN	CR CD	CST TYP	ADDR_LINE_1	ADDR_LINE_2	ADDR_LINE_3
PK						
003531	0059	A	C	JOHN BLOGGS	25 MAIN ST.	DALLAS, TEXAS
094425	0047	B	C	SAM HOSER	19 REDUNDANT	HOUSTON, TEXAS
976531	0099	I	I	IBM DEPT 344	3500 STORY	BOCA RATON, FLORIDA

Exhibit H-20. Customer Table

CUSTOMER

CUSTNO	BRAN	CR CD	CST TYP
PK			
003531	0059	A	C
094425	0047	B	C
976531	0099	I	I

Exhibit H-21. Customer Address Table

CUSTOMER ADDRESS

CUSTNO	LINE NO.	ADDR_LINE
PK		
003531	01	JOHN BLOGGS
003531	02	25 MAIN ST.
003531	03	DALLAS, TEXAS
094425	01	SAM HOSER
094425	02	19 REDUNDANT
094425	03	HOUSTON, TEXAS
976531	01	SALES DEPT 355
976531	02	3500 STORY
976531	03	BOCA RATON, FLORIDA

is multivalued has been disguised by the use of unique column names. The give-away is in the similarity of names. Additional examples of give-aways are names like:

- CURRENT_SALESMAN, PREVIOUS_SALESMAN
- FIRST_BRANCH_OFFICE, SECOND_BRANCH_OFFICE,...

Second Normal Form (2NF)

Each attribute depends on **THE WHOLE KEY**

The second step in normalization is to remove attributes that depend on only a part of the key and form them into a new entity.

Let us examine Exhibit H-22, in which the entity (PRODUCT MODEL) is an entity consisting of all the products and their models. The key is PROD-NO + MODNO. Let us assume that each product has a single SOURCE OF SUPPLY and that it is necessary to know the QTY ON HAND of each model.

Exhibit H-22. Product Model Table

PRODUCT MODEL

PRODNO	MODNO	PROD DESCRIPT	MODDESCRIPT	QTY ON HAND	SOURCE SUPPLY
PK					
3084	032	4_PLEX CPU	SMALL MEMORY	3	FUJISAWA
3084	064	4_PLEX CPU	MORE MEMORY	2	FUJISAWA
3084	0C8	4_PLEX CPU	OODLES OF MEMORY	0	FUJISAWA
3180	001	TERMINAL	TWINAX CONNECTION	55	DALLAS
3180	002	TERMINAL	COAX CONNECTION	83	DALLAS
3274	A41	CONTROL UNIT	BIG MODEL (LOCAL)	15	SAO PAULO
3274	C41	CONTROL UNIT	BIG MODEL (REMOTE)	29	SAO PAULO
SAO PAULO	C61	CONTROL UNIT	DESK TOP MODEL	11	

PRODDESCRIPT and SOURCE_OF_SUPPLY in Exhibit H-23 are PRODNO and are removed to form a new PRODUCT entity in Exhibit H-24.

The old PRODUCT MODEL entity is now dependent on the new PRODUCT entity. New models can be added without maintaining product descriptions and source of supply information. Models can be deleted while still retaining information about the product itself.

Dependence of attributes on part of a key is particularly evident in cases where a compound key identifies occurrences of an entity type.

Exhibit H-23. Product Table

PRODUCT

PRODNO	PRODDESCRIPT	SOURCE
PK		SUPPLY
3084	4_PLEX CPU	FUJISAWA
3180	TERMINAL	DALLAS
3274	CONTROL UNIT	SAO PAULO

Exhibit H-24. Product Model Table

PRODUCT MODEL

PRODNO	MODNO	MODDESCRIPT	QTY ON HAND
PK			
FK			
3084	032	SMALL MEMORY	3
3084	064	MORE MEMORY	2
3084	0c8	OODLES OF MEMORY	0
3180	001	TWINAX CONNECTION	55
3180	002	COAX CONNECTION	83
3274	A41	BIG MODEL (LOCAL)	15
3274	C41	BIG MODEL (REMOTE)	29
3274	C61	DESK TOP MODEL	11

What would be the effect on the above entities if a product could have multiple sources of supply?

Third Normal Form (3NF)

Each attribute depends on **NO OTHER BUT THE KEY**

The third step in normalization is to remove attributes that depend on other non-key attributes of the entity.

At this point it should be noted that a non-key attribute is an attribute that is neither the primary key nor a candidate key. A candidate key is an attribute, other than the primary key that also uniquely identifies each occurrence of an entity. (For example, a personnel file, is keyed on employee serial number and also contains social insurance number, either of which uniquely identifies the employee. The employee serial number might function as the primary key, while the social security number would be a candidate key.)

Consider the entity ORDER in Exhibit H-25, each occurrence of which represents an order for a product. As a given, assume that the UNIT PRICE varies from machine to machine and contract to contract.

Exhibit H-25. Order Table

ORDER

ORDNO	PRODNO	MODNO	CUSTNO	CONTRACT TYPE	UNIT PRICE	QTY	EXTENDED PRICE
PK	FK	FK					
XN223	4068	067	112339	EMPLOYEE	$1,098	1	$1,098
XQ440	4068	067	990613	INTERNAL	$875	5	$4,375
4068	4068	067	574026	DEALER	$1,170	20	$23,400
XB229	5160	020	390651	RETAIL	$2,960	2	$5,920
ZC875	5360	020	740332	BUSINESS	$33,600	1	$33,600
YS8/13	5360	B40	468916	GOVERN'T	$28,400	4	$113,600

Here we see a number of attributes that are not dependent on key. UNIT PRICE is dependent on CONTRACT TYPE, PRODNO and TENDED PRICE is dependent on both QTY and UNIT PRICE.

Reduction to third normal form requires us to create a new entity, PRODUCT/MODEL/CONTRACT, whose key is PRODNO + MODNO + CONTRACT TYPE, with UNIT PRICE an attribute of the entity. EXTENDED PRICE is calculated from the values of the other attributes and can be dropped from the table and computed as required. This is known as a derived attribute.

The third normal form should look like those displayed in Exhibit H-26 and Exhibit H-27.

In this form, prices and quantities may be changed. Data from both entities is joined together to calculate an EXTENDED PRICE. What changes to the model might be required to protect the customer against price changes? What would be the effect on the application if it were decided to maintain the EXTENDED PRICE as an attribute of the ORDER entity?

Model Refinement. This section discusses additional refinements that can be (and, in a real situation, usually must be) incorporated into a data model.

Exhibit H-26. Order Table

ORDER

ORDNO	PRODNO	MODNO	CUSTNO	CONTRACT TYPE	QTY
PK	FK	FK		FK	
XN223	4068	067	112339	EMPLOYEE	1
XQ440	4068	067	990613	INTERNAL	5
XL715	4068	067	574026	DEALER	20
XB229	5160	020	390651	RETAIL	2
ZC875	5360	B40	740332	BUSINESS	1
YS8/13	5360	B40	468916	GOVERN'T	4

Exhibit H-27. Product/Model/Contract Table

PRODUCT/MODEL/CONTRACT

PRODNO	MODNO	CONTRACT TYPES	UNIT PRICE
PK			
4068	067	EMPLOYEE	$1,098
4068	067	INTERNAL	$875
4068	067	DEALER	$1,170
5160	020	RETAIL	$2,960
5360	B40	BUSINESS	$33,600
5360	B40	GOVERN'T	$28,400

What is important about these refinements is that they introduce constraints in the model, which must be documented in the design and incorporated into the application.

Entity Subtypes. Frequently it is necessary to decompose (break down) a defined entity into Subtypes.

A Definition. Entity Subtypes

- Have attributes peculiar to the subtype, and/or
- Participate in relationships peculiar to the subtype, and
- Are identified by a subset of the key of the entity

An entity subtype is not the same as a dependent entity. A dependent entity is identified by a compound key, consisting of the key of the major entity plus additional qualifying attributes.

This need not be so in the case of an entity subtype, which has the same key as the major entity and is, in fact, merely a subclassification of that entity.

For example, all of us are employees and hence are occurrences of the EMPLOYEE entity. Some employees, however, are also marketing reps with attributes (marketing unit, team, territory, quota, etc.) that are unique to their occupation. The MARKETING REP entity is a subtype of the EMPLOYEE entity.

Additional subtypes of the EMPLOYEE entity might be:

- Employee as manager
- Employee as stockholder, employee as beneficiary

The existence of entity subtypes raises issues of referential integrity, which we shall discuss in the next section.

Referential Integrity.

Integrity Rule

> For any foreign key value in a table, there must be a corresponding primary key value in the same or another table.

As stated, the rule is very simple. To enforce this rule may require a great deal of complicated application code, preceded (of course) by a significant design effort. Fortunately, some database management systems have built-in features that make the provision of referential integrity much simpler (e.g., the logical insert, replace and delete rules in IMS/VS).

Exhibits H-28, 29, and 30 illustrate the problem by means of three entities (customer, product, and order).

Exhibit H-28. Customer Table

CUSTOMER

CUSTOMER NUMBER
PK
221356
840723
737174

Exhibit H-29. Product Table

PRODUCT

PRODUCT CODE
PK
3084XC8
4260067
5360A23

Exhibit H-30. Order Table

ORDER

ORDER NUMBER	CUSTOMER NUMBER	PRODUCT CODE
PK	FK	FK
ZA8845	221356	4260067
YB4320	737174	3084XC8
XN7691	840723	4260067
ZL3940	221356	5360A23

In practical terms, adherence to the referential integrity rule means:

1. A customer can be inserted without integrity checks.
2. A product can be inserted without integrity checks.
3. An order can be inserted, *but* the customer number foreign key must exist in the CUSTOMER entity, and the product code foreign key must exist in the PRODUCT entity.
4. A customer may not be deleted if its primary key exists in the order entity as a foreign key.
5. A product may not be deleted if its primary key exists in the order entity as a foreign key.
6. An order can be updated, *but* the customer number foreign key must exist in the CUSTOMER entity and the product code foreign key must exist in the PRODUCT entity if the values of those attributes are being altered.

Sometimes, adherence to the integrity rules can be more complicated. For example, we might want to permit the creation of a CUSTOMER at the time the order is entered, in which case the application must be coded to enforce a modified rule:

- An order can be inserted, *but* the customer number foreign key must exist in the CUSTOMER entity or must be inserted along with its attributes during order insertion. The product code foreign key must exist in the PRODUCT entity.

If these restrictions seem unduly harsh, ask yourself if you would want a salesman to enter orders for customers and products that do not exist.

Integrity constraints apply to entity subtypes as well. In a sense, a subtype simply has a special (1:1) relationship with another entity in which the primary key of the subtype is also a foreign key into the other entity type. In other words, we cannot appoint Joe Bloggs as a marketing rep unless he is already an employee.

> Referential integrity rules must be documented as part of the data model.

The rules, based on the dependency constraints, in this case would be:

1. An order can be inserted without dependency checks (although to do so without inserting at least one order line might be meaningless).
2. An order line item can be inserted, *but* the order number foreign key must exist in the ORDER entity or must be inserted along with its attributes during order line insertion.
3. An order line can be deleted without dependency checks.
4. An order cannot be deleted unless all its dependent order lines have been previously deleted

OR

5. Deletion of the order must trigger the guaranteed deletion of all dependent order lines.

The dependency constraints must be documented as part of the data model.

Dependency Constraints

Constraint Rule

> A dependent entity cannot exist unless the entity on which it depends also exists.

The dependency constraint rule is a special form of referential integrity constraint applicable to dependent entities. Some database management systems automatically enforce most dependency constraints. Other do not.

APPENDIX H

Exhibit H-31 and H-32 are illustrations of dependency as an ORDER with multiple LINE-ITEMS:

Exhibit H-31. Order Table

ORDER

ORDER NUMBER
PK
ZA8845
XN7691

Exhibit H-32. Line-Item Table

LINE-ITEM

ORDER NUMBER	LINE NUMBER	QTY	PRODUCT CODE
PK			FK
FK			
ZA8845	1	10	4260067
ZA8845	2	1	3084XC8
ZA8845	3	5	5160002
XN7691	1	2	5360A23
XN7691	2	18	3180001
XN7691	3	2	3520002

Recursion

A recursive relationship is a relationship between two entities of the same type.

Recursive relationships are found more frequently than one might think. Two of the most common recursive relationships are:

- Bill-of Materials Explosion/Implosion
- Organizational Hierarchies

Recursive relationships are a special case among the common relationships (i.e., 1:1, l:M, M:M) and are modeled in exactly the same way. We can start out by making an EMPLOYEE entity represent the organizational structure of a company, as in Exhibit H-33.

Exhibit H-33. Employee Table

EMPLOYEE

EMPLOYEE NUMBER	EMPLOYEE NAME	DEPT NUMBER
PK		
00100	CODD	220
00135	KENT	220
00171	NIJSSEN	220
00190	DATE	220
00326	BOYCE	220
00529	KAGOOL	354
00558	MONGO	354
00721	STEIGLITZ	354
00843	STROHEIM	955

The relationship between a manager and his employee (the organizational structure) is a one-to-many relationship. The manager's employee number as a foreign key is shown in Exhibit H-34.

Exhibit H-34. Employee Table

EMPLOYEE

EMPLOYEE NUMBER	EMPLOYEE NAME	DEPT NUMBER	MGR_EMP NUMBER
PK			FK
00100	CODD	220	00326
00135	KENT	220	00326
00171	NIJSSEN	220	00326
00190	DATE	220	00326
00326	BOYCE	220	00843
00529	KAGOOL	354	00721
00558	MONGO	354	00721
00721	STEIGLITZ	354	00843
00843	STROHEIM	955	NULL -

APPENDIX H

Recursive relationships impose additional integrity constraints. In this case:

1. A manager cannot work for himself. This implies that the topmost level of the hierarchy must contain a null value in the MGR_EMP_NUMBER column.
2. A manager cannot work for one of his employees; neither can he work for anyone who works for one of his employees ... and so on *ad infinitum*.

A bill of materials processing model is an example of a many-to-many recursive relationship in which each component is used in many subassemblies and finished products and in which each product contains many components.

As an exercise:

1. What would such a model look like?
2. What constraints should be placed on the model? Would they differ from the constraints placed on the previous model?

Using the Model in Database Design. All the work of modeling is of no use unless it directly contributes to the database design. In converting the model to a physical database design, some compromises with normalization may be necessary in order to obtain satisfactory performance. The compromises will be:

Least in implementing a relational design
Moderate in implementing a hierarchical design
Greatest in implementing a flat file design

It is not the intent of this section to give complete guidance for implementing the model using a specific database management system (DBMS). This material will be covered in IMS database design and relational database design courses.

Relational Design. The first cut at implementing the model using a relational DBMS is to implement the model as it stands:

- Each entity and relationship becomes a table.
- Group logically related entities into databases.
- Each attribute becomes a column in the table.
- A unique index is defined for each primary key (to ensure ROW uniqueness).
- Additional indices are created to support known access paths.
- For each table, an index is chosen by which the data will be clustered, to support the most frequently used access sequence.
- Space calculations are performed.

Subsequent modifications may be required to achieve acceptable performance.

H11: DECISION TABLES

Decision tables are a technique for representing combinations of actions for the respective set of decisions and are an alternative to flow chart analysis. Each column, therefore, comprises a test case, or path through a flow chart.

Consider the following small program, which reads records from a file and tallies the numerical ranges of a field on each record to illustrate the technique.

PROGRAM: FIELD-COUNT

```
Dowhile not EOF
    read record
    if FIELD_COUNTER > 7 then
        increment COUNTER_7 by 1
    else
        if FIELD_COUNTER > 3 then
            increment COUNTER_3 by 1
        else
            increment COUNTER_1 by 1
        endif
    endif
End_While
End
```

The respective decision table is displayed in Exhibit H-35, and there are four test cases to test the program using decision tables.

H12: DESK CHECKING

Desk checking is a human error-detection process which is in the form of a one-person walkthrough. The typical application is where an individual reads a program, checks it with a checklist, and manually talks test data through it. It can also be applied to requirements and design as a check on the work. This technique provides an evaluation of the quality of the program after it has been written or after the design has been completed.

H13: EQUIVALENCE PARTITIONING

The equivalence partitioning testing technique is a black-box testing technique that partitions the input domain into a set of input classes that can cause multiple behaviors.

Exhibit H-35. Decision Table

DECISIONS					
	EOF	Y	N	N	N
	FIELD_ COUNTER > 7	-	Y	N	N
	FIELD_ COUNTER > 3	-	-	Y	N
ACTIONS					
	End Program	X			
	Increment FIELD_COUNTER_7 by 1		X		
	Increment FIELD_COUNTER_3 by 1			X	
	Increment FIELD_COUNTER_1 by 1				X

From the requirements, each input is divided into partitions. Using this technique, one representative value from each partition is selected and tested. It is assumed that the results predict the results for other values in the partition, which demonstrates the power and economy of this technique.

It is more complicated than a simple range test because a range is divided into a series or one or more ranges because of the different behaviors that can occur. Consider the following application. The income needs to be broken up into three equivalence classes, as the behavior (or tax) varies according to the income value.

An IRS program computes the amount of state income tax based on the income, as is displayed in Exhibit H-36 and Exhibit H-37.

Exhibit H-36. Income vs. Tax Percent

Income Range	Tax % Due
$1 and $30,500	25%
$30,501 and $62,500	27%
$62,501 or more	38%

The following are some other examples of how to apply the technique.

Numeric Input Data

Field Ranges. Ex. "Input can range from integers 0 to 100," e.g., a test case could be 45 (any arbitrary number between 1 and 100).

Exhibit H-37. Income/Tax Test Cases

Test Case Number	Test Value	Expected Value	Equivalence Partition
1	$25,000	$6,250	$1 and $30,500
2	$40,500	$10,935	$30,501 and $62,500
3	$85,200	$32,376	$62,501 or more

Ex. "Input can range from real numbers 0.0 to 100.0," e.g., a test case could be 75.0 (any arbitrary number between 0.0 and 100.0).

Numeric Output Data

Output Range of Values. Ex. "Numerical range outputs of actuarial tables can be from $0.0 to $100,000.00," e.g., a test case could be $15,000.00 (any arbitrary number between $0.0 and $100,000.00).

Non-Numeric Input Data

Tables or Arrays. Ex. a test case could be to input from any table row with alphabetic contents.

Number of Items. Ex. "Number of products associated with a model is up to 10," e.g., a test case could be 5 products (any arbitrary number of products between 0 and 10).

Non-Numeric Output Data

Tables or Arrays. Ex. Update, write, delete any table row.

Number of Outputs. Ex. "Up to 10 customers can be displayed," e.g., a test case could be 7 customers displayed (any arbitrary number of customers between 0 and 10).

H14: EXCEPTION TESTING

With exception testing, all the error messages and exception handling processes are identified, including the conditions which trigger them. A test case is written for each error condition. A test case/error exception test matrix (Exhibit H-38) can be helpful for documenting the error conditions and exceptions.

H15: FREE FORM TESTING

Free form testing, often called error guessing, *ad hoc* testing, or brainstorming, is a "blue-sky" intuition of where and how errors are likely to occur and is an add-on technique to other testing techniques.

Exhibit H-38. Test Case/Error Exception Test Matrix

Test Case Name	Error Message/Exception	Passes/Failed	Date	Tester
1				
2				
3				
4				
5				
6				
7				
8				
9				

Some testers are naturally adept at this form of testing, which does not use any particular testing technique. It involves intuition and experience to "smell out" defects. There is no particular methodology for applying this technique, but the basic approach is to enumerate a list of potential errors or error-prone situations and write test cases based on the list.

H16: GRAY-BOX TESTING

Black-box testing focuses on the program's functionality against the specification. White-box testing focuses on the paths of logic. Gray-box testing is a combination of black- and white-box testing. The tester studies the requirements specifications and communicates with the developer to understand the internal structure of the system. The motivation is to clear up ambiguous specifications and "read between the lines" to design implied tests. One example of the use of gray-box testing is when it appears to the tester that a certain functionality seems to be reused throughout an application. If the tester communicates with the developers and understands the internal design and architecture, a lot of tests will be eliminated, because it might be possible to test the functionality only once. Another example is when the syntax of a command consists of 7 possible parameters which can be entered in any order as follows:

Command parm1, parm2, parm3, parm4, parm5, parm6, parm7 (enter)

In theory, a tester would have to create 7! or 5,040 tests. The problem is even more compounded if some of the parameters are optional. If the tester uses gray-box testing, by talking with the developer and understanding the parser algorithm, if each parameter is independent, only 7 tests may be required to test each parameter.

H17: HISTOGRAMS

A histogram is a graphical description of measured values organized according to the frequency or relative frequency of occurrence. In Exhibit H-39, the table consists of a sample of 100 client/server terminal response times (enter key until a server response) for an application. This was measured with a performance testing tool.

Exhibit H-39. Response Time of 100 Samples (seconds)

2	4	1	6	5	12	4	3	4	10
5	2	7	2	4	1	12	4	2	1
1	2	4	3	5	1	3	5	7	12
5	7	1	2	4	3	1	4	1	2
1	3	5	2	1	2	4	5	1	2
3	1	3	2	6	1	5	4	1	2
7	1	8	4	3	1	1	2	6	1
1	2	1	4	2	6	2	2	4	9
2	3	2	1	8	2	4	7	2	2
4	1	2	5	3	4	5	2	1	2

The histogram in Exhibit H-40 illustrates how the raw performance data from the above table is displayed in a histogram. It should be noted that the design specification is for response times to be less than 3 seconds. It is obvious from the data that the performance requirement is not being satisfied and there is a performance problem.

Exhibit H-40. Response Time Histogram

Average = 3.47 seconds

0	23	25	10	16	10	4	5	2	5
0 to .9	1 to 1.9	2 to 2.9	3 to 3.9	4 to 4.9	5 to 5.9	6 to 6.9	7 to 7.9	8 to 8.9	9 to ∞

H18: INSPECTIONS

Inspections are the most formal, commonly used form of peer review. The key feature of an inspection is the use of checklists to facilitate error detection. These checklists are updated as statistics indicate that certain types of errors are occurring more or less frequently than in the past. The most common types of inspections are conducted on the product design and code, although inspections may be used during any life cycle phase.

Inspections should be short because they are often intensive; therefore, the product component to be reviewed must be small. Specifications or designs that result in 50 to 100 lines of code are usually manageable. This translates into an inspection of 15 minutes to one hour, although complex components may require as much as two hours. In any event, inspections of more than two hours are generally less effective and should be avoided.

Two or three days before the inspection, the producer assembles the input to the inspection and gives it to the coordinator for distribution. Participants are expected to study and make comments on the materials before the review.

The review is led by a participant other than the producer. Generally, the individual who has the greatest involvement in the next phase of the life cycle is designated as reader. For example, a requirements inspection would likely be led by a designer, a design review by an implementer, and so forth. The exception to this is the code inspection, which is led by the designer. The inspection is organized and coordinated by an individual designated as the group leader or coordinator.

The reader goes through the product component, using the checklist as a means to identify common types of errors as well as standards violations. A primary goal of an inspection is to identify items that can be modified to make the component more understandable, maintainable, or usable. Participants discuss any issues that they identified in preinspection study.

At the end of the inspection, an accept or reject decision is made by the group, and the coordinator summarizes all the errors and problems detected and gives this list to all participants. The individual whose work was under review (e.g., designer, implementer, tester) uses the list to make revisions to the component. When revisions are implemented, the coordinator and producer go through a minireview, using the problem list as a checklist. The coordinator then completes management and summary reports. The summary report is used to update checklists for subsequent inspections.

H19: JADS

A JAD is a technique which brings users and development together to design systems in facilitated group sessions. Studies show that JADs increase the productivity over traditional design techniques. JADs go beyond the one-on-one interviews to collect information. They promote communication, cooperation, and teamwork among the participants by placing the users in the driver's seat.

JADs are logically divided into phases: customization, session, and wrap-up. Regardless of what activity one is pursuing in development, these components will always exist. Each phase has its own objectives.

1. Customization

   This phase is key to a JAD and largely consists of preparation for the next phase. Participants include the session leader and JAD analysts. The tasks include organizing the team, defining the JAD tasks and deliverables, and preparing the materials for the next JAD session.

2. Session

   This phase consists of facilitated sessions where the analysts and users jointly define the requirements and the system design. The session leader facilitates the session and the analyst documents the results.

3. Wrap-Up

   In this final phase, formal JAD outputs are produced. The facilitated session leader summarizes the visual and other documentation into a JAD document. The design results are fed back to the executive sponsor.

A given development effort may consist of a series of the three phases until the final requirements and design have been completed. When a project has multiple design activity, e.g., different portions of the overall design, a final wrap-up occurs at the completion of the design where the design is reviewed as a whole.

H20: ORTHOGONAL ARRAY TESTING

Orthogonal array testing is a statistical technique pioneered by Dr. Taguchi in manufacturing which helps in the selection of test cases to get a handle on the potentially enormous number of combination factors. It calculates the ideal number of tests required and identifies variations of input values and conditions, e.g., it helps in the test selection process to provide maximum coverage with a minimum number of test cases.

Taguchi methods, developed by Dr. Genichi Taguchi, refer to techniques of quality engineering that embody both statistical process control (SPC) and new quality related management techniques. Most of the attention and discussion of Taguchi methods have been focused on the statistical aspects of the procedure; it is the conceptual framework of a methodology for quality improvement and process robustness that needs to be emphasized.

An example is when the syntax of a command consists of three possible parameters in which there can be three possible values as follows:

```
Command PARM1, PARM2, PARM3 (enter)

PARMx = 1,2,3
```

In theory, a tester would have to create 3^3 or 27 test combinations, as shown in Exhibit H-41.

Exhibit H-41. Parameter Combinations (with total enumeration)

Test Case	PARM1	PARM2	PARM3	Test Case	PARM1	PARM2	PARM3
1	1	1	1	14	2	2	2
2	1	1	2	15	2	2	3
3	1	1	3	16	3	2	1
4	2	1	1	17	3	2	2
5	2	1	2	18	3	2	3
6	2	1	3	19	1	3	1
7	3	1	1	20	1	3	2
8	3	1	2	21	1	3	3
9	3	1	3	22	2	3	1
10	1	2	1	23	2	3	2
11	1	2	2	24	2	3	3
12	1	2	3	25	3	3	1
13	2	2	1	26	3	3	2
-	-	-		27	3	3	3

Applying orthogonal array testing (OATS), the technique selects test cases so as to test the interactions between independent measures called factors. Each factor also has a finite set of possible values called levels. In Exhibit H-41, there are three factors (PARM1, PARM2, and PARM3). Each has three levels (1, 2 and 3). The technique calls for the tester to locate the best fit of the number of factors and levels to the possible orthogonal arrays (found in most statistical texts). In Exhibit H-42, the orthogonal array with 3 factors and 3 levels is chosen. Each column in the array corresponds to a factor and each row corresponds to a test case. The rows represent all possible pairwise combinations of possible levels for the factors. Thus, only nine test cases are required, which demonstrates the power of the technique.

H21: PARETO ANALYSIS

Pareto diagrams are a special form of a graph that points to where efforts should be concentrated. By depicting events or facts in order of decreasing frequency (or cost, or failure rate, etc.), it allows for a quick separation of

Exhibit H-42. Parameter Combinations (OATS)

$L_9(3)^3$ (Orthogonal array, 3 factors, 3 levels)

Test Case	PARM1	PARM2	PARM3
1	1	1	3
2	1	2	2
3	1	3	1
4	2	1	2
5	2	2	1
6	2	3	3
7	3	1	1
8	3	2	3
9	3	3	2

the "vital few" from the trivial many. The Pareto chart is more commonly known to information systems personnel as the 80-20 rule, i.e., 20% of the causes make up 80% of the frequencies. A Pareto chart is a histogram showing values in descending order, which helps identify the high-frequency causes of problems so that appropriate corrective action can be taken. It is an organized ranking of causes of a problem by type of cause. The objective is to select the most frequent cause or causes of a problem in order to direct action to eliminate those causes.

The four steps in using a Pareto chart include:

- Identify a problem area
  One problem example is an excessive number of defects discovered during software testing.
- Identify and name the causes of the problem
  This is the most time-consuming step because it requires the collection of information from various causes. Causes of defects include: architectural, database integrity, documentation, functionality, GUI, installation, performance, and usability. For most problems, there is little need to identify more than 12 causes. When more than 12 causes can be identified, one approach is to select 11 causes and the 12th cause can be classified as "Other." If the "Other" category becomes significant, then it may need to be broken down into specific causes.
- Document the occurrence of the causes of the problem
  The occurrences of the causes need to be documented. Samples from the defect tracking database can be used to obtain these frequencies.

- Rank the causes by frequency, using the Pareto chart
  This involves two tasks. The first is to count the problem occurrences by type. The second is to build a bar chart (or Pareto chart), with the major causes listed on the left-hand side, with the other causes listed in descending order of occurrence.

In Exhibit H-43 there are eight defect causes. Approximately 1,050 defects have been recorded. Of those, 750 are caused by functionality and database integrity. Thus, 20% of the causes account for 71 (or approximately 80%) of the frequency. In our example, functionality is the major cause, and database integrity is the second cause. Emphasis should be placed on eliminating the number of functional and database problems. One approach might be increased unit testing and reviews.

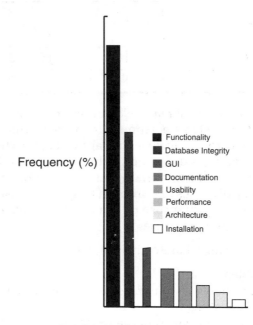

Frequency (%)

- Functionality
- Database Integrity
- GUI
- Documentation
- Usability
- Performance
- Architecture
- Installation

Exhibit H-43. Pareto Chart

H22: POSITIVE AND NEGATIVE TESTING

Positive and negative testing is an input-based testing technique that requires that a proper balance of positive and negative tests be performed. A positive test is one with a valid input, and a negative test is one with an invalid input. Since there typically are many more negative than positive tests, a suggested balance is 80% negative and 20% positive tests.

For example, suppose an application accepts stock market or mutual fund five-character symbols and then displays the respective stock or mutual fund name. An example of a positive test is "PHSTX," which is the mutual fund symbol associated with a health science fund. If this symbol displayed some other fund, this would entail a positive test that failed.

Values that are not valid stock or mutual fund symbols are negative tests. Typically, a negative test produces an invalid error message. For example, if "ABCDE" is entered and an invalid error message is displayed, this is a negative test that passed.

Some considerations of negative testing are how much negative testing is enough and how do we anticipate unexpected conditions. Testing the editing of a single alphabetic character field can be complex. One negative test would be "("and should be detected by the system. Should")" be tested? How many other nonalphabetic characters should be tested? Unanticipated conditions are also sometimes difficult to detect. For example, "&" and """" have special meaning with SQL. Should both of these be tested in every field?

H23: PRIOR DEFECT HISTORY TESTING

With prior defect history testing, a test case is created or rerun for every defect found in prior tests of the system. The motivation for this is that defects tend to cluster and regress back to the original problem. Some causes include poor software configuration management procedures, poor coding and unit testing during defect repair, the tendency for bugs to cluster, etc.

A defect matrix is an excellent tool which relates test cases to functions (or program units). A check entry in the defect matrix indicates that the test case is to be retested because a defect was previously discovered while running this test case. No entry means that the test does not need to be retested.

If this approach is not economical because a large number of defects have been discovered, a test case should be retested on or above a certain defined severity level.

H24: PROTOTYPING

Prototyping is an iterative approach often used to build systems that users are initially unable to describe precisely. The concept is made possible largely through the power of fourth-generation languages (4GLs) and application generators. Prototyping is, however, as prone to defects as any other development effort, maybe more so if not performed in a systematic manner. Prototypes need to be tested as thoroughly as any other system. Testing can be difficult unless a systematic process has been established for developing prototypes.

The following sections describe several prototyping methodologies. They are presented to show the diversity of concepts used in defining software life cycles and to illustrate the effects of prototyping on the life cycle in general.

Cyclic Models

This concept of software development with prototyping consists of two separate but interrelated cyclic models: one consisting of a classical software development cycle and the other of a prototyping cycle that interacts with the classical model during the phases of analysis and design. The major operations are:

Classical cycle

- User request
- Feasibility
- Investigation
- Consideration of prototyping
- Analysis
- Design
- Final proposed design
- Programming
- Testing
- Implementation
- Operation
- Evaluation
- Maintenance
  (the cycle is repeated)

Prototyping cycle

- Prototype is designed
- Prototype is used
- Investigation is conducted using the prototype
- Analysis is performed on the investigation
- Refinements are made, or a new prototype is built
  (this cycle is also repeated)

The interaction of the two cycles occurs when investigation in the classical cycle uncovers the need to prototype, at which time the prototyping cycle is entered. Prototyping is terminated when analysis, design, or the final proposed design of the classical cycle can be completed based on information discovered or verified in the prototyping cycle.

Fourth-Generation Languages and Prototyping

This method proposes the following life cycle steps:

1. A prototyping team of one analyst/programmer and one end user is formed.

2. User needs are identified by interviewing several end users to define the problem and elicit sample user expectations.
3. A prototype is developed quickly to address most of the issues of the problem and user expectations.
4. The prototype is demonstrated to the end user. The user experiments with it and performs work within a specified time period. If the prototype is not acceptable, it is scrapped.
5. The prototype is refined by including changes identified through use. This step and the previous one are iterated until the system fully achieves the requirements.
6. An end-user test group is formed to provide more feedback on the prototype within a specified period of time.
7. A determination is made as to whether the prototype will be implemented or the system will be rewritten in a conventional language. This decision is based on maintenance considerations, hardware and software efficiency, flexibility, and other system requirements.

Iterative Development Accounting

This model is based on the view that a system is a sequence of specification levels with an increasing amount of detail at each level. These levels are:

- Informal requirements
- Formal requirements
- Design
- Implementation
- Configuration
- Operation

Each level contains more detail than the one preceding it. In addition, each level must be balanced with upper-level specifications. Iterative development imposes development accounting on each level (i.e., a change in one specification level can be made only if the next higher level has been modified to accommodate the change).

A complete history of development is maintained by this accounting technique to ensure that consistency remains throughout all levels. A prototype is developed at each level to show that the specifications are consistent. Each prototype concentrates on the functions to be evaluated at that level. The final prototype becomes the implemented system once testing, installation, and training have been completed.

Evolutionary and Throwaway

Two models are presented here. In the first, the prototype is built and gradually enhanced to form the implemented system. The second is known as the throwaway model.

End users are integral parts of the prototype development in both models and should be trained in the use of a prototyping tool (e.g., a simulation language or 4GL). The two models are described briefly as follows:

- Method 1:
  - The user experiments with and uses a prototype built to respond to the end user's earliest and most tentative needs to perform work.
  - The analyst watches the user to see where prototype refining needs to take place. A series of prototypes, or modifications to the initial prototype, evolve into the final product.
- Method 2:
  - A prototype is implemented. The initial design is developed from this and the end user's feedback. Another prototype is produced to implement the initial design. The final system is implemented in a conventional language.

Application Prototyping

This method proposes the following steps:

1. Identification of basic needs — Concentrate on identifying fundamental goals, objectives, and major business problems to be solved and defining data elements, data relations, and functions.
2. Development of a working model — Build a working prototype quickly to address the key needs.
3. Demonstration of prototype — Present the prototype to all interested users and obtain additional requirements through user feedback.
4. Completion of prototype — Iterate between demonstration and enhancement of the prototype until users are satisfied that the organization could provide the service needed from the prototype. Once users agree that the prototype fits the concept of the service needed, it can be enhanced into the final system or rewritten in a more efficient language.

Prototype Systems Development

The stages for this approach are as follows:

1. Management states the organization's objectives. These are described in terms of information requirements and the scope of the system boundaries and capabilities. Prototype screens and reports are developed.
2. End users and management review and approve the prototype. Full system design, equipment selection, programming, and documentation are completed.
3. Management reviews and commits to implementing the system. System tests of the prototype are run in parallel with the old system.

Work begins on the next release, which causes an iteration of all three stages.

Data-Driven Prototyping

This methodology consists of the following six steps:

1. Operational review — Define the project scope and evaluate the environment, current organization, and information structures.
2. Conceptual design — Define proposed metadata (i.e., the structure of data and relationships between individual structures), the scenarios needed to describe service functions that change data states, and types of retrievals.
3. Data design — Normalize the metadata.
4. Heuristic analysis — Check consistency of requirements against metadata through the use of real data values; this step is iterated with the data design step.
5. Environment test — Build programs to support data entry and retrieval (prototype).
6. Performance monitoring and application tuning.

Replacement of the Traditional Life Cycle

In this model, the steps include:

1. Rapid analysis — Results in an incomplete paper model that shows the system context, critical functions, an entity–relationship model of the database, and conceptual tables, screens, attributes, reports, and menus.
2. Database development — Uses a relational architecture to create a working database for the use of the prototype.
3. Menu development — Expands on the initial concepts defined in rapid analysis and fixes the hierarchical structure of the application.
4. Function development — Groups functions by type into modules.
5. Prototype demonstration — Iterates by redoing parts as necessary and tuning if possible.
6. Design, coding, and testing — Completes the detailed design specifications.
7. Implementation — Is based on the evolution of the prototype and completion of all programs, tests, and documentation.

Early-Stage Prototyping

This model can assist in specifying user requirements, verifying the feasibility of system design, and translating the prototype into the final system. The procedure includes the following:

1. A preliminary analysis and requirements specification establish a baseline for future reference.
2. A prototype is defined and implemented, emphasizing the user interface. The prototype is developed by a small development team using prototype development language and tools to assist in rapid development.
3. The prototype is tested in the user's workplace.
4. The prototype is refined by incorporating user comments as quickly as possible.
5. Baseline requirements are refined by incorporating lessons learned from the prototype.
6. The production system is developed through the use of a traditional life cycle with requirements derived from the prototype.

User Software Engineering

This is based on a model of software development that is part formal and part informal and includes the following steps:

1. Requirements analysis — Activity and data modeling and identification of user characteristics.
2. External design — Develop transactions and user-program interfaces.
3. Facade development — Used as a prototype of the user–program interface and revised as needed.
4. Narrative text — Used to informally specify the system operations.
5. Preliminary relational database — Designed as the basis for a functional prototype of the system.
6. Functional prototype — Developed to provide at least some, and perhaps all, of the functions of the proposed system.
7. Formal specification of the system operations — May be optionally developed at this point.
8. System architecture and modules.
9. System implementation — In a procedural language.
10. Testing and verification — Performed on the system before the system is released into the production environment.

H25: RANDOM TESTING

Random testing is a technique in which a program or system is tested by selecting at random some subset of all possible input values. It is not an optimal testing technique, because it has a low probability of detecting many defects. It does, however, sometimes uncover defects that standardized testing techniques might not. It should, therefore, be considered an add-on testing technique.

H26: RANGE TESTING

The range testing is a technique that assumes that the behavior of any input variable within a predefined range will be the same. The range over which the system behavior should be the same is first selected. Then an arbitrary representative from the range is selected and tested. If it passes, it is assumed that the rest of the values do not have to be tested.

For example, consider the following piece of coding, which calculates the results Z from two input values X and Y:

$$Z = \sqrt{(X^2 - Y^2)}$$

If X and Y are positive integers ranging from 0 to 5 and X is greater than or equal to Y, there are 21 possible test cases, as depicted in Exhibit H-44.

Applying this technique has the potential of saving a lot of test generation time. However, it does have the limitation of the assumption that selecting an arbitrary input sample will produce the same system behavior for the rest of the inputs. Additional tests such as the conditions X and Y positive integers and Y greater than X need to be tested as well as the verification of square roots results, e.g., we need to determine if the Z variable will accept fractional values as the result of the calculation or truncation (also see Boundary Value Testing).

H27: REGRESSION TESTING

Regression testing tests the application in light of changes made during a development spiral, debugging, maintenance, or the development of a new release. This test must be performed after functional improvements or repairs have been made to a system to confirm that the changes have no unintended side effects. Correction of errors relating to logic and control flow, computational errors, and interface errors are examples of conditions that necessitate regression testing. Cosmetic errors generally do not affect other capabilities and do not require that regression testing be performed.

It would be ideal if all the tests in the test suite were rerun for each new spiral, but due to time constraints, this is probably not realistic. A good regression strategy during spiral development is for some regression testing to be performed during each spiral to ensure that previously demonstrated capabilities are not adversely affected by later development spirals or error corrections. During system testing after the system is stable and the functionality has been verified, regression testing should consist of a subset of the system tests. Policies need to be created to decide which tests to include.

Exhibit H-44. Range Testing Test Cases

Test Case	X Value	Y Value	Z (Expected Result)
1	0	0	0
2	1	0	1
3	1	1	0
4	2	0	2
5	2	1	$\sqrt{3}$
6	2	2	0
7	3	0	3
8	3	1	$\sqrt{8}$
9	3	2	$\sqrt{5}$
10	3	3	0
11	4	0	4
12	4	1	$\sqrt{15}$
13	4	2	$\sqrt{12}$
14	4	3	$\sqrt{7}$
15	4	4	0
16	5	0	5
17	5	1	$\sqrt{24}$
18	5	2	$\sqrt{21}$
19	5	3	4
20	5	4	3
21	5	5	0

In theory, the reliability of a system that has been modified cannot be guaranteed without a full regression test of all tests. However, there are many practical considerations:

- When defects are uncovered, additional regression tests should be created
- A regression test library should be available and maintained as it evolves
- There should be a methodology of isolating regression tests which focus on certain areas (see retest and defect matrices)
- If the overall architecture of a system is changed, full regression testing should be performed

- Automated testing with capture/playback features should be strongly considered (see Section IV, Modern Testing Tools)

H28: RISK-BASED TESTING

The purpose of risk management testing is to measure the degree of business risk in an application system to improve testing. This is accomplished in two ways. First, high-risk applications can be identified and subjected to more extensive testing. Second, risk analysis can help identify the error-prone components of an individual application so that testing can be directed at those components.

Risk analysis is a formal method for identifying vulnerabilities (i.e., areas of potential loss). Any area that could be misused, intentionally or accidentally, and result in a loss to the organization is a vulnerability. Identification of risks allows the testing process to measure the potential effect of those vulnerabilities (e.g., the maximum loss that could occur if the risk or vulnerability were exploited).

Risk-based testing is a technique in which test cases are created for every major risk factor which has been previously identified. Each condition is tested to verify that the risk has been averted.

H29: RUN CHARTS

A run chart is a graphical representation of how a quality characteristic varies with time. It is usually a line graph that shows the variability in a measurement or in a count of items. For example, in Exhibit H-45, a run chart can show the variability in the number of defects detected over time. It can show results from a sample of a population or from 100%.

Exhibit H-45. Sample Run Chart

x (week)	y
1	10
2	50
3	30
4	60
5	25
6	50
7	75
8	45

A control chart, a special form of run chart, places lines on the chart to represent the limits of permissible variability. These limits could be determined by a design specification or an agreed upon standard. The control limits are frequently set to show the statistical limit of variabilities that could be due to a chance occurrence. This is calculated by using the averages and range of measurement from each sample of data. Control charts are not only used as an alarm when going outside the limits, but also to examine trends occurring within the limits. For example, if the sequence of 10 measurements in Exhibit H-45 is shown to fall above the expected average, it can be assumed that this is not due to mere chance and, therefore, an investigation is in order.

H30: SANDWICH TESTING

Sandwich testing uses top-down and bottom-up techniques simultaneously and is a compromise between the two. The approach integrates from the top and bottom at the same time, meeting somewhere in the middle of the hierarchical control structure. The meeting point in the middle is defined by the program structure.

It is typically used on large programs but is difficult to justify on small programs. The top level of the hierarchy usually includes the user interfaces to the system, which requires stubs to mimic business functions. The bottom level includes primitive level modules, which requires drivers to simulate lower level modules.

H31: STATEMENT COVERAGE TESTING

Statement coverage is a white-box technique that ensures that every statement or line of code (LOC) is executed at least once. It does guarantee that every statement is executed, but it is a very weak code coverage approach and not as comprehensive as other techniques, such as branch coverage, where each branch from a decision statement is executed.

Consider the following small program, which reads records from a file and tallies the numerical ranges of a field on each record to illustrate the technique.

PROGRAM: FIELD-COUNT

```
Dowhile not EOF
    read record
    if FIELD_COUNTER > 7 then
    increment COUNTER_7 by 1
    else
        if FIELD_COUNTER > 3 then
            increment COUNTER_3 by 1
        else
```

```
        increment COUNTER_1 by 1
     endif
  endif
End_While
End
```

The test cases to satisfy statement coverage are as follows:

Test Case	Values (FIELD_COUNTER)
1	>7, ex. 8
2	>3, ex. 4
3	<= 3, ex. 3

H32: STATE TRANSITION TESTING

State transition testing is a testing technique in which the states of a system are first identified. Then a test case is written to test the triggers or stimuli that cause a transition from one condition to another state. The tests can be designed using a finite-state diagram or an equivalent table.

Consider the following small program, which reads records from a file and tallies the numerical ranges of a field on each record to illustrate the technique.

PROGRAM: FIELD-COUNT

```
Dowhile not EOF
   read record
   if FIELD_COUNTER > 7 then
       increment COUNTER_7 by 1
   else
       if FIELD_COUNTER > 3 then
           increment COUNTER_3 by 1
       else
           increment COUNTER_1 by 1
       endif
   endif
End_While
End
```

Exhibit H-46 illustrates the use of the testing technique to derive test cases. The states are defined as the current value of COUNTER_7, COUNTER_3, and COUNTER_1. Then the possible transitions are considered. They consist of the end of file condition or the value FIELD_COUNTER for each successive record input. For each of these transitions, a definition of how each respective state is transformed is performed. Each transition becomes a test case and the final state is the expected result.

587

Exhibit H-46. State Transition Table

Initial State	Test Case (Transition)	Final State
COUNTER_7 = X1	1. EOF	COUNTER_7 = X1
COUNTER_3 = X2		COUNTER_3 = X2
COUNTER_1 = X3		COUNTER_1 = X3
		Exit Program
COUNTER_7 = X1	2. Next Record with FIELD_COUNTER > 7	COUNTER_7 = (X1+1)
COUNTER_3 = X2		COUNTER_3 = X2
COUNTER_1 = X3		COUNTER_1 = X3
		Successful
COUNTER_7 = X1	3. Next Record with FIELD_COUNTER < = 7 and FIELD_COUNTER >3	COUNTER_7 = X1
COUNTER_3 = X2		COUNTER_3 = (X2+1)
COUNTER_1 = X3		COUNTER_1 = X3
		Successful
COUNTER_7 = X1	4. Next Record with FIELD_COUNTER < = 3	COUNTER_7 = X1
COUNTER_3 = X2		COUNTER_3 = X2
COUNTER_1 = X3		COUNTER_1 = (X3+1)
		Successful

H33: STATISTICAL PROFILE TESTING

With statistical profile testing, statistical techniques are used to develop a usage profile of the system. Based on the expected frequency of use, the tester determines the transaction paths, conditions, functional areas, and data tables which merit focus in testing. The tests are, therefore, geared to the most frequently used part of the system.

H34: STRUCTURED WALKTHROUGHS

Structured walkthroughs are more formal than the code-reading reviews. Distinct roles and responsibilities are assigned before the review. Preview preparation is greater, and a more formal approach to problem documentation is stressed. Another key feature of this review is that it is presented by the producer. The most common walkthroughs are those held during design and coding; however, recently they have been applied to specifications documentation and test results.

The producer schedules the review and assembles and distributes input. In most cases, the producer selects the walkthrough participants (although this is sometimes done by management) and notifies them of their roles and responsibilities. The walkthrough is usually conducted with less than seven participants and lasts no more than two hours. If more time is needed, there should be a break or the product should be reduced in size. Roles usually included in a walkthrough are producer, coordinator, recorder, and representatives of user, maintenance, and standards organizations.

Although the review is opened by the coordinator, the producer is responsible for leading the group through the product. In the case of design and code walkthroughs, the producer simulates the operation of the component, allowing each participant to comment based on that individual's area of specialization. A list of problems is kept, and at the end of the review, each participant signs the list, or other walkthrough form, indicating whether the product is accepted as is, accepted with recommended changes, or rejected. Suggested changes are made at the discretion of the producer. There are no formal means of follow-up on the review comments. If the walkthrough review is used for products throughout the life cycle, however, comments from past reviews can be discussed at the start of the next review.

H35: SYNTAX TESTING

Syntax testing is a technique in which a syntax command generator generates test cases based on the syntax rules of the system. Both valid and invalid values are created. It is a data-driven black-box testing technique for testing input data to language processors, such as string processors and compilers. Test cases are developed based on rigid data definitions. The valid inputs are described in Backus Naur Form (BNF) notation.

The main advantage of syntax testing is that it ensures that no misunderstandings about valid and invalid data and specification problems will become apparent when employing this technique.

H36: TABLE TESTING

Table testing is a technique that tests the table which is usually associated with a relational database (the same approaches can be applied to arrays, queues, and heaps). Tables usually come in two forms: sequential and indexed. The following are general tests that need to be performed against tables.

Indexed Tables

    a. Delete the first record in the table
    b. Delete a middle record in the table
    c. Delete the last record in the table

d. Add a new first record in the table
e. Add a new middle record in the table
f. Add a new last record in the table
g. Attempt to add a duplicate record
h. Add a record with an invalid key, e.g., garbage in the key field
i. Change the key field(s) on a existing record, e.g., change an order number
j. Delete a nonexisting record, e.g., enter a delete key which does not match table entries
k. Update and rewrite an existing record

Sequential Tables

a. Attempt to delete a record from an empty table
b. Read a record from an empty table
c. Add a record to a full table
d. Delete one record from a one-record table
e. Read the last record
f. Read the next record after the last record
g. Scroll sequentially through the table
h. Insert an out-of sequence record
i. Attempt to insert a duplicate record

H37: THREAD TESTING

Thread testing is a software testing technique that demonstrates key functional capabilities by testing a string of program units that accomplishes a specific business function in the application.

A thread is basically a business transaction consisting of a set of functions. It is a single discrete process which threads through the whole system. Each function is tested separately, then added one at a time to the thread. The business transaction thread is then tested. Threads are in turn integrated and incrementally tested as subsystems, and then the whole system is tested. This approach facilitates early systems and acceptance testing.

H38: TOP-DOWN TESTING

The top-down testing technique is an incremental approach in which the high-level modules or system components are integrated and tested first. Testing then proceeds hierarchically to the bottom level. This technique requires the creation of stubs. When a module or system component is tested, the modules or components it invokes are represented by stubs, which return control back to the calling module or system component with a simulated result. As testing progresses down the program structure, each stub is replaced by the actual code it represents. There is no correct rule of which module to test next; the only rule is that at least one of the modules or system component calling modules must have been tested previously.

Top-down testing allows early discovery of major design flaws occurring at the top of the program, because high-level functions and decisions are tested early, and they are generally located at the top of the control structure. This verifies the program design early. An early prototype or initial design facilitates early demonstrations. Since the menus are often at the top of the control structure, the external interfaces can be displayed early to the user. Stubs need to be created but are generally easier to create than drivers. On the other hand, critical low-level modules or system components are not tested until late in the process. In rare cases, problems with these critical modules or system components may force a redesign.

H39: WHITE-BOX TESTING

White-box testing, or structural testing, is one in which test conditions are designed by examining paths of logic. The tester examines the internal structure of the program or system. Test data are driven by examining the logic of the program or system, without concern for the program or system requirements. The tester has knowledge of the internal program structure and logic, just as a mechanic knows the inner workings of an automobile. Specific examples in this category include basis path analysis, statement coverage, branch coverage, condition coverage, branch/condition coverage.

An advantage of white-box testing is that it is thorough and focuses on the produced code. Since there is knowledge of the internal structure or logic, errors or deliberate mischief on the part of a programmer have a higher probability of being detected.

One disadvantage of white-box testing is that it does not verify that the specifications are correct, i.e., it focuses only on the internal logic and does not verify the logic to the specification. Another disadvantage is that there is no way to detect missing paths and data-sensitive errors. For example, if the statement in a program should be coded "if |a-b| < 10" but is coded "if (a-b) <1," this would not be detectable without specification details. A final disadvantage is that white-box testing cannot execute all possible logic paths through a program, because this would entail an astronomically large number of tests.

Glossary

Adaptive Maintenance. Modifications made to a system to accommodate changes in the processing environment.

Algorithm. A set of rules that are supposed to give the correct answer for solving a particular problem.

ANSI. Acronym for the American National Standard Institute, an institute that creates standards for a wide variety of industries, including computer programming languages.

Architecture. Similar to the architecture of a building, the architecture of a computer refers to the design structure of the computer and all its details.

Archive. To store information, to back it up, with the idea of preserving it for a long time.

ASCII. Stands for the American Standard Code for Information Interchange, which is a standardized coding system used by almost all computers and printers.

Assumption. Proposition that must be allowed to reduce the relevant variables of a problem to be manageable.

Attribute. The descriptive characteristic of something.

Backup. The process of making copies of files to enable recovery.

Baseline. (1) A defined set of executables or documents of a specific product, put into a state in which all development and change activity are closely managed in order to support a defined activity at a set time. Examples: Integration Test, Pilots, System Test, Reviews. (2) A product, document, or deliverable that has been formally reviewed, approved, and agreed upon; thereafter serving as a basis for further development, and to which a change can only be implemented through formal change control procedures. Examples: Initial deployment of a product. Evolution of existing products.

Baseline Measurement. A measurement taken for the specific purpose of determining the initial value of a state.

Benchmark. A test used to measure the relative performance of hardware or software products.

Button. On a computer screen, it is the visual equivalent of a button on a machine.

593

Cascade. A command in applications that automatically organizes all the windows on the screen in a tidy stack.

Cause-Effect Diagram. A tool used to identify possible causes of a problem by representing the relationship between some effect and its potential cause.

Client-Server. A system architecture in which a client computer cooperates with a server over a network.

Control Chart. A statistical method for differentiating between common and special cause variations as demonstrated by a process.

Corrective Action. The practice and procedure for reporting, tracking, and resolving identified problems both in the software product and the development process. The resolution provides a final solution to the identified problem.

Corrective Maintenance. The identification and removal of code defects.

CPU. The central processing unit, the brains of the computer.

Customer. The individual or organization that receives a product.

Database. A collection of information stored in computerized form.

Defect. Producer's view — product requirement has not been met. Customer's view — anything that causes customer dissatisfaction.

Download. To receive information, typically a file, from another computer.

Drag-and-Drop. Perform tasks by using the mouse to drag an icon onto some other icon.

Emergency Repair. Software repair required immediately.

Entrance Criteria. Quantitative and qualitative measures used to evaluate a products' readiness to enter the next phase or stage of development.

Error. A discrepancy between actual values or conditions and those expected.

Exit Criteria. Quantitative and qualitative measures used to evaluate a products' acceptance for that specific stage or phase of development.

Flowchart. A diagram that shows the sequence of steps of a process.

Formal Review. A type of review typically scheduled at the end of each activity or stage of development to review a component of a deliverable or in some cases, a complete deliverable or the software product and its supporting documentation.

GUI. Graphical User Interface — a user interface in which graphics and characters are used on screens to communicate with the user.

Histogram. A graphical description of measured values organized according to the frequency of occurrence.

Icon. A miniature picture used to represent a function.

Impact Analysis. The process of determining which system components are affected by a change to software or hardware.

Incident Report. A report to document an issue or error arising from the execution of a test.

Inputs. Products, services, or information needed to make a process work.

Integration Testing. (1) The testing of combinations of individual, unit-tested pieces of code as they are combined into a complete unit. (2) A testing event driven by temporal cycles determined before the start of the testing phase. This test phase is conducted to identify functional problems with the software product. This is a verification activity.

Intermediate Repair. Software repair before the next formal release, but not immediately (e.g., in a week or so).

ISO9000. A quality series that comprises a set of five documents, which was developed in 1987 by the International Standards Organization (ISO).

Legacy System. Previous application system in production.

Maintenance. Tasks associated with the modification or enhancement of production software.

Management. A team or individual who manage(s) resources.

Management Review and Approval. A management review is the final review of a deliverable. It is conducted by the project manager with the project sponsor to ensure the quality of the business aspects of a work product.

Mean. A value derived by adding several items and dividing the sum by the number of items.

Network. A system that connects computers together and shares resources.

Perfective Maintenance. Enhancement to software performance, maintainability, or understandability.

Policy. Managerial intents and goals regarding a process or products.

Problem. Any deviation from predefined standards.

Problem Reporting. The method of identifying, tracking, and assigning attributes to problems detected within the software product, deliverables, or within the development processes.

Procedure. Step-by-step method which is followed to ensure some standard.

Process. Specific activities that must be performed to accomplish a function.

Process Improvement. To change a process to make it produce a product faster, more economically, or of higher quality.

Productivity. Ratio of output to the input of a process using the same unit of measure.

Quality. The totality of features and characteristics of a product or service that bear on its ability to meet stated or implied needs.

Quality Assurance. An overview process that entails planning and systematic actions to ensure that a product or service conforms to established requirements.

Quality Assurance Evaluation. A type of review performed by the QA organization to ensure that a project is following good quality management practices.

Quality Assurance Organization. A permanently established organization or unit whose primary goal is to review the project and products at various points to ensure that good quality management practices are being followed. Also to provide the testing efforts and all associated deliverables for testing on supported projects. The QA organization must be independent of the project team.

Quality Control. Process by which product quality is compared with standards.

Quality Improvement. Changing a process so that the rate of defects is reduced.

Quality Management. The execution of processes and procedures that ensures quality as an output from the development process.

Regression Testing. Tests used to verify a previously tested system whenever it is modified.

Release Management. A formal release process for non-emergency corrective, perfective, and adaptive projects.

Requirement. A performance standard for an attribute or a function, or the process used to verify that a standard has been met.

Reviews. A process or meeting during which a work product, or a set of work products, is presented to project personnel, project and program managers, users, customers, sponsors, or other interested parties for comment or approval.

Root Cause Analysis. A methodical process based on quantitative data to identify the primary cause in which a defect has been introduced into the product. This is typically more than just repairing the product affected, but establishing how the process or method allows the defect to be introduced into the product to begin with.

Run Chart. A graph of data points in chronological order used to detect trends of a characteristic being measured.

Scatter Plot. A graph which shows whether there is a relationship between two factors.

Software Maintenance. All changes, corrections, and enhancements that occur after an application has been placed into production.

Standard. A measure used to evaluate products or processes and identify non-conformance.

Statistical Process Control. The use of statistics and tools to measure a process.

System Testing. The functional testing of a system to verify that it performs within the limits of the system requirements and is fit for use.

Test Coverage. A measure of the portion of a system under test that is actually tested.

Test Cycle. A set of ordered test conditions that will test a logical and complete portion of a system.

Test Event. A generic term used to describe one of many levels of test. Examples: Unit Test, Integration Test, System Test.

Testing Tool. A manual or automated procedure or software used to test a system.

Test Readiness Review. A formal review conducted primarily to evaluate that all preliminary and entrance criteria have been satisfied and are verifiable before proceeding into a formal test event.

Unit Testing. Testing performed on individual programs to verify that they perform according to their requirements.

User. The customer who uses a product or process.

Validation. A type of evaluation conducted at the end of the development process to assess the software product's ability to meet the specified requirements.

Values. The ideals and customs toward which individuals have a positive regard.

Verification. A type of evaluation to determine if the software products at a given development phase satisfy the imposed conditions, which were determined at the start of that phase.

Vision. A statement that describes the desired future state of something.

Walkthrough. A testing technique to analyze a technical work product.

Window. A rectangle on a screen which represents information.

Bibliography

Arthur, Lowell Jay. 1993. *Improving Software Quality: An Insider's Guide to TQM.* New York: John Wiley & Sons, Inc.

Beizeir, Boris. 1984. *Software System Testing and Quality Assurance.* New York: Van Nostrand Reinhold Company.

Beizeir, Boris. 1991. *Software Testing Techniques,* Second Edition. New York: Van Nostrand Reinhold Company.

Beizeir, Boris. 1995. *Black-Box Testing: Techniques for Functional Testing for Testing of Software and Systems.* New York: John Wiley & Sons.

Boehm, Barry W. 1981. *Software Engineering Economics.* Englewood Cliffs, NJ: Prentice Hall.

Brooks, Frederick P., Jr. 1995. *The Mythical Man-Month,* Anniversary Edition. Reading, MA: Addison-Wesley Publishing Company.

Bruce, Phillip and Sam M. Pederson. 1982. *The Software Development Project: Plan and Management.* New York: John Wiley & Sons.

Buckley, Fletcher J. 1989. *Implementing Software Engineering Practices.* New York: Wiley Series in Software Engineering Practice.

Caplan, Frank. 1980. *The Quality System,* Second Edition. Philadelphia: Chilton Book.

Card, David N. with Robert L. Glass. 1990. *Measuring Software Design Quality.* Englewood Cliffs, NJ: Prentice Hall.

Charette, Robert N. 1990. *Applications Strategies for Risk Analysis.* New York: McGraw Hill.

Chen, Peter. 1977. *The Entity-Relationship Approach to Logical Database Design.* New York: Q. E. D. Information Sciences.

Cho, C. K. 1980. *An Introduction to Software Quality Control.* New York: Wiley Interscience.

Cho, C. K. 1987. *Quality Programming: Developing and Testing Software with Statistical Quality Control.* New York: John Wiley & Sons.

Crandall, Vern J. 1995. *The Software Product Development Life Cycle. Proceedings of the 1995 International Information Technology Quality Conference,* Orlando, Florida, April 6, 1995.

Creech, Bill. 1994. *The Five Pillars of TQM.* New York: Truman Valley Books/Dutton.

Davis, Alan M. 1990. *Software Requirements: Analysis and Specification.* Englewood Cliffs, NJ: Prentice Hall.

DeCarlo, Neil J. and W. Kent Sterett. 1990. *History of the Malcolm Baldridge National Quality Award. Quality Progress,* March 1990, pp. 21-27.

DeMarco, Tom. 1979. *Structured Analysis and System Specification.* Englewood Cliffs, NJ: Prentice Hall.

DeMarco, Tom. 1982. *Controlling Software Projects: Management, Measurement, and Estimation.* Englewood Cliffs, NJ: Yourdon Press.

Deming, W. E. 1986. *Out of the Crisis.* Cambridge MA: Massachusetts Institute of Technology, Center for Advanced Engineering Study.

BIBLIOGRAPHY

Deming, W. E. *The Deming Management Method.* New York, New York, Perigee Books.

Dickensen, Brian. 1980. *Developing Structured Systems.* Englewood Cliffs, NJ: Yourdon Press.

Dijkstra, Edsgar. 1968. *Go To Statement Considered Harmful. Communications of the ACM,* Vol.11, No.3: 147-178.

Fagan, Michael E. 1976. Design and code inspections to reduce errors in program development. IBM Systems Journal, Vol.15, No.3, pp. 182-211.

Fagan, Michael E. 1986. *Advances in Software Inspections.* IEEE Transactions on Software Engineering, July 1986, pp. 744-751.

Flavin, Matt. 1981. *Fundamental Concepts of Information Modeling.* Englewood Cliffs, NJ: Yourdon Press.

Freedman, Daniel and Gerald Weinberg. 1977. *Technical Inspections and Reviews.* Boston, MA: Little, Brown and Company.

Freedman, Daniel P. and Weinberg, Gerald M. *Handbook of Walkthroughs, Inspections, and Technical Reviews,* Third Edition. New York: Dorset House Publishing Co., 1990.

Gane, Chris and Trish Sarson. 1979. *Structured Systems Analysis: Tools and Techniques.* Englewood Cliffs, NJ: Prentice Hall.

Gilb, Tom. 1977. *Software Metrics.* New York: Winthrop.

Gilb, Tom. 1988. *Principles of Software Engineering Management.* Reading, MA: Addison-Wesley Publishing Company.

Gilb, Tom. 1991. *Software Metrics: Practical Approaches to Controlling Software Projects.* Paper presented at YSG Conference, Cardiff, Wales. April 1991.

Giles, A. C., 1992. *Software Quality: Theory and Management.* New York: Chapman & Hall.

Glass, Robert L. 1991. *Software Conflict-Essays on Art & Science of Software Engineering.* Englewood Cliffs, NJ: Yourdon Press (Prentice-Hall).

Glass, Robert L. 1991. *Building Quality Software.* Englewood Cliffs, NJ: Prentice-Hall.

Grady, Robert B. 1989. Dissecting software failures. *HP Journal.* April 1989: pp. 57-63.

Grady, Robert B. 1992. *Practical Software Metrics for Project Management and Process Improvement.* Englewood Cliffs, NJ: Prentice Hall.

Grady, Robert B. and Deborah L. Caswell. 1987. *Software Metrics: Establishing a Company-Wide Program.* Englewood Cliffs, NJ: Prentice Hall.

Gub, Tom et al. 1993. *Software Inspection.* Reading, MA: Addison-Wesley Publishing Co.

Hahn, Gerald J. 1995. Deming's impact on industrial statistics: some reflections. The American Statistician, Vol.49, No.4, November 1995, pp. 336-341.

Halstead, M. 1977. *Elements of Software Science.* New York: Elsevier.

Hansen, Kirk. 1983. *Data Structured Program Design.* Topeka, KS: Ken Orr and Associates.

Hetzel, Bill. 1988. *The Complete Guide to Software Testing,* Second Edition. Wellesly, MA: QED Publishing Group

Hetzel, Bill. 1993. *Making Software Measurement Work: Building an Effective Measurement Program.* Wellesly, MA: QED Publishing Group.

Higgins, David. 1979. *Program Design and Construction.* Englewood Cliffs, NJ: Prentice Hall.

Higgins, David. 1983. *Designing Structured Programs.* Englewood Cliffs, NJ: Prentice Hall.

Hollocker, Charles P. 1990. *Software Reviews and Audits Hand Book.* New York: John Wiley & Sons.

Humphrey, Watts S. 1989. *Managing the Software Process.* Reading, MA: Addison-Wesley Publishing Company.

Humphrey, Watts S. 1995. *A Discipline for Software Engineering.* Reading, MA: Addison-Wesley Publishing Company.

IEEE Standard for Measures to Produce Reliable Software. 1988. Washington, D.C.: IEEE, Std. 982.

IEEE Standard for Software Verification and Validation Plans. 1986. Washington, D.C.: IEEE, Std. 1012-1986 (R1992).

IEEE Standard Glossary of Software Engineering Terminology. 1990. Washington, D.C.: IEEE Std. 610.12-1990.

Jackson, M. A. 1975. *Principles of Program Design.* New York: Academic Press.

Jackson, M. A. 1983. *System Development.* Englewood Cliffs, NJ: Prentice Hall.

Jarvis, Alka S. 1988. *How to Establish a Successful Test Plan.* EDP Quality Assurance Conference, Washington, D.C., November 14-17, 1988.

Jarvis, Alka S. 1994. *Applying Software Quality.* The Seventh International Software Quality Week, San Francisco, California, May 17-20, 1994.

Jarvis, Alka S. 1995a. *Applying Metrics.* First World Congress for Software Quality Conference, San Francisco, California, June 20-22, 1995.

Jarvis, Alka S. 1995b. *Exploring the Needs of a Developer and Tester,* Quality Conference 95, Santa Clara, California, April 4-7, 1995.

Jones, Capers. 1986. *Programming Productivity* New York: McGraw-Hill

Jones, Capers. 1993. *Assessment and Control of Software Risks.* Englewood Cliffs, NJ: Yourdon Press Computing Services.

Jones, Capers, 1993. *Critical Problems in Software Measurement.* Carlsbad, CA: Infosystems Management.

Jones, Capers. 1991. *Applied Software Management: Assuring Productivity and Quality.* New York: McGraw-Hill.

Kaner, Cem, Jack Falk, and Hung Quoc Nguyen. 1993. *Testing Computer Software,* Second Edition. New York: Van Nostrand Reinhold.

Lewis, William E. 1998. *Spiral Testing.* Quality Assurance Institute Annual International Information Technology Quality Conference, April 13-17, Orlando, Florida.

Lewis, Robert O. 1992. *Independent Verification & Validation: A Life Cycle Engineering Process for Quality Software.* New York: John Wiley & Sons.

Linger, R. C., H. D. Mills, and B. I. Witt. 1979. *Structured Programming: Theory and Practice.* Reading, MA: Addison-Wesley.

Maples, Mike. 1995. Interview. *Information Week.*

Marca, David A. and Clement L. Mcgowan. 1988. *SADT: Structured Analysis and Design Technique.* New York: McGraw-Hill.

Marciniak, J. 1994. *Encyclopedia of Software Engineering.* New York: John Wiley & Sons.

Marks, David M. 1992. *Testing Very Big Systems.* New York: McGraw-Hill.

Martin, James. 1989. *Information Engineering Book I Introduction.* Englewood Cliffs, NJ: Prentice Hall.

Martin, James. 1990a. *Information Engineering Book II Planning & Analysis.* Englewood Cliffs, NJ: Prentice Hall.

Martin, James. 1990b. *Information Engineering Book III Design & Construction.* Englewood Cliffs, NJ: Prentice Hall.

BIBLIOGRAPHY

Martin, James, Kathleen Kavanagh Chapman, and Joe Leben. 1991. *Systems Application Architecture: Common User Access.* Englewood Cliffs, NJ: Prentice Hall.

McCabe, J. J. and C. W. Butler. 1989. Design complexity measurement and testing. *Communications of the ACM,* Vol.32, No.12, December 1989, pp.1415-1424.

McCabe, Thomas J. 1982. *Structured Testing: A Software Testing Methodology Using Cyclomatic Complexity Metric.* National Bureau of Standards Special Publication, December 1982: 500-599.

McConnell, Steve. 1993. *Code Complete: A Practical Handbook of Software Construction.* Redmond, WA: Microsoft Press.

McMenamin, Stephen M. and John F. Palmer. 1984. *Essential Systems Analysis.* Englewood Cliffs, NJ: Yourdon Press.

Metzger, Phillip W. 1981. *Managing a Programming Project,* Second Edition. Englewood Cliffs, NJ: Prentice Hall.

Mills, Harlan D. 1983. *Software Productivity.* Boston, MA: Little, Brown and Company.

Mills, H. D., R. C. Linger, and A. R. Hevner. 1986. *Principles of Information Systems Analysis and Design.* New York: Academic Press.

Murine, Gerald E. 1988. Integrating software quality metrics with software QA. *Quality Progress,* November 1988: 38-43.

Musa, J. D., A. Iannino, and K. Okumoto. 1987. *Software Reliability: Measurement, Prediction, Application.* New York: McGraw-Hill.

Myers, Glenford J. 1976. *Software Reliability Principles & Practices.* New York: John Wiley & Sons.

Myers, Glenford J. 1978. *Composite/Structured Design.* New York: Van Nostrand Reinhold.

Myers, Glenford J. 1979a. *Reliable Software Through Composite Design.* New York: Van Nostrand Reinhold.

Myers, Glenford J. 1979b. *The Art of Software Testing.* New York: John Wiley & Sons.

Norwell, MA: Kluwer Academic Publications, 1993.

Davis, Brendan. 1994. *The Economics of Automatic Testing.* Second Edition, New York: McGraw-Hill.

Orr, Ken. 1981. *Structured Requirements Definition.* Topeka, KS: Ken Orr and Associates.

Page-Jones, Meilir. 1988. *Practical Guide to Structured Systems Design,* Second Edition. Englewood Cliffs, NJ: Yourdon Press.

Page-Jones, Meilir. 1985. *Practical Project Management: Restoring Quality to DP Projects and Systems.* New York: Dorset House Publishing.

Parnas, D. L. 1972. On the criteria to be used in decomposing systems into modules. *Communications of the ACM,* December 1972, pp.1053-1058.

Perry, William E. 1986. *How to Test Software Packages: A Step-by-Step Guide to Assuring They Do What You Want.* New York: John Wiley & Sons.

Perry, William E. *Quality Assurance for Information Systems: Methods, Tools, and Techniques.* Wellesley, MA: Q.E.D. Information Sciences, Inc., 1991.

Peters, Lawrence. 1987. *Advanced Structured Analysis and Design.* Englewood Cliffs, NJ: Prentice Hall.

Pressman, Roger S. 1988. *Making Software Engineering Happen: A Guide to Instituting the Technology.* Englewood Cliffs, NJ: Prentice Hall.

Pressman, Roger S. 1992. *Software Engineering: A Practitioner's Approach,* Third Edition. New York: McGraw-Hill.

Radice, R. A., J. T. Harding, P E. Munnis, and R. W Phillips. 1985b. A programming process study. *IBM Systems Journal,* Vol.24, No.2, pp.91-101.

Radice, Ronald A. and Richard W. Phillips. 1988. *Software Engineering: An Industrial Approach, Volume I.* Englewood Cliffs, NJ: Prentice Hall.

Roper, Marc. 1993. *Software Testing.* New York: McGraw-Hill.

Ross, D. T., and K. E. Schoman. 1977. *Structured Analysis for Requirements Definition.* IEEE Transactions on Software Engineering, Vol. SE-3, No.1, January 1977, pp.6-15.

Royer, Thomas C., 1992. *Software Testing Management: Life on the Critical Path.* Englewood Cliffs, NJ: Prentice-Hall.

Rubin, Howard. 1993. *Practical Guide to the Design and Implementation of IS Measurement Programs.* Englewood Cliffs, NJ: Prentice-Hall.

Sanders, Joe. 1994. *Software Quality: A Framework for Success in Software Development.* Reading, MA: Addison-Wesley Publishing Company.

Schulmeyer G. Gordon. 1990. *Zero Defect Software.* New York: McGraw-Hill.

Schulmeyer, W. Gordon and McManus, James. 1992. *Total Quality Management for Software.* New York: Van Nostrand Reinhold.

Sharp, Alex. 1993. *Software Quality and Productivity.* New York: Van Nostrand Reinhold.

Sommerville, L. 1985. *Software Engineering,* Second Edition, Reading, MA: Addison-Wesley Publishing Company.

Stevens, Roger T. 1979. *Operational Test & Evaluation: A Systems Engineering Process.* New York: Wiley-Interscience.

Stevens, Wayne P. 1981. *Using Structured Design: How to Make Programs Simple, Changeable, Flexible, and Reusable.* New York: Wiley-Interscience.

Stevens, Wayne, Larry Constantine, and Glenford Myers. 1974. Structured design. *IBM Systems Journal,* Vol.13, No.2: 115-139.

Ward, Paul T. and Stephen J. Mellor. 1985a. *Structured Development for Real Time Systems. Volume 1: Introduction and Tools.* Englewood Cliffs, NJ: Yourdon Press.

Ward, Paul T. and Stephen J. Mellor. 1985b. *Structured Development for Real Time Systems. Volume 2: Essential Modeling Techniques.* Englewood Cliffs, NJ: Yourdon Press.

Ward, Paul T. and Stephen J. Mellor. 1986. *Structured Development for Real Time Systems. Volume 3: Implementation Modeling Techniques.* Englewood Cliffs, NJ: Yourdon Press.

Warnier, Jean-Dominique. 1974b. *Logical Construction of Programs,* Third Edition. New York: Van Nostrand Reinhold.

Warnier, Jean-Dominique. 1981. *Logical Construction of Systems.* New York: Van Nostrand Reinhold.

Weinberg, Gerald M. 1992. *Software Quality Management: Vol.1: Systems Thinking.* New York: Dorset House Publishing.

Weinberg, Gerald M. 1993. *Software Quality Management: Vol.2: First-Order Measurement.* New York: Dorset House Publishing.

Weinberg, Gerald M. 1992. *Quality Software Management: Systems Thinking, Vol. I,* New York: Dorset House Publishing.

Weinberg, Gerald M. 1993. *Quality Software Management: First-order Measurement, Vol.2,* New York: Dorset House Publishing.

BIBLIOGRAPHY

Weinberg, Gerald M. and Daniela Weinberg. 1979. *On the Design of Stable Systems.* New York: Wiley-Interscience.

Weinberg, Victor. 1978. *Structured Analysis.* Englewood Cliffs, NJ: Yourdon Press.

Whitten, Neal. 1990. *Managing Software Development Projects: Formula for Success.* New York: John Wiley & Sons.

Yourdon, Edward. 1975. *Techniques of Program Structure and Design.* Englewood Cliffs, NJ: Prentice Hall.

Yourdon, Edward. 1985. *Structured Walkthroughs,* Third Edition. Englewood Cliffs, NJ: Yourdon Press.

Yourdon, Edward. 1989. *Modern Structured Analysis.* Englewood Cliffs, NJ: Yourdon Press.

Youll, David P. 1990. *Making Software Development Visible: Effective Project Control.* New York: John Wiley & Sons.

Yourdon, Edward and Larry L. Constantine. 1979. *Structured Design: Fundamentals of a Discipline of Computer Program and Systems Design.* Englewood Cliffs, NJ: Prentice Hall.

Zachman, John. 1987. A framework for information systems architecture. *IBM Systems Journal,* Vol.26, No.3.

Index